THE BREAST-PLATE
OF
FAITH AND LOVE

16th – 17th Century Facsimile Editions

The Breast-plate of Faith and Love

John Preston

THE BANNER OF TRUTH TRUST

THE BANNER OF TRUTH TRUST
3 Murrayfield Road, Edinburgh EH12 6EL
P.O. Box 621, Carlisle, Pennsylvania 17013, USA

*

First Published 1630
This Banner Facsimile Reprint of the
Fifth Edition, 1634, first published 1979
ISBN 0 85151 289 5

*

Printed in Great Britain
Photo-litho reprint by W & J Mackay Limited, Chatham
from earlier impression

THE BREAST-PLATE OF *FAITH AND LOVE.*

A TREATISE,

Wherein the ground and exercise of *Faith* and *Love*, as they are set upon Christ *their Object, and as they are ex-* pressed in *Good Works*, is explained.

Delivered

In 18. Sermons upon three severall Texts,
By the late faithfull and worthy Mini- ster of Jesus Christ,
JOHN PRESTON,
Dr. in Divinity, Chaplaine in ordinary to his *Majestie*, *Master* of Emmanuel *Colledge in* Cambridge, and sometime Preacher of *Lincolnes* Inne.

The fifth Edition.

But let us who are of the day be sober, putting on the Breast-plate of Faith and Love, 1 Thes. 5. 8.
What will it profit, my Brethren, if a man say he have Faith, and hath not Workes? Can Faith save him? James 2. 14.

Imprinted at *London* by *R. Y.* for *Nicholas Bourne*, and are to be sold at the South entrance of the *Royall Exchange*. 1634.

ILLUSTRISSIMO, NOBILISSIMOQUE VIRO,
ROBERTO COMITI WARVVICENCI,
JOHANNIS PRESTONI S. T. D. ET
COLLEGII EMMANUELIS Q. MAGISTRI
(CUJUS TUTELÆ,
DUM IN VIVIS ESSET, PRIMOGENITUM SUUM
IN DISCIPLINAM ET LITERIS EXPOLIENDUM
TRADIDIT)
POSTHUMORUM TRACTATUUM PARTEM
DE NATURA FIDEI, EJUSQUE EFFICACIA,
DEQUE AMORE ET OPERIBUS BONIS,
DEVOTISSIMI, TAM AUTHORIS DUM VIVERET,
QUAM IPSORUM QUI SUPERSUNT, OBSEQUII
TESTIMONIUM.

M. D. D. D.

RICHARDUS SIBS.

JOHANNES DAVENPORT.

To the Christian Reader.

Christian Reader,

INnumerable are the sleights of Satan, to hinder a Christian in his course towards Heaven, by exciting the corruption of his owne heart to disturbe him, when hee is about to doe any good; or by discouraging him with inward terrours, when he would solace himselfe with heavenly comforts; or by disheartning him under the feares of sufferings, when he should be resolute in a good cause. A type whereof were the Israelites, whose servitude was redoubled, when they turned themselves to forsake Ægypt: Wherefore wee have much neede of Christian fortitude, according to that direction; Watch ye, stand fast, quit your selves like men: especially since Satan, like a Serpentine Crocodile pursued, is by resistance put to flight. 1 Cor.16.13.

But as in warres, (which the Philistims knew well in putting their hope in Goliah) the chiefe strength of the Souldiers lyeth in their Captaine, so in spirituall conflicts, all a Christians strength is in Christ, and from him. For, before our conversion, we

 were

were of no strength: *since our conversion,* wee are not sufficient of our selves to thinke a good thought. *And, to worke out from the Saints all selfe-confidence, God, by their falls, teacheth them* To rejoyce in the Lord Jesus, and to have no confidence in the flesh.

Whatsoever Christ hath for us, is made ours by Faith, *which is the hand of the soule enriching it by receiving Christ, who is* the treasure hid in the field, *and with him, those* unsearchable riches *of grace, which are revealed and offered in the Gospell: Yea, it is part of our spirituall armour. That which was fabulously spoken of the race of Gyants, is truly said of a Christian, he is borne with his armour upon him; as soon as he is regenerate, he is armed. Its called a* Breast-plate, *because it preserves the heart; a* long, large shield, *(as the word signifieth) which is usefull to defend the whole man from all sorts of assaults: Which part of spirituall armour, and how it is to be managed, is declared in the former part of the ensuing Treatise, in ten Sermons.*

1 Thes. 5. 8. Θώραξ Eph. 6. 16. Θυρεὸς of θύρα.

Now as all rivers returne into the sea, whence they came, so the beleeving soule, having received all from Christ, returneth all to Christ. For thus the beleever reasoneth; Was Gods undeserved, unexpected love such to me, that he spared not his onely begotten Sonne, but gave him to dye for mee? Its but equall that

that I ſhould live to him, die for him, bring in my ſtrength, time, gifts, liberty, all that I have, all that I am, in his ſervice, to his glory. That affection whence theſe reſolutions ariſe, is called Love, which ſo inclineth the ſoule, that it moveth in a direct line, towards that object wherein it expecteth contentment. The ſoule is miſerably deluded in purſuing the wind, and in taking ayme at a flying fowle, whileſt it ſeekes happineſſe in any creature: which appeares in the reſtleſneſſe of thoſe irregular agitations, and endleſſe motions of the minds of ambitious, voluptuous, and covetous perſons, whoſe frame of ſpirit is like the lower part of the elementary region, the ſeate of windes, tempeſts, and earthquakes, full of unquietneſſe; whileſt the beleevers ſoule, like that part towards heaven, which is alwaies peaceable and ſtill, enjoyeth true reſt and joy. And indeed the perfection of our ſpirits, cannot be but in union with the chiefe of ſpirits, which communicateth his goodneſſe to the creature according to its capacity. This affection of Love, as it reflecteth upon Chriſt, being a fruit and effect of his Love to us apprehended by faith, is the ſubject of the ſecond part of the following Treatiſe, in ſeven Sermons.

The judicious Author out of a piercing inſight into the methods of the Tempter, knowing upon what rockes the faith of many ſuffers ſhipwracke; that

neither

neither the weake Christian might lose the comfort of his faith, through want of evidences, nor the presumptuous rest upon a fancy in stead of faith, nor the adversaries be emboldened to cast upon us, by reason of this doctrine of Justification by faith onely, their wonted nick-names of Soli-fidians, *and* Nulli-fidians, *throughout the whole Treatise, and more especially in the last Sermon, he discourseth of* good Workes, *as they arise from faith and love. This is the summe of the faithfull and fruitfull labours of this reverend, learned and godly Minister of the Gospel, who whilest he lived, was an example of the life of faith and love, and of good workes, to so many as were acquainted with his equall and even walking in the wayes of God, in the severall turnings and occasions of his life. But it will be too much injury to the godly Reader to be detained longer in the porch. We now dismisse thee to the reading of this profitable worke, beseeching God to increase faith, and to perfect love in thy heart, that thou maist be fruitfull in good works.*

Thine in our Lord Jesus Christ,

RICHARD SIBS,

JOHN DAVENPORT.

OF FAITH.

The first Sermon.

ROM. 1. 17.

For by it the righteousnesse of God is revealed from Faith to Faith: as it is written, The just shall live by Faith.

IN the words I have read unto you, S. *Paul* tels them, that he is not ashamed of the Gospell of *Christ*. For it was a shame to him, partly, because the Gospel was then in persecution; and partly, because he was plaine in speech. He came not with excellency of words, or mans wisedome; and therefore you may observe what adoe he had to defend himselfe in his Epistles to the *Corinthians*, a wise people, who partly hated, and partly despised his manner of delivery: but, saith he, *I am not ashamed of it, for it is the power of God to salvation:* it is that which, being received, will bring men to heav n; being rejected, will shut men up in hell, and therefo e it is of no small moment. Hee gives a reason in th se words, why it is the power of *God* to salvation: *For*, saith he, *by it the righteousnesse of God is revealed:* That is, the righteousnesse which is of *God*, which only *God* accepts, and by which alone men can be saved, is revealed by the Gospel, and no other way.

But to what purpose is this revealed, if I know not how to come by it? Many things are revealed, but how sh ll I know that they are mine? Therefore he addes, *It is the power of God to salvation, to every one that beleeves.* As it is revealed by the Gospel, so something is to be done on our part; as *God* manifests it, and layes it open, so you must receive it by faith.

Y a, but I have not so strong a faith, I cannot beleeve as I would, and as I should. Saies he, faith hath degrees, *it is revealed from faith to faith:* That is, one receives it in one degree, and the same afterward receives it in a greater degree, and so forward. All are alike justified, but there is a difference in faith, some is stronger, some is weaker, which I will afterward shew at large.

The point to be gathered out of these words is this:

Doct. *That Righteousnesse, by which alone wee can be saved now in the time of the Gospel, is revealed and offered to all that will take it.*

You heare this, it may be you may not have such a conceit of the thing as you should have: but it is not a matter of light moment, but an exceeding great thing to see the righteousness of *God* revealed. It is the great, glorious mystery of the Gospel; which the Angels desire to pry into, which made S. *Paul* in his Ministery so so glorious, which swallowed up his thoughts, that he could not tell how to expresse it: that now in this last age, *Christ hath revealed* through us *the unsearchable riches of his Grace*: that is, Riches which I know not how to expresse. Therefore he prayes that *God would open their eyes, that they might comprehend with all the Saints, the height, and length, and breadth of that* Redemption, which *Christ* hath wrought for them. It passeth our comprehension, yet he prayes that they may comprehend it in such a measure as is possible, though there be a height, and breadth, and depth therein, which could not be measured. And this is it that is revealed to the soules of men, the escaping of Hell and Death, such free accesse to the Throne of Grace, as none before had; this liberty to be made the Sonnes of *God*, and heires of heaven, yea Kings and Priests to *God*, and making good of all promises, and the entailing of them to our posterity, and making them Yea & Amen. All this, I say, is now revealed, which before was not.

Why this righteousnesse is said to be revealed.

1. It was not written in mens harts by nature.

1. It is said to be revealed, partly, because this, of all other things, was never written in the hearts of men. The Morall Law was written therein, but they had not the least inkling, the least crevice of light to see this; partly, because it is now opened in a larger measure than it was heretofore, in the times of the Prophets: the doore was a little open before, but now it is wide open, and nothing is hid from the soules of men, that is necessary for them to know.

2. In respect of those that reveale it.

3. In regard of those that hear it.

Againe, it is revealed, not onely in regard of the Preachers that make it knowne, but likewise in regard of them that heare it: for there is a greater measure of the spirit of Revelation dispensed under the Gospel.

Therefore, *Eph*. 1. 18. the Apostle prayes that *the eyes of their underſtanding might be opened, that they might know what is the hope of their calling, and the riches of his glorious inheritance in the Saints*. For what is it to have a light ſhining, if their eyes be ſhut to whom it ſhines? So the thing revealed is the Righteouſneſſe of *God*. And laſtly, it is that Righteouſneſſe, by which alone man can be ſaved.

This is the maine point, which, that you may underſtand, I will open by anſwering theſe ſixe Queſtions.

6. Queſtions about this righteouſneſſe.

1. How this Righteouſneſſe of *God*, (*i.e.* which is accepted of *God*) ſaves.

2. How it is offered to us.

3. To whom it is offered.

4. Upon what qualifications.

5. How it is made ours.

And laſtly, What is required of us when we have it. Theſe hang one upon another, but for memory ſake I have thus diſtinguiſhed them.

Queſt. 1. How it ſaveth.

Anſw. 1.

First, How doth it ſave? I anſwer: 1. This righteouſneſſe ſaves after the ſame maner that the unrighteouſneſſe of *Adam* did condemne: let us ſet theſe two together, and the thing will be plaine.

A paralell betweene the unrighteouſneſſe of the firſt, and the righteouſneſſe of the ſecond Adam, in 3. things.

Firſt, as *Adam* was one man, yet the common root of all mankinde, of whom all that are guilty of death, and ſhall be damned, muſt be born: ſo *Chriſt*, the ſecond *Adam*, ſtands as a publike perſon, and the root of all that ſhall be ingrafted into, and borne of him.

Secondly, as *Adams* firſt unrighteouſneſſe, the firſt ſin he committed, is communicated to men, and made theirs by imputation; and not ſo onely, but by inherency alſo (for it hath bred in them originall ſinne:) After the

the ſame maner the righteouſneſſe that *Chriſt wrought*, is made ours by imputation; and this imputative righteouſneſſe of *Chriſt* worketh a righteouſneſſe which qualifies the perſon, and is inherent in us. Laſtly, as after this unrighteouſneſſe comes death, which rules and reignes in us, bringing every thing into ſubjection, ſo that all the comforts men poſſeſſe, are overcome in ſome degree, while we live here; (all ſickneſſes, & troubles, and croſſes, being as ſo many skirmiſhes which death hath with us, before the main Battell comes:) So in *Chriſt* life reignes over all, and brings all into ſubjection to him: that is, it brings all the troubles man ſuſtaineth, all the enemies he hath, yea death and ſin into ſubjection, by degrees in this life, and after death perfectly. There is a compariſon made in *Rom*.5.14. which you ſhall finde more fully to expreſſe, and more largely to ſet this out than I have done. The firſt *Adam* was a figure of him that was to come: and 1 *Cor*.15.45. *Chriſt* is called the *ſecond Adam*. Now you doe ſee the miſerable fruit of *Adams* fall, you ſee by lamentable experience, what originall ſin is, and how much it hath corrupted us; why then ſhould you thinke it a ſtrange thing, that the righteouſneſſe of Chriſt ſhould bee imputed? Againe, death, you ſee, reignes over all by one; why then will you not beleeve that life ſhall reigne over all men, that is, bring every enemie of ours into ſubjection, by the other? For the righteouſneſſe of one ſaves, as the unrighteouſneſſe of the other condemnes.

Another expreſſion I finde in 2 *Cor*.5.21. *As Chriſt was made ſin for us, who knew no ſinne, ſo are we made the righteouſneſſe of God in him*: That is, though *Chriſt* was a man without ſin in himſelfe, yet our ſin was imputed *Anſw*.2.

to him, and he was by *God* reckoned as a ſinner; and then he kils him, putting our curſe upon him: ſo to us that are free from righteouſneſſe, *Chriſt* is made righteouſneſſe, ſo that *God* lookes on us as if we had performed perfect righteouſneſſe, and when that is done, he ſaves us. And ſo much for the firſt Queſtion.

How we ſhall come by it.

Ob. But now when wee heare that this righteouſneſſe ſaves, the Queſtion is, How ſhall we come by it? In that it ſaves, it is good and comfortable; but it may ſave ſome men, and yet I have no ſhare nor part in ſalvation.

Anſw. I anſwer, it is freely given to us, even as Fathers give Lands and inheritances to their children, and as kings give Pardons, and Titles, and Honours, and Riches, out of their clemency, becauſe they will, to ſhew their magnificence, and goodneſſe to their ſubjects; So doth *God* give this righteouſneſſe; as you ſhall find it expreſſed, *Eſay* 9.6. *To Us a Childe is borne, to Us a Son is given*: a place worth your marking and obſervation. And *Joh*.3.16. *God ſo loved the world, that he gave his only begotten Son, &c.* And *Rom*.5.17. it is called *the gift of Righteouſneſſe*: That is, a thing which *God* freely, ſimply, voluntarily, and only becauſe he will, beſtowes on men, not looking on any worthineſſe in them of the ſame: (as we ſay, nothing is ſo free as gift.) The paſſage is this: For, *if through the offence of one, Death reigned in all, much more they which receive aboundance of grace, and the gift of righteouſneſſe, ſhall reigne in life by one Jeſus Chriſt.* So that *God* gives it freely out of his meere love, without any other motive or end, but to ſhew his magnificence, and to make manifeſt in the ages to come the unſearchable riches of *Chriſt*, the great

and

and exceeding glorious riches that hee hath provided for them that love him.

But what is the reaſon that *God* will have it communicated to the ſonnes of men no other way but by gift? You ſhall ſee it, *Rom.* 4.5. that it is for theſe cauſes. Reaſons why it is by gift.

Firſt, *That no man might boaſt in himſelfe, but that he that rejoyceth, may rejoyce in the Lord.* If any other bargaine or manner of conveyance had beene made, wee ſhould have had ſomething to boaſt of, but comming meerely from *God* as a gift, we have cauſe to glory in *God*, and nothing elſe. Againe, its a gift, that men may learne to depend upon *God* for it: *God* will have no man challenge it as due; for it is a meere grace. Laſtly, it is a gift, *that it may be ſure to all the ſeed.* If there had bin any thing required at our hands, (This doe, fulfill this Law, and you ſhall have this righteouſneſſe:) it had not bin ſure, nay none had been ſaved; for by the Law is tranſgreſſion and wrath: but being by gift, it is firme and ſure to all the ſeed: for when a thing is freely given, and nothing expected, but taking it, and thanks-giving for it, what is more ſure? 1. That none might boaſt. 2. That it be of grace. 3. That it might be ſure to all the ſeed.

But, when you heare this righteouſneſſe is given, the next queſtion will be, To whom is it given? If it be only given to ſome, what comfort is this to me? To whom it is given.

But (which is the ground of all comfort) it is given to every man, there is not a man excepted; for which we have the ſure word of *God*, which will not faile. When you have the Charter of a King well confirmed, you reckon it a matter of great moment: What is it then, when you have the Charter of *God* himſelf? which you ſhall evidently ſee in theſe two places, *Marke ult.* 15.

Goe and preach the Gospel to every creature under Heaven: What is that? Goe and tell every man without exception, that there is good newes for him, *Christ* is dead for him, and if he will take him, and accept of his righteousnesse, he shall have it; restraine it not, but goe and tell every man under Heaven. The other Text is, *Rev. ult. Whosoever will, let him come, and take of the waters of life freely.* There is a *quicunque vult*, whosoever will come, (none excepted) may have life, and it shall cost him nothing. Many other places of Scripture there be, to prove the generality of the offer: and having a sure word for it, consider it.

Object. But if it be objected, It is given onely to the Elect, and therefore not to every man.

Answ. 1. In the ministry of the Gospel, Christ is offered to every one in foure respects.

I answer, when we have a sure Word, that it is given to every man under heaven, without any restraint at all, why should any except himselfe? Indeed, when *Christ* was offered freely to every man, and one received him, another rejected him, then the Mystery of Election and Reprobation was revealed; the reason why some received him being, because *God* gave them a heart, which to the rest he gave not; but, in point of offering of *Christ*, we must be generall, without having respect to election. For otherwise the Elect of *Christ* should have no ground for their faith, none knowing he is elected, untill he hath beleeved and repented.

Object. But *Christs* righteousnesse being offered to men in state of unregeneration, how shall I know it belongs to me?

Answ. There is no other ground but this Syllogisme: This righteousnesse belongs to every man that beleeves: but I beleeve; therefore it belongs to me. Therefore, though it be applied only to beleevers, yet it

must

must bee offered to every man.

Againe, we are bound to beleeve that the thing is true, before we can beleeve our share in it; we doe not therefore make it true, because we beleeve; but our beleeving presupposeth the object of our Faith, which is this, that *Christ* is given: now the very beleeving doth not cause *Christ* to be given; but he is given, and therefore we beleeve. In all actions, the object is in order of nature before the action it selfe; my beleefe makes not a thing true, but it is true in it selfe, and therefore I beleeve it. It being true that *Christ* is offered to all men, therefore I beleeve that I am reconciled and adopted, and that my sins are forgiven. *Answ.2.*

Againe, if he should not be offered to every man, we could not say to every man, If thou dost beleeve, thou shalt be saved; but this we may say to all, even to *Judas*, If thou beleevest, *Judas*, thou shalt be saved. *Answ.3.*

Again, if he were not offered to all, then wicked men should be excluded as much as the Divels; but *Christ* took their nature on him, therefore it is possible for them, if they beleeve, to be saved. *Answ.4.*

Object. But how differs this from the doctrine of the Adversaries; for they also say that *Christ* is offered equally to all?

Answ. I answer, In two respects: (not to run through all) The first is this; We say, Though *Christ* be offered, and freely given to all, yet *God* intends him onely to the Elect. They say, His intention is the same to all, to *Judas* as to *Peter*. The other is, they affirme, that as *Christ* is offered to all men, so all men have sufficient grace to receive him, there is an ability by that as well as a freedome, and universality in the offer. This we altogether deny.

1. God intends him only to the Elect.

2. God gives power onely to them to receive him.

deny. Though *Christ* be given to all, yet the gift of faith is a fruit of election. *God* gives faith & repentance, and ability to receive him, where he pleaseth. The gate is open to all, we shut out none; but none will come in, but those whom *God* enables. A pardon may be offered to all, and yet none accept it, but those whose minds *God* hath inclined. Therefore that he is offered to all, it is without question. They that question it, doe it because they doe not understand the Doctrine of our Divines; for wee propound it no otherwise in substance than they doe, onely we differ in the method: but it will be your wisedome to looke to that which will be of use, and yeeld comfort when you come to die. As this you may build on, The Gospell is preached to every creature under heaven, and therefore I have my share in it. If a Pardon be offered to some, whose names alone are inserted therein, you cannot say on any good ground, I am pardoned: but when the Pardon is generall, and offered to all, then I can beleeve the Pardon belongs to me. Were it only to the Elect, whose names are written in the Pardon, we should first enquire whether we be elect or no, but that 's not the method. Build you on the sure promise, they that are pardoned, shall take hold of it, they that take not hold of it, shall be excluded.

Quest. 4. Unto what qualifications it is given.

The next thing a man will desire to know is this; What qualifications are expected? Doth not *God* require to finde something in us, if he give it us?

I answer, that it is offered to all, and no qualification at all is required as præexistent to be found in us, but any may come and take it. *God* requires no qualification as concerning our sins; hee saith not, you

shall

ſhall be pardoned, ſo your ſinnes be of ſuch a number, or of ſuch a nature, but though they be never ſo many, though of never ſo extraordinary a nature, though they may bee aggravated with all the circumſtances that can be, yet there is no exception at all of you, the pardon runnes in generall termes, *This is the Lambe of God that taketh away the ſinnes of the world.* And ſeeing it is in generall termes, why will you interline and reſtraine it? You ſee it runs in generall, and ſo you may take it. Inſtance: 1. in ſins.

And as it is propounded generally, ſo it is generally executed: 1 *Cor.* 6.9. You ſhall find, the greateſt ſinnes that can be named are there pardoned: *Be not deceived,* you know how *no fornicator, nor adulterer, nor unclean perſon, &c. ſhall enter into the kingdome of God, and ſuch were ſome of you: but now you are iuſtified, now you are ſanctified, now you are waſhed.* Though they had committed the greateſt ſins, you ſee, it is generally executed, without exception.

But there is another ſort of qualification. Is there not ſomething firſt to be done? I know that though I have committed all the ſins of the world, yet they ſhall not prejudice my pardon; but I muſt doe ſomething to qualifie me for it. No, not any thing as antecedarious and precedent to the pardon: it is onely required of thee, to come with the hand of faith, and receive it in the middeſt of all thy unworthineſſe, whatſoever it be, lay hold on the pardon, and embrace it, and it ſhall be thine. 2. In graces.

But you will object, then to what end is the doctrine of humiliation? to what end is the Law preached to be a Schoolemaſter, if no qualification be required? *Ob.* 1.

I an-

Answ. 1. I answer, humiliation is not required as a qualification; for no teares of ours can give satisfaction. And againe, it hath beene found in a Reprobate; for *Judas* had it. Neither is it any part of sanctification.

Object. But how is it required then?

Answ. 2. How humiliation is required before we come to *Christ.* As that without which we will not come to *Christ.* As for example: If we say to a man, The Physician is ready to heale you; before you will be healed, you must have a sense of your sicknesse: this sense is not required by the Physician (for the Physician is ready to heale him): but if he be not sicke, and have a sense of it, hee will not come to the Physician. *Simile.* If at a generall Dole it be proclaimed, Let all come hither that be hungry; a man is not excluded, if he be not hungry, but else hee will not come: therefore we preach, that none receive the Gospel but the poore, those that be humble, and touched with sense of sin and wrath; and wee preach so, because indeed no man will come without it.

Quest. 4. How *Christs* righteousnesse is made ours. In the next place, the Question will be, How this righteousnesse of Christ is made ours? or, what is to be done of him to whom it belongs?

Answ. To this I answer; though no precedent qualification be required, yet this must be taken, a man must not reflect on himselfe, and consider, Am I worthy of it? but he must take it as a Plaister, which if it be not applyed, will not heale; or as meat, which if it be not eaten, doth not nourish. *Simile.* In what sense faith is required. As the husband wooes his spouse, and saies thus, I require nothing at thy hands, no condition at all, I doe not examine whether thou art wealthy, or no; whether thou be faire or no; whether thou be out of debt, or well conditioned, it is no matter what thou art: I require thee simply to take me for thy husband. After

this

this manner comes *Christ* to us; we must not say, Am I worthy to make a Spouse for *Christ*? Am I fit to receive so great mercies? Thou art onely to take him. When we exclude all conditions, we exclude such a frame and habite of mind, which we think is necessarily required to make us worthy to take him. As if a Physician come and offer thee a Medicine, by which thou maist be healed, and say, I require nothing at your hands, onely to drinke it, for else it will doe you no good: So *God* offers the Righteousnesse of *Christ*, which is that that heales the soules of men, *God* lookes for nothing at your hands, it matters not what your person is, onely you must take it. So you shall finde himselfe expressing it, *Esay* 55.1. where he compares this to the offer of wine and milke: *Come, buy wine and milke without money*: Let him that is a thirst come and he that hath no money. As if he had said, it is freely offered, you are onely to take it.

In what sense conditions are excluded. *Simile.*

Quest. But when you heare you must take it, the question will be, What this taking is.

Answ. I answer, This taking is nothing else but that which we call *Faith*: and therefore that we may not erre in the maine, I will declare what Faith is. And it is nothing else but this, when these two things concurre, that *God* the Father will give his Son, and freely offers righteousnesse, and we receive this righteousnesse, taking *Christ* for our Husband, our King and Lord.

What this taking is.

Faith what.

Ob. But you will say, Faith is more: for *Fides est actus intellectus*, it is an act of the understanding, assenting to Truthes for the authority of the Speaker; therefore the mind and will must concurre to make up this Faith.

Answ.

Faith in the understanding & will both.

Answ. For the better understanding of it, marke this word, *The righteousnesse of God is revealed:* wherein is likewise implyed, (though it be not expressed) that it is offered: for to what purpose, or what comfort is it to see that there is such a righteousnesse, if it be nothing to us? but it is so revealed, that it is also offered. Now being both revealed, and offered, you must finde something in men answerable to both these: to the revelation of it, the understanding assenting to it as a Truth, that *Christ* is come in the flesh, and offered to all men.

Againe, to answer to the matter of the offer, there is also an act of the will, whereby it comes in, and takes or imbraceth this righteousnesse. Both these, 1 *Tim.* 1. 15. are put together; *This is a faithfull saying, & worthy to be received, that Jesus Christ came into the world to save sinners.* It is true, saith the understanding, and therefore that beleeves it; but it is worthy to bee received saith the will, therefore that comes in, takes and accepts it. As in matter of marriage, if one come and tell a Woman, There is such a man in the world that is willing to bestow himselfe on you, if you will take him, and accept him for your Husband: Now (marke what it is that makes up the marriage on her part:) first, she must beleeve that there is such a man, and that that man is willing to have her; that this message is true, that it is brought from the man himselfe, and that it is nothing else but a true declaration of the mans minde. This is an act of her minde or understanding. But will you take him, and accept of him for your Husband? now comes the will, and the concurrence of these two makes up the match. So we come and tell you, There is such a one, the *Messiah*, that is willing

Simile.

willing to bestow himselfe on you; if you beleeve that we deliver the message from *Christ*, & doe consequently imbrace and take him, now are you justified, this is the very translation of you from death to life, at this very instant you are delivered from Satan, possessed of a kingdome, and salvation is come to your house.

Now because this taking of *Christ* is the main point which makes *Christ* ours, and the want whereof is the cause that every man is condemned, (it comming nearest to life and death) that you may know what it is, we must tell you, that this is required therein: 3. things must concur in receiving *Christ*.

First, there must not be *Error personæ*, errour of the person.

Secondly, you must understand aright what this taking is.

Thirdly, there must be a complete deliberate will, which must concur to this action of taking.

These three being declared, we shall not easily bee deceived in it.

First, when you heare of this righteousnesse of *Christ*, & it being made ours; you must know that first *Christ* himselfe is made ours, and then his righteousnesse: as first you must have the husband, and then the benefits that come by him. I say, take heed that there be not an error of the person, that you mistake him not. And this excludes all ignorant men, that take not *Christ* in deed, but onely in their owne fancie. Therefore when you come to make this marriage, you must know that *Christ* is most holy, that he is also such a one as will bring persecution with him, as he saies of himselfe, that hee knowes not where to lay his head: such a one as for whose sake you must part with every thing; such a one 1. There must be no error about the person.

one as is hated in the world, and for whose sake you must be hated: Some would have the man, but they know not the man; and so many thousands are deceived, that are willing to take *Christ*, but they know not what they take, they understand not *Christ* aright: there is an errour of the person, and so a misse of the match, and consequently of justification: for, so as to make him their Lord, so as to be subject to him, they take him not, they do not consider that he requires such and such things at their hands.

2. The right forme must be observed.

Secondly, if there be no mistake of the person, yet what is this taking? In marriage there is a certaine forme to be observed, and if that forme be mist of, there is a misse of the match. This taking therefore is nothing but this, so to take him, as to be divorced from all other Lovers; so to serve him, as you serve no other master; so to be subject to him, that you be subject to nothing in the world besides. This is properly to take *Christ*; and this excludes the greatest part of men, they being ready to take *Christ*, and yet they will love the world too: but *God tels* them, that *if they love the world, the love of the Father, nor the Son, is not in them.* You must have your affections weaned from every kind of vanity. Goe thorow the whole Universe, looke on all the things that are, Riches, and Pleasures, and Honours, Wife, and Children; if your heart be not weaned from every of them, you take him not as a Husband.

Christ must be taken onely.

Againe, others will serve *Christ* and their riches too, their credit too, their owne praise with men too; but *Christ* tels them, no man can serve both; you must serve him alone, and be obedient to none but him: if you doe so, you take him for your Lord indeed. So likewise,

many

many will be subject to him as a King, but they will be subject to their lusts too: if their lusts command them, they cannot deny them, some they will reserve; and you know how many this excludes. Therefore you shall find that no man can take *Christ* and his wealth: you know the young man was shut out because he would not let goe his possessions, which he must part with, or else have none of him. So *Joh.* 5.44. *If you receive the praise of men, how can ye beleeve?* That is, if you be not weaned and divorced from all, you cannot beleeve. Though you be the off-scowring of men, though you be mocked and scorned, it matters not; but if you seek the praise of men, you cannot beleeve. Where by the way you may mark something, and add it to that I said before. What is the reason that the seeking praise of men should hinder from beleeving? Certainly, if faith were only an act of the understanding, assenting to the truth for the authority of its speaker, it would be no hinderance or impediment to the act of the mind, in beleeving that such a thing is true; so that it must needs have reference to the will. Therefore, saith *Christ*, While you seek the praise of men, how can you beleeve? that is, take me for your *God* and *Lord*, whom you will serve altogether. So that to take *Christ* with a justifying faith is nothing else but to receive him, as it is expressed in many other places of Scripture: *John* 1.11. *He came unto his owne, and his own received him not; but to as many as received him he gave power to become the sons of God, even to them that beleeve on his name.* And so it is not (as the Papists say) a meere act of the understanding, but a taking of him for your

John 5.44.

Joh. 1, 11, 12.

God, your Saviour, to whom alone you will be subject, and give your selfe.

3 Christ must be taken with a complete and deliberate will.

Last of all, when these two are done and effected, so that there is no errour either in the person or in the forme, there is yet one thing more remaines behind, and that is, to take and accept him with a complete, a deliberate, and true will. For, even as in other matches, put the case the person be knowne, and the forme duly observed, yet if there doe not concurre a complete will, it is not properly a match: and therefore those matches are unlawfull which are made before yeeres of discretion, when a man hath not the use of his will, or when a man is in a phrenzie, because there is then no complete or deliberate will: so in this spirituall match you shall see how many the want of such a will excludes.

Three things required in the will in taking Christ.

1 It must be complete.

First, I say, it must be complete; which excludes all wishers and woulders, that prize *Christ* a little, that could be content to have *Christ*, but it is rather an inclination than a complete will, that are in an *æquilibrio*, that would have *Christ*, but not yet; that would live a little longer at ease, and have a little more wealth, but are not come to a resolute peremptory will, that have onely a weake inclination, which is not enough: for in a match the will must be complete; and it is needfull it should be so, it being a thing that must continue all a mans life.

2 Deliberate.

Againe, it must be a deliberate will: and this excludes all those that will take *Christ* in a good mood, on some sudden flash, when they are affected at a good Sermon, and have some good motions cast into their minds,

minds, that will (at ſuch a time) be content to take *Chriſt*, to ſerve him and obey him, to forſake their ſins, and give over their former luſts, but the will is not deliberate.

Laſt of all, as it muſt be complete and deliberate, ſo it muſt be a true will, that is, it muſt be free: and that excludes all them that meerely for ſervile feare, at the time of death, in the day of ſickneſſe and trouble, when hell and heaven are preſented to them, will take *Chriſt*. Indeed you can ſcarce come to any, but, in ſuch a caſe, he will profeſſe that he is now content to take *Chriſt* for his Lord and Saviour: but this is done by conſtraint, and ſo the will is not free. So I ſay, when all theſe concurre, the match is now made, and you are juſtified. 3 True, or free.

But after the match is made ſomething is required. Therefore there is one Queſtion more, and that is, What is this that is required after the making of the match? *Queſt.6.* What is required of us when we have it.

I anſwer, it is required that you love your husband *Jeſus Chriſt*, that you forſake father and mother, and become one Spirit with him, as a man is one fleſh with his wife: for you are now bone of his bone, and fleſh of his fleſh. *Anſw.* 1 To love Chriſt.

2. Againe, it is now required that you ſhould repent. And that is the meaning of that place, *Repent, for the Kingdome of heaven is at hand.* I tell you of a Kingdome, and a great Kingdome, but no man can come into that Kingdome except he repent: you muſt walke no longer after the fleſh, but after the Spirit: you muſt have your fleſh crucified, with all the affections and luſts of it. 2 To repent. Mat.3.2.

3 Part with all for him.

3. You must part with every thing for his sake, whether it be riches, or honours, or credit, or whatsoever, it is no matter, you must be ready to let them all goe.

4 To suffer for him.

4. You must be ready to undergoe any thing for his sake: you must have him for worse as well as for better: *you must be content to be hated of all men for his sake: you must take up your crosse and follow him.*

5 To doe for him. Tit. 2.14.

5. You must doe much as well as suffer much for him: he died to this end, *that he might purchase to him a peculiar people, zealous of good works:* you must respect him as a wife doth her husband, not as a servant doth a hard Master: you must not looke on his commandements as a hard task whereof you could willingly be excused, but as one that hath his heart inflamed to walk in them; as a loving wife, that needs not to be bidden to doe this or that, but if the doing of it may advantage her husband, it will be a greater griefe to her to let it lie undone, than labour to doe it.

Ob.

But now men say, This is a hard condition, I little thought of it.

Answ. None take Christ upon his own conditions, till they be throughly humbled.

It is true, the condition is hard, and that is the reason that so few are willing to come-in, when they understand these after-clap conditions, that they must part with all, that they must be persecuted, that their will must be perfectly subject to the will of *Christ*, that they must be holy as he is holy, that the same mind must be in them that is in *Christ Jesus*, that they must be of those peculiar people of God. And therefore have wee told you that none will come in to take *Christ* for their husband, till they have been bitten with the sense of their

their ſins, till they be *heavie laden*, and have felt the weight of Satans yoke, till then they will not come under the yoke of *Christ*: but thoſe that be humble, that have their hearts broken, that know what the wrath of God is, that have their conſciences awaked to ſee ſin, will come-in, and be glad they have *Christ*, though on theſe conditions; but the other will not. If you will have *Christ* on theſe conditions you may. But we preach in vaine, all the world refuſeth *Christ*, becauſe they will not leave their covetouſneſſe, and idleneſſe, and ſwearing, and their ſeverall ſports and pleaſures, their living at liberty, their company-keeping, they will not doe the things that *Christ* requires at their hands, and all becauſe they are not humbled, they know not what ſin means; whereas ſhould God ſhew it to them in its right colours, ſhould they be but in *Judas* his caſe, had they taſted of the terrours of the Almighty, were their conſciences enlightned, and did it ſet them on, they would take him with all their heart. Note.

But another objection comes in, I would come in, but how ſhould I doe it? I want power and ability, I cannot mortifie the deeds of the body: could I doe that, I would not ſtand on the buſineſſe. *Ob.*

To this I give a ſpeedy anſwer: If thou canſt come with this reſolution to take him, take no care for doing it; for aſſoone as thou art his, hee will give thee another ſpirit, hee will enable thee to all things. *Joh.* 1.12. *To as many as received him, to them he gave power to become the ſons of God*: What is that? is it an empty title? No, *he made them ſons, not born of the fleſh, or of the will of man, but of God.* It is true, with thy own

Anſw. When we reſolve to take Chriſt, God gives us power. John 1.12, 13.

heart

heart thou art not able to doe it; but what if God give thee a new heart, and a new ſpirit? When the match is made, and concluded betweene him and us, he ſends his Spirit into our hearts, and this Spirit gives us ability, making us like *Chriſt*, changing us, and cauſing us to delight in the duties of new obedience in the inward man. Therefore take no care for abilitie, onely labour for an honeſt heart, armed with this reſolution; I am reſolved to take *Chriſt* from henceforth, and you ſhall find another Spirit to enable you exceedingly. And now, that we may not let all this goe without ſome application, we will hereof make two Uſes.

Uſe 1. To ſee the greatneſſe of mans ſin, and Gods juſtice in condemning.

First, this great uſe is to be made of it, to learn hence to ſee how great the ſin of men is, and how juſt is their condemnation for the ſame, that when this *righteouſnes of God is revealed* from heaven by this Goſpel which we now preach, they reſiſt it, caſting it at their heeles, not regarding it, but deſpiſing theſe glad tidings of ſalvation, which is ſo glorious a myſtery. This very thing that we preach to you, is it that was ſo many thouſand yeeres agoe fore-told, and as long expectd, being the greateſt worke that ever *God* did. This is that which *Paul* magnified ſo much, and ſtood ſo amazed at. Therefore if you reject it, know that your ſin is exceeding great. We that preach the Goſpel are Meſſengers ſent from the Father to invite every one of you to come to the Marriage of his Son: if you will not come (as ſome of you are young, and mind other things; others of you have gone long in an old tract, and will not turne; ſome have married a wife, others have

Aggravation of ſins againſt the Goſpel.

have other businesse, and therefore you will not come; or if you doe come, it it without your Wedding Garment, you come not with a conjugall affection) I say, if you refuse, the *Lord* will deale with you as with them in the Gospel, he will have you brought and slaine before his face. And we come not from the Father onely, but we are also sent from the Son; he is a suitor to you, and hath dispatched us as Embassadours to wooe you, and *to beseech you to be reconciled.* If you will come, he hath made knowne his mind to you, you may have him; if you will not come, you will make him angry; and you had need to *kisse the Son lest he be angry:* though he be so mercifull, as *not to quench the smoaking flax, nor to break the bruised Reed,* yet notwithstanding, that Son hath *feet like burning brasse, he hath a two-edged Sword in his hand, and his eyes are like flames of fire:* so you shall find him to be if you refuse him. As he is a corner stone for some to build on, so he is a corner stone to grind them to powder that refuse him. When the better is the suitor, and is rejected, what wrath, what indignation breeds it among men? And so take all the sins you have committed, there is none like this; none shall be so much laid to your charge at the day of Judgement, as your rejecting of the Son, and of his righteousnesse revealed, and freely offered to you. What *Christ* said (*It shall be easier for Sodome and Gomorrah than for such a Citie*) I may apply to every one that's come to heare me this time. If you will not give eare to my invitation, it shall be easier for *Jewes* and *Turkes*, for the *Salvages* at the *East-Indies*, than for you. It had beene better for you

Rejecting Christ the greatest sin.

Mar. 16. 16.

 that

that *Christ* had never come in the flesh, that his righteousnesse had never beene offered to you. Therefore is that added, *Mar.* 16.16. *He that beleeveth not, is damned:* of such consequence is the Gospel. When *Moses* was on Mount *Ebal,* he set before them a blessing and a curse, life and death: so doe I now; If you will not accept of *Christ*, you are cursed. Therefore when you heare this offer, let every man examine himselfe how he stands affected unto it. For all hearers are divided into these two sorts, some are worthy, and some unworthy. As when *Christ* sent away his Disciples, *If any were worthy, their peace was to rest upon them*; if they were not worthy, they were to *shake off the dust of their feet against that Citie.* I say, consider if you be worthy of this righteousnesse: for if you find your hearts to long after it, if you find you prize it much, so that you can reckon all as drosse and dung in comparison of it, and will sell all to buy this pearle, then are you worthy: but if when you heare of it you neglect it, and attend unto it coldly, you are unworthy, and against such wee are to shake off the dust of our feet; that is, *God* shall shake you off as dust when you come for salvation to him at the day of Judgement.

Mar. 16.16.

Hearers of two sorts.

To be worthy of Christs righteousnes what.

If in examination you find your selves unworthy, that this worke hath not beene wrought in you, (wherein it is your best way to deale plainely with your selves) then give no rest to your selves, but enter into a serious consideration of your sins, attend on *Gods* ordinances, make use of all that hath beene delivered concerning humiliation, and give not

not over untill you have attained this eager desire after *Christ*. Indeed this is wrought by God himself, but give not you over. This is it S. *John* calls drawing: *None can come to me, except the Father draw him*: and that is done when *God* gives another will, when, on the propounding of *Christ*, he gives *agninam voluntatem*, the nature of a Lamb, changing the heart, and working such an inclination to *Christ*, as is in the Iron to follow the Loadstone, which never rests untill it be attained.

John 6.44.

Thus it was with the woman of *Canaan*, she would have no deniall; and *Cant*.3. with the Spouse that would not be at quiet untill she had found her Beloved, seeking him day and night; finding him not within, she inquires of the *watchmen*, and never gives over till she had found him *whom her soule loved*. As *God* puts an instinct in the creature, such a violent, strong, impetuous disposition and instigation is in them that shall be saved, and belong to *Christ*: *God* puts into them such a disposition as was in *Sampson* when he was athirst, *Give me water, or else I die*; so are they athirst after *Christ*, Give me *Christ*, or else I die. And this you must have, for *God* will put you to it, he will try whether you be worthy commers or no. Commonly, at the beginning, he is as a man that is in bed with his children, and loath to rise, but you must knocke and knock againe; and as it was with the unjust Judge, importunity must doe it; though your desire be strong, yet for a time, in his ordinary course, he with-holds and turnes a deafe eare, to trie if thou hast an eager desire: for if it ceaseth quickly, he should have lost his labour

Cant.3.

God works a strong desire in the Saints after Christ.

How God trieth the strength of our desires after Christ.

labour in bestowing Christ on thee. But if nothing will make thee give over, if thou wilt beseech him, and give him no rest, I'll assure thee *God* cannot deny thee; and the longer he holdeth thee off, the better answer thou shalt have in the end. And when thou hast *Christ*, thou hast that that cannot be expressed; for with him thou hast *all things*. When you have him you may go to him for justification, and say, *Lord*, give me remission of sins: I have *Christ*, and thou hast promised that all that are in *Christ* shall have pardon, that they shall have thy Spirit, and be made new creatures; now, *Lord*, fulfill these promises. I say, it is a condition beyond expression: next to that we shall have in heaven, and far above that which any Prince or Potentate in the world hath, farre beyond that which any man that swimmes in pleasures and aboundance of wealth hath; which, if it were known, would by all the world be sought after. Therefore when you heare of such a condition offered, take heed of refusing it: for if you doe, your sin is hainous, and your condemnation will be just.

What we have together with Christ.

Use 2. Not to deferre the taking of Christ.

The second Use I will onely name. Consider what it is to refuse, yea, what it is to deferre your acceptance of it: *God* may take your deferring for a deniall: you that thinke, Well, I will take it, but not yet, take heed lest you never have such an opportunity againe. I say, be exhorted, be moved, be besought to take it. This I speake to you that be humble, to so many among you as have broken hearts. Others may take him if they will, but they will not, they mind not this doctrine, they regard not things of of this nature, they will when they lie a dying, but now they have something else to doe. But you that *mourne in Sion*, you that have broken hearts, that know the bitternesse of sinne, to such as you is this Word of salvation sent: others have nothing to doe with it, and let them not thinke much to be excluded, for *Christ* excludes them: *Come unto me all ye that are heavie laden, and ye shall find rest.* Not but that others shall have him if they will come, but they will not take him on the precedent conditions named before. It may be they would have redemption, and freedome, and salvation by him, but they will not take him for their King. They that be humble, that have their hearts wounded with the sense of sin, are willing to take him on his owne termes, to keep his Commandements, and not thinke them grievous; to beare his burden, and thinke it light; to take his yoke, and count it easie; to give all they have for him, and thinke all too little; to suffer persecution for his sake, and rejoyce in it; to be content to be scoffed at, and hated of men; to doe, to suffer any thing for his sake: and when all this is done, to regard it as nothing, to reckon themselves *unprofitable seovants*, to account of all as not worthy of him. Therefore be not thou shie in taking of him, for you have free liberty.

Mar. 11.28, 29.

They that be willing to take Christ, how they be affected.

But before I dismisse you, let me speake a word to you that be not yet humble, let me beseech you to consider three things to move you. First, the great danger that is in not taking of him. If you could be well without him, you might sit still as you are; but you

Three considerations to move men to take Christ.

1. The danger in not taking him.

you shall die for want of him. If a wife can live without a husband, she may stay unmarried: but when a mans case is this, I see without *Christ* I must perish, I must lose my life, that is the penalty, such is the danger if I refuse him; me thinks this should move him.

2 The benefit in taking him.

Secondly, as the danger of refusing him, so consider the benefit of taking him: if you will have him, you shall with him have a Kingdome, you shall change for the better; for whatsoever you part withall, you shall have an hundred fold in this life: if you forgoe any pleasure or lust, you shall have for it the joy of the *Holy Ghost*, farre exceeding them: if you part with riches, you shall be truely rich in another world, yea, you shall there have a Treasure: if you lose friends, you shall have *God* for your friend, and shall be a Favourite in the Court of heaven. In a word, you shall have an hundred fold.

3 The certainty of having him.

Thirdly, you shall be sure to have him, you shall not be deceived: for *God* hath put out his word, he hath declared that to be his will, and it stands now with his justice as well as with his mercie, to give *Christ*: his word is a corner stone, and you may build on it. Nay, *by two immutable things* he hath confirmed it, his Word and his Oath; and *Heaven and Earth may passe, but they shall not passe*: you may build on them, to have *Christ*, and salvation by him. When *Paul* had delivered *Gods* mind, if an Angell from heaven should tell them the foundation is sandy, nay, if he himselfe should preach another doctrine, they were not to beleeve him. Therefore if you will take him and have him, *trust perfectly in the grace that is reveal-*

The certainty of Gods promise.

led

led by Jesus Christ: doe it not by halves; It may be I ſhall be ſaved, it may be not: thou maiſt build on it, thou maiſt venter thy life on it. All theſe things conſidered, the greatneſſe of the danger in refuſing, of the benefit in accepting: and if it be thus ſure, if we will take him, then put it to venture; why doe you ſtand off? what can we ſay more to perſwade you? If you will take him and his righteouſneſſe, you may have it. *God* hath committed this to us, *What we looſe on Earth, ſhall be looſed in Heaven.* He hath given us the Keyes of Heaven and Hell, and if we open the gates of Heaven to any, they ſhall ſtand open: but now in the preaching of the word the gates of heaven ſtand open to every one of you; therefore come in while it is called to day, before the Sun ſet on you, as you know not how ſoone it may. Indeed if we had not made the offer, the danger had bin ours, and we ſhould have periſhed for your ſakes: but ſeeing we have *made manifeſt the whole counſell of God, we are now free from the bloud of every one of you*; for we have made known the will of *God* to the full. You know what is offered to you, and if you take him not, your bloud ſhall be upon your owne heads. Therefore conſider whether you will take him or refuſe him: this is the queſtion, Will you take him or not take him? You that now refuſe and ſleight this offer, the day may come when you would be glad to have it. You that are now in the height and flower of your youth, and you that are more ancient, living in health and wealth, and having your fill of pleaſures, it may be, for the preſent, you have other things to take up your minds; but the

time

time will come when the Bridegroome ſhall enter in, and the doores ſhall be ſhut, when your houre-glaſſe ſhall be out, and your time ſpent, and then this relation of righteouſneſſe, and remiſſion of ſins now offered, would be reckoned glad tidings: but take heed that it be not too late, beware leſt you cry, and *God* refuſeth to hear. Not but that *God* will hear every man, if his cry comes from unfeigned faith and love; but it may be, *God* will not give you that unfeigned faith and love, when you be come to that extremity: ſeeing you would not come when he called, it may be he will not come when you call; it may bee hee will not breathe the breath of life, nor give ſuch a ſpirit and diſpoſition as he will accept of. *Chriſt* died to purchaſe to himſelfe a peculiar people, zealous of good works, and not onely to ſave men. He died for this end, that men might do him ſervice: and if you will not come-in in time of ſtrength and youth, when you are able to doe him ſervice, I ſay, in his ordinary courſe, he will reject you in your extremity, you may not then expect mercie at his hands. Therefore doe not ſay, I will follow my covetouſneſſe and idleneſſe, my pleaſures and buſineſſe, my luſts and humours, and hereafter come in; for you are not to chuſe your owne time. If he call you, and you refuſe to come, take heed leſt in his wrath he ſweare that you ſhall not enter into his reſt.

FINIS.

THE SECOND SERMON.

ROM. 1. 17.

For by it the righteousnesse of God is revealed from Faith to Faith: as it is written, The just shall live by Faith.

THe next point that these words afford us is this, That,

Faith is that whereby the righteousnesse of God is made ours to salvation. Doct. 2.

The righteousnesse of God (saith the Apostle) *is revealed from faith to faith:* that is, it is so revealed and ffered by *God*, that it is made ours by faith, we are made partakers of it by faith: you see it ariseth cleerly from the words.

Now for the opening of this point to you, you must understand that there are two wayes or Covenants whereby *God* offereth salvation to men. One is the Covenant of workes, and that was that righteousnesse by which *Adam* had beene saved if he had stood in his innocency: for it was that way that God appointed for him, *Doe this, and live:* but *Adam* performed not Two Covenants.

not the condition of that Covenant, and therefore now there is another Covenant, that is, the Covenant of Grace, a Boord given us against Shipwrack. Now this Covenant of Grace is double:

Either absolute and peculiar,

Or conditionall.

1 Absolute. Absolute and peculiar onely to the Elect; so it is expressed *Jer.* 31. *I will put my Law into your inward parts, and write it in your hearts, and I will be your God, and you shall be my people.* So likewise in *Ezech.* 36. *I will give you a new heart, and put a new spirit within you, and I will take your stony hearts out of your bodies.* Here the Covenant is expressed absolutely, and this is proper onely to the Elect.

Jer. 31. Ezek. 36.

2 Conditionall. But now beside this there is a conditionall Covenant of Grace, which is common to all: and that is expressed in these termes, *Christ* hath provided a righteousnesse and salvation, that is his worke that he hath done already. Now if you will beleeve, and take him upon those termes that he is offered, you shall be saved. This, I say, belongs to all men. This you have thus expressed in the Gospel in many places: *If you beleeve, you shall be saved:* as it is *Marke* 16. *Goe and preach the Gospel to every creature under Heaven: he that will beleeve shall be saved, he that will not beleeve shall be damned.* It is the same with that *Rom.* 4. 5. *To him which worketh not, but beleeveth in him which justifieth the ungodly, his faith is accounted righteousnesse.* (Marke it) *To him that beleeveth on him that justifieth the ungodly*, that is, there is a certaine justice of righteousnesse that *Christ* hath prepared or purchased

Mar. 16. Rom. 4. 5.

purchased for men, though they be ungodly, he requires nothing of them before-hand, though they be wicked and ungodly, yet this righteousnesse is prepared for them; that which is required of them is onely that they take it. Now he that will beleeve *God* that he hath prepared this for him, and will receive it, it is enough to make him a righteous man in *Gods* acceptation: so that this is the onely way now by which men shall be saved. The worke is already done on *Christs* part, there is righteousnesse that *God* hath prepared, which is therefore called the righteousnesse of *God*; and there is nothing precedently required or looked for on our part but taking and applying of it. Note.

Quest. But, you will say, Is there nothing else required of us? Must *God* doe all? and must we doe nothing but onely take that righteousnesse that is prepared for us?

Answ. Though holinesse be required, it is Gods worke.

I answer, it is true indeed, we must lead an holy life, a religious, sober, and righteous life: for, *for this end hath the grace of God appeared*, saith the Apostle: yet thou must know withall that we cannot worke in our selves this holinesse, this religious and sober conversation, that must be *Gods* worke altogether: we are onely to take this righteousnesse, and the other is but a consequent that followeth upon it. To illustrate this unto you by a similitude: A Wheele or Bowle runneth, not that it may be made round, that is the businesse of the workeman, who makes it round, that it may run. So it is in this case: God doth not look that we should bring holinesse and piety with us, *Simile.*

D for

for we have it not to bring: we are at the first onely to beleeve and accept this righteousnesse that is offered us: when that is done, it is *Gods* part to frame us, and to fit and fashion us for an holy life. Such a kind of speech you have it expressed in, *Eph.* 2.10. *We are Gods workmanship, fashioned in Christ Jesus to walke in good workes, which he hath ordained, &c.* Marke it: it is not an action of our owne, but *God* is the workman, we are the materials, as the clay and the wood, that he takes into his hands: when we have but taken this righteousnesse that is offered, it is *Gods* worke to cast us into a new mould, to give us a new heart, and to frame a new spirit within us, that so we may walke in good workes before him: this is the great mysterie of godlinesse: for we have much adoe to perswade men to beleeve that the righteousnesse prepared by *Christ* should be offered to them, and nothing be required but receiving of it: this will not sinke into the hearts of men by nature, they thinke they must doe something precedently, or else this righteousnesse is not offered them. But, my Beloved, we must learne to beleeve this, and know that it is the worke of *God*, to sanctifie us after he hath justified us. I confesse it is not so in other things, there is still some action of our owne required to gaine this or that habit or abilitie: as you see in naturall things, there are some kind of habits that we get by some precedent actions of our owne, as the learning of Arts and Sciences, to learne to write well, &c. here there is some action of our owne required to fit us for it, and then we get the ability to doe it.

Habits of two sorts.

But

But besides these there are other habits that are planted by nature in us, as an abilitie to heare, to see, to taste, &c. Now for these we need not any action of our owne for the attaining of them, because they are planted in us by nature. So it is in these things that belong to salvation. It is true indeed, we may get habits of morall Vertues by labour and paines of our owne, there are actions of our owne required to them; and in that the Philosopher said right, that *we learne to be temperate, and sober, and chaste, &c.* But now for the Graces of the Spirit, there it is not so; those habits that nature hath planted in us, we exercise them naturally, without doing any action of our own to attaine them; as we doe not by seeing oft learne to see, but it is a facultie naturally planted in us: so it is in all the workes that we must doe, which are the way to salvation, *God* workes them in us, he infuseth those habits into us. Therefore this conclusion is good, that it is faith alone by which this righteousnesse is made ours to salvation.

This is evident by the Apostle, *Gal. 2. ult.* Saith he, it is not by the Law, *If righteousnesse had beene by the workes of the Law, then Christ had died without a cause.* As if he should have said, salvation must needs be by one of these two.

Either by something that we doe our selves, some actions that we our selves have wrought, or else it must be meerly by faith. Now if it had beene attainable by any worke of our owne, *Christ* died without a cause: as if he should say, *Christ* could have given you abilitie to doe those workes without his dying; but for this very cause *Christ* came into the World, and died, that he might work righteousnesse, and make satisfaction to *God:* so that you have nothing to doe for the first attaining of it, but to receive it by faith.

Foure reasons why God will save men by faith.

And if you would know the reason why *God* that might have found out many other wayes to lead men to salvation, yet hath chosen this way above all others to save men, onely by faith, receiving the righteousnesse of *Christ*, which he hath wrought for us; you shall find these foure reasons for it in the Scriptures: two of them are set downe *Rom.*4.16. *Therefore it is by faith, that it might come by grace.* (Marke it:) This is one reason why *God* will have it by faith, *that it might be of grace.* For if any thing had beene wrought by us (as he saith in the beginning of the Chapter) it must have beene given as wages, and so it had been received by debt, and not by favour: but this was *Gods* end in it, to make known the exceeding length and bredth of his love, and how *unsearchable the riches of Christ are:* his end was to have his grace magnified. Now if there had beene any action of ours required but meerely the receiving of it by faith, it had not beene meerely of grace; for faith empties a man, it takes a man quite off his owne bottome; faith commeth as an empty hand, and receiveth all from *God*, and gives all to *God*. Now that it might be acknowledged to be free, and to be altogether of grace, for this cause *God* would have salvation propounded to men, to be received by faith onely.

*Reas.*1. That it might be of grace.

Reas 2. That it might be sure.

Secondly, as it is by faith, that it might come by grace, so also *that it might be sure*, that the promise might

might be sure; if it had beene any other way, it had never beene sure. Put the case that *God* had put us upon the condition of obedience, and had given us grace and abilitie, as he did to *Adam*, yet the Law is strict, and the least failing would have bred fears and doubts, and would have caused death. But now, when the righteousnesse that saveth us is wrought already by *God*, and offered to us by him, and offered freely, and that the ground of this offer is the sure Word of *God*, and it is not a conjecturall thing, now we may build infallibly upon it: for unlesse faith have footing on the Word, we cannot say it is sure; all things else are mutable, and subject to change: therefore when God hath once said it, we may firmely rest in it, and it is sure. And this is the second reason why it is onely by faith.

Thirdly, it is by faith, *that it might be to all the seed*, not onely to those that are of the Law, but also them which were strangers to the Law. If it had beene by the Law, then salvation had beene shut up within the compasse of the Jewes: for the Gentiles were strangers to the Law of God, they were uncleane men, shut out from the Commonwealth of *Israel*: but when it is now freely propounded in the Gospel, and nothing is required but onely faith to lay hold upon it, when there is no more looked for but beleeving and receiving; hence it comes to be to all the seed: for *Abraham* himselfe, before he was circumcised, he was as a common man, the vaile was not then set up; yet even then his *faith was imputed to him for righteousnesse*.

Reas. 3. That it might be to all the seed.

Reas.4. That no flesh might rejoyce in it selfe.

The last reason why it is of faith, is, that no man might boast, *that no flesh might rejoyce in it selfe:* for if it had beene by any other meanes, by any thing done in our selves, we had had cause to rejoice in our selves: but for this cause, saith the Apostle, 1 *Cor.*1. 30. *Christ is made to us wisedome, righteousnesse, sanctification, and redemption, that he that rejoyceth might rejoyce in the Lord.* As if he had said, If God had given us a wisedome of our own, we had had cause to have rejoyced in our selves; but we are *darknesse, Ephes.*4. there is nothing but foolishnesse and weakenesse in us, to the end *that no flesh might rejoyce in his presence.*

1 Cor.1.30.

Ephes.4.

Againe, if we had had grace put into our selves, (though it had beene but little) for which *God* might have accepted us, the flesh would have boasted; therefore his *righteousnesse* is made ours.

But when this is done, yet if after justification it had beene in our power and abilitie to have performed the workes of sanctification by any power or strength of our owne, we should yet have beene ready to boast thereof, *Christ is made sanctification* too; so that *wee are not able to thinke a good thought,* we are not able to doe the least good thing without him: *It is I* (saith the *Lord*) *that doth sanctifie you:* it is I that doe act every Grace: it is I that doe put your hearts into a good frame: *Christ is made sanctification to us:* so that take a holy man after he is justified, it is *Christ* that sanctifieth him, and that carries him thorow his life in an holy and righteous conversation: and all this is done that *no flesh should rejoyce in it selfe.*

And

And yet one thing more is added by the Apostle; for if a man could rid himselfe out of miserie, if a man could helpe himselfe when he is under any crosse or trouble, he would then be ready to boast in himselfe: therefore, saith he, *Christ is made to us redemption also:* so that take any evill, though it be but a small evill, a small disease, a little trouble, no man is able to helpe himselfe in this case; it is *Christ* that redeemes us from the least evill, as well as from hell it selfe. For you must know that all the miseries that befall us in the World, they are but so many degrees, so many descents and steps towards hell: now all the redemption that we have it is from *Christ:* so that let us looke into our lives, and see what evils we have escaped, and see what troubles we have gone thorow, and see what afflictions we have beene delivered from, it is all through *Christ*, who *is made redemption for us.*

Christ delivers from the least evils, as well as from hel.

It is true indeed, there are some generall workes of Gods providence that all men taste of; but there is no evill that the Saints are freed from, but it is purchased by the blood of *Christ*: and all this *God* hath done *that no flesh might rejoyce in it selfe:* and for this cause salvation is propounded to be received onely by faith, there is no more required at our hands but the taking of *Christ* by faith; and when we have taken him, then he is all this to us.

Freedome from evill to the Saints, whence it is.

So that now you see the point cleered, and the reasons why it is by faith onely, that the righteousnesse of *Christ* is made ours to salvation.

Now in the next place if to this that we have said we adde but one thing more, to cleere the point, we ſhall then have done enough to ſatisfie you in this point; and that is this, to ſhew you what this faith is: for when we ſpeak ſo much of faith (as we doe) every man will be inquiſitive to know what this faith is: therefore we will endevour to doe that at this time.

First, Faith, if we ſhould take it in the generall, it is nothing elſe but this:

Faith, what in generall.

An act of the underſtanding, aſſenting to ſomething.

But now this aſſent is of three ſorts:

Aſſent of three ſorts.

1 Opinion.

First, there is ſuch an aſſent to a truth, as that a man is in a great feare leſt the contrary ſhould be true; and this we call *opinion*, when we ſo aſſent to any propoſition, as that that which is contrary may be true for ought we know.

2 Science.

There is a ſecond kind of aſſent, which is ſure, but it is grounded upon reaſons and arguments, and that we call *ſcience* or *knowledge*: that is, when we are ſure of the thing we aſſent to, we make no doubt of it, but we are led unto it by the force of reaſon.

3 Faith.

Againe, there is a third kind of aſſent, which is a ſure aſſent too; but we are led to it by the authority of him that affirmeth it: and this is that which is properly called *Faith*. So that a generall definition of Faith is this:

It is nothing elſe but *a firme aſſent given to the things contained in the holy Scriptures, for the authority of God that ſpake them.*

This is properly *Faith*, or *beleeving*, if we take the word in the generall.

Juſtifying faith.

But if we ſpeak of juſtifying Faith, we ſhall find that that

that is not commonly expressed in the word *beleeving* only, but *beleeving in Christ*, which is another thing; and therefore you shall find that it differeth in two things from this common and generall faith.

First, in regard of the object, and indeed that is the maine difference: for whereas the other faith lookes upon the whole Booke of *God*, and beleeves all that *God* hath revealed, because *God* hath revealed it, this justifying Faith pitcheth upon *Christ*, and takes him, with his benefits and priviledges: so that the difference lieth not in the habit of Faith, but in the object; for with the same faith that we beleeve other things, we beleeve this; as with the same hand that a man takes other writings with, he takes a Pardon: with the same eyes that the *Israelites* saw other things, they looked upon the brazen Serpent: the difference was not in the facultie, but in the object upon which they looked, by which they were healed: so it is in this, between this faith and the other, they differ not in the habit, but in the object. How it differs from generall faith. 1 In the object.

There is a second difference, which is a maine difference too; the other faith doth no more but beleeve the truth that is revealed, it beleeveth that all is true that is contained in the Scriptures; and the Divels may have this faith, and wicked men may have it: but justifying faith goeth further, it takes *Christ*, and receives him, so that there is an act of the Will added to that faith, as it is expressed, *Heb.* 11.13. *They saw the promises afarre off, and embraced them thankfully.* Others (it may be) see the promises, and beleeve them, but they take them not, they doe not embrace them. 2 In the act of the will.

So

So that if I should define justifying faith unto you, it may be thus described:

Definition of justifying faith.

It is a grace or a habit infused into the soule by the Holy Ghost, whereby we are enabled to beleeve, not only that the Messias is offered to us, but also to take and receive him as a Lord and Saviour.

That is, both to be saved by him, and to obey him: (Marke it) I put them together, to take him as a Lord, and as a Saviour: for you shall find that in the ordinary phrase of Scripture these two are put together, *Jesus Christ our Lord and Saviour.* Therefore we must take heed of dis-joyning those that *God* hath joyned together, we must take *Christ* as well for a Lord as a Saviour. Let a man doe this, and he may be assured that his faith is a justifying faith. Therefore marke it diligently, if thou wilt take *Christ* as a Saviour onely, that will not serve thy turne, *Christ* giveth not himselfe to any upon that condition, onely to save him; but we must take him as a Lord too, to be subject to him to obey him, and to square our actions according to his will in every thing. For he is not onely a Saviour, but also a Lord; and he will be a Saviour to none but those to whom he is a Master. *His servants you are to whom you obey*, saith the Apostle; if you will obey him, and be subject unto him in all things, if you make him your Lord, that he may have the command over you, and that you will be subject to him in every thing; if you take him upon these conditions, you shall have him as a Saviour also: for as he is a Priest, so you must know that he is a King, that *sits upon the Throne of David*, and rules those that are to be saved by

Christ must be taken as a Lord as well as a Saviour.

by him. Therefore, I ſay, you muſt not onely take him as a Prieſt, to intercede for you, to petition for you, but to be your King alſo; you muſt ſuffer him to rule you in all things, you muſt be content to obey all his Commandements. It is not enough to take *Chriſt* as a head, onely to receive influence and comfort from him, but you muſt take him alſo as a head to be ruled by him, as the members are ruled by the head; you muſt not take one benefit alone with the members, to receive influence from the head, but you muſt be content alſo to be guided by him in all things, elſe you take him in vaine.

Againe, this muſt be marked that I ſay, you muſt *take* or *receive* him: you muſt not onely beleeve that he is the ***Meſſias***, and that he is offered, but there is a taking and receiving that is neceſſary to make you partakers of that that is offered. Thoſe words, *John* 3. make it plaine; *God ſo loved the World that he GAVE his onely begotten Son, &c. Giving* is but a Relative, it implies that there is a *receiving* or *taking* required: for when *Chriſt* is given, unleſſe he be taken by us, he doth us no good, he is not made ours. If a man be willing to give another any thing, unleſſe he take it, it is not his. It is true indeed, there is a ſufficiencie in *Chriſt* to ſave all men, and he is that great Phyſician that heales the ſoules of men; there is righteouſneſſe enough in him to juſtifie all the world: but, my *Beloved*, unleſſe we take him, and apply him to our ſelves, we can have no part in that righteouſneſſe: this is plainly expreſſed in *Mat*.22. where it is ſaid, the King ſent forth his ſervants to bid men to the Marriage of his

We muſt not onely beleeve, but receive.

John 3.

Though there be ſufficiencie in Chriſt to ſave all, yet none benefit by it, but thoſe that receive him.

Mat.22.

his Son. And ſo in *Epheſ.*5. the ſame ſimilitude and compariſon is uſed by the Apoſtle, where he ſetteth forth the union that is between *Chriſt* and the Church, by that union there is betweene the Husband and the Wife. Put the caſe that an Husband ſhould offer himſelfe to a woman to marry her, and ſhe ſhould beleeve it; yet unleſſe there be a taking of him on her part, the match is not made: and ſo it is here, and in this thing the eſſence of faith conſiſts, when *Chriſt* offereth himſelfe unto you, you muſt beleeve that there is ſuch a thing, and that *God* intendeth it really, but it is the taking that conſummates the marriage; and when the Wife hath taken the Husband, then all that is his is hers, ſhe hath an intereſt in all his goods: ſo alſo it is here, there muſt be a beleeving that *Chriſt* is offered, that he is the *Meſsias*, and that there is a righteouſneſſe in him to ſave us; but that is not enough, we muſt alſo take him, and when that is done, we are juſtified, then we are at peace with *God*.

Wherein the eſſence of faith conſiſteth.

But that you may more fully underſtand what this faith is, I will adde theſe foure things more.

Four things touching faith.

First, I will ſhew you the object of this faith.
Secondly, the ſubject, or place where it is.
Thirdly, the manner how it juſtifieth us.
Fourthly, the actions of it.

1 The object of it, Chriſt

Note.

I ſay, that you may more fully underſtand what this faith is, conſider firſt the object of it, and that is *Chriſt* (as I told you before:) and herein this is to be marked, that a man muſt firſt take *Chriſt* himſelfe, and after, the priviledges that come by him. And this point I could wiſh were more preſt by our Divines, and that our

our hearers would more intend it. I ſay, firſt remember that you muſt firſt take *Chriſt* himſelfe, and then other things that we have by him, as the Apoſtle ſaith, *Rom.* 8. *If God have given us him*, that is, *Chriſt, he will with him give us all things elſe*: but firſt have *Chriſt* himſelfe, and then all things with him. And ſo 2 *Cor.* 1. *All the promiſes IN HIM are Yea and Amen*: That is, firſt we muſt have *Chriſt*, and then looke to the promiſes: this muſt be ſtill remembred, that we muſt firſt take his perſon, we muſt have our eyes fixed upon that. And ſo that place before named, *John* 3. *God ſo loved the World, that he gave his onely begotten Son*: he gives his Son as a father gives his ſon in marriage; the father gives the ſon, and the ſon himſelfe muſt be taken. So that we muſt firſt take *Chriſt*, we muſt fixe our eyes upon him: for faith doth not leape over *Chriſt*, and pitch upon the promiſes of Juſtification and Adoption, but it firſt takes *Chriſt*. The diſtinct and cleere underſtanding of this will helpe us much in apprehending and underſtanding aright what juſtifying faith is: wee muſt remember to take *Chriſt* himſelfe; for it is an adulterous affection for a Wife not to thinke of the perſon of her Husband, but to thinke onely what commoditie ſhe ſhall have by him, what honours, what riches, what conveniences, as if that made the match, to be content onely to take thoſe: will this, thinke you, make a match amongſt men? Surely no, there muſt be a fixing of the eyes upon the perſon, that muſt doe it. Doe you love him? are you content to forſake all, that you may enjoy him? It is true

True love lookes firſt to Chriſts perſon.

true indeed, you ſhall have all this into the bargaine, but first you must have the perſon of your Husband: therefore remember to fixe your eyes upon *Chriſt*, take him for your Husband, conſider his beauty and his excellencies, (which indeed are motive to us;) as a Woman that takes a Husband is encouraged by the benefits that ſhe ſhall have by him: but still remember that he himſelfe must be taken. As it is in other things, if you would have light you must first have the Sun; if you would have strength, you must first take meat and drinke before you can have that benefit by it: ſo you must first have *Chriſt* himſelfe before you can partake of thoſe benefits by him: and that I take to be the meaning of that in *Mar.* 16. ***Goe preach the Goſpel to every creature under heaven; He that beleeves and is baptized, ſhall be ſaved:*** that is, he that will beleeve that *Jeſus Chriſt* is come in the fleſh, and that he is offered to mankind for a Saviour, and will be baptized, that will give up himſelfe to him, that will take his marke upon him: for in that place by baptizing is meant nothing elſe but the giving up of a mans ſelfe to *Chriſt*, and making a publike testimony of it, although there be ſomething more meant generally by baptizing: but here is meant a testification to all the world that we have taken *Chriſt*. Now every one that will beleeve, and be baptized, that is, every one that will doe this, ſhall be ſaved: ſo that a man must first take *Chriſt* himſelfe, and then he may doe as the Wife after ſhe hath her Husband, ſhe may thinke of all the benefits ſhe hath by him, and may take them, and uſe them as her owne. This is the first thing.

We may looke to the benefits we have by Christ, but not principally.

Baptizing, what meant by it in Mar. 16.

The

The second thing that I promised, was to shew you the subject of faith, and that is the whole heart of man; that is to say, (to name it distinctly) both the mind and the will. Now to shew you that both these are the subject of faith, you must know that these two things are required: 2 The subject of faith, both the mind and will.

First, on the part of the understanding it is required that it beleeve, that is, that it conceive and apprehend what *God* hath revealed in the Scriptures: and here an act of *God* must come in, putting a light into the understanding. For, my Beloved, faith is but an addition of a new light to reason, that whereas reason is purblind, faith comes and gives a new light, and makes us see the things revealed by *God*, which reason cannot doe; by faith we apprehend these great and glorious Mysteries, which otherwise we could not apprehend, as we see it expressed in 2 *Cor*. 4. *The god of this world hath blinded their eyes, that the light should not shine into their hearts, by which they should beleeve this glorious Gospel.* So then there must be a light put into the mind, that a man may be able by that to elevate and raise his reason to beleeve this: that is, to conceive and to apprehend the things that are offered and tendered in the Gospel. What required in the understanding touching faith. Faith an addition of a new light to reason.

But this is not all, there is an act also of the will required, which is to take and receive *Christ*: for this taking is an act of the will, therefore there must be a *consent* as well as an *assent*. Now it is the act of the understanding to assent to the truth which is contained in the promises wherein *Christ* is offered: but that is not all, there is also an act of the will requisite to consent What required of the will touching faith.

unto

unto them, that is, to embrace them, to take them, and to lay hold upon them, and to apply them to a mans selfe. This I will the rather cleere, because it is a thing controverted. I say, there is a double act, an act of the mind, and an act of the will: to this purpose consider that in *Rom.*5.17. *For if by the offence of one death reigned by one, much more they which receive abundance of grace, and the gift of righteousnesse, shall reigne in life by one, Jesus Christ.* (Marke it) you may see what faith is in those words, Those that receive the gift of righteousnesse: righteousnesse is given and offered by *God*, and those that receive that gift of righteousnesse shall reigne in life: so that taking and receiving being an act of the will, it must needs be that the will must come into this worke as well as the understanding. Like unto this is that 1 *John* 12. *To as many as received him, &c.* That is, *to as many as beleeved in his Name:* for so the words afterward expresse. That is, when we are willing to take *Christ*, which is nothing else but the consent of the will, when the will is resolved to take him, being so apprehended as he hath beene described, as a Lord, and as a Saviour, this is faith; this, I say, is an act of the will, because it is an act of receiving. It is evident, *John* 5.44. *How can ye beleeve which receive honour one of another? &c.* If beleeving in *Christ* were onely an act of the mind, as the Papists affirme, and some other besides; if beleeving were nothing else but an assenting to the truth of God, which is an act of the understanding, how could the praise of men be opposite to beleeving? But the meaning is, How can you beleeve, and take me for

for your Husband, and yet seeke praise of men too? for that will come in competition with me, and then you will forsake me. I say, this makes it evident that justifying faith is not onely an act of the mind, but an act of the will also; because otherwise the seeking praise with men could be no impediment to the act of beleeving.

This act of the will wrought by God.

Now this also, as well as the former, must be wrought by *God*, and *God* puts a new light into the understanding: as he raiseth that up to see and beleeve these truths, so there is another act which *God* also workes on the will, and unlesse he worke it, it is not done: for come to any man that is in the state of nature, and aske him, Will you be content to take *Christ*? that is to say, to receive him in that manner as he hath beene described; his answer would be, No. Beloved, the lives of men expresse it, though they speak it not in so many words: Therefore till *God* come and draw a man, and change his will, the work is not done. If you take a bough, and offer it to a Swine or a Wolfe, they will refuse it, and trample it under their feet; but offer it to a Sheepe, and the Sheepe receives it, and followes it: so when *Christ* is offered to men upon these conditions that we have named, men refuse him, they reject him and sleight him: but when *God* takes away these wolvish and swinish hearts of ours, and turns our wills another way (which is the drawing the Scripture speakes of) then we are willing to take *Christ*. If you take other metall than Iron, the Load-stone will not stirre it; but turne the metall into Iron, and it will follow the Load-stone.

The heart must be changed before a man can be willing to take Christ.

So let the hearts of men continue in that condition wherein they are by nature, and they will never take *Christ*, they will never accept him; but when *God* puts into them such a strong and impetuous instigation and disposition, as that of the Spouse in the *Canticles*, that had no rest till she found her Beloved, then they will take *Christ* upon his owne conditions. So then we see that faith is an action both of the mind and the will, wrought by *God*, enlightning the mind, and changing the will; which is that which our Saviour *Christ* calls drawing, ***None comes to me unlesse the Father draw him:*** that is, except his will be set on worke, unlesse *God* change him, and put such a disposition and instigation into him, that he can find no rest till he come to *Christ*.

How faith justifieth.

Thirdly, the next thing we are to speake of is, ***How this Faith justifieth.***

Now for this know that this faith is considered two wayes:

A twofold consideration of faith.

Either { As it workes, or, As it receives.

Either as a qualitie, or as an instrument.

As a qualitie it workes, and in this sense it hath nothing to doe with justification.

Faith altereth not the nature of sin.

Note.

It justifieth us as it is an instrument, and that not by altering the nature of sin, that is, by making sin to be no sin, but by taking away the efficacie of sin. As for example; when a man hath committed sins, Faith doth not make his sins to be no sins, indeed *it scattereth them*

them as a Cloud. You may consider it after this manner: First, it cannot be that that sin that is committed should be made to be no sin; for what is once done cannot be undone: *God* himselfe cannot doe that, because it is a thing that cannot be: for when the sins are committed, they doe remaine so: and therefore, I say, it cannot be that that which is sin should be made to be no sinne. We cannot make adultery to be no adultery, for the nature and essence of the thing must remaine. Well, now what doth faith? It doth this, though the sinne be the same that it was, yet it takes away the sting and the guilt of sinne, by which it puts us into the state of condemnation, and by which it bindes us over to punishment. As the Lions to which *Daniel* was cast, they were the same as they were before, they had the same propensenesse and disposition to devoure as they had before, they had the ordinary nature of Lions; but at that time *God* tooke away from them that fiercenesse that was in them, so that they did not devoure him, though they were there still: so it is with sinne, the nature of sin is to condemne us; but now when *God* shall take away this efficacie from it, it doth not condemne: and this is that that faith doth.

Faith takes away the efficacie of sin, that it doth not condemne us.

Even as the Viper that was upon *Pauls* hand, though the nature of it was to kill presently, yet when *God* had charmed it you see it hurt him not: so it is with sin, though it be in us, and though it hang upon us, yet the venome of it is taken away, it hurts us not, it condemnes us not: thus faith, by taking away the efficacie and power of ſin, it juſtifies, as an inſtrument, as a hand that takes the Pardon.

The King when he pardoneth a Traitour, he doth not make his treaſon to be no treaſon, for the act of the treaſon remaines ſtill; but the taking of the Pardon makes the Traitor not to be under condemnation: So, my Beloved, faith is that act that takes the Pardon from *God*, ſo that though the ſin remaine the ſame, and of its owne nature is of power to bind us over to death, yet by this faith taking the Pardon from *God*, it comes to paſſe that it hurts us not, we are not condemned for it.

You know debts in a mans booke, the writing remains ſtill, the lines are not blotted out; yet when they are once croſſed, the Creditour cannot come and aske his debt any more, becauſe it is croſſed: So it is in this, our ſins are the ſame after we are juſtified as they were before; but faith is that that croſſeth the booke: faith, I ſay, by apprehending the Pardon, and taking the acquittance at *Gods* hands that he offers.

If a man have an acquittance, although the debt remaine the ſame in the Booke, yet there can no more be required at the hands of him that hath taken the acquittance.

Thus, I ſay, faith juſtifies us as an inſtrument, by accepting, receiving, and taking the acquittance that *God* hath given to us through *Chriſt*.

Let me adde one word more of the next thing; which is, What are the acts of faith?

4 The acts of faith three.

They are theſe three:

First,

First, To reconcile, or to justifie.
Secondly, To pacifie the heart.
Thirdly, to purifie, or sanctifie.

The first thing that Faith doth, is to reconcile: that is, (as I said before) by faith we are pitched upon *Christ*; we take him first, and then we take the priviledges, they all follow upon it, forgivenesse, and adoption: this is the first act of faith, to reconcile us to *Christ* himselfe, and upon this we have boldnesse to goe to *Christ* for forgivenesse, to goe to *Christ* to make us heires of all things. For after this manner Faith doth it, *All things are yours*, *whether* Paul *or* Apollo, *&c.* And why? Because you are *Christs*. (Marke it) you must first be *Christs*: that is, even as the Wife is the Husbands, so you must be knit and united to *Christ*, and then all things are yours: so that Faith first makes us *Christs*, it reconciles us to him, and makes us one with him, and in him, one with *God* the Father; and then all things are given unto us, and made ours. 1 To reconcile us.

The second act of Faith is to quiet and pacifie the heart; to comfort us, in assuring us that our sins and transgressions are forgiven; and this is different from the former. There are two acts of faith: 2 To pacifie the heart.

The one is the direct act, by which we apprehend and take *Christ*, and the righteousnesse that is offered through him, by which we take forgivenesse. Direct and reflect act of faith.

And the second is the reflect act, by which we know that we have taken *Christ*, and have taken out our Pardon: and this act is very different from the

the former, we may have the former without this.

We commonly thinke that we are not justified by *Christ*, unlesse we have assurance of it; and when we looke for that, and find it not presently, all our hopes are gone: but it should not be so. It is one act of Faith to take *Christ*, and another act of Faith to comfort and pacifie the heart; and that these are two distinct things, consider but this in a word.

Difference betweene them in three things.

The first act is constant: when a man hath once taken and accepted of *Christ*, he is alwaies his: after we once have *Christ* there is no divorce. But the other act of assurance whereby we know that we have taken him, that is a thing that may faile and deceive a man.

Againe, the first act admits of no degrees: for when a man is once in *Christ*, he is alwaies *Christs*, when he is once married to him. Marriage you know admits of no degrees; so Justification is equall to every man, it admits of no degrees, it is alwaies the same, we are not now lesse justified, and then more, but we are alwayes alike justified, being once justified: but the other act of faith whereby I am assured that I have taken *Christ*, that admits of degrees, a man may have sometimes more comfort, sometimes lesse: and therefore righteousnesse is said here to be revealed *from faith to faith.*

Lastly, the first act of faith, whereby we take *Christ*, and those priviledges by him, as the Wife takes the Husband, that is founded upon the sure Word of *God*; *God* hath tendred it to us upon his word and promise, and he must performe it, it cannot be altered nor changed: he that builds upon it, builds upon the corner-stone, that will not faile him. But now the second act

whereby

whereby I come to know that I have done this, that is grounded upon experience. Indeed we are helped by the *Holy Ghost* to know it, but it is chiefly grounded upon our owne experience: for it is no more but the act of a mans owne heart, reflecting upon what he hath done, when he considers, Have I taken *Christ* or no? as a Lord, and as a Saviour; as a Priest to save me, as a King to live by his Lawes? This is a looking upon an act of mine owne, therefore the understanding and knowing of it must come from experience.

The last act of faith is to purifie and to sanctifie. I cannot stand upon it at this time, nor make Use, and apply this as I desired: therefore I will break off here. So much for this time. 3 To purifie the heart.

FINIS.

THE THIRD SERMON.

ROM. I. 17.

For by it the righteousnesse of God is revealed from Faith to Faith: as it is written, The just shall live by Faith.

THe last point that we delivered out of these words was this, That,

Faith is that whereby we are made partakers of the righteousnesse of Christ.

We come now to the uses of it.

Use 1. Not to be discouraged to come to God.

And first of all, if it be by faith only by which we are made partakers of that righteousnesse that saveth us, the first consectary that we will draw from hence is this, That we should learne to come to *Christ* with an empty hand, and not to be discouraged for any want that we find in our selves, nor for the greatnesse of our sins; we should not be discouraged for the want of a perfect degree of repentance and godly sorrow, or for the want of whatsoever good worke you thinke is requisite to salvation. For, my beloved, you must know that this is the nature

nature of faith, that it doth its worke best alone; and faith is so farre from requiring any thing in the party that shall have *Christ*, that necessarily he must let goe all things else, otherwise he cannot beleeve: and this is a point necessarily to be considered: for every man is apt to conceive and thinke that it is impossible that *God* should accept him, unlesse there be something in him why *God* should regard him. If he find himselfe to be exceeding ungodly, he thinkes that *Christ* will never looke after him.

Faith worketh best alone.

And againe, if he have nothing at all to give, if he have nothing to bring with him in his hand, he thinkes that he shall have no pardon. But you see that faith requires nothing in the first apprehension of *Christ*: if a man be never so ungodly it is all one, the offer notwithstanding is made unto him.

Againe, why should you looke for righteousnesse in your selves? The work of faith (and it hath nothing else to doe) is to take that righteousnesse of *Christ* that is none of your owne: so that there is nothing else at all required; for all that faith hath to doe, is onely to take from *Christ* that righteousnesse that we want our selves. So that I say there is no reason why any man should be discouraged in his first comming, for any want that he finds in himselfe, or for any condition that he is in, because faith onely is that that makes us partakers of a righteousnesse to justifie us, because we our selves have it not. I say, faith is so farre from requiring any thing to be added to it, to help it in the act of justifying, that of necessitie it excludes all things else: for faith hath this double qualitie,

The worke of faith, what.

A double qualitie in faith.

qualitie, not onely to lay hold of *Christ* offered, but to empty a man of all things else whatsoever. As for example: Faith is not onely the beleeving of a truth which is delivered from the authority of him that doth deliver it; but it is a resting upon *Christ*, a casting of our selves upon him. Now when a man leanes upon any other thing, he stands not upon his own legges, hee stands not upon his owne bottome; for if hee did, hee could not properly be said to leane. If a man trust and depend upon another, hee provides not for himselfe; but he that so lookes to himselfe, that he provide so as to make himselfe safe if another should faile him, so farre he trusts himselfe; so that, beloved, if you trust *Christ*, it is of necessitie required that you must be unbottomed of your selves, you must alogether leane upon him, you must cast your selves wholly upon him. For faith hath such an attracting vertue in it, that it fils the heart with *Christ*. Now it cannot fill the heart with *Christ* unlesse the heart be emptied first. Therefore, I say, faith hath a double quality, not onely to take, but to empty; and they are reciprocall, the one cannot be without the other.

Faith emptieth a man of himselfe.

Hence it is that we say, faith ingrafts a man: a man cannot be ingrafted into a new stocke, unlesse he be quite cut off from the former root: therefore faith drives a man out of himselfe, and makes him nothing in himselfe; so that when he comes to lay hold on the promise of *God*, he lookes at no quality or excellency of his owne, he lookes at no fitnesse or worthinesse in himselfe, but he comes with a hand and a heart altogether empty: so that when a man comes to beseech

God to receive him to mercy, and to grant him a pardon of his sins, when he comes to take hold of the righteousnesse of *Christ* for his justification, if he think that there is any little worthinesse in him, or that there be no fault in him at all, and from thence shall thinke that *God* will receive him, this man is not fit to take *Christ*: he must be wholly emptied of himselfe, and then God will speake peace to him.

But you will aske, What is that that faith doth empty a man of? *Quest.*

Faith emptieth a man of two things: *Answ.*

First, of all opinion of righteousnesse in himselfe.

Secondly, of opinion of strength and ability to help himselfe: for if either of these remaine in the heart, a man cannot receive *Christ*.

First, I say, a man must be emptied of all opinion of worthinesse in himselfe, of all conceit that he hath the least righteousnesse in himselfe: therefore when the young man came to *Christ*, and *Christ* told him that he must keep the Law, and he said he had done all those things from his youth, *Christ* knew that he was not yet fit: therefore saith he, *Goe and sell all that thou hast*: *Christs* end was nothing else but to discover to him his owne unworthinesse. If thou wilt be perfect (saith *Christ*) take this triall; Canst thou be content to let thy wealth goe, to follow me? Canst thou be content to suffer persecution? This shewed that he was not perfect, but that he was still a sinfull man; this was the way to prepare him for *Christ*, this course we see *Christ* alwaies tooke: we see it expressed in the Parable of the Publican and of the Pharisee, the Publican went

1 All opinion of worth in himselfe.

went away justified, because he was wholly emptied of all conceit and opinion of worth in himselfe.

Why the Pharisee was not justified.

But the Pharisee was not justified, not because he was not a juster man than the Publican (for he was in outward performances better than he) but because he had an opinion of his owne righteousnesse; he was conceited of a worthinesse in himselfe, therefore he went home not justified.

What was it that excluded the Jewes? was it not an opinion of something they had of their owne?

The *Laodiceans* they thought they were rich, and increased, and wanted nothing, therefore they never came to buy of *Christ*. That which a man thinkes he hath already of his owne, he will never be at the cost to buy. Therefore that is the first thing that a man must doe, he must thinke himselfe of no worth at all, he must be empty of all opinion and conceit of his owne excellency.

2 Of all opinion of strength to help himselfe.

But this is not all, although a man be perswaded of this, that he hath no worthinesse in himselfe, yet if he think he is able to helpe himselfe, and can stand alone without *God*, he will not come to take *Christ*; and therefore this further is required, that a man see that he hath no abilitie to help himselfe, that all his redemption must come from *Christ*: for if you ask many men whether they have any opinion of worth in themselves, they will be ready to answer, No. What then is the reason that they come not to *Christ*? It is because they are in health and prosperity, and they can doe it soone enough hereafter, they can yet for the present subsist without *Christ*; but when *God* shall shew

ſhew a mans heart to himſelfe, when *God* ſhewes a man his danger, and ſhewes it him at preſent, and how unable he is to help himſelfe out of danger, then a man will have no reſt till he have *Chriſt*. Therefore you ſhall ſee both theſe required, 1 *Cor.* 1.30. *Chriſt* muſt be to us *wiſedome, righteouſneſſe, ſanctification, and redemption* too. Firſt, if a man think that there is anything in him, either *wiſedome, righteouſneſſe*, or *ſanctification*, that excludes him; for he will rejoyce in himſelfe: and that concerns the firſt condition required, to be empty of all opinion of worth.

But yet if a man thinke that he is able to ſtand ſafe and ſecure for a time, that he is able to be a Buckler to himſelfe, that he hath ſomewhat whereunto he may leane, and doth not ſee that *Chriſt* muſt be his redemption alſo, he will not come at *Chriſt*.

That which kept the Prodigall ſon away, it was not an opinion of any worth in himſelfe, but becauſe he thought he could live without his father, he had his portion in his owne hands, and at his own diſpoſing; and he would not come home to his father, till he could live of himſelfe no longer: ſo that though we have an opinion of no worth in our ſelves, yet if we conceive or thinke that we can live without *Chriſt*, we will not care for him.

This was the fault of thoſe that were invited to the marriage: they refuſed to come, not becauſe they thought that themſelves were of worth, but they were perſwaded that they needed not thoſe things to which they were invited. Therefore, I ſay, theſe two things muſt be done, a man muſt be be emptied of all opinion of worth in himselfe.

And secondly, of all abilitie in himselfe to help himselfe: and when faith hath done both these, then it brings a man to *Christ*: when a man seeth that there is nothing in him why *God* should regard him, and that he cannot stand longer, nor be in safetie longer than *Christ* helps him, and speakes peace to him, now a man is fit to take hold upon *Christ*: and therefore we must learne to come to *Christ* with an empty heart.

Ob. Many men complaine that they would beleeve, but they want that sorrow that they should have, they want that repentance that they would have, they think they are not yet fit, therefore they dare not apply the promises.

Answ. Double complaint in sense of want. To these we say now, that there is a double kind of complaint:

1 Sinfull. One is, when a man lookes upon these things as upon things that make him fit; which if he have, he thinks *God* will respect him; and if he have it not, he thinkes that *God* will not looke after him. If thy complaint be thus, it is sinfull; for in this thou seekest some thing in thy selfe.

2 Lawfull. But if a mans complaint be this, that he is not yet awaked enough, that he is not yet sensible enough of his sins, the doctrine of the remission of his sins, and free justification doth not affect him as it should. Indeed here is just cause of complaint, for these things are necessary before you come to take *Christ*. Therefore that place in *Mat.* 10.11. will explaine this, and answer an objection that may be made against it: when the Apostles were sent out to preach the Gospel, when they

they came to any house, they were bidden to *enquire who were worthy*; *If any man be worthy* (saith *Christ*) your *peace shall come upon him*: but if he be not worthy, *shake off the dust, &c.* A man would thinke by this that there were some worthinesse required in the party that comes to *Christ*, and that before he can apply the first promise of justification. *Object.*

To this we answer, the worthinesse that is required here, is nothing else but abilitie to prize *Christ*, to set him at a high rate, to long after him, to hunger and thirst after his righteousnesse, your *peace shall come upon such a man.* That is, if there be a broken-hearted man that lookes after *Christ*, whose heart yearnes after him, that he is able to prize him aright, he shall be accepted: but if they be such men as will not receive you, such as will not set meat before you, such as will give you no respect, *shake off the dust of your feet, &c.* So that, I say, such a complaint we may make, if we find a want of desire after *Christ*, for that is required: but if wee looke upon any thing as a *qualification* in our selves, such a worthinesse is not required, we must be driven out of all conceit of it, or else we cannot take *Christ*. So much for that Use, that seeing it is onely faith whereby we lay hold of *Christs* righteousnesse, that then we have no reason to be discouraged in respect of any want: nay, we must find a want of all things, before we can be made partakers of this righteousnes. *Answ.*

Againe, secondly, if it be by faith onely by which we are made partakers of this righteousnesse, and by which we are saved, then we should learne hence to rejoyce onely in *God*, and not to rejoyce in our selves; for *Use 2.* To rejoyce in God.

for this is the very end why *God* hath appointed this way of salvation: *Eph.1.6. For he hath chosen us to the praise of the glory of his grace, in his Beloved:* That is, that he might have the praise of the glory of his grace, as it is in *Ephes.2.* Therefore it is of faith, and not by workes, that no man should boast of himselfe: 1 *Cor.* 1.30. Therefore *Christ is made to us wisedome, righteousnesse, sanctification, and redemption*, that no flesh should rejoyce in it selfe. Now if that be *Gods* end, if that be his aime, why he will have us saved by faith, let not us disappoint him of his aime, let us not take from him the glory of his grace, but let us glory in the *Lord*.

We are prone naturally to rejoyce in our selves.

This point we should especially looke to, not to rejoice in our selves, but in *God*: for, my Beloved, we are all naturally exceeding apt to rejoice in our selves, we would faine find some excellencie in our selves, every man is apt to reflect upon himselfe, and he would faine see some worth there that he might rejoyce in; and if he be no body at all there, it is contrary to his nature to thinke that he shall be accepted: there is nothing in the world that we are so backward to as this. It was *Adams* fault in Paradise; whereas he should have trusted *God*, and have beene wholly dependant upon him for all, he would needs know good and evill, he would have something of his owne; and this was it that lost him all, and brought the curse upon him, because he would not be dependant.

Now in the Gospel *God* comes by a second meanes of saving men, and in this the *Lord* would have the creature to have nothing in himselfe to glory in; but man

man is hardly brought to this, but exalts and lifts up himselfe, and would faine have some worth and excellencie of his owne; but as long as we doe thus, we cannot be saved: that is the argument that is used *Rom.*6 4. why *Abraham* was justified by faith. If there had beene any other way, *Abraham* had had wherein to rejoyce in himselfe: but faith excludes this rejoycing, and onely faith: we should, I say, learn to do this in good earnest, to see that there is no worth in our selves, to have *Christ* to be to us all in all. *Col.*3. 11. is an excellent place to this purpose: Saith the Apostle there (in the matter of salvation) *There is neither Jew nor Gentile, bond nor free, but Christ is all in all*: that is, when we come to be justified before *God*, when we come to the matter of salvation, *God* lookes at nothing in a man, he lookes at no difference betweene man and man; one man is vertuous, another man is wicked; one man is a Jew, and hath all those priviledges, another man is a Gentile, an Alien from the Commonwealth of *Israel*; one man is circumcised, another man is uncircumcised: but all this is nothing. Why? For *Christ is all in all*. (Marke it:) First, he is all; that is, there is nothing else required to justifie. Indeed if we were something, and he were not all, we might then looke at something besides, but he is all.

Col.3.11. opened.

Christ all in all.

Againe, he is *all in all*: that is, goe thorow all things that you may thinke will helpe you to salvation, in all those things *Christ* is onely to be respected, and nothing but *Christ*; whatsoever is done without *Christ*, *God* regards it not. If you will do any work of your own to help your selves in salvation, if you wil rest upon any priviledges, *Christ* is not all in all; but *Christ* must be all in all in every thing: and if onely *Christ* be all, then we must come onely with faith; for it is faith onely that layes hold upon *Christ*.

Now a naturall man he will not have *Christ* to be all, but himselfe will be something; or if *Christ* be all in some things, he will not have *Christ* to be all in every thing, to have *Christ* to be his wisedome, his righteousnesse, his sanctification; to doe nothing but by *Christ*, to have *Christ* to be his redemption, not to be able to helpe himselfe without *Christ*, but that *Christ* must helpe him out of every trouble, and bestow upon him every comfort; this, I say, is contrary to the nature of man: therefore we must be thorowly emptied of our selves in this matter of rejoycing, as well as

Note.

in the matter of taking: for in what measure any man sets any price upon himselfe, so farre as he hath any opinion of himselfe that hee is something, just so farre he detracts from *Christ*: but when a man boasts not of himselfe at all, such a man rejoyceth in *God* altogether, such a man will stand amazed at the height, and breadth, and length, and depth of the love of *God*; such a man will be able to see that there are unsearchable riches in *Christ*, such a man will be able to say with *Paul*, that he cares for nothing, he reckons *all things dung*, *Phil.*3. I have all the priviledges (saith he) that other men have, I am a Jew, I am a Pharisee, but I reckon all these things as dung; that is, I care for none of them if I had a hundred more. It is true, I have beene as strict as any man, yea, I went beyond

beyond others, for I was zealous in that course wherein I was, yet I have beene taught thus much, that all these things are nothing; for *God* regards them not, he regards nothing but *Christ* and his righteousnesse: therefore I looke not after these things, but that I may be found in him, not having mine owne righteousnesse, but that righteousnesse that *God* accepteth, which is *through faith in him*. Therefore, my brethren, learne thus to rejoyce in *Christ* and in *God*, and not in your selves; this is the most excellent worke that we can performe, it is the worke of the Saints and Angels in Heaven, we should learne to come as neere them now as we can. In *Rev.* 7. 11. they cried with a loud voice, saying, *Salvation commeth by our God, that sitteth upon the Throne, and by the Lamb, and therefore praise, and wisedome, and glory be given to God for evermore*; because salvation is from the *Lord*, and from the Lamb, and not from our selves at all: hence it is that they fell downe and worshipped him, and for this cause they all cry, *Wisedome, and glory, and praise be to our God for evermore.*

The ground of praising God, what.

If salvation had beene from our selves, if we had done any thing to helpe our selves therein, there had not been ground of giving all praise and glory to *God*; and if this be the worke of the Saints and Angels, we should labour to performe it as abundantly as we can now; and let us doe it in good earnest: for if men could be brought to this, to rejoyce in *God* alone, their mouthes would be filled with praise exceedingly, they would regard nothing else, and in the course of their lives they would make it evident to the world that they were ſuch as made no account of the world, ſo they might have *Chriſt*, they would be content with any condition; for *Chriſt* is all in all to them.

Uſe 3. To labour for faith above all.

Thirdly, if it be by faith onely by which we are made partakers of the righteouſneſſe by which we are ſaved, then it ſhould teach us to let other things goe, and principally to mind this matter, to labour to get faith, whatſoever become of other things; for it is that by which we have ſalvation.

The Papiſts they teach that workes are the maine, and many things they preſcribe that men muſt doe: our doctrine is, you ſee, that faith only is required. Indeed many things follow upon faith, but faith is that you muſt only labour for, and then the reſt will follow upon it.

This Doctrine of ours you ſhall find that it is delivered cleerely in *Gal.* 5. 5, 6. *We wait, through the Spirit, for the hope of righteouſneſſe, which is through faith:* that is, we looke for nothing from the Law, we regard no workes at all in the matter of juſtification; that which we looke for is only that righteouſneſſe which is taken by faith: and why doe we ſo? For, ſaith he, *in Chriſt Jeſus neither circumciſion is any thing, nor uncircumciſion, but faith, &c.* as if he ſhould ſay, There is good reaſon why we ſhould expect ſalvation onely by faith, becauſe nothing elſe will helpe us in that worke: *circumciſion is nothing, nor uncircumciſion is nothing:* by thoſe two he meanes all other things; that is, in the having of all the priviledges in the world, in the doing of all the workes that can be be done, faith is all in all; but it must be such a faith as workes by love: though it be by faith only, yet it is not an idle faith: therefore you are especially to labour for faith.

Without faith God regards not morall vertues.

There are many other excellencies that we are capable of, many morall vertues, such as *Aristotle* and *Socrates* have described; but without faith *God* regards none of these: take one that is a wicked man, and take another, let him be never so vertuous, as *Socrates* and *Seneca*, that were the strictest in Moralitie of all the Heathen; nay, take any man that lives in the Church, that lives the most strict and exact life, and yet is not justified by faith, *God* makes no difference betweene these men, the one is as neere to heaven as the other, *God* lookes upon them both with the same eye; for he regards nothing without faith. He that is the most profane and ungodly, if he come with faith he shall obtaine *Christ*; the other that hath all morall Vertues in the most exact maner, without faith, they shall doe him no good: therefore we are to seeke for nothing in the matter of justification, but how we may be enabled to beleeve; we are principally to study this matter of faith.

Difference betweene faith and morall vertues.

Take such a one as *Socrates*, and such a one as Saint *Paul*, it may be *Socrates* might be outwardly as temperate, and as patient, and be indued with as many excellencies, he might appeare in his carriage as strict as Saint *Paul*; but here is the great difference, the one doth what he doth of himselfe, and through himselfe, and for himselfe; the other doth what he doth of *Christ*, and through *Christ*, and for

Christ: Therefore faith mainely is requisite.

If we had all other excellencies, yet we shall find this in them, that they doe alway give something to the creature.

Againe, if you goe never so farre in them, yet you shall find that there is some imperfection in them.

But faith, it emptieth the creature of all things, it leaveth nothing in a man, it makes him leane and rest onely upon *Christ*, and upon his righteousnesse for salvation.

Againe, faith worketh in us a love to *God*: for we have nothing in our selves, but all that we have being from him, we cannot but love him againe.

Againe, faith presenteth to *God* a perfect righteousnesse, and therefore *God* onely accepts it: for *God* must be just, and nothing can satisfie the justice of *God* but a righteousnesse that is perfect; nothing can attain a righteousnesse that is perfect, but onely faith: labour therefore to beleeve this, and to turne all your study and care how to get faith. My Beloved, this is a thing that we are bound to preach to you; this is the summe of that doctrine that *Christ* so often preached when he was upon the earth, *Beleeve, for the Kingdome of God is at hand*: this is the summe of all the Doctrine of the Apostles; it was all they had to doe, to perswade men to beleeve. What was the summe of all Saint *Pauls* doctrine? *We goe up and downe* (saith he) *from place to place, witnessing both to Jewes and Gentiles, &c.* So it is our part when we come to preach to you, when we come to dispense to you that which is for the nourishment of your soules, we must doe as those

The summe of the preaching of Christ and his Apostles.

those Stewards, that set bread and salt upon the Table, whatsoever other dish there is: so we should alwayes preach *Christ*, and perswade you to beleeve in him, and stirre you up to turne the streame of your endevours after the obtaining of that faith that taketh this righteousnesse: the principall thing we are to looke unto, is, to see from what Fountaine that that we have comes: if a man have never so many vertues in him, if they arise not from this fountaine, if they spring not from this root, they are nothing, *God* lookes upon them without acceptance or delight.

Againe, this is that that you are to doe in hearing, that which you are chiefly to looke after, is, how to get faith; and therefore if men will imploy their strength and their endevours, and busie themselves to attaine such and such vertues, it is but as the watering of the branches, and to let the root alone. Faith is the root, that is, it is that that makes all acceptable to God: for what is the difference betweene Christianitie and Moralitie? and without this what is our preaching? We may gather well neere as good instructions to resist vice out of *Plutarch*, and out of *Seneca*, as out of *Pauls* Epistles, but this differenceth it, that we preach *Christ*, and from *Christ* we derive abilitie and strength to doe all things else, and that makes all els to be acceptable: so that this is it that you must look after, to have *Christ*, to receive all from him, to doe all for him; for these are reciprocall. Unlesse you think you have all from *Christ* you will never doe all for him; when we think *Christ* is all-sufficient we will be perfect with him againe. Note.

Difference betweene faith and shewes of holinesse.

But, by the way, in this you see not onely the difference betweene morall vertues, and those in a true Christian, which is godlinesse, that they come from different fountaines, and looke to different ends; but you see also the difference betweene those shewes of strictnesse that are among the Papists, and that sincerity of life that we preach unto you, which is an effect of this faith: for if you marke it you shall find that all that they doe either is without *Christ*, or addes to *Christ*; they thinke they shall be saved for doing such and such things, which prepare and fit them for salvation, they looke mainely to the workes of humbling the body, and doing many actions of mortification, but still *Christ* onely is not sought after in all this. But now looke to the Doctrine that wee have delivered, it is *Christ* that we preach, it is faith that we preach unto you. It is true, wee preach those things too, we lay the same necessitie upon you of doing good workes, we stirre you up to holinesse of life, and mortification: but here is the difference, we derive it all from *Christ* by faith, we say that faith doth all.

Indeed, when you have faith, if that faith be right, it will work by love: here then you see the difference, we doe the same things, but we derive all from a justifying faith, laying hold upon *Christ*; and so love to him, and all other graces doe arise from this.

Use 4. To apply the promises with boldnesse.

Againe, a fourth Use of this point is this, if salvation be onely by faith, then we should learne hence to goe with boldnesse to *God*, to take the promises, and to reckon them sure to us. If something else had beene

beene required on our part, we should then have gone with a great deale of doubting to *God*; but now, seeing there is nothing required but onely to goe and take it, this should make us to goe with boldnesse to the Throne of grace, to come with assurance that we shall speed.

And therefore in the businesse of seeking to *God* for the remission of our sins (which indeed is the greatest businesse that we have to doe) what greater comfort can there be than to have this assurance, that if we come to *God* for it, we shall not faile, nor be deceived of it?

For the present occasion of receiving the Sacrament. What is the end of the Sacrament, but to preach faith? The Sacrament preacheth that to your outward senses that we doe to your understandings; it presenteth to the eye that which we now preach to the eare: for what is the Covenant of *God* in the Gospel but onely this? *God* offers *Christ* unto you freely, as the Bread and Wine is given unto you. *To us a Sonne is given, &c.*

The Sacrament preacheth faith.

Againe, we take him, and bind our selves to obey him, and to love him, to be to him alone, to marry him, to make him our Lord and our Husband. Now in the Sacrament both these are done: when the Bread and Wine are offered they are but a resemblance of the offer of *Christ*. Indeed there is a blessing in it: for it is *Gods* Ordinance, it increaseth this grace of faith. And againe, there is a bond on our part wherein we tie our selues to obey *Christ*.

Now if any of you will offer to come, and yet have

not

To receive the Sacrament unworthily, what.

not given up your selvs to *God* in good earnest, you receive your own condemnation, you are divorced from *Christ*, and married to the World; and this is to receive the Sacrament unworthily. The maine end of the Sacrament is to increase faith; and salvation is ours by faith: therefore we should come with boldnesse, and lay hold upon the promises of it.

Gods free promise should encourage us to come with boldnesse.

We should doe in this case as *Joab* did, lay hold upon the hornes of the Altar, that is, take hold upon *Christ*, and remember that sure word of promise, *To us a Son is given, to us a child is borne.* And, *Let whosoever will, come and take of the waters of life freely.* Goe thorow the whole Booke of *God*, all the promises therein are as so many grounds for faith to build upon: it is impossible that *God* should slay you if you come and lay hold of the hornes of the Altar. If you will take *Christ*, and receive these promises, and rest on them, it is impossible but that *God* should performe them, he hath bound himselfe to performe what he hath said: *If we acknowledge our sins, he is faithfull and just to forgive them*, 1 *John* 1.9. as if he were unjust and unfaithfull if he should not doe it. His Oath is passed, he hath added an Oath to his promise, that by two immutable witnesses it should stand firme.

We should doe in this case as *Jacob* did after he had once a promise from *God*: when he meets his brother *Esau*, *Lord* (saith he) *thou hast promised to doe me good, therefore deliver me from the hand of my brother.* So when we have a promise, and *God* hath said, He that will take *Christ* shall be saved: and *Christ* is freely given, and the pardon is generall, therefore what

should

ſhould hinder us? Urge *God* upon his promiſe, wreſtle with *God* as *Jacob* did, and let him not goe without a bleſſing: *wreſtling* implies reſiſting; it is a ſigne *God* reſiſted him for a time: ſo it may be *God* will denie thee a great while, yet continue thou to ſeeke him, let him not goe, he cannot denie thee in the end, thou ſhalt have the bleſſing at the laſt: we ſhould learne thus to importune God; tell him, *Lord*, I have a ſure promiſe, and thou haſt made the pardon generall, and I am ſure I come within the number of that Commiſſion, *Goe and preach the Goſpel to every creature*: goe and tell every man under heaven that *Chriſt* is offered to him, he is freely given to him by *God* the Father, and there is nothing required of you but that you marry him, nothing but to accept of him: here is a word ſure enough if there were nothing elſe but this. Therefore learne to doe in this as the woman of *Canaan* did, though *Chriſt* denied her, yet ſhe would not give over: for ſhe had this ground to build upon, that he was *Jeſus*, he was *the Son of David*, he was mercifull, and ſhe had exceeding great need of him, and therefore ſhe would not give over: ſo, I ſay, having this ground for your faith, goe to *God* with boldneſſe, and never give over; it is impoſſible (if you ſeeke him in good earneſt, with all your heart) but that he ſhould receive you.

Jacob wreſtling with God.

It is true indeed, he gives to ſome ſooner than he doth to others; with ſome he deales as he did with the woman of *Canaan*: to ſome he gives an anſwer quickly, ſome againe he deferres longer, and he will put us to the triall. *Chriſt* dealeth differently with his children,

God anſwers ſome ſooner, and ſome later.

dren, he doth with us sometimes as the unjust Judge, he turnes the deafe eare to us: or like the man that was in bed with his children, and was unwilling to rise; but what saith the Text? *Luke* 11. 6. though he would not doe it for him as a friend, yet his *importunity* makes him rise and lend him: so thou thinkst (it may be) *God* is not thy friend, yet by thy importunitie he will rise at the last: therefore though thou find *God* to be as an enemy, though he be never so backward to rise, yet give not over: I can assure thee, as certainely as there is any truth in the Booke of *God*, thou shalt be heard in the end, *Heaven and earth shall passe away before this sure Word* shall perish. It is *Gods* maner to put men to the triall, and it is his wisedome so to doe, otherwise he would have many that would be forward at the first, yet fall off in the end.

Note.

The reason of it.

It was *Naomies* wisedome to bid her Daughter *Ruth* goe backe to her kinred, but she would not, she stood out: *I will goe* (saith she) *where thou goest, and nothing but death shall part betweene me and thee.* When *Naomi* saw that she was stedfastly minded, she tooke her along with her. So if *God* should receive men at the first, many men would come in, and take hold upon *Christ*, and make a profession of his Name, but they would not hold out to the end with him. But when *Christ* shall tell them, I have not so much as a place to lay my head in, if thou wilt have me, thou must deny thy selfe, and take up thy Crosse, and thou shalt find a great deale of trouble, and suffer persecution; if a man now, notwithstanding this, will not be beaten off from *Christ*, but, though *Christ* turne

turne the deafe eare to him for the present, and present to him all maner of difficulties, yet if he will, notwithstanding all this, be constant still in importuning *God* to have *Christ*, when *God* shall see that his mind is thus set, he will take him along with him, he will be thine, and thou shalt be his, his people shall be thy people: this is it that knits the knot betweene you: *My Beloved is mine, and I am his*; his Word is passed for it, he hath promised his consent, now if we will give ours, the match is made.

If it were doubtfull whether we should have his consent, it were another case; but we have a sure Word for it, we should learne therefore to importune him.

Now when we have done this, when we are come with this boldnesse, and have laid hold upon *Christ*, then let us looke to the priviledges, then let us take the pardon of our sins, adoption, and reconciliation, and all things else, onely remembring that condition of after-obedience; that though we may come freely, and come with this boldnesse, and though nothing be required, but that we take this Sonne of *God* that is offered, yet, I say, there is a condition of after-obedience, we must resolve to serve him, and to love him with all our heart, we must resolve to doe that that *Ruth* promiseth to *Naomi*, to live with him, and to be with him, and that his people shall be our people, &c.

After we have Christ, look to the priviledges by him.

Ob.

But you will say, I am willing to doe this, to part from my lusts, and to be to *Christ* alone, but I am not able, my lusts are strong and prevalent.

Answ.

To this I answer, if thou be but willing, *Christ* desires

no

Christ requireth but a willingnesse to mortifie our lusts.

no more: I would but aske thee this; Suppose that thou wert able to overcome those lusts; take a man that is strongly given to good-fellowship (as they call it) to company-keeping, that is given to fornication, to swearing, or whatsoever the sin be, take any prevalent lust that is in any man that now heareth me, I would aske him this question; Put the case thou wert able to get the victorie over thy lust, wouldest thou be content to part with it, and to take *Christ*? If thou sayest, No, I had rather enjoy the sweetnesse of my lusts still, art thou not now worthy to be condemned? But if thou answer, I would upon condition I were able to overcome my lusts, I assure thee *God* will make thee able, *God* requires no more but a willingnesse to come and take *Christ*, the other is *Gods* worke.

Object. I, but I have tried, and have not found it so.

Answ. I answer, it cannot be, thou hast not yet resolved to part with thy lusts, thou hast not yet set downe this peremptory conclusion in thy selfe, that thou wilt forsake every thing, that thou maist have *Christ*. If any man say, he is willing to take *Christ*, and to part with the sweetnesse, and the pleasantnesse, and the profitablenesse that his lust brings to him, if he could get the victory, if he were freed from the solicitations of them; let me tell thee, thou must first resolve to take *Christ* upon his owne conditions, and for the other, *God* hath promised to doe that himselfe: 1 *Cor.* 8.9. *God will confirme you, and keepe you blamelesse; for he is faithfull that hath called you to the fellowship of his Sonne:* as if he should have said, Doe you thinke

He that is under the dominion of his lusts, never yet resolved to part with them.

thinke that *God* will call men to *Christ*, that he will beseech men to take his Sonne? Will he call you to the fellowship of his Son, and will he not keepe you blamelesse? he hath promised it, and sworne it, if he should not doe it he should be unfaithfull. When *God* calleth you to come unto *Christ*, he promiseth that the vertue of *Christs* death shall kill sin in you, and that the vertue of *Christs* resurrection shall raise you up to newnesse of life: *God* hath promised that he will give the *Holy Ghost*: for he never gives his Son to any, but he gives them the Spirit of his Son too. Now, *He that hath called you is faithfull, and he will doe it.* So that, I say, if thou wilt come in, that is, if thou wilt accept of *Christ* upon his conditions, it is certaine *God* will receive thee: and if thou find thy selfe troubled with the violence of any lust, or of any temptation, presse upon *God*, urge him with his Word and Promise, that he would assist thee by his owne strength, that he would enable thee to overcome, that he would give thee the Spirit of his Sonne, and resolve as *Job*, *Though he kill me, yet will I trust in him*: for I have a sure promise, *Heaven and earth shall passe, but not one tittle of his sure Word shall passe till it be fulfilled.*

Two things in laying hold on the promises.

Now because this is a point of much moment, this laying hold upon the promises, and because it is a thing that is not easily done, therefore I will shew you these two things.

The first is this, that the understanding must be rightly informed what ground a man hath to doe it: when a man comes to beleeve the forgivenesse of his sins, let

let him not thinke, I have a perswasion that my sins are forgiven, therefore they are forgiven; but a man must labour to see the ground of it: for a thing is not true because we are perswaded it is so, but the thing is first true, and then we beleeve it: *God* hath first offered forgivenesse of sins to you, and then you looke upon his Word, and so beleeve it. But, I say, when a man is perswaded in a confused manner, without any just ground, without a cleere knowledge of the progresse of faith, how it goeth along, this is not right, this keepeth many from assurance, because they are not cleerely instructed in it. For to the end that faith may take hold of the promise, that it may be sure to us, we must conceive of the right method, and that stands in these foure things:

Four things in the understanding touching the promises.

1 To see our miserable condition.

First, we must see our owne condition, we must be sicke before we can seeke to the Physician, we must see our selves to be condemned men, that there is nothing in us to help our selves; we must be broken in heart in some measure, we must see our selves to be children of wrath, and then we will come and seek for a remedy; and that is,

2 To look to the promises.

By looking into the Booke of *God*, (and that is the second thing) and there I find all the promises, *Christ* is there cleerely offered, onely with this condition required, that I must obey him, and serve him, and love him; so that that is the second thing, *Christ* is offered in the Scripture to every one, and if you have him, you shall have a pardon of your sins with him; onely he is offered with condition of obedience. Well, when you see this cleerely, now you come to consider

it,

it, you begin to ponder this Word, whether it be ſo or no; a man begins to thinke, Is this a ſure promiſe? and then he ſees, that looke what certainty there is of the Scriptures in generall, there is the ſame certainty in theſe particular promiſes: ſo that with the ſame faith that a man is to beleeve the Word of *God*, with the ſame faith hee is to beleeve this offer of *Christ*.

I, but is it ſure *to me*?

Then a man looks to the generalitie of the promiſe, that it is offered to all, none excepted, and therefore, ſaith he, it is offered to *me*.

But will *Chriſt* doe to me as he hath promiſed? is he powerfull and willing to doe it? Then a man lookes into the world, and finds that he is Almighty, that he is able to make him the Sonne of *God*, that whatſoever *Chriſt* hath by nature, he ſhall have it by matching with him. Indeed *Chriſt* hath it immediately, as he is the Son of *God*, but we have it mediately, as the wife hath the riches of her husband. If a woman marry the Kings ſon, ſhe hath the ſame priviledges, and the ſame inheritance that he hath: ſo whatſoever *Chriſt* hath becomes ours: *Paul*, and *Apollo*, and all are *Chriſts*, the World is *Chriſts*, and all things preſent and to come are *Chriſts*, and they are all made ours. Now when this is well pondered, and we find that we have a ſure Word to confirme this:

Then in the third place we come and take him; and this no man will doe indeed, till he have well conſidered, as the ſaying is of marriage, that it is a 3 To take Chriſt.

 beſtowing

bestowing of ones self upon such an one, so it is in this; every one therefore should consider before-hand, what it is to bestow himselfe upon *Christ*. And when this is done, that we have made the match, and bestowed our selves upon *Christ*, then,

4 To see what we have by him.

In the next place, wee come to see what wee shall have by him, and then we come to make use of all that *Christ* brings with him: reconciliation, and pardon of sinne, and all things else that hee hath, I have with him, I am the sonne of *God*, and I shall bee sanctified, (for together with him I have his Spirit) all my prayers shall bee heard, all the promises in the Booke of *God* are mine; for *In him they are all Yea and Amen*: as all the world is his, so it is all the wealth of a Christian after hee hath taken *Christ*. Now when this is distinctly propounded to us, and wee conceive it aright, it makes the way much more easie to us; but when we goe on in a confused manner, because the Gospell is not cleerely understood by us, hence it is that we labour much, and yet the thing is not done: therefore, my Beloved, if you have a perswasion of the forgivenesse of your sinnes, if it bee but a meere perswasion, it will alter exceedingly, it will goe and come in the time of temptation: but when you have a sure Word, when you have built your selves upon the Scriptures, it is not dependent upon your perswasion, but it is the Word that you rest upon: For fancie, and opinion, and perswasion, it will grow sometimes longer, and sometimes shorter, as the shadow doth, whereas the body of the thing is the same; but when your eye is upon

upon the Word, when you rest upon that, then your perswasion will continue the same as the Word continues. Indeed your comfort may be sometimes more, sometimes lesse; but when it is pitched upon the sure Word, that is it that will bring you comfort in the working of it, to observe the method and degrees of it. Indeed, my Beloved, it is a point of another nature to beleeve than the world thinkes of; therefore examine, and recall, and understand this Doctrine that we have now taught you distinctly, it will be worth all your labour: for the present you shall have a good conscience, and the assurance of *Gods* favour, and when death comes, the right understanding of it will be worth all the world besides.

It is said of the second ground, that they fell away, because *they had no root in themselves*: they had some root, but their faith was pitched upon a generall Doctrine, upon a generall perswasion, that hath a kind of root, but it hath no root in it selfe: so many Christians goe farre, and they doe much, but they have no root in themselves, that is, they doe not understand distinctly, and throughly, the grounds upon which their faith is built, they see not a sure ground for it in the Word of *God*, they know not how faith is built upon the sure corner stone; for *Christ* is that sure corner stone, he that is built upon him shall never be ashamed: we should learne therefore not to give over till wee be rooted and grounded. If a man should aske many people, What is the reason that you are perswaded that your sinnes are forgiven? (for you ought to build that upon an infallible

 ground.)

Upon what grounds we should be perswaded of forgivenesse.

ground.) If it be no more but because you are perswaded, it is nothing; but if you can say, My sins are forgiven, because I have *Christ*, and *he that hath the Sonne, hath life:* I have the sure Word of *God* for it, *God* cannot lie, he is Truth it selfe that hath said it, and he hath offered *Christ* to every creature under heaven: then is the ground good, thou maist take him boldly, being within that number.

So much for this time.

FINIS.

THE FOURTH SERMON.

ROM. I. 17.

For by it the righteousnesse of God is revealed from Faith to Faith: as it is written, The just shall live by Faith.

THe next thing to be done is this, To draw the will to take the promises; for though the understanding rightly apprehend all that is delivered in the Word, yet except the will be bowed, except we incline, and be willing to embrace these offers, and willingly take *Christ* upon these conditions, the thing is not done: for, I say, justifying faith is as well in the will as in the understanding: for that which I deliver now is built upon that which I delivered before; and I speake chiefly to those that understand the promises, or else you will not fully understand what we are now about. Of drawing the will to take the promises.

But seeing that the will hath a part in faith as well as the understanding, the second thing is to draw the will. But how is that done? This is the work of *God*, God only boweth the heart.

 he

he onely hath the soveraignty over the will and affections of a man, it is the great prerogative of *God*, when a businesse is to be done with the will and affections, *God* must perswade it, as in *Noah*'s speech, *God perswade* Japheth *to dwell in the Tents of* Sem: as if he should say, I may perswade in vaine, except *God* put to his hand to the worke. So it is the propertie of the Spirit to convince, as *John* 16. *The Spirit shall convince the world of sin and righteousnesse*: that is, he shall shew men their sins, and their need, and withall convince them, and perswade them to take *Christs* righteousnesse. Thus, I say, it is *God* that draweth the will, it is he that puts a strong instinct into the heart of man, it is he that must worke on the heart, as in *John* 6.44. *None can come to me except the Father draw him*. How shall that be done? If *God* doth once draw a man, he will have no rest till he have *Christ*, he will not be at quiet till he have gotten him. Compare that place, *None can come to me except the Father draw him*, with that *Cant.* 2.3. *Draw us, and we will runne after thee*: it is not such a drawing as when a man is drawne by force, but it is a drawing which is done by changing the will and affections. When *God* alters the bent of the mind, when *God* justifies a man, he will affect a mans heart so, that he shall be so affected with *Christ*, as that he shall have no rest till he have him; when he doth see his need of him, he shall not give over till he be assured that he is reconciled to him: *Draw us, and we will runne after thee*. It is such a drawing as is called the teaching of *God*: *John* 6.45. *Ye shall be taught of God*: that

How God draweth the will.

is,

is, when *God* comes to teach a thing he boweth the will and affections to doe it. We heretofore exemplified this by the similitude of the *Ant*, and the *Bee*, and other creatures; they are said to be taught of *God*, when *God* puts a strong instinct into them to doe such and such a thing, he teacheth them to doe this and this. So *God* teacheth men to come to *Christ*, that is, he puts a strong inclination into their hearts, and when that is there once, they can have no rest, as the Iron cannot rest till it come to the Loadstone, and as the Stone cannot rest till it come to the Center: so the heart of man, when *God* draweth it, when he hath changed the will, then he finds such a disposition in him as was in the Spouse, *Cant*.2. She sought him whom her soule loved, she sought him by night, and by day, she sought him in the street, and among the Watchmen, and never rested untill she had found him. So when *God* hath drawne a mans heart, when he hath inclined a mans will to embrace *Christ*, he is never satisfied untill he hath found him.

But, you will say, *God* doth this by meanes, he useth Arguments to draw the will.

It is true; the question therefore is, How *God* doth this. We will propound three meanes by which *God* doth usually doe it.

First, the will is drawne, by being perswaded what the miserable condition of a man is that is not yet come to *Christ*, that hath not yet taken him, that hath not gotten the pardon and forgivenesse of his sins, that hath not got assurance that *Christ* hath received him to mercy. The will drawne by three means.

The second thing is, the good that hee shall get by it.

The third thing is, that he shall not lose his labour if he doe attempt it.

1 The consideration of our miserie out of Christ.

The first thing, I say, that drawes us to *Christ* is to consider how miserable we are without him: if men were perswaded of this, they would more seeke him. It is true, if a man could live alone, he would not come to him. Take Rebels, and Pyrates, if they were able to maintaine themselves abroad, if they could be as happy in rebellion as in receiving mercy, they would never come in. So it is in this case, if we be brought to this exigent, that we see we cannot hold out any longer, we are not stronger than he, as the Apostle saith, 1 *Cor.*10. *Are we stronger than he?* When a man is perswaded of that, when a man seeth this necessitie is laid upon him, or else he perisheth, then he will come in. So take a son, or a servant, if he be able to live from his Father, or Masters house, perhaps he will runne at riot still; but when he seeth he cannot have so much as huskes, hee can have nothing to sustaine him, that is it will bring him home. So take a Wife, a Spouse, if one come to wooe her, if she be able to live without him, it may be she will refuse him; but if the case be so that she cannot subsist, but the Creditors will come upon her, she must needs have a Husband to protect her, to be a barre and a covering unto her, now she seeth a necessitie of it. Therefore we say the Law drives men unto *Christ*, and the Law doth it by shewing a man his sin, and the curse due to it, by shewing a man his vilenesse: and if this

Simile.

will

will not doe it, then it shewes him the curse: when a man sees the miserie that the Law brings upon him, and pronounceth against him, that he is condemned, that perswades him. Therefore the Law drawes a man, and the sense of his miserie shewing him that he is out of *Christ*, this drawes him to consider that *God* is his enemy, that all the creatures are his enemies: for if *God* be thine enemy, then needs must all the creatures be so, because they turne with him to and fro; as an Armie turnes at the becke of the Generall. Now to have *God* and the creatures to be a mans enemies, to have every thing to worke for a mans hurt, *prosperitie slaies him*, and adversitie is not a Plaister or Medicine, but a poison to him, every thing joynes for his hurt; the Word, which is the *savour of life* to others, is the *savour of death* to him; the Sacraments, which are a meanes to convey grace and assurance to others, are a meanes to convey Satan to his heart; it increaseth his condemnation and his judgement, for *the wrath of God abides upon a man*; that is, it shall be upon him for eternity hereafter: for he that hath not the Son, hath not life, *Joh. 3 ult.* When a man seriously considers all this, when he seeth what case he is in, that he cannot live without *Christ*, this will be one thing that boweth and inclineth the will to come in and take *Christ*. But this is not all.

The Law drawes men to Christ, how.

In the second place a man will know what good he shall have by such an Husband: and indeed, if this were all, he could never marry out of love; and if he doe not, it can be no match: therefore we must find some good, some excellencie in *Christ*. And this is the second

The consideration of the good by Christ.

ſecond thing that drawes the will. If we take him we ſhall have all his wealth, and all his honour, all the joy and pleaſure he can afford. We ſhall have all his wealth; that is, goe to the whole Univerſe, and ſee what there is profitable or comfortable to the ſons of men, and all that is ours, whether it be *Paul*, or *Apollo*, or *Cephas*, *or the world*, *or life*, *or death*, *or things preſent*, *or things to come*, *all is yours*, *you are Chriſts*, *and Chriſt is Gods*: all this is yours. As for the things of this world, if we take him once, we have all theſe. Would not a man deſire all theſe? Is not this a ſtrong argument to move a man to take *Chriſt*, that all the Angels in heaven, all the excellent Miniſters on the earth, (that are next to Angels) they are all his ſervants? *God* hath beſtowed theſe gifts for his ſake, they are ſet a worke for the furthering of his ſalvation: and *the Angels*, you know, *are miniſtring Spirits*, *ſent forth for the good of the Elect*: for the world, as the Apoſtle ſaith, that is, whatſoever is in the world, all the good and all the evill in the world, even that evill doth him ſervice: the afflictions, and perſecutions, and ſtormes drive him to his haven as well as faire gales; every thing ſcoures him, doth him ſome good or other; all in the world is his, both life and death, that is, whatſoever belongs to this life or another, all is for his ſervice; and not that onely, but when death comes, that a man thinkes is the greateſt enemie, that there is no good in death, yet that doth him good, it heales our ſins, it is a meanes of happineſſe. In a word, when the Apoſtle could ſay no more, *things preſent*, *or things to come*, for a man ſhould looke to both: as heaven will not content him without the things of this life, so the things of this life will not content him without Heaven; but when there is both, the mind is satisfied.

Now when a man considers what wealth he hath by *Christ*, and againe, that he shall have all his honour, now looke what honour *Christ* hath, the same he hath by matching with him; having him we have all things. If a man could enter into a serious consideration of this, to thinke that he is a King, that he is an heire of all things, that all the promises doe belong to him. Doe but thinke with your selves, if any of you should be raised from a meane ordinary condition to be made an earthly Prince, how would you be affected with it? would it not put other thoughts into you? Why should you not beleeve spirituall priviledges to be as reall? Why should you not rejoyce more in them? they are more durable, they are more excellent, they have all in them the other have. Indeed they are things that are not seene with the eye, they are spirituall, they are things that are enjoyed and reserved for afterward, but yet there is much for the present. Learne to consider this, and it would draw and move you; but because these things are looked on with a generall eye, as matters of fancie and speculation, they are looked on as things that are rather talked of, we see no such thing, we have no feeling of them, therefore we doe not affect them: but we should labour to beleeve this, the Scripture often mentions and repeats this, *Ye are a royall Priesthood, heires with Christ*. Labour to come to this disjunction, if

Why we are not affected with spirituall priviledges.

Note. if these things be not so, why doe you beleeve them at all? if they be so, why doe you not rejoyce in them proportionably to these priviledges? And so for Joy; *at his right hand there are Joyes and pleasures for evermore.* And as it is so for eternity, so the neerer we draw to him in this life, the more pleasure we have; for he is *the God of all comfort*; the neerer we are to him, the more comfort, *all the wayes of wisedome are wayes of pleasure,* because they leade neerer to *God,* who is the cause of all comfort. So that is the second thing to consider, the good you shall have by *Christ,* when once you see how miserable you are without him, and that you shall gaine so much by him.

3 That we shall not lose our labour in attempting it.

Then in the third place there is one thing remaining. How shall I have him? I may attempt it, and goe without him; I may seeke, and be denied: and therefore, in the third place, you shall be sure to obtaine; that is a great meanes to encourage us to come unto him, when you see you shall not faile, there is nothing can hinder on your part, as you have heard in the precedent condition; there is required but an earnest hunger and thirst after him, *he justifies the ungodly*, and therefore nothing can hinder on your parts: and therefore if any thing hinder it, it must be on *Gods* part. Now what is there on *Gods* patt that hinders? He hath promised, and bound himselfe, and he will not goe from his Word, he will not denie himselfe: and therefore when there is no hinderance on neither part, then why doe you not beleeve? If you will consider *Christ*, and see how he describes himselfe in the Word, if you looke unto all those arguments

arguments that are propounded unto us therein, to perswade us, you will make no question; but if you are willing to come, you are sure to receive him, you shall have remission of all your sins. If you consider, first, those speeches in *Ezekiel*, *I desire not the death of a sinner*: and, *Why will yee die, O yee house of Israel?* Such expostulations are very frequent; *O that my people would returne*: and, *How often would I have gathered you as the hen gathereth her chickens?* I say, these are the speeches of *God*, and *God* speakes as he meanes; you shall find by the maner, and the fashion, and the figure of the speeches, that *God* desires it earnestly: *Why will ye die, O ye house of Israel?* by way of interrogation: and, *O that my people would* doe thus and thus. Even this *God* desires, that a sinner would returne. There is no action that *God* doth, but he doth it willingly; that he forgives sinners, that he receives those men that will come home unto him. You see in the Father of the Prodigall, that doth expresse the disposition of *God*, he runs to meet his Son, he was the forwarder of the two, he falls upon him, and kisseth him, he could not expresse his joy for his comming home: such is the disposition of *God*: *I take no delight, as I live*, (saith the Lord) *in the death of a sinner*, but rather that he should live. And therefore when *God* saith it we have a surer Word, you should better thinke of it, undoubtedly he will receive you to mercy.

Seven arguments to perswade us of Christs willingnesse to receive sinners.

1 By expressions in Scripture.

Againe, consider how *Christ* did in the dayes of his flesh, how he behaved himselfe then: was he not exceeding gentle to all that came unto him, exceeding compassionate

2 By Christs practice when he was on earth.

compaſſionate and pitifull, ready to heale every one, ready to doe any thing that was requeſted of him, that he denied not any that was importunate with him? Doe you thinke that he hath put off that diſpoſition? Is he not the ſame ſtill? As it is in the *Hebrewes*, Is he not a mercifull High Prieſt ſtill? and that the bowels of compaſſion in him melt over a ſtraying ſinner, and is ready to receive him, his bowels yearne within him, and therefore doubt not but the Lord will receive you.

3 Elſe Chriſts bloud were ſhed in vain

Againe, of neceſſitie he muſt receive you, or elſe the bloud of *Chriſt* were in vaine, his Croſſe and death were of none effect. What now can make the death of *Chriſt* to be of none effect, but when it is not regarded, when his bloud is trampled under feet and deſpiſed of men, when it doth no good, when it is not improved for the purpoſe it was ſhed for? Doe you think that *God* ſent his only Son from heaven to die a curſed death, and would he have his bloud ſhed in vaine? Now except he ſhould receive poore ſinners when they come, the death of *Chriſt* ſhould be of none effect. And therefore it cannot be but *God* muſt be ready to receive them. So that there is no difficultie in him, all the difficultie is in our ſelves, we are not willing to come.

4 By the example of others pardoned.

Againe, if we conſider what he hath done for others, how many he hath received to mercie: when one ſees ſuch Rebels received to mercie, and conſiders with himſelfe, and thinkes how he gave pardon to *Manaſſes* of his ſins, which were crying ſins, and of an extraordinary nature, ſinnes that were of long continuance:

continuance: he forgave *Marie Magdalens* sins, he forgave these greater sinners, and why should he not forgive me? If one should come to a Physician, of whom he hath heard a great fame, and if he should meet with hundreds by the way of his Patients, and all of them should tell him he hath cured them, and healed them, it would encourage a man to goe on with confidence. Or if one should come to a Well, of which he hath heard much, and should meet with hundreds of people by the way, and all of them should tell him, we have beene at the Well, and it hath cured us, and made us whole; this would encourage a man to goe with confidence, because of the multitude that have tried the experience of it: so we should run to *Christ*; when so many thousands have beene forgiven, why should not these perswade us that he is ready to forgive us? as *Paul* saith, *he hath shewed mercy to me, that others might beleeve in God.* I am an example for them to trust in *God*: therefore when we see he hath forgiven others so many and so great sins, why should we doubt?

Againe, if *Christ* should not be ready to receive us, *no flesh should be saved*, there is no man that would feare him, or heare him: *Psal.* 130. 3: there the same argument is used, *If thou, Lord, shouldst marke iniquity; who should stand? but there is mercy with thee that thou maist be feared*: that is, if *God* should not be pitifull to mankind, and ready to receive them, notwithstanding their manifold failings, and infirmities, and rebellions they are subject unto, no flesh should be saved, but all the world should perish. 5 Else no flesh should be saved.

Againe,

6
God should not else be worshipped

Againe, not so onely, but *God* himselfe should not be worshipped, men would not regard him, men would not serve him: therefore I say, of necessitie *God* must have mercy upon men, that they may feare him, and serve him, and that men may be willing to serve him.

Take a hard Master, a cruell King, a man that shuts out men, and excludes them, that they have no hope: there is none that will serve such a man, there is no man that will come in to him; but there is mercy with the Lord that he may be feared and worshipped, and men may come in and worship him: and therefore doubt not that *Christ* is willing to receive you.

7
By the infinitenesse of Gods mercy.

If all this will not perswade you, yet in *Esay* 55. there is one thing more. It it will not enter into your thoughts, if you thinke your condition be such, if you thinke your sins so circumstantiated, as I may say, that they are committed in such a manner, that you thinke, though others have beene forgiven, yet you cannot, it passeth your thoughts, you know not how to imagine it; yet know, his mercy is above your thoughts: a man must hold that conclusion still.

And if this alone will not perswade me, yet when all this is put together, when I see the miserie of a man without *Christ*, when I see I shall be happy with him, when I see it is of necessitie, and, if I come, I shall certainly be received, he cannot refuse me, all this will help to perswade a man; this you should learn to presse upon your own hearts. We that are the Ministers of *Christ* are bound to doe it: and therefore he hath sent us out to compell men to come in, that his house may

be

be full: therefore he commands them to goe unto the high way, and unto the hedges, and *compell men to come in*. (And what is that?) That is, be so importunate with them, promise them, threaten them, command them in the name of *Christ* to consent and come in: *God* would faine have his House filled, *he hath killed his fatlings*, he would not have his Table ready, and have no guests; he would have his house filled, that his Table might not be prepared in vaine: and that it may not be in vaine, we are to invite you to this Marriage, we are to invite you to these Fatlings, to this Wine and Milke: it is a banquet, and a banquet you know what it is: in a banquet there is as much as will cheer the body, a concourse of all pleasant things: such things are in *Christ*, there is spirituall comfort, a concourse, a heap of all spirituall joy and comfort, of all precious things you can find; and if you will come and take, you shall have all his Jewels, all his Graces, to beautifie and to adorne you withall. Let this perswade you to come in.

To compell men to come in, what.

But some may object, If I come in, I must lose my right eye, or my right hand, I must part with my lusts, which are as deere to me as these members.

Object.

I will be brife in this point, because I will finish the text at this time, and will answer it even as *Christ* doth *Matth*. 5. It is true, we must doe so, but then remember we shall have heaven for our labour. If heaven be not worthy losing of a right eye, or a right hand, keepe thine eye still, if thou wilt needs keep it, but thou shalt be sure to goe to hell. There needs no other answer: doe but seriously consider of this: If I will,

Answ. Though we part with that which is deere for Christ, we shall have better.

I may keepe this lust, this fleshly desire, but certainely that will leade me to hell. Let that answer serve for this.

*Ob.*2. But it may be further objected, If I doe thus I must denie my selfe, and this is a difficult thing for a man to offer violence to himselfe, to crosse himselfe in all his desires: a man is able to doe much, he may be willing to take great paines, and to suffer much, but to crosse himselfe still of his most inward desires that he hath, those that are most rooted in the soule, that sticke neer and close unto him, this is difficult.

Answ. By denying our selves we enjoy our selves better.

I answer; *Christ* is worthy of all these, thou shalt better provide for thy selfe by doing this, there is another life in the regenerate part, and it perfects that: though you destroy the flesh, and offer violence unto that, yet there is the inward man, that is growing up daily, though the outward man faile. It is true, violence must be offered to the flesh, you must be content to part with pleasures, and the outward man, in that sense, must suffer somewhat; but remember what you gaine, there is the inward man that so much the more provides for it selfe, and if you wil not then denie your selfe, you denie not your disease that will slay you. If a man have a disease that cries hard to him to have such and such things given it, it is wisedome for him to denie it, because he nourisheth that that would destroy him: so herein himselfe is his disease, and to give to that is his destruction. So that that which you call your selfe, is your disease; and when you feed your selfe, you feed your disease: and therefore every one is to be ruled by the Physicians advice,

A mans carnall selfe is his disease.

advice, who teacheth to doe otherwise. *Christ* teacheth us another way, which is for our health and safety: I cannot stand to presse that.

Ob. But I shall endure persecution, and losse of friends, nay, perhaps losse of life.

Answ. Yea, but thou shalt receive an hundred fold, thou shalt have no losse by that bargain, thou shalt find *Christ* worth all that thou givest for him. More I should adde, but I come to the last point.

If we endure persecution for Christ, we shall have an hundred fold.

The righteousnesse of *Christ* is revealed from faith to faith.

The first point ye have heard, that,

Doct. 1. Righteousnes is revealed and offered in the Gospel to as many as will take it. As also

Doct. 2. The second, that it is by faith by which we are made to partake of this righteousnesse: it is revealed from faith to faith, that is, it is so revealed as that it is taken by faith.

The third point that we are now to handle is this, that,

Doct. 3. *Faith admits degrees, and every Christian ought to grow from degree to degree.*

Faith admits degrees.

In this proposition, *Faith admits of degrees, and that we ought to grow from one degree to another*, I find two parts:

Two parts in the Doctrine.

First, that there are degrees of faith.

Secondly, that we ought to grow from degree to degree.

For the first, that I may run thorow them as briefly as I can: There are degrees in faith in these foure respects: as there are two acts of faith, one whereby

Faith admits of degrees in foure respects.

we take *Christ*, and that we call a direct act, by which we truely lay hold on him, and receive him as our Lord and Saviour. The second is that act of faith by which we know we have received him, the reflect act, which is assurance, both these receive degrees. The first receives degrees in three respects, the last receives degrees in one respect, which shall make up the fourth.

1 In perswasion.

The first act by which we receive and take *Christ* the Messias offered unto us, it admits this first degree, there is a great degree of perswasion that *Christ* is offered, and that he is ours, that he is given by *God* the Father: and though I find this proposed in the Word, that *Christ* is given to us, yet there are degrees of the perswasion of the truth of this: and this we need not wonder at; for though it be faith, and though the perswasion be true, and good, and firme, yet notwithstanding it may admit of degrees, else any man might object,

Object. If a man be fully perswaded, what needs he more? If he be not fully perswaded, it is not faith; if he be fully perswaded, that makes it faith, and how can that admit degrees?

Answ. I answer, it may, because there are degrees in the very perswasion: though the perswasion be good and true, yet there are degrees in it. As for example: There is such a proposition of Truth, which I am perswaded to beleeve by arguments that overcome me: I must needs yeeld to it, and yet there are more arguments and reasons that may be brought, that may work a greater perswasion, as we say, that may be more immediate

immediate to perſwade us of that concluſion: As a man that ſees a thing by a little glimmering light of a candle, he may ſee it certainly and firmely, but when there come more candles or a torch in, he may ſee more cleerely, although he ſaw it certainely before: So the promiſes of *God*, wee may behold them, and apply them to our ſelves to be ſure and firme, and yet this may admit more degrees. When there is more light, and more arguments, when the Spirit of Adoption ſpeakes more cleerely and fully to us, there may be a greater degree of perſwaſion: and therefore that objection, that either it is not faith, if there be doubting, or if it be firme in a man, he needs no more; I ſay it is not ſo: for faith admits degrees, there is a full perſwaſion, *Col.*2. which intimates there is a leſſer faith than that. As, you know, a Ship may be carried with a gentle gale of wind as well as with a ſtronger gale, though it goe not ſo faſt; but it may be moved, it may be put on with a gentle wind as well as with a ſtrong gale. *Simile.* *Simile.*

So a Tree may be rooted, and rooted ſtrongly and firmly, and yet may be more rooted afterward. The phraſe of Scripture carries it ſo, *Oh ye of little faith:* there is a little faith, and therefore it implies there is a ſtrong faith, yet the leaſt is accounted faith. So, *Lord I beleeve, help thou my unbeliefe:* it was unbeliefe, and yet it was reckoned for beliefe. *Simile.*

So our Saviour ſaid to *Peter*, *Why doſt thou doubt?* Certainely *Peter* beleeved, or elſe he could not caſt himſelfe upon the water; and yet there was doubting mingled with it. And indeed, if faith were not mixed with doubting, who ſhould have faith? Did not *David* truſt *God* much? and yet his faith was mixed with doubting: ſaith he, *I ſhall periſh one day by the hand of Saul:* and yet he had faith. Therefore, I ſay, there may be faith, though we have not ſo full a perſwaſion.

Object. But you will ſay, How differs it from opinion?

Wherein faith and opinion differ.

Anſw. Opinion is an aſſent to a truth, with a feare leſt the contrary may be true. It differs from opinion in the object: the object of opinion is ſomething in its owne nature uncertaine, but faith pitcheth upon the Word of *God*, which is in its owne nature infallible, and cannot deceive.

1 In the object.

Againe, opinion is a matter of ſpeculation and no more: faith is a matter of practice; but that is not all.

2 In the working.

Opinion goeth no further, but ſtayes in a doubt, but faith proceeds to full aſſurance: and therefore it hath the denomination of full aſſent. As we ſay of a Wall that is a little white, it is white, becauſe it tends to full whiteneſſe; and as we ſay water is hot, that is a little hot: ſo faith that is but in a little degree, yet it may be true, firme, and ſubſtantiall.

3 In overcomming doubts.

Simile.

But what is the leaſt degree of faith, the leaſt aſſent, the leaſt beliefe of the promiſes, without which it cannot be ſaid to be faith?

The leaſt degree of faith, what.

I anſwer, the leaſt degree of faith is that which brings us to *Chriſt*, which makes us willing to take him. Marke this point, for it will be of much uſe to you, when the promiſes of *God* are preached to you, and made

made knowne unto you, when the arguments that move you to come to *Christ* are declared and made manifest. Now if a man stands and knowes not whether he were best to take him or no, this is not faith, such a man acteth nothing, he is such an one as is spoken of in *James* 1. (for that I take to be the meaning of that place) a man that knowes not whether he should come to *Christ* or no, that stands in a doubt, and sometimes he will goe, and sometimes he will not, he is off and on, to and fro; such a man hath not faith, such an one *Christ* rejects: but now when there is so much weight as will cast the Ballance the right way, though there be something left in the other end of the Ballance, that is, though there be some doubting, some feare, yet if I so farre beleeve the promises, and the Word of *God*, as that I am willing to take *Christ* for my Husband, I am willing to rest on him, to pitch on him, to bestow my selfe upon him; this is faith, though it come not to the full degree.

As for example, if one be a spokesman for a Suitor, he comes and tels the Spouse to whom he is a Suitor, that such a man is of such parentage, hath such honour, and such wealth, and is thus qualified; now if she be but so farre perswaded as that she is willing to take him for her husband, that is enough to bring her to make the match, that perswasion will bring her to doe it; afterward she may come to know the thing more fully, and to be better perswaded, but that adds to the degrees. So if there be but so much assent, so much firmnesse of perswasion to bring us to *Christ*, to make us willing to come to take him for our Saviour, and for our Lord; that is the least degree of faith: and though there be doubting left, and though there be some feares, yet if there be but so much as will produce that, it is faith. Let me exemplifie it in some other thing: Take *Hester*, when she was to come to the King she knew not what successe she should have, she was fearefull, as we may see by the maner of going about the businesse; yet seeing there was so much as drew her to the action, she comes and sayes, *If I perish, I perish*; as if she had doubted she might have perished, yet she resolved to doe it: this may be said to be an act of faith that put her on the worke. Take a martyr that comes to suffer, he hath many doubts and feares, and yet if there be but so much perswasion as will produce the act in him, as that he is moved to doe the thing, he may properly be said to doe it out of faith.

And so of all other actions. The three Children, *God can deliver us if he will* (say they) *if he doe not, we will not worship that Image that thou hast set up.* There might be some doubting in them, and yet because there was so much trust in *God* as to bring them to do the thing, here was faith enough to make them acceptable in the sight of *God*. So, I say, if there be so much faith as will bring us to *God* and to *Christ*, that is the least degree; other degrees there are that may be added afterwards: but this is thy comfort, if thou have but so much as will produce such an effect, thou maist be sure that thou hast faith.

2 In respect of difficulties.

Secondly, faith admits degrees in regard of the difficulty and hardnes of the things that are to be beleeved.

As

As for example, *Martha* and *Mary* both beleeved in *Christ* when he feasted with them, but when *Lazarus* was dead, and had beene in the grave foure dayes, that put them to a stand. Now if they had beene able to beleeve this, there had beene a greater degree of faith. And that was it that magnified *Abrahams* faith so, that when there was so great difficultie that he must goe and offer his sonne, the sonne in whom *God* had promised that his seed should be blessed, who was called *the sonne of the promise.* Now here was a great degree of faith, because there was great difficultie. *Instances. Martha and Mary.*

Moses, we see, when he came to beleeve the promise of *God* in *Numbers* 11. that so many, even six hundred thousand should be fed with flesh, and that they should be so fed a whole moneth together, it set *Moses* at a stand, he knew not what to say: Not one day (saith he) not ten dayes, not twenty dayes, but a whole moneth together, and six hundred thousand people! *If all the Flockes and Herds should be killed, and all the fishes in the Sea should be gathered together, how should this be done?* This was a great thing to beleeve, and therefore *God* pitied *Moses*: *God* seeth when things are hard to be beleeved, and pities man: *God* beares with *Moses* in that case, because the thing was difficult and high: there are some things which are above hope, and in such cases *God* is willing that his people should aske him a signe, he knowes their strength, they had need of something to confirm them. And therefore in such a case, when *God* comes in such a manner, if they aske him a signe, *God* is *Moses.* In what cases God is willing to give a sign, or not give it.

is willing to give them a ſigne: Indeed when men will aske a ſigne to tempt *God: an adulterous generation askes a ſigne:* that is, for triall or temptation, not for love of *Chriſt*, and to be perſwaded he is fit for them, but an adulterous generation, they did it not out of love: but, I ſay, when either the thing is high, or elſe when the meanes of perſwaſion is weake and ſlender. As, we know, *Chriſt* ſaid unto *Nathaniel*, Doſt thou beleeve for this? as if he ſhould ſay, This ſhewes thy faith is great, that for ſo ſmall a thing as this thou beleeveſt; I ſaid no more but *I ſaw thee under the Fig-tree.* And this ſhewed the weakneſſe of *Thomas* his faith, that he would not beleeve, unleſſe he might put his finger into the print of *Chriſts* wounds, and his hand into his ſide: ſo that when a man beleeves by ſlender meanes, or when hee beleeves things of a higher nature, which is more above hope, when there is great difficultie, in this ſenſe faith admits degrees.

Joh. 1. 5.

4 In regard of extent.

Thirdly, faith admits degrees in regard of the extent of it, when there are more things revealed to them: and, I take it, this place will carry that, *the righteouſneſſe of God is revealed from faith to faith*; that is, the righteouſneſſe of *Chriſt* was revealed in the time of the Law and the Prophets, it was revealed obſcurely, and there was a little faith among them to beleeve, it was enough to ſave them; but when the time drew neerer, there were greater revelations, as we know in the time of the Prophets, their faith was great; as there were more revelations, ſo there was more faith. So, I ſay, it admits degrees in regard of the

the extent of revelation; as the Apostles, when *Christ* was upon the earth, they had a degree of faith, but when *Christ* ascended, then there were more revelations, then they grew *from faith to faith*, because they grew from revelation to revelation, then the Spirit of *God* was sent into their hearts to reveale all things, and to leade them into all truth: you know they had abundance of revelations afterwards. So in this regard, in regard of the extent, faith receives degrees, not because the habit is increased, but because the revelations and objects are more. And therefore that is the comfort of poore Christians, those that are yet ignorant, they may have a true habit, and as true a grace in the heart: and though a man be more conversant in Scripture, and knowes more than they, he hath more revelations, and in that sense, though he have a greater faith than the other, yet the other hath a like precious faith with him in regard of that grace.

So we see how faith receives degrees in these three respects.

4 The reflect act of faith admits degrees.

Now, last of all, that faith that gives assurance, that pacifieth and comforteth the heart, which is nothing but a reflect act, by which we know and are perswaded that we have taken *Christ*, and that our sins are forgiven, this admits of degrees of proofe. And here, as the evidences of sanctification are more, so is the assurance; as the Apostle saith, *The Spirit witnesseth to our spirits*: he discovers good things to us, we had need of the light of the Spirit to judge aright of the sinceritie of the graces that we have, we shall goe amisse else, we shall not be able except we have the

Spirit

Spirit to help and assist us, and so we grow from assurance to assurance.

2 We must labour to grow in these degrees.

Now for the second part, that we must grow in all these.

First, as faith admits of degrees, so we must labour to grow in all these degrees.

1 In perswasion.

First, labour to grow to a more full and firme assent, by that meanes we shall draw neerer to *Christ*, and receive him in a greater measure. Marke, this very act of taking *Christ*, that immediately justifies, but it is fed with assurance in the understanding, it is that which doth increase, and strengthen, and supplie this action of the will in taking *Christ*. So that the more strong assent the mind and understanding of a man gives to those truths which concerne justification, delivered in the Scripture, the stronger his will is in taking *Christ*. As in the act of marriage, a woman takes such a one to be her husband, but yet there are degrees in the will, one may take him with greater greedinesse, with a more full perswasion that it is best for her, with more love, and with more resolution. So the stronger the assent is that we give to the promises of *God*, wherein he assures us of the pardon of our sins, wherein *Christ* is offered freely unto us, the more we take *Christ*, and so the union is greater betweene us, we are linkt and knit together, and married, as it were, in a greater degree.

2 To beleeve difficulties.

Secondly, in regard of difficultie, which is the second thing wherein faith admits degrees, when we beleeve hard things, or easie things propounded with slender arguments. Labour to grow in this, for this is is very profitable for you: I will give you but these two instances.

You know what *Moses* lost, and what *Abraham* got: *Moses* lost *Canaan*, he lost the honour of carrying in the people, he lost the honour of concluding his worke, when he had taken so much paines, and all because he did not beleeve when he strooke the Rocke, for want of faith. *Abraham* now that beleeved things that were of a high, of a difficult nature, you see what he got by it: for this cause, saith the *Lord*, I will doe thus and thus, *because thou hast not spared thine onely Son*: which is repeated *Rom*.4. *Abraham being strong in faith, gave glory to God*. And therefore you see *Abraham* is set above all men, he is the *Father of all the faithfull*, he is the head, the top of those to whom *God* shewed mercy, he shewed mercy to all for *Abrahams* sake: *Abraham*, *Isaac*, and *Jacob*: *Abraham* is first, this did *Abraham* get for ever, because he beleeved in *God* in so great a matter. This you shall gain, if you will beleeve, it will bring a great reward, yea, it will not onely bring a reward, such as *Abraham* had, but it will bring increase of the same faith, *God* will reveale more to you, and give you more of his Spirit, as he did to *Nathaniel*. Beleevest thou for this, saith *Christ*? thou shalt see greater things than these. If wee beleeve in difficult cases, *God* will make us with facilitie to beleeve them another time.

Thirdly, for the multitude of revelations, for the extent of faith, that way we should labour to be filled full of faith, as *Barnabas* is said to be *full of faith*. 3 To abound in revelations.

And

And how is that? By studying the Word much, for therein will *God* reveale this: this is it that *Paul* magnifies so much in 2 *Cor*. 12. that which he gloried in; he doth not name it in his owne person, but saith, *I knew a man in Christ* that had such a revelation: he glories not in this, that he had wealth, or honour, but in the multitude of revelations; that of all other might have exalted *Paul*, but he was wise, he knew what he did when he was so apt to be exalted, in that it seemes there was some extraordinary excellencie in it.

4 Grow in assurance. Motives to grow in assurance.

Lastly, labour to get full assurance; the more assurance you have, the more love.

Again, you shall doe the more work when once you are assured that your *labour shall not be in vaine in the Lord*: as 1 *Cor*. 15. *ult*. It will make you *abound in the workes of the Lord*.

Againe, it establisheth a man in well-doing, he shall never hold out and be constant till he come to have assurance that he shall not lose his reward. I cannot stand on this point: I will name the uses, that so I may not leave the point unfinished.

Use 1. To comfort those that have faith, though in a lesse degree.

The first is a use of much comfort. If there be such degrees in faith, then let us not be discouraged, though we come to the highest: if we have but a little, yet since there are degrees, this is enough to make us partakers of the righteousnesse of *Christ*, and of salvation. The end of this is to comfort those which are apt to be discouraged. A little graine of true muske is able to sweeten a great deale: So if faith be true, a little true faith will perfume all the heart and soule, it hath influence into every thing, and it puts a good tincture

tincture upon all that a man doth; though it be but little, yet the influence is great. Therefore though thou have not a great measure of faith, if thou have a little, comfort thy selfe with that; we know the least bud drawes sap from the root, as well as the greatest branches, as truely: so they that bud, that are but yet in the beginning of faith, yet they are as truely graffed into *Christ*, and receive life from him, as those that are growne Christians. And therefore be not discouraged because thou hast not as yet a great measure of faith: say not, Because I am not as strong as such, therefore I am no body; reason not so, if thou have but as much as will bring thee within the doore, within the Covenant, within compasse once. It is true, when a man is within the doore, there are greater degrees, he may goe farther into the house, or a little way in, but all is well when he is in once. So in faith, a little faith is enough to put a man within the Covenant, to put one within the Gate of Heaven, as it were; indeed when they are in, some goe further, and some goe not so farre: but if thou be in at all, comfort thy selfe with that, and thinke not that every little infirmitie shall breake the Covenant when thou art in. No, that which makes a divorce betwixt *God* and you will doe it, but every infirmitie doth not that. Take heed therefore of robbing *God* of his glory, and your selves of comfort; you know what a Father he is, he is a tender and a wise Father: we reckon it is wisedome in parents when they consider the infirmities of their children: *God* is wise, let us goe to him. A father will beare with his son, and receive him againe and againe,

Infirmities breake not the Covenant.

againe, though he have infirmities. So *God* is thy Father, what though he see many failings in thee? what though he see we have little grace, or little faith? yet we are sons, *God* will spare us: and therefore *cast not away your hope*, but labour to know, that though you be but as *smoaking flax*, yet there is fire there, as well as if it were all on a flame.

Satan labours to discourage.

Now it is Satans end indeed to discourage: and remember but that, that the thing he labours is to perswade you that you have no faith, and that a little will not serve the turne, and that because thou art not so strong as the strongest Christians, that therefore thou hast a false heart, and art no body at all: his end is to discourage, labour to resist him. And we that are Ministers of *Christ*, we are in this case to comfort and encourage you, as Saint *Paul* saith, *we were gentle among you, as a Nurse among her children*: we should be tender over you, and comfort, and encourage you, *we are not Lords of your faith*. And therefore in *Ezekiel* 33. it was the fault of the Shepheards, they ruled over the people with rigour, *but we are helpers of your joy*: for what have we to doe, but what our Master hath set us about to doe? as he did. How did he behave himselfe? The smoaking Flax, he did blow it with a tender breath to kindle it more, he dealt not roughly with it. So the Ministers of *God* should labour to build men up, to draw them on. Indeed sometimes the Minister must be sharpe, to wake men when they sleepe, to discover hypocrites and temporizing professours, to teach those to know themselves, that have a forme of godlinesse without the power thereof:

thereof: here the Word preached must be *a two-edged sword, that must pierce between the marrow & the joynts*; here the Word must be as the Thunder and Lightning, it must have terrour in it. So *Christ comes with his Fan in his hand*, and with his Axe in his hand, *he will burne the chaffe with unquenchable fire*, and hew downe the unfruitfull Trees. But this is to be understood of those that are false-hearted, those that are not sound, that have *Christ* offered them, but doe not receive him. Indeed to those our Ministerie is sharp, but for others it is not so. And therefore in *Ezek.* 34. we are to doe as the Shepheards doe there with their Flocks, some Sheepe are weake, and are not able to goe the pace of the rest; some are broken, some are lost, and some are gone astray, and some are great with young: our businesse is to seeke those that are lost, to drive on according to the pace of the weakest, to bind up the broken, to carrie them in our armes: thus *Christ* did, and if we faile in this, *Christ*, who is the great Shepheard of the flock, he sees it; if we goe astray, he fetches us in; if we be broken, and have lost our wooll, and be not in right order, he binds us up, he feeds us, and tenders us; thus *Christ* deales with you. And therefore be not discouraged, though thou be not so strong as the strongest, yet if thou be a Sheepe, if thou be in the fold, if thou hast the least degree of faith, it is able to make thee partaker of this righteousnesse, although thou have not the highest degree, though thou have not that excellencie that others have.

Use 2. For exhortation to grow in faith.

The second use is, to exhort you to grow in faith (and so I end.) Content not your selves with a little, a ſmall meaſure of faith, though notwithſtanding a little will ſerve to put you in the ſtate of ſalvation, yet it ſhould be your wiſedome to get a great degree, as the Apoſtle ſaith, 1 *Pet.*1.13. *Truſt perfectly in the grace brought in by the revelation of Chriſt.* (Marke it, for it is an excellent place for this purpoſe, ſtudie it, and thinke well of it.) Truſt perfectly in the grace revealed; that is to ſay, doe it not by halves, let not there be ſome odde reckonings betweene *God* and thee, ſtand not in diſtance from him, but truſt upon him perfectly, beleeve fully and aſſuredly that your ſins are forgiven you, beleeve fully the grace that is given you through *Chriſt*, doe it perfectly, throughly; truſt perfectly in the grace brought in by *Chriſt*, that is our fault that we doe it not in ſuch a manner: hence it is that our joy is weake, our grace is weake: truſt perfectly, *that your joy may be full*, that you may have full communion and fellowſhip with *Chriſt*: the benefit is exceeding great when we truſt perfectly, and why will you not? why ſhould you limit the *Holy One of Iſrael?* It was their ſin and tranſgreſſion to limit him in his power and all-ſufficiency, as if he were not able to doe ſuch and ſuch things, and is it not as great a ſin to limit him in his mercy and goodneſſe? Why cannot he forgive ſins and tranſgreſſions, that in all circumſtances are the greateſt ſins, in what nature ſoever? To thinke otherwiſe is to limit the *Holy One of Iſrael:* truſt perfectly therefore. It is not a little that will ſerve the turne, as the Apoſtle ſaith 2.*Pet.*3.*ult.* *Grow in grace.* There is need of it, you ſhall find that as you wade further in the profeſſion

Motives to grow in faith.

on of Christianitie, so you shall have need of more strength, you shall have greater imployment, therefore you have more need of growth to goe forward and persevere. 1 We need more strength daily.

Againe, you shall meet with greater temptations and assaults; if you be not more strong than at the first, you are not able to resist. 2 We meet greater assaults.

Againe, if you grow in faith, you shall grow likewise in joy; and that is a thing which we have continuall use of, that is of hourely use to comfort and strengthen us, to make us abound in the works of the *Lord*, that helps us to goe thorow all variety of conditions, that enables us to abound, and to want, to passe *thorow good report and evill report*, to suffer and endure persecution. Now the more you grow in faith, the more you grow in joy, as the Apostle saith *Rom.* 15.13. *The God of peace fulfill you with all joy by beleeving.* So that the more we beleeve, the more joy, the more consolation we have. 3 We shall hereby grow in joy.

Againe, the more you grow in faith, the more you shall gaine the favour of *God*, the more you shall win his love: there is nothing in the World doth so much win the favour of *God* as a great degree of faith: and therefore though thou maist be saved with a lesse degree, yet that thou maist be in a greater degree of favour, seeke more faith: and this, though it be reckoned a small matter to have a great degree of *Gods* favour, yet it is the greatest dignitie in the world. Looke upon all the difference of men, it is their difference in the favour of *God* that makes them so. Why was *Moses* a man above all the rest? Saith

What it is that differenceth men.

God, I will have compassion upon whom I will have compassion, and I will shew mercie to whom I will shew mercy; I have chosen *Moses*: look to what difference of men you will: looke into what estate, what condition thou wouldest have, either for thy soule or thy body, whatsoever it be, it is by the grace and favour of *God* in *Christ Jesus* that all thy comfort and consolation increaseth.

Quest. What shall make me grow in the favour of *God*?

Answ. Faith maketh us grow in the favour of God.

I answer, there is nothing that causeth *God* to set so much by us as faith. The woman of *Canaan*, see what cause *Christ* had to give her such a great commendation, *great is thy faith*; and because her faith was great, therefore he set her at so high a rate. So the Centurion; saith *Christ*, *I have not found so great faith in Israel*, and that is the thing that he set so great a price upon. So *Jacob* when he got the name of *Israel*, when he prevailed with *God*, certainely it was the greatest blessing that ever he had. Why was that? Because he shewed the greatest faith that ever he did, it was a strong faith that prevailed with *God*. And what set him at so high a rate in *Gods* Booke? It was the faith he had in *God*, and therefore he was remembred in the whole Booke of *God* for his faith. Therefore the more faith you have, the more *God* prizeth you, it is it that wins his love. I cannot stand upon the arguments why we should grow in faith; they are many: the more faith we have, the more powerfull are our prayers in prevailing with *God*, for faith gives strength to them.

5 The more we prevaile in prayer.

Againe, the more faith you have, the more you bring

bring glory to *God*; if there be much faith, there will be much fruit, it is the root of all grace: as *John* 15.8. *Herein is my Father glorified, that you bring forth much fruit.* Get much faith then if you will have much fruit, that you may bring glory to *God*: as if he should say, If a man have but some faith he brings forth fruit, yet there shall be something wanting: but when a man is eminent, when he is conspicuous, when he is as a great light that every man turns his eye to, when he is as a Tree that brings forth much fruit, which turns the eyes of the beholders to it. So it is with Christians; herein, saith Christ, is my Father glorified, &c.

6 The more glory we bring to God.

A Christian hath no such motive as this, he shall glorifie *God* exceedingly, if he have abundance of faith, he shall have abundance of every grace, he shall grow *rich in good works*: this is that which we should all labour for: I cannot stand to presse it further. So much for this time, and for this Text.

FINIS.

A TREATISE OF EFFECTUALL FAITH.

Delivered in six Sermons upon 1 *Thes* 1.3.

By the late faithfull and worthy Minister of JESUS CHRIST,

JOHN PRESTON,

Doctor in Divinitie, Chaplaine in ordinary to his Majestie, Master of *Emanuel* Colledge in *Cambridge*, and sometime Preacher of *Lincolnes Inne*.

HAB. 2. 4.

The just shall live by faith.

HEB. 11. 33, 34.

Who through faith subdued Kingdomes, wrought righteousnesse, obtained promises, &c.

LONDON,

Printed by *Robert Young* for *Nicolas Bourne*.

M. DC. XXXVII.

OF EFFECTUALL FAITH.

The first Sermon.

1 THESS. 1. 3.
Remembring your effectuall Faith, &c.

IN the former verses the Apostle setteth downe this generall, *we give thanks alwaies for you, making mention of you in our praiers, without ceasing.* First, he tels them that he praies for them; and then he tels them more particularly that his prayer was a Thanksgiving. And this giving of thankes for them he expresseth by the continuance of it, he did it constantly, *without ceasing,* (not by fits) *making mention* Coherence.

of

of you in my prayers. Then he names the particulars for which he gives thankes, namely these three:

For their { *Effectuall Faith.* / *Diligent Love.* / *Patient Hope.* }

Now these three Graces he describeth and setteth forth three wayes:

First, from a certaine propertie or character which distinguisheth the true faith from the false faith, the true love from the false love, the true hope from false hope. I give not thankes for every faith, but for such a faith as is *effectuall:* (that is the propertie or character by which the truth of faith is discerned.) Again, not for every love, but for such a love as is *laborious*, (for so the word signifieth.) Thirdly, not for every hope, but for such a hope as makes you *patient*, (that is the character by which to know hope.) And this is the first way whereby he describeth these Graces.

Secondly, he describeth them from the object upon which these graces are pitched, and that is *Jesus Christ* our Lord. That is to say, I give thankes for the faith you have in *Christ*, for the love you have towards him, for the hope you have of what he will doe for you: I give thanks for that faith, for that love, for that hope, that hath *Christ* for the object of it.

Thirdly, he describeth these graces from the sinceritie of them: I give thankes for all these graces that you have in the sight of *God*, that is to say, not in the sight of man onely; as if he should have said, Many make a profession of faith, and goe for beleevers in *God*, and for lovers of *God*, and men judge them so: but

but you have it in the ſight of *God*; that is, not onely in the ſight of men, not onely in your owne fancie, apprehenſion, and opinion, but in deed, in good earneſt, in ſinceritie.

Laſtly, *In the ſight of God our Father*: he deſcribes *God* by this propertie, he is a Father. I need not ſay more for the opening of the words. We will come to that point for which we have choſen them, which is the firſt thing for which he gives thankes.

Remembring your effectuall Faith.

This point we will deliver to you out of them, that, *The faith that ſaves us muſt be effectuall.*

Doct. The faith that ſaves us muſt be effectuall.

This Doctrine we have need to adde to that which we formerly delivered: for having ſaid ſo much of faith, that faith is that that ſaveth men, and that there is no more required of you but to take the *gift of righteouſneſſe*, onely that you receive *Chriſt*, onely that you *beleeve in God that juſtifieth the ungodly*; that is, that you onely accept of that juſtification that *God* is ready to give every man, be he never ſo ungodly. Now (when we heare ſo much of faith, and that there is nothing at all required of us but a meere taking, leſt any man ſhould be deceived, and run away with a falſe opinion, that if he have but a naked apprehenſion, and no more, he ſhall doe well enough) I have choſen this Text, that you may know what kind of faith it is that is required of us, namely, *Effectuall Faith*. The faith that ſaves us muſt be effectuall.

Men are apt to deceive themſelves.

Now Saint *Paul* adding this word to it, (*Remembring your Effectuall Faith*) he gives us this intimation, that there is a faith which is not effectuall: there

is

That many men have a false faith, proved by instances both in the Old and New Testament.

is a faith in the world that goes for true faith, which, if it be examined, is not a faith that saves. We see, through the Scriptures, much mention made of a certaine faith which men had, which yet was not a saving faith: we see *many came and beleeved* in our Saviour, *but he would not commit himselfe to them: for he knew what was in their hearts* *John* 2.23,24. Here was a faith to beleeve in him: nay further, it was such a faith as had some effect too (for it made them come to him) and yet, for all this, it was not such a faith as *God* accepts, it was not an effectuall faith.

So when *John Baptist* came before *Christ*, there were many hundreds that came to him, and *rejoyced in his light*, *John* 5.35. but it was not effectuall, but a counterfeit faith that they had, notwithstanding all that.

Mat.22.8,9,10,11. opened.

Wedding garment, what.

So there came many that were *invited to the Wedding*, *so that the house was full*; but yet every man *had not a Wedding garment*. There was a certaine faith which brought them to the house, but they had not true faith, they had not the Wedding garment; that is, they had not such a faith as could produce and bring forth in them a conjugall affection, which is the Wedding garment. So two of the foure grounds had faith, they brought forth some fruit, that faith strengthened and enabled them to doe so much as they did; but yet it was not true faith, it was not the faith which the fourth ground had.

Mat.3.

And not onely in the New Testament, but in the Old Testament also there is often mention made of such a faith, and of such a trust in *God*, as enabled men

to

to doe much, but it was not an unfeigned trust, it was not effectuall, but as it is *Jer.*3.10. *Trecherous* Judah *hath not turned to me with her whole heart, but feignedly, saith the Lord.* Therefore certainly, saith the Lord, their turne of evill and misery shall come: they trusted in *God*, but not with their whole heart.

So likewise *Deut* 5.25. the people there desire *Moses* to goe and receive the Commandements from *God* for them, and whatsoever *God* should say to them, that would they doe: here was a faire profession, it is likely themselves thought it to be sound and good, yet *Moses* tells them they were deceived in it: *Oh* (saith he) *that this people had an heart* to doe this indeed, ver.29. So, we see, there is a faith that is not effectuall, and therefore we have the more need to looke to it, because there is so much false faith in the world. As, when you that are Tradesmen doe heare that there are so many counterfeit Drugges, or so many counterfeit Colours, or whatsoever you deale in, you will looke the more to it: so we should the better to our faith in this regard. Therefore to open this point a little we will doe these three things:

Simile.

First, I will shew the cause why there is so much uneffectuall faith, why there is so much faith that is not sound and substantiall.

Three things opened.

Secondly, I will shew wherein the efficacie of faith consists, what it is for faith to be effectuall.

Thirdly, I will shew the reasons why *God* will accept no other faith at our hands, why we cannot be saved unlesse we have such a faith.

For

1 The causes why the faith of many is uneffectuall, which are five.

For the first, namely, the causes of uneffectuall faith, the reasons why the faith of many is uneffectuall, that it works not powerfully, that it is not substantiall, you shall find them to be these five.

Cause 1. Taking Christ upon mis-information.

Instances.

1 The young man that came to Christ. Luke 18.

First, the vanitie or uneffectualnesse of faith ariseth upon our taking of *Christ* upon mis-information, when we know not who it is that we take, when there is an errour in the person we take, when we understand not aright what we doe. Many doe as the young man that came running to *Christ*, he came hastily, he made account to be his follower; but *Christ* tels him that he might mistake him: and therefore he lets him know what it was to follow him, what a Master he had betaken himselfe unto: saith he, *If thou wilt be my servant goe sell all that thou hast.* As if he should have said, Mistake me not, if thou wilt be mine, thou must be mine altogether, thou must take up thy Crosse, thou must part with any thing. Now if the young man had gone away with this mistake, that he had not understood *Christ*, hee had become a Disciple of *Christ*, as well as others, but it had beene upon a mistake.

2 The Scribe. Mat. 8. 20. opened.

And so likewise that Scribe to whom *Christ* said, *The Son of man hath not whereon to lay his head:* as if he should have said, It may be thou lookest for ease, for bed and boord with me, thou lookest for a pleasant life; but it will not be so, I lead not a pleasant life my selfe, I have not whereon to lay my head, I am not in so good a condition as many Fowles are, as many Beasts are, I have not a nest, I have not a den; that is, I have not that which should be in stead of these to me, me, and therefore know what thou dost before thou betake thy selfe to my service. Now men, not considering this, they put themselves upon *Christ*, they take upon them the profession of his Name, before they enter into a serious consideration, and this is it that causeth faith to be uneffectuall: as one speaking of false fortitude, names this for one amongst the rest: Many (saith he) are valiant for want of experience; that is, they know not what the wars are, they know not what hardnesse they must endure, and therefore when they come to feele it, when they come to see what paines they must take, and what they must endure, they shrinke. So it is in this, many men enter upon the profession of Christianitie, upon that warfare (for so our profession is called) I say, many enter upon it out of mistake, they understand not what it is, they have not experience of it, they know not how many will come against them, they know not that the force of their enemies is so great, they know not that they have so many thousands to meet them, therefore they undertake the businesse, they goe about the enterprise, and it comes to nought, because they considered not what they did. Therefore, saith *Christ*, *Let him that builds a house set downe before what it will cost*: That is to say, If a man consider not what *Christ* looks for at his hands, if he consider not before-hand that if he will be *Christs* he must *crucifie the flesh, with the affections thereof*, that he must *denie himselfe* in those things that are deerest to him, he must be content to be *hated of all men*, this is a thing that will goe hard. This is that that a man can hardly endure, to be scoffed at,

Cause of false fortitude.

What Christ expects of his followers.

at, to have every man his enemie, to part with all his friends, to live a despised man, to suffer persecution, that the end of one persecution should be the beginning of another, and the end of one suffering the beginning of another.

Againe, for a man to have his inward lusts and desires so mortified, and so crucified, and so restrained, to be so strait-laced in every thing; I say, because men consider not this, what it is to take this profession on them, when the time comes what doe they? They goe backe againe. Hence it is that many, out of flashes, and in good moods, will be ready to embrace Religion; but we see by experience how soone there is an end of it. As the people when *Christ* came to *Jerusalem*, how ready were they to receive him with *Blessed is he that commeth in the Name of the Lord*, and *Hosanna, &c.* But how soone were they gone againe? So many young commers on in this Citie, and many, even of our profession, in the beginning of their time are ready to take upon them the profession of *Christ*; but afterwards, when they come to see what must be done, when they see that *Christ* and the world cannot stand together, that *Christ* and pleasures cannot stand, but they must be content to goe another course, then they goe backe, and their faith proves uneffectuall. This (I say) is the first cause, when men are not throughly informed what they doe.

Cause 2. Taking Christ out of feare.

A second cause of the uneffectualnesse of faith is, when men take *Christ* out of feare, when they are in some present distresse, and would have ease, and upon this they take *Christ*, not because of any true love

love to him, but because they would be delivered out of that present exigent which they are in; and this is as usuall as the other. How many are there that when *God* affrights them a little with the terrours of the Law, when their consciences are troubled, when they begin to apprehend Hell, so long as they are in such a condition, they are willing to take *Christ*, but as soone as these stormes are over, and their hearts are at peace againe, when their consciences returne to some quiet, and when there is an end of those terrours, then there is an end of their religion, and of their faith, so that their faith proves uneffectuall? So many men, when they are in some great calamitie, as, you know, *Pharaoh*, when he was in the present strait, then he would doe any thing: so many men under great crosses, afflictions, and disgraces in the world, then they will be religious; but let them have peace and prosperitie, let them abound in all things againe, and they will forget *God.* Such *Esay* complaines of, chap. 58. *They hang downe their heads for a day:* that is, when the storme is on them, when they have some affliction, for such a time they will doe any thing, there is nothing more usuall than this. When men come to have sicknesse, and to apprehend death, what will not a man doe for his salvation at such a time? And therefore you find by experience that few of those that make such promises in their sicknesses, when they apprehend death, doe keepe them afterward; for they come from feare, and therefore they last not.

Esay 58. opened.

Promises made in sicknesse seldome performed.

Take any man, the most ambitious man in the world,

when he comes to die, the praise of men is then nothing to him, then he will part with any thing. Take a covetous man, to save his life what will not he doe? A Merchant that loves his goods never so well, yet when the Ship is ready to sinke he will cast them out, he is willing to lose them rather than to lose his life. So when a man comes to such an exigent, when he comes to stand in the gate of destruction, as it were, when he sees Heaven and Hell before him, he is ready to doe any thing then, not because indeed he loves *Christ*, or is willing to take him, but to save himselfe: as the foolish Virgins, when the gate was shut, then they cry, *Lord, Lord, open to us.* They would faine have had *Christ* then, not out of love to *Christ*, for then they would have taken him before: it was not out of any love to the Bridegroome, but out of feare, and sense of their owne miserie that they had when they were shut out, and that made them cry, *Lord, Lord, open to us.* And this is the second cause that makes the faith of men to be uneffectuall, when they take *Christ* out of feare.

Simile.

Men in extremity would fain have Christ, but not out of love.

Cause 3. Taking Christ for love of the good things by him, and not for love to his person.

Note.

The third cause is, when men take *Christ*, not out of love to his person, but out of love to those commodities and advantages they shall have by him, when they looke not upon him, when they fixe not their eies upon his person, and the beauty that is in him: but they looke upon the Kingdome, they looke upon the wealth they shall have, they looke to what they shall get by him. This faith proves uneffectuall, because when other commodities are presented that are present and sensible, and in their apprehension greater than

than these, then they let *Christ* goe againe. Men doe in this case as those that marry for wealth; if that be their end, when they have gotten the wealth that they would have, when they have that which they desire, they care for their wives no longer: so in this case, when men looke at nothing but simply at Heaven disjoyned from *Christ*, or when they looke at some other advantages, when they look at an earthly Kingdome, (as many of the Disciples did) when they looke for great matters by *Christ* in this world; when they find it quite otherwise, when they lose in the world, and all that they have is in hope, it is in things spirituall, that are not seene with the eye, things that are not sensible, then they are ready to slip from *Christ* againe. So it is usually among us, many take *Christ* for advantages, as *Christ* tells them plainely, *John 6.* saith he, *You seeke me, not for the Miracles which I did, but for the loaves:* that is to say, not out of love to the work, not because you judge aright of the things of the spirit, not because you love grace, but because you love some advantage that we have by religion, some profit that it brings you for the present, and because you would be freed from Hell for the future, such things as carnall men may see and be affected with: but this will not hold out.

Simile.

John 6. 26. opened.

The manner of these men is to seeke mercie, and not grace. If they can be but assured that it shall goe well with them, that they shall be freed from the feares they might have of Hell, that they may have some hope of being in a better condition, this is that they looke for: but as for grace, for repairing the

Some men seek mercy, and not grace.

the Image of *God* in their hearts, to be enabled to obey *Christ* in all things, this is a thing that they desire not, this is a thing they long not for: therefore the secret inquisition of their heart is, What good shall we get by it? They enquire not what excellencie and what beauty there is in *Christ*, what maner of one he is, that they may love him; but what good shall we get by him? what advantage will it be to us? Contrary to that in *Cant*.5.12. when the Spouse is there asked what the reason was that she followed her Beloved so much, and that she magnified him so much; she doth not tell them, Because I shall have such things by him, or he is thus wealthy, or I shall have this honour by matching with him: but mark her answer, *My Beloved is white and ruddy, the chiefe among ten thousand; his head is as the most fine Gold, his lockes are blacke as a Raven, his eyes are as the eyes of Doves by the Rivers of waters, washed with milke, and fitly set*: and so she goes along in a holy delectation, *This is my Beloved, O yee Daughters of Jerusalem*. I say, so it is with those that take *Christ* in good earnest, that looke upon the excellencies of *Christ*, as he is considered in himselfe, not that the other is excluded: for we may looke at the advantages and commodities that we have by him, but not upon that alone: but marke, in her answer she describeth what a one he was, and therefore she loved him. My Beloved is white and ruddy, the fairest of ten thousand, such a one is my Beloved: therefore Chap. 1. Ver.2. she describes him to be such a one as he is; and (saith she) *therefore the Virgins love thee*: as if she had

Cant.5.12. opened.

We may look to our own advantages by Christ.

had ſaid, there is a Harlots love, that lookes only what they ſhall have by him: but none but Virgins, that is, thoſe that have chaſte and good affections, thoſe that have holy and right affections, indeed *the Virgins love thee*, but the others doe not, for they have adulterous and Harlot-like affections (as we may call them, when a man lookes not unto *God* himſelfe, but to his owne advantage and profit.) And this is the third cauſe that makes faith prove uneffectuall.

Harlots love.

Virgins love.

Fourthly, faith proves uneffectuall for want of preparation and humiliation that ſhould goe before it, becauſe the heart is not circumciſed, the heart is not broken yet, it is not emptied of thoſe things that it muſt be emptied of before a man can take *Chriſt*: and therefore in *Deut.* 30.6. *Moſes* ſaith, *The Lord your God will circumciſe your hearts, and then you ſhall love him with all your ſoule, and with all your ſtrength.* As if he ſhould have ſaid, It is impoſſible you ſhould cleave to *God*, to love him indeed, to take him in good earneſt, unfeignedly, with all your hearts, except firſt your hearts be circumciſed; therefore the *Lord your God will circumciſe your hearts*; that is, he will humble you, he will breake your hearts, that your luſts ſhall be mortified in you, he will take away thoſe ſtrong, violent, thoſe carnall and ſinfull deſires that abounded in your hearts before, and when that is done, then you ſhall love the Lord in good earneſt; not feignedly, but with all your hearts. Now if a man come to take *Chriſt* before he be thus circumciſed, he takes him in vaine, he takes him ſo as that he cannot hold him, nor continue with him.

Cauſe 4. Want of humiliation.

Deut. 30.6. opened.

Now this circumcision is done by a certaine worke of preparation or humiliation, by which those strong lusts are broken in us: therefore when men come to *Christ*, before the Law hath beene a sufficient Schoolmaster to them, before it hath indicted them, before it have put them in prison, and told them that they must pay every farthing, (when a man comes to this, he seeth that he cannot doe it, then he goeth to *Christ*, and beseecheth him to pay his debt) before the Law have done this, men care not for *Christ*, they take him negligently, and therefore they hold him not. And for this it was that before *Christ* came into the world he would make way before him: so before he will come into a mans heart, the Mountaines must be brought downe, the Spirit of *Elias* must make way; that is, there must be a sharp ministry to shew men their sins, that they may be throughly humbled and prepared, or else they will never take *Christ* so as to keepe close to him.

The Spirit of *Elias*, what.

A man must be brought to have a present apprehension of death, and of the wrath of *God*, and damnation, or else he will not lay hold on the Hornes of the Altar: as *Joab*, when he saw that *Salomon* would slay him indeed, and take away his life, then he layes hold on the Hornes of the Altar, and would not let goe: so when a man sees present death, he will keepe close to *Christ*; and till this be wrought a man may take *Christ*, but his faith will be uneffectuall, because, indeed, till a man be soundly humbled he never accounts and rekons sin to be the greatest evill; and till he doe that, he never accounts *Christ* to be the greatest good; and if

Without sound humiliation sin is not accounted the greatest evill, nor Christ the greatest good.

if a man doe not reckon *Christ* to be the chiefe good of all other, there will be somewhat propounded which will be esteemed before him; and when that comes, he lets goe *Christ*. But when there is a sound humiliation, which makes a man prize *Christ* above all other things, then faith proves effectuall; that is, a man holds out, he goes thorow with the worke, he cleaves so to *Christ* as that he will not part with him: but for want of this, because mens hearts are not circumcised, because way is not made, because the Mountaines are not brought downe, because the Ministry is not sharp enough to prepare them, hence it is that their faith is vaine, and comes to nothing.

Cause 5. Because faith is not grounded aright.

Fifthly and lastly, the faith of men proves uneffectuall, because it is not well grounded: they take to themselves a perswasion of the remission of their sins, upon an uncertaine ground, they are not built upon the Rocke, they take *Christ*, but they are not well bottomed: for there is a certaine false perswasion, which is nothing else but a strong fancie which makes a man to thinke that his sins are forgiven, and that he is in a good estate; but when it comes to examination, he can give no sound reason for it. When men take *Christ* on this manner, when they are perswaded their sins are remitted, and yet have no good ground for this perswasion and peace, it holds not out, it continues not. Therefore to such as these Saint *Paul* speaks, *Eph.* 4. 10. *Be not children* (saith he) *in understanding, to be carried about with every wind of doctrine.* As if he had said, Indeed you are such as have embraced *Christ*, but you must not doe as children doe, that

False perswasion, what.

Eph. 4. 10. opened.

being not able to use their owne judgement, they see what other men doe, and heare what they say; but, saith he, you must learne to be men, that you may use your owne understanding, that you may see with your owne eyes, or else you will be *like a Ship tossed and carried about with every wind.* That is to say, it was a false perswasion that drave you to *Christ*, and another wind will drive you from him: therefore be not children in understanding. So, I say, when you have a perswasion of the remission of your sins, of beleeving in *Christ*, be not children in understanding, see that it be soundly grounded. That is a condition required by the Apostle, *Colos.1.23. Christ hath reconciled us to God the Father, to be blamelesse, and without fault.* But (saith he) I must put in this condition, *If you continue grounded and stablished in the faith, that you be not moved from the hope of the Gospel.* As if he should have said, There is a certaine faith by which you may take *Christ*, and so you may be perswaded of reconciliation: but, saith he, that will not doe, unlesse you be grounded and stablished in the faith. The word in the Originall signifieth, Except you be so built as a house is built upon a sure foundation, as a Tree that is soundly rooted; when you are so pitched upon *Christ*, that when new objects come, new temptations come, things that you never thought on, yet nothing can move you from the hope of the Gospel. If you be not grounded, you may take a hope to your selves of reconciliation, and of being without fault in the sight of *God*, but it will never hold out unlesse it be soundly grounded. Hence you see therefore

Col.1.23. opened.

Hope that is not well grounded holds not out.

therefore that if a man be not well rooted, if he be not built upon the Rocke, if this perswasion of the remission of his sins be not well bottomed, that causeth him not to hold out, but to fall off againe. Whereas it is required of us that we keep so close to *God*, in such a case our faith should be built on so sure a ground that nothing in the world should move us, no not the most probable arguments that may be brought in: as we see *Deut.* 13. Saith *Moses*, *If a Prophet, or a dreamer of dreames come, and give you signes and wonders, and the thing that he foretold come to passe*, hat you could not answer any thing, you can see no reason but that he should be a true Prophet: saith he, *God* will put you to such trialls to prove you, to see if you be soundly grounded. All that are saved he will have them so fixed, he will have them take their salvation upon so good a ground, upon such infallibilitie, that whatsoever shall be brought against them, they shall keepe them close to *God*. This is that that we should labour for, and for want of this, when men have a confused perswasion that their sins are forgiven, and thinke it enough if their hearts be quiet, if they have rest in their consciences, that they be not troubled, and never examine what the grounds are; I say, for want of this it is that in temptation they fall away: when other men come and preach other doctrines, then they *are plucked away with the errour of the wicked*, as Saint *Peter* saith, 2 *Pet.* 3. 17. *Be not plucked away with the errour of the wicked, but grow in knowledge.* As if he should have said, If you have but some perswasion, but some good opinion that

Deut. 13. 1, 2, 3. opened.

that *Christ* is yours, and that it is best for you to cleave to him, this will not hold, you will be plucked away with those errours that other men are plucked away with. This is the first thing which we have done with, to shew the causes of the uneffectualnesse of faith.

2 Wherein the efficacie of faith consists. Three things opened.

In the next place I am to declare unto you what it is that maketh faith effectuall, wherein the effectualnesse of faith consists. In this we will shew you three things.

First, in what sense it is called effectuall faith: for the very opening of this word which the Apostle useth will open a window to us, it will open a crevice of light to see into the nature of the thing it selfe.

Secondly, we will shew you particularly and distinctly wherein this effectualnesse of faith consists.

Thirdly, we will shew you how it is wrought, how this faith is made effectuall in us; and when we have done these three, you will fully understand what effectuall faith is.

1 In what sense faith is called effectuall. Things are said to be effectuall in foure respects.

First, for the opening of this very appellation, this name *effectuall faith:* you shall find that a thing is said to be *effectuall* in foure respects.

1 When they doe their proper office. The proper function of faith, what.

First, we say a thing is *effectuall* when it doth its office, when it exerciseth that proper function that belongs to that qualitie, or that grace, or that gift, or that creature whatsoever it is; and when it doth not that, then we say it is uneffectuall, when it doth not the thing that we looke for from it. In this sense *faith* is said to be effectuall, when it doth the thing for which faith is, when it doth the thing that *God* expects of faith, that is the proper function of faith: and

and what that is you heard before, namely, to take *Christ*. If faith take *Christ*, it is effectuall faith.

Now for the opening of this a little further to you, to shew you what this proper function of faith is. It is when a man is so far perswaded of the truth of the Scriptures, of the truth of the promises, and doth so farre appropriate them to himselfe, that he is willing to take *Christ*; though there be some doubtings and waverings in him, yet if there be so much faith as to doe the thing, this is properly effectuall faith, though it be not perfect faith: for you must know that there is a doubting mingled with the best faith. Therefore when we say *effectuall faith*, we doe not meane that it is such a faith as is without doubtings, and without feares mingled with it: but if it be such a faith as doth the thing it selfe, for which faith is appointed, it is properly said to be effectuall faith. It is a point necessary for you to understand: and if you compare this that we have said (concerning this description of this first explication of effectuall faith) with that in *James* 1.7,8. we shall see what the meaning is. He speakes there of doubting, and tels you, that those that doubt, *they are like a wave of the Sea, tossed to and fro, and* in the end *they vanish away*. Saith the Apostle, *Let not such a man thinke to obtaine any thing at Gods hands, for he is a double-minded man*, and *is unstable in all his wayes*. The meaning is, that there is such a faith that makes a man doubt, when he knowes not what he should doe, but is unstable, as a wave of the Sea that is tossed to and fro; he is sometimes going towards *God*, sometimes from him againe, and in the end

Faith may be effectuall, though it be mingled with doubting.

Jam. 1. 7, 8. opened.

end he goes quite away. Saith he, ſuch a man ſhall not receive any thing. Why? Becauſe he is a double-minded man. Now by a double-minded man is not meant a man that hath one thing in his face, and another in his heart; one that pretends one thing, and intends another; (though the word be ſometimes ſo taken, yet in that place it is not ſo to be underſtood) but by a double-minded man this is meant, when the mind is divided betweene two objects, that it knowes not which to chuſe, but ſtands as one in *bivio*, that hath two wayes before him, and knowes not whether to goe this way, or that way: a man that is diſtracted in his owne mind, he knowes not what to reſolve on. Now when a mans faith comes to this, that he knowes not whether to take *Chriſt* or the world, he doubts whether he ſhould chuſe *God* or the world, there is an uncertainty in his mind, that it is divided: ſometimes he thinks it is beſt, and ſometimes he thinkes it not beſt; *aliud ſtans, aliud ſedens*; when he thus wavers, this is not effectuall faith. But now, if a man goe beyond this, and pitch upon *Chriſt* reſolutely, when he goeth ſo farre, as that he reſolves to take him, although he have many pluck-backs, although there be many things that may diſſwade him from it, though there be ſome reluctancie in his mind, ſome feare whether it be the beſt way or no, yet if he pitch upon *Chriſt*, he chuſeth him rather than the world: though he have ſome inclination to the world ſtill, though there be ſomewhat offenſive in his heart, though, as I ſaid, there be ſome doubts, ſome feares whether it be the beſt way or no, yet if faith come ſo farre as to pitch on

Double-minded man, who.

on *Christ*, to chuse him, to take him, this is properly effectuall faith. Indeed it is farre from perfect faith, but it is effectuall faith, and such as shall save you. Therefore you shall find this rule among the Schoole-men (I name them because they were Papists, and their doctrine of faith is contrary to this) they say, it is not faith except it be a full perswasion; they speake not there of resting on *Christ*, that is not the thing, but of the full perswasion of the truth of the thing to be beleeved: yet notwithstanding you shall find this rule among some of the Schoole-men, ***Fides non excludit omnem dubitationem***, faith doth not exclude all doubting, but that doubting that overcommeth, that doubting that casteth the ballance the contrary way: if it be such a doubting as doth not overcome, it may stand with true and sound faith. So, I say, if you would know now what it is to pitch on *Christ*, and so to take him, though there be some reluctancie, some doubt, some feare, you shall know it by this; if a man have so taken him, that still he is growing, still his faith is prevailing, still his faith is overcomming those doubts and feares from day to day, he is better and better resolved; I say, though his faith be not perfect at the first, yet if it be still thus on the growing hand, it is saving and effectuall faith. Whereas another man, that is not soundly rooted, that is divided thus, he takes *Christ*, but it is not upon any good ground, but as the weathercock stands such a way, while the wind blowes that way; not because the weathercocke is fixed, (for when the wind turnes, the weathercocke turneth too) so such men cleave to *Christ*, not because they have any good

Papists tenent of doubting.

What doubting it is that faith excludeth.

How to try truth of doubting.

Simile.

Some men cleave to Christ for want of temptations.

good ground, but because they want temptations to a contrary way: let temptations from the Word come, let there come reasons that they knew not before, let there come new objects, new allurements, which they knew not of before, they will forsake *Christ* againe: but when the heart is fixed, when there is an Anchor that holds the soule, though the ship waver, when there is an Anchor to hold it fast, though it be much tossed to and fro, though there be much doubting, thou maist be sure it is true and effectuall faith.

This point you must marke: when, I say, it is effectuall, it is no more but when it thus pitcheth on *Christ*, though there be some doubting. It is so farre from being true that faith must be without all doubting, that we may boldly say, it is not faith except it have much doubting, unlesse there be some feares, unlesse there be some troubles within that resist this faith, and strive against it; otherwise it is no faith: for certainly there is no man that hath perfect faith, especially at the first, or afterward either, so as to set his heart fully at peace, and then if it be not perfect faith, if there be no doubting, there must be perfect flesh, that is, there is nothing but flesh; and if there be some faith which is imperfect, alway in the beginning there must needs be doubting, because there is some flesh, and some spirit; there is fire and water, and therefore there must needs be striving. We may say of doubting in this case, as we say of Thistles, they are ill weeds, but the ground is fat and good where they grow: so doubting is a thing that resists faith, it is bad, but it is a sign the heart is good where it is. So that where there is all peace, where

True faith not without doubtings and fears sometimes.

Note.

Simile.

Doubting a signe of a good heart.

where there is no questioning, where the heart is not perplexed and troubled, and complaines not, it is a sign that the strong man possesseth the house wholly, it is a sign there is nothing but flesh there. Therefore mark this point to your comfort, that if there be but so much faith as will produce this worke of taking *Christ*, though there be some doubtings mingled with it, yet it is properly effectuall faith, because it doth the thing, though not perfectly. That is the first acceptation of the word *effectuall.* a thing is said to be effectuall when it doth the proper function of it; though it doe it not perfectly and throughly, yet if it doe it, it is said to be effectuall: so faith, if it pitch upon *Christ*, though not so perfectly as afterwards it may, it is effectuall.

Secondly, a thing is said to be *effectuall* as it is opposed to that which is vaine and empty, to that which is but a name, a shadow of it, but is not such a thing indeed. So faith is said to be effectuall, when it is true, reall, and substantiall: you know there be empty clouds, we see the heavens many times full of clouds, but there is no raine followes, they are driven away with the winds, they are empty clouds, they are not clouds indeed: so there is a great shew of faith sometimes, that makes a man shew like these clouds, and yet it is vaine and empty, no raine followes. A counterfeit Piece, although it shew to be good money, yet when we find it counterfeit, when we find it clipt, we cast it away: so true faith is said to be effectuall when it is opposed to vaine faith. In *James* 2. the latter end of the Chapter, the Apostle speaks to that purpose, to shew the difference betweene true faith and dead faith, which

2 A thing is effectuall in opposition to that which is vaine and empty.

Simile.

Simile.

which is but the name of faith, but is not faith indeed.

3 A thing is said to be effectuall when it is operative.

Thirdly, a thing is said to be effectuall when it lieth not idle and still, but is doing something. As a Pilot in a Ship, he sitteth not still there, if he doe sit still and doe nothing, we may say he in an uneff ctuall Pilot, he were as good not be there: so when faith lies still in the heart, and is not stirred and moved, nor shewes it selfe in the fruits of it, this we say is uneffectuall faith; whereas faith should be in the soule as the soule is in the body, which is never there in vaine, but still it is stirring, and shewing it selfe by motion, by action, by doing somewhat or other. And in this sense *faith* is said to be *effectuall*, when it is a stirring faith, when it is a lively and fruitfull faith, that is, doing somewhat in the soule of man.

4 When it goes thorow with the worke in hand.

Last of all, a thing is said to be effectuall when it goes thorow with the worke that it hath in hand: this differeth from that which I named first, therefore the Greeke word that is rendred effectualnesse, signifieth perfectnesse to bring a thing to an end; so that faith is said to be effectuall, that goes thorow with the worke it undertakes, that is, when it sanctifieth the heart throughout in respect of parts, and throughout in regard of time; when it brings a man to the end of his salvation, when it carries a man thorow all impediments, when it leapes over all difficulties: so that a growing, prevailing, overcomming faith, that is said to be an effectuall faith, such a faith as leaves not the worke halfe done, such a faith as leaves not the building in the beginning, in the rudiments, but sets it up, and puts the roofe upon it; such a faith which though it may sinke as a Corke for a time, yet it riseth againe: such a faith as overcomes, and perfects the worke of our salvation; in this sense faith must be effectuall, and this differs from the other three: so that in these foure senses *faith* is said to be *effectuall*. And this is the first thing.

The second thing which we undertook was to shew you wherein the effectualnesse of faith consists. It consists in these foure things. That which we said before to you, when we shewed you the causes of the uneffectualnesse of faith, will make good way to this.

2 The effectualnesse of faith consists in four things.

The first thing wherein the effectualnesse of it is seene, is in being well built; that is, when the preparation is sound and full, that makes way for it.

The second is, when the understanding is cleere, and a man beleeveth the promise of *God* upon sure and infallible grounds, when he seeth them perspicuously and distinctly.

The third is, when the will takes *Christ*, and takes him out of love, not out of feare, not out of love to the advantage onely by him, not out of mistake.

The fourth is, when it turnes not only the will, but all the affections; when it turnes the whole man, when it shoots it selfe into life and practice.

I. When the preparation is good.

First, I say, faith is effectuall when there is a good way made for it, when the rubbish and false earth is taken away where it should be built, that is, when the humiliation is sound and good, when the preparation is perfect, when it is such as makes a man fit for the Kingdome of *God*. For I finde that phrase used, *He that puts his hand to the Plow, and lookes backe,*

Luke 9. 62 opened.

 is

is unfit for the kingdome of God. As if hee had said, There are certaine men which come to the profession of Christianity, as many come to husbandry, which is an hard employment; some there be which doe this, and goe backe againe. Why? because they are not fit for the kingdome of *God*: that is, they are not throughly prepared for it: that is to say, when a man is not throughly humbled to know what sinne is, and what the wrath of God is, hee is not fit for the kingdome of *God*: but if he doe come to *Christ*, if hee doe begin to beleeve, he will goe backe againe. So a man is properly said not to be fit for the kingdome of *God*, till he be throughly humbled, till hee have tasted the bitternesse of sinne, till he have felt what the Divels yoke is. As it was with the *Israelites*; put the case they had been carried out of *Egypt* before the time that they were, indeed they had not been fit for the land of *Canaan*, because they would have beene ready to have turned backe in their hearts into *Egypt*; and though the *Lord* laid load on them, though their yoke were hard, though he caused them to wander up and downe long, yet all was little enough, still they were lingering after *Egypt*: and if they had been taken out of *Egypt* before the tale of bricke was required of them without giving them straw, before the Taske-masters had dealt hardly with them, what would they have done? Might it not truely be said of them, they would not have been fit for *Canaan*? So in this case, if a man will take *Christ*, it is a laborious worke, as laborious as husbandry, as laborious as putting the hand to the Plow, as taking the yoke. Now before a man have felt

Sound humiliation fits men for Christ.
Instances.
I.
In the Israelites.

felt how hard the yoke is that he hath already (for there be many that weare the yoke of Satan, and see no hardnesse in it, but goe in a faire course, their consciences are not wounded with the sense of their sinnes, they never had afflictions wherein they tasted the wrath of God) alas, such men may come to put their hand to the Plow, but when they come to see what worke they have in hand, they goe backe, they are not fit for the kingdome of Heaven. *Till a man be weary, and heavie laden* with the burden of Satan; till he see Satans yoke to be intolerable, he will never continue under the yoke of *Christ*: therefore let us consider whether we be fitted or no: this fitnesse is first required. Many wear Satans yoke and feele it not heavie.

So againe, we may take example from the Prodigall sonne: he was in his fathers house, but hee would not continue there when he was there at the first, and lived as the other sonne did, because he had not beene abroad in the world, to finde the misery of being away from his father, he was never pinched with affliction, with want of meat; till he was from his father he never knew what it was to be at his fathers finding, till he had his stocke in his owne hand, hee was not fit, and wee see he continued not there: So, take a man that is brought up in his Fathers house, as it were, that hath tasted nothing but the sweetnesse of the promises, and all is well with him; hee hath drunke in the truth of the Gospel with his education; you shall finde, that this will not usually hold out: because hee hath not found what misery it is to bee out of his Fathers house, therefore hee prizeth it not; such an one is not fit to continue, he is unfit for the kingdome

2 In the Prodigall.

Men hold not without sound humiliation.

of *God.* Therefore the first thing that is required to make faith effectuall, wherein the effectualnesse of faith consists, by way of preparation, to make way for it, is, when a man is soundly humbled and prepared, when it is such as will make him continue. You have a phrase used *Rev.*2.25. *Hold fast till I come that which thou hast already.* As if he should say, Many have hold of the Truth, they have hold of *Christ*, they have hold of the promises, but they hold them not fast; they hold them a while, but they hold them not fast till I come. *To him that overcommeth, &c.* and, *him that continueth to the end will I make ruler over Nations, &c.* So, I say, till a man be thus made fit, he may take hold for a while, but he shall not hold fast till *Christ* come, but he will let goe his hold, because he is not prepared with humilitie. This is that which is required in that place I formerly named, *Matth.*10.6. *If there be any worthy* (saith he) *let your peace come upon them:* that is, if there be any, when you come to preach the Gospel, that are so farre broken and humbled, if there be any that are so farre convinced of their sins, that they prize me indeed, so that they hold me, and will not let me goe for any thing, but they are content to let all goe rather than me; such a man is worthy of me, such a man prizeth and esteemeth me, and your peace shall come upon him; that is, it shall come effectually upon him, it shall abide with him, and save his soule for ever. So, I say, when there is so much humiliation wrought in the heart, when the Spirit so farre convinceth a man of sin, that he comes to prize *Christ*, this is the

Rev.2.25. opened.

Mat.10.6. opened.

the first thing wherein effectuall faith consists: for though it be not the very thing wherein beleeving consists, yet it is that preparation without which faith can never be found sound and effectuall.

Secondly, when this is done, this is not all; when there is such a preparation made that a man is willing to take *Christ* upon any conditions, yet now, if he shall not be well built, if he see not just ground to take him, if his understanding shall not see the truth of the promise so cleerely, that he can build on it, that he can rest on it, that all the arguments in the world cannot draw him from it againe, his faith will not be effectuall. Therefore the second thing wherein the effectualnesse of faith consists, is to have it well built in the mind and understanding of a man, when he cleerely seeth the truth of the promises, that he can build upon it infallibly. For your better understanding of this, you must know that then a man is said to be well built, to be rooted and grounded in faith, when he hath the first ground right, that so he proceeds from one to another, that it is not a confused superficiall knowledge, to assent to the truth and promises that are delivered in the Word; but when he hath a sure ground, the first ground, and the next, and so he proceeds along. As for example: the first thing that a man must doe, is to beleeve the Scriptures, to know that they are true and infallible, that they are the sure Word of *God*; when a man can say, this I know, and this I build upon. And besides that, then we looke upon the promises which the Scriptures containe, wherein *Christ* and forgivenesse of sinnes is offered.

II. When the understanding is cleer

When a man is said to be well built.

1 When he beleeves the Scriptures in generall.

2 The promises in particular.

Now if the first ground faile you, that is the bottome upon which the promises stand; therefore have that sure: when that is sure, you must have the promises sure, that is, you must consider the promises, and examine them, and see if this be the sense of the Scriptures, if there be so much light in you as to say, I find it so, I find the Scriptures true, I beleeve them, I find these promises in the Scriptures, I find *Christ* offered to every creature under Heaven, I find that I have a warrant to take him: when a man, out of himselfe, out of an inward principle, out of his owne proper judgement seeth this, and is convinced of the truth of this, that the promises are so, and that they belong unto him, that he may justly, upon good ground, appropriate them to himselfe; so that when he lookes round about him, and considers all the objections that may be made, yet he can answer all arguments; when he falls downe, and is fully convinced, and perfectly perswaded in his own mind, when a man thus apprehends the promises, when his understanding is rooted and grounded in the faith, that is the second thing wherein the effectualnesse of faith consists. And we see that described in *Ephes.* 2. saith the Apostle there, *You are no longer strangers and forreiners, but Saints, of the houshold of God, and are built upon the foundation of the Prophets and Apostles, Jesus Christ being the chiefe corner stone.* Marke; saith he, you are built upon the foundation of the *Apostles* and *Prophets*, that is, you that are Saints must consider what ground you have to take that name to your selves; saith he, you are built upon the foundation of the Apostles and Prophets, that

Applicati-on of the offer of Christ.

Eph. 2. 19, 20. opened.

that is, you are not built upon the foundation, upon the word of a man, you are not built upon this Doctrine that I teach, meerely because I teach it; but you are built upon the foundation of the Prophets and Apostles, that is, you see the Prophets and Apostles deliver this Doctrine. I, but one may seeke a further ground than that. What foundation have the Prophets and Apostles? Saith he, *Christ* is the chiefe corner stone on which they are built. So that when you have this tract of consequence, I see the promise is sure. Why? Because it is built upon the foundation of the Apostles and Prophets, they have affirmed it. But how shall I know that they are sure? Because *Christ* himselfe hath spoken by them, he is the chiefe corner stone: when faith is thus grounded, then we are truely said to be built, and rooted, and grounded in faith. Therefore as the *Samaritans* said, *John* 4.44. *We beleeve, not because thou toldst us,* not for thy words, *but we have heard him our selves, and we know that he is the Messias, and Saviour of the world.* Now if those *Samaritans* had onely beleeved because the woman brought that relation, their faith might have failed them; but when they heard *Christ* themselves, when they saw him with their owne eyes, when they could say, in good earnest, out of their owne knowledge, we know that this is *Christ* the Saviour of the world, that is such a faith as will hold out. So when a man doth onely take a perswasion out of the generall preaching of the Word, without a certaine ground, it proves uneffectuall faith; but when men beleeve, because themselves have seene, and out of that know-

To be built upon the foundation of the Apostles and Prophets, what.

Note.

Particular knowledge.

 ledge

ledge can ſay, they know *Chriſt* to be the *Meſsias*; when they know *Chriſt* to be theirs, when they know *Chriſt* to be the Saviour of the world, and ſo, by conſequence, of them which are part of the world; then they may be truely ſaid to be built, to be rooted and grounded in faith. This is that that Saint *John* ſaith, 1 *John* 1.19. *We know that we are of God, and that all the world lieth in wickedneſſe.* We know that we are of *God*, that is, it is not a thing that we are uncertainely perſwaded of, but it is a thing that we know as certainely as any man knowes a thing that is before his eyes, as a man knowes a thing of which he doubts not. We know that although all the world be againſt us, though all the world run another way, though all the world condemne us for vaine men, idle men, for truſting in *Chriſt* crucified, yet we know that we are of *God*, and that all the world lieth in wickedneſſe. I ſay, when a man holds out thus, when he is put to the triall, when a man knowes in his owne knowledge that it is ſo, as Saint *Peter* ſaith to *Chriſt*, *John* 6.68. many had taken *Chriſt* that went away againe. Saith *Chriſt* to his Diſciples, *Will you alſo goe away?* Marke the anſwer that Saint *Peter* gives: No, ſaith he, *whither ſhould we goe? Thou haſt the words of eternall life. I know and beleeve that thou art Chriſt the Son of the living God.* As if he ſhould ſay, It is impoſſible that I ſhould goe away, for I know and beleeve; that is, I know upon good ground, I have another manner of ground than they had: If I had no more ground than the reſt, I ſhould goe away as well as they; but I know and beleeve that thou art *Chriſt* the Son of the living *God*, therefore it is impoſſible

John 6.68. opened.

impossible that I should ever forsake thee, although all should forsake thee. This is to be rooted and grounded in faith, in this second sense, when we see an infallible ground, a sure Rocke upon which our faith is built, and we are willing to adventure our selves upon it, to adventure our goods, our name, our life, our libertie, that if a man be brought to Martyrdome, he can adventure himselfe, and put all that he hath upon it. This ground will hold out, I say, when the understanding of a man is thus built upon the Word, when a man is examined every way, when he is able to answer all arguments, and all objections that may be brought against it. This is the second thing wherein the effectualnesse of faith consists. I should adde more, but I must defere them till the afternoone.

FINIS.

THE SECOND SERMON.

1 THESS. 1.3.

Remembring your effectuall Faith, &c.

The third thing wherein the efficacie of faith consists, to take Christ.

THe third thing wherein the efficacie of faith is seene, is when we take *Christ*; this is the action of the will, when we take him in a right maner, when we take him so as to hold him, when we take him in such a manner as that we are knit and united to him. That this is required,

First, I will shew it in the generall. It is a point that we have often mentioned heretofore; but to all that I have said, I will adde that in *Heb.* 10.22. *Let us draw neere with a true heart, and full assurance of faith.* Marke it, first, there must be an assurance of faith, that is in the understanding and mind of a man, and to that must be added drawing neere, and that is an act of the will: for when we are assured of the truth of the promises, and have appropriated them to our selves, then followes the act of the will: therefore in verse 38. of that Chapter it is said, *The just shall live by faith: but if*

Heb. 10.22. opened.

if any man draw backe, my soule shall have no pleasure in him. That Antithesis, that opposition that is made in that withdrawing of a mans selfe from *God*, is opposed to faith, to drawing neere to him, when a man not onely beleeveth the promises, but accepts and receives them. Now to doe this in a right manner, is that wherein the efficacie of faith doth principally consist. Now what is that? It is to take *Christ*, to draw neere to him in a right manner; and then it is done, when you so take him, that you bring *Christ* into your hearts, to dwell there, as it is expressed *Eph*.3.17. *That Christ may dwell in your hearts by faith:* that is, when there is an union made betweene *Christ* and us, when he comes into the heart, when he dwels in us, and we in him; when *Christ* is so brought into our hearts, that he lives there; and when we are so united to him, that we live in him; when he growes in us as the Vine in the branches, and we grow in him as the branches in the Vine: when faith hath done this, then it is an effectuall faith, when it knits and unites us to *Christ*, as he saith, *Rev*.3.20. *I will come in, and sup with him:* that is, I will continue with him, I will live in him, and rule over him.

What taking of Christ is effectuall.

Now when *Christ* is in the heart, he is not there to no purpose, but, as Saint *Paul* saith, *I live in Christ, and he in me.* I say, when our taking of *Christ* shall proceed so farre as to make this union betwixt us, therein this efficacie lieth: when the heart is knit to him, as the soule of *Jonathan* was to *David*, and when *Christ* shall be knit to us againe, that we shall be content to leave father and mother, and to become one

spirit

ſpirit with him, as it is *Eph.5.23.* It is a ſimilitude expreſſing the union betwixt Chriſt and the Church. *A man ſhall forſake Father and Mother, and ſhall cleave to his wife.* The Word in the Originall, κολλᾶσθαι, ſignifieth to glew: if there be any conjunction that is neerer than other, it is ſignified in that word: there is not a word in all the Greeke Language that ſignifieth a neerer conjunction than the word there uſed for cleaving or glewing. When a man ſhall forſake all, even Father and mother, the deereſt things in the world, and ſhall cleave to *Chriſt*, (it is a repetition of what is ſaid, *Gen.2.24.* concerning *Adam* and *Eve*) when faith hath done this worke, it is an effectuall faith.

But yet adde this againe, a man may take *Chriſt*, and ſeeme to draw neere to him, when it may be it is done out of feare, it may be out of love to his, and not out of love to him, it may be done out of miſ-information and miſtake; but when we draw neere to *God*, and doe it out of love, (put theſe two together) that we ſo take *Chriſt*, as that there is an union made betweene us and him, and when it is done out of love, as that condition is put in, 1 *Tim.1.5.* *The end of the Commandement is love out of a pure heart, and a good conſcience, and faith unfeigned.* As if he ſhould ſay, There is a double kind of faith, a falſe faith, and a faith that is not hypocriticall, that is the word uſed in the Originall. Now, ſaith he, the end of the Commandement is love, &c. That is, all that *God* lookes for is ſuch a love as comes from faith that is unfeigned, that is not counterfeit. Herein is faith ſeene not to be counterfeit, if it beget love, and out of that love we cleave

We muſt draw neere out of love to Chriſt.

to

to *Christ*. So that this is the third thing that makes faith effectuall.

Fourthly, faith is then said to be effectuall, when it hath not onely done all this, when there is not onely a good preparation made for it, when it is well built in the understanding, and when the will hath thus taken *Christ*; but there must be a further act, and that is the turning of the whole soule, and a seconding of it in our whole lives and practice, a seconding of it in our executions, and doing the things that *Christ* commands, as in *Gal.* 5. *In Christ Jesus neither circumcision availeth any thing, nor uncircumcision, but faith that worketh by love.* Such a faith as workes that, that is effectuall faith. As if he should have said, Many will be ready to beleeve in *Christ*, but will doe nothing for him, they will not worke. Now working is in doing or in suffering: for in suffering there is a worke as well as in doing, onely it is a worke with more difficultie, a worke with more impediments. Againe, if they will doe any thing for *Christ*, it is not out of love, but for other respects; perhaps out of some flash or good mood, or some other respects: but to doe it as being rooted and grounded in love, if faith have this work, it is effectuall faith: and therefore when faith hath once taken *Christ*, it must shoot it selfe into all the affections: for when they are all set on worke, endevour will follow. If the will be so set on worke indeed, the rest will follow after it. *Love* will follow, *Desire* after *Christ* will follow, *Feare* to offend him will follow, *Repentance* and turning from Satan will follow, bringing forth *Fruits* worthy amendment of life and

The fourth thing wherein the efficacie of faith consists.

The turning of the whole soule

Working in doing and suffering.

Obedience,

Obedience, &c. will follow. Therefore you ſhall find, that the promiſes are made promiſcuouſly, ſometimes to one thing, ſometimes to another: ſometimes, he that *repenteth* ſhall be ſaved: ſometimes, he that *beleeveth* ſhall be ſaved: ſometimes, he that *obeyeth* ſhall be ſaved: you ſhall finde them promiſcuouſly; becauſe that when faith is effectuall, it hath all theſe with it, it purifieth the heart, and *bringeth forth fruit worthy amendment of life*. Therefore this muſt bee added, to ſhew the efficacy of faith; and, if this be wanting, faith is not effectuall; not that it can be diſ-joined from the other, but that it is that wherein it conſiſts with the reſt.

Why the promiſes are made promiſcuouſly.

And therefore it is *Gods* uſuall manner, when men ſeeme to take *Chriſt*, and to beleeve in him, hee puts them to the triall, to ſee what they will doe, whether their faith will worke or no. Thus he did with *Abraham*, when he would prove him; hee was a faithfull man before, *God* had experience of him before, but yet he would prove *Abraham* by offering his ſonne, and when he ſaw he did it, he concluded that hee had faith: indeed it was a ſtrong faith, for it endured the tryall. I ſay, *God* will put men to it. So likewiſe thoſe in *Joh*. 12. 42. *Many of the chiefe Rulers beleeved in him, but they durſt not confeſſe him for feare of the Jews, leſt they ſhould be caſt out of the Synagogue*. There was a faith in them, a taking of *Chriſt*, but when it came to the tryall, it held not out, they durſt not confeſſe him, becauſe they feared to be caſt out of the Synagogue; that is, when they came to ſuffer a little for *Chriſts* ſake, when they came to ſuch an action as confeſſing his name, when they came to endure but ſuch a thing

God tryeth mens graces.

thing as to be cast out of the Synagogue, they forsook him, which shewed that their beliefe was uneffectuall. So that let a man seeme to have all the other three, yet when the praise of men shall come in competition with any command of *God*, when *God* shall put him to doe any thing, to part with any thing that is deare to him, as he did *Abraham*, if his faith worke not, if his faith hold not out in the tryall, *but start aside, like a broken Bow*, it is not effectuall faith. So you see the things wherein the efficacie of faith consisteth.

First, in the soundnesse of the preparation.

Secondly, when the mind apprehends the promises, and sees good ground to pitch upon them.

Thirdly, when the will so takes *Christ*, as to bring *Christ* into the heart (so that *Christ* lives in us) and that out of love.

And fourthly, when faith worketh, and that in the time of tryall, when *God* shall put us to it. I say, when you finde these foure things, you may conclude that your faith is effectuall.

The last thing I propounded, is to shew how this is wrought, how our faith is made effectuall. It is made effectuall by the Spirit of *God*, it is not in our owne power, we are not able to beleeve; nay, we are so farre from it, that we strive against it, the spirit in us resists it; so that if *God* himselfe put not his hand to the work, no man is able to beleeve.

3 How effectuall faith is wrought.

It is not in mans power to beleeve.

You may thinke, when you see such generall propositions as these, that *Christ is offered to every creature under Heaven*, and that *whosoever beleeveth shall bee saved*; you may thinke, I say, that it is easie to bring this

this home in particular, to say, Surely this pardon belongs to me. My Brethren, it is another thing for a man indeed to beleeve, for him to take *Christ* so, as to *denie himselfe* for him; to take him so, as to *mortifie his lusts*; so, as to *take up his Crosse*; so, as to obey *Christ*, to *follow* him in all things; this is a thing that no man is able to doe, unlesse *God* enable him to it with his Almighty power. For the heart of every man by nature is so shut up against *Christ*, that it will give no entrance to him; he may stand and knock long enough, unlesse *God* himselfe shake off the bolts, and open the gates, and break open these *everlasting doors, that the King of glory may come in*, we will not admit him, but keepe him out.

Every man naturally hath an hard *heart that cannot repent*, that cannot turne from sin: he will be content perhaps to take *Christ* for a Saviour; but to take him so as to obey him, and feare him, so as to love him, this no man will doe, or can doe, unlesse the Holy Ghost enable him.

Quest. But you will aske, How doth the Holy Ghost doe it?

How the HolyGhost worketh faith: by three things
1
Putting an efficacie in the Law.

The Holy Ghost doth it by these three acts: First, by putting an efficacie into the Law, and making that powerfull, to worke on the heart, to make a man poore in spirit, that so he may be fit to receive the Gospel. For the Law, though it be fit to humble a man, yet it is no worker of sanctification. If a man were able to doe any thing, he were able to see the righteousnesse the Law requires, and how farre he is from it, and to discerne the curse upon the not doing of it; and yet this

this hee is not able to doe, without the *spirit of bondage*: the spirit of bondage must make the Law effectuall, as well as the *spirit of Adoption* doth the Gospel. That is, except the Lord himselfe presse the Law on our hearts, so as to cause it to make sinne appeare to us, we that are the Ministers of *God*, may discover your sinnes, wee may shew you the rectitude required in the Law, we may shew you the danger, yet all will be to no purpose, unlesse *God* awaken you: if hee will set sinne upon the conscience to worry a man, to plucke him downe, when *God* shall charge sinne on him, that hee shall feele the weight and burthen of it, when he shall sharpen sinne, and cause it to use its sting, this makes a man fit to receive *Christ*: otherwise, if the *sonnes of Thunder* should speake to men, if we should *come in the spirit and power of Eliah*, nay, if *God* himselfe should thunder from heaven, all would not move the heart of a man, all would not awaken him to see his sinnes, till *God* himselfe shake the heart.

To convert the *Gaoler* in *Acts* 16. the foundation of the Prison was shaken, which was a resemblance of the shaking of his heart: wee may as well shake the earth as strike the heart of a sinner without the worke of *God*. For though the Law bee a sword, yet unlesse *God* take that sword into his hand, and strike therewithall himselfe, it shall not be able to wound a sinner. Therefore the first worke of the *Holy Ghost* is to awaken a sinner, to set sinne upon him, that he may be fit to receive *Christ*.

Secondly, when this is done, that the heart is thus

By shewing the excellency and the riches of Christ. Eph. 1.18, 19. opened.

prepared by the Spirit, then the *Holy Ghost* shewes us what we have by *Christ*, hee shewes *the unsearchable riches of Christ, what is the hope of our calling, and the glorious inheritance prepared for the Saints. and what is the exceeding greatnesse of his power in them that beleeve.* I say, wee need the Spirit to shew these things.

Ob. But, you will say, a man may see these things without the helpe of the Spirit.

No man can so see the riches of Christ, as to be affected with them, without the help of the Spirit.

Ans. It is true, in some manner you may, but not in such a manner as shall affect you. For there is a manner of seeing proper onely to the Saints, and that is the proper worke of the Spirit in them, when wee shall so see them, as to be affected with them. Otherwise, you may read the Scriptures a thousand times over, you may understand them, yet you shall not bee affected with them, till the *Holy Ghost* shew them unto you. This is the secret of *God*, that hee revealeth to those whom he meaneth to save, that is, when hee presents these spirituall things prepared for us in *Christ*, in such a manner, as that wee shall love them, and embrace them; when we shall not onely see the truth of them, but the goodnesse of them; when *God* shall not onely shew us the advantages we have by *Christ*, but the excellency of *Christ*, so that we shall be in love with his person, as well as to be ready to receive the priviledges with him.

1 Cor. 2. 12. opened.

Now this is done by the Spirit, 1 *Cor.* 2. 12. *Wee have received the Spirit of God, by which we know the things that are given us of God, and they are revealed to us by the Spirit.* They are two or three times repeated in in that Chapter: as if he ſhould have ſaid, if you ſaw them no more than other men doe, than naturall men doe, you would be no more affected with them than they are: but when you have the Spirit of *God* to ſhew you the things that are given you of *God*, that is the thing that works upon you and affects you. And ſo in *John* 14.21. ſaith *Chriſt*, *I will come to him, and ſhew my ſelfe to him*: When *Chriſt* ſheweth himſelfe to a man, it is another thing than when the Miniſters ſhall ſhew him, or the Scriptures nakedly read doe ſhew him: for when *Chriſt* ſhall ſhew himſelfe by his Spirit, that ſhewing draweth a mans heart to long after him, otherwiſe wee may preach long enough, and ſhew you that theſe ſpirituall things, theſe priviledges are prepared for you in *Chriſt*, but it is the Holy Ghoſt that muſt write them in your hearts; we can but write them in your heads. Therefore the *Lord* taketh that as peculiar to himſelfe: *I will write my Law in your hearts*: That is, I will make you affected with the things that I ſhew you, and this is the teaching of *God*. There is a teaching by men, and a teaching by *God*; that is, when *God* ſhall enable a man to ſee things in good earneſt, otherwiſe it will bee but as a man that ſees a thing, when his minde is upon another matter: ſo, wee ſhall ſee, and not ſee: but when the Holy Ghoſt ſhall ſhew you theſe things, you ſhall ſee indeed; till then you may hear oft enough of theſe things, but your hearts wil be minding other matters; ſome about their profits, and ſome their pleaſures, &c. but when the Holy Ghoſt ſhall ſhew you theſe things; that is, when he preſents them

Joh.14.21. opened.

Jer.31.33. opened.

Teaching of God, what.

to us, that draweth the heart from minding other things, to seeke after *Christ*, to long after him, and not to content your selves till you bee united to him.

3 By assuring us that these things are ours.

But besides this, there is a third act of the *holy Ghost*, by which he workes it, and maketh this faith effectuall, and that is the testimony that the Spirit gives to our spirits, telling us, that these things are ours: when the heart is prepared by the Law, and when these things are so shewed unto us, that we prize them, and long after them, yet there must be a third thing, that is, to take them to our selves, to beleeve that they be ours; and there needeth a worke of the Spirit for this too: for, though the promises be never so cleare, yet, having nothing but the promises, you will finde that you will never bee able to apply them to your selves: but when the *Holy Ghost* shall say, *Christ is thine*, and these things belong to thee, and *God* is thy father: when he Spirit shall beare witnesse with our spirits, by an immediate worke of his owne, then we shall beleeve. This is necessarily required, and without this we shall not beleeve. It is true, the holiest man doth it two wayes.

This also must be wrought by the Spirit.

The testimony of the Spirit wrought two waies.

1 By clearing the promises.

One is by clearing of the promises shining into our hearts, by such a light as makes us able to discerne them, and to beleeve them, and to assent to them.

2 By an immediate voice.

But besides that, he doth it by an immediate voice, by which he speaketh immediately to our spirits, that we can say, as they said, *John* 16. *Now thou speakest plainely, and speakest no parable*; we understand thee fully: so till the *Holy Ghost* speake to us, wee are in a cloud,

cloud, *God* is hid from us, we cannot see him clearly; but when we have this Spirit of Adoption, to give us this witnesse, then we beleeve plainly indeed. Therefore in *Isai.* 57.19. saith the Lord, *I create the fruit of the lips, Peace, &c.* That is, the Ministers may speake peace to you, but unlesse I goe and joine with the Minister, except I adde a power of mine owne; that is, such an almighty power as I used in the creation, it shall never bring peace to you. I create the fruit of the lips; that is, the words of the Minister to be peace, otherwise they would be uneffectuall. Therefore, I say, there must be a worke of the Spirit to perswade a man in such a case. And you shall finde by experience, let a Minister come to them that are in despaire, they will not apprehend the promises; though we use never so cleare reasons, though wee argue with them never so long, and never so strongly, we shall finde that all will doe nothing, it will be but labour spent in vaine, till *God* himselfe open the clouds, till he will smile on a man, and send his Spirit into the heart, to give a secret witnesse to him, till there be a worke of his owne joyning with the promises, we finde by experience, that our labour is lost.

Isai. 57.19. opened.

All arguments without the Spirit prevaile not.

It is true, wee ought to doe this, and every man is bound to looke to the word: for *faith commeth by hearing*; and to hearken to the Ministery, for it is *Gods* ordinance to breed faith in the heart, but yet till there be a work of the Spirit, a man shall never be so perswaded, as to have any sure and sound comfort by it.

Now all this is done by the Spirit, it is the wonderfull worke of God: for when *Christ* is propounded to men, when he is offered (as we have often offered him to you; we have shewed you what accesse you have to him, that no man is excluded, that he is offered to every creature under heaven; we have shewed you the generalitie of the promise, that it takes-in all, that you are contained under it, that you may apply it to your selves; I say, when all this is done, yet) when a man comes to performe this, to apply it to himselfe, he is no more able to doe it, than a dead man is able to stirre himselfe. Therefore the same power that raised *Christ* from the dead, is required to worke faith in our hearts, as it is in *Ephes.*1.19. *According to his mighty power which he wrought in Christ, when he raised him from the dead.* So that it is as great a worke to move a mans heart to *Christ*, as to put life into a dead man; we are as unapt and backward to it, as a dead man is to receive life. For what else is the reason, that when we preach *Christ* to you, when he is offered to you, that there be so few that are affected with him, that there be so few that take him? Doth it not shew that you are dead? Yea, so dead, that unlesse *God* call you, and that there be a mighty worke of the Spirit, the hearts of men will never answer unto us. Therefore that is required as a condition in all them who will come, *Acts* 2.59. *So many as the Lord our God shall call*: that is, when we preach, except there be a secret voice of the Spirit of *Christ* speaking to your hearts, as we doe to your eares, and saying, *Come and take Christ*, no man will come. We see *Christ* said to his Apostles, *Follow me*; and presently they followed him: (for it was not the outward voice that did it, there was a secret

Eph.1.19. opened.

As great a worke to move the heart to take Christ, as to raise the dead.

a secret voice within) so when *God* shall call men to take *Christ*, then they doe it, but not before. That word that is used *Luke* 14.23. *Goe and COMPELL them to come in, that my house may be full*, it intimates a great backwardnesse in us. When men are compelled, it shewes, that not only the arguments are strong and forcible, but that there is a great backwardnesse in men, that they must (as it were) be constrained, that they must be put on it by force, and against their will; such is the unaptnesse that is in men.

Luk. 14.23. opened.

That men are compelled to come in, what it implies.

So saith *Christ*, *No man can come to me except the Father draw him*. That phrase of the Holy Ghost shewes that there is an extreme backwardnesse, that if they be not forced to come (as it were) they will not doe it; not but that when a man is once wrought upon by the Holy Ghost, he commeth of himselfe: but that phrase is used onely to shew that backwardnesse that is in man by nature. For when the Holy Ghost hath wrought upon the will, and hath turned that, then a man commeth upon his owne legs, and is moved from an inward principle of his owne: therefore men are so *drawne*, that withall *they runne after him*, as it is *Cant.* 1. but it shewes this thing for which I have used it, that there is a wondrous backwardnesse in all of us by nature, and that this must be done by a great worke of the Spirit.

What is implied by drawing. Joh. 6.44. opened.

How the Holy Ghost draweth.

Therefore the Apostle *Paul*, in *Ephes.* 1. in all the former part of the Chapter, to the 18. Verse, having declared the great mysterie of salvation, he takes himselfe up on the sudden, and begins to thinke with himselfe, though I shew you all this, it is to no purpose, if *God* send not the spirit of revelation, &c. Therefore hee lifts up his heart to *God*, beseeching him *to give them the spirit of revelation, to open the eyes of their understanding, that they might see the hope of their calling, and the riches of their inheritance with the Saints.* So should Ministers learne to doe, to pray for the people, that *God* would infuse, and send his Spirit into their hearts, that they may be able to perceive these things effectually, with a right apprehension to see the secrets of *God* in them: you also should goe to *God*, and beseech him to helpe you with his Spirit, that so you may be able to apprehend these things, and that they may be powerfull to worke the same thing for which we deliver them to you: and so we have shewed you these three things; First, what effectuall faith is: namely, in shewing you why it is called effectuall faith.

Secondly, wherein the efficacie of faith consists: and thirdly, how it is wrought.

4 Why God will accept no faith but that which is effectuall.

Now last of all, we are to shew you the reason why *God* accepts no faith but that which is effectuall.

And there is good reason why no faith should be accepted of *God*, but that which is effectuall.

1 Because else it is not faith, because it is dead.

First, because otherwise it is not faith at all, if it bee not effectuall; and if it be not faith, it is no wonder that he doth not accept of it. I say, it is no more faith than a dead man is said to be a man: you give the name of a man to him, yet he is not a man; no more is faith that is not effectuall any faith; it hath onely the name of faith, and there is no more in it: but as dead Drugs, which have no efficacy in them; or as dead Plants, or dead Wine which is turned into Vinegar, it ceaseth to

Simile.

bee

be Wine, it is no longer Wine, but Vinegar; so it may be said of ineffectuall faith, it is not faith, it hath the name and the shadow of faith onely, and therefore *God* accepts it not.

Againe, *God* will save none unlesse they be reconciled to him, and be such as love him, for that condition is every where put in. *All things shall worke together for good to them that love him:* and he hath *prepared a Crowne for them that love him.* Now if faith be not effectuall, there will be no love; and if love be necessarily required, *God* cannot accept that faith that is ineffectuall. 2 Because such faith hath no love. Rom. 8. 28.

Againe, if *God* should accept of a faith that is ineffectuall, the Divels have such a faith, by which they apprehend the Word, and a faith that brings forth effects: for they feare and tremble; but this is not the faith that purifieth the heart, it is not an effectuall, it is not a purging lively faith. 3 Because the Divels have such a faith.

Againe, *Christ* receives none but them that deny themselves, and are willing to *take up their crosse and to follow him,* that *mortifie the deeds of the body by the Spirit.* Now an ineffectuall faith doth none of these, and therefore that faith that saveth must be a working faith, or else these things should not be necessarily required. 4 Because it workes no mortification.

Againe, it was *Christs* end in comming into the World, *That he might destroy the workes of the Divell,* and *for this end hath the grace of God appeared, that men should deny ungodlinesse and worldly lusts:* and for this end did he give himselfe, *to purifie to himselfe a people zealous of good workes.* He comes to be a King, as well 5 Because else Christ should lose the end of his comming into the world.

as

as a Saviour, to rule among his people, to have men obey him, which could not be, if faith were not effectuall, if it did not purifie the heart, and enable men to deny all worldly lusts, *and to live soberly, ighteously, and godly in this present world.*

6 Good works are the way to salvation.

And last of all, good workes are required of necessity, as the way to salvation: *Ephes.2.10. We are Gods workmanship, created in Jesus Christ unto good workes, which he hath ordained that we should walke in them.* Good workes are required of necessity; *God* judgeth us according to our workes, *Rom.2.* and at the last day the reward is pronounced according to that which men have done; *When I was in prison you visited me, when I was naked you cloathed me, &c. Mat. 26.35,36.* And if they be required for necessity, then it is not a dead, livelesse, worklesse faith, but a powerfull, energeticall faith, a faith that is stirring and active, a faith that is effectuall which *God* requires, without which we cannot be saved. We come now to make some use of what hath beene said.

Mat.26.35, 36.

Use 1. To try our faith whether it be sound.

First, if *God* accepts no faith but that which is effectuall, it should teach us not to be deceived in a matter of so great moment, it should teach us to looke to our faith, to consider whether it be a right faith or no. If a man have Evidences upon which his lands and whole estate dependeth, if one should come and tell him that they were false Evidences, it would affect him, he would at the least be ready to looke and to examine them: and yet these are matters of lesse moment.

Simile.

If one be told that his corne is blasted, that all the Trees in his Orchard are dead, that all his money is counterfeit, a man would looke even to these things; a man would have that which he hath to be sound, and not counterfeit: and shall not we then look to the faith that we have, upon which the salvation of our soules depends, seeing *God* accepteth none unlesse it bee sound, and seeing there is so much counterfeit faith in the World? It should teach us to looke about us, and consider what our faith is: For, as S. *James* saith, Faith without workes cannot save us. *What availeth it, my brethren, if a man say he hath faith, and hath not works? can his faith save him?* So I say to every man in such a case; thou that thinkest thou hast faith, if there be not workes too, if it be not effectuall, if it be not a lively faith, will such a faith save thee? If a man should come and say to one that bragges of the balsome or drugges which he hath (that are dead, and have lost their efficacy) Will such a balsome heale thee? If a man have a gilded Target made of Paper, a man may say to him, Will that Target defend thee? And so I say, when a man hath a counterfeit faith, Will such a faith as this save thee? It will not save you; you may please your selves in it, as a man is pleased with a false dreame, but, when you are awaked, you shall finde that you are deceived. Learne therefore to consider of your faith, to see if it be effectuall. Jam.1.14.

When the *Lord* proclaimed himselfe to be a *mercifull God, forgiving iniquity, transgression, and sinne;* yet it is added, *He will not hold the wicked innocent.* So when we have said so much of faith, and that faith saveth; yet know, that it must be a working faith that saveth us: it must be such a faith as purifieth the heart, it Exod.34.6, 7.

it must be such a faith that may shew it selfe in fruits worthy amendment of life. And therefore St. *James* taketh so much paines in this case, as you shall finde in his first Chapter, and the beginning of the second; he layeth downe rules, and tels them, that if they keepe the whole Law, and yet faile in one point, they are guilty of the whole.

Ob. Now having dealt so strictly, some might bee ready to object; *God* is mercifull, and I shall be saved through *faith.*

Ans. It is true (saith hee) if you have a right faith, you shall bee saved by it; but yet know this, that unlesse your faith be such a faith as enableth you to doe what I say, it is a faith that will doe you no good, it will not save you: for though faith saveth you, yet it must be such a faith as worketh. And that he proveth by many arguments; (it is a place worth the considering, and fit for this purpose) I say hee useth some arguments to prove, that that faith which is not effectuall, will not save us.

Five arguments of St. James against worklesse faith.

1. It is vain.

As first, saith he, if a man should say to one, *Be warmed, or be filled:* as this is but vaine liberality, when as yet a man doth nothing; so for a man to professe that he beleeveth in *Christ*, and yet doth nothing for him, it is a vaine faith.

2. True faith is working.

Note.

Secondly, some man might say, *Thou hast faith, and I have workes, shew me thy faith by thy workes.* That is, if a man have faith, he will shew it by his workes. As if he should have said, if the sunne be the greatest light, let it give the greatest splendor; if the load-stone be of such a vertue, let it shew it by attracting the iron to it:

So

So if thy faith be effectuall, shew it by thy works: that is, if thy faith be a true faith, it must be a working faith, or else it is nothing, *God* will not accept it.

Thirdly, unlesse it be a working faith, an effectuall faith, the Divels have the same: *Thou beleevest that there is one God, the Divels doe the same and tremble.* 3 The Divels have such a faith.

Fourthly, if any man could bee justified by faith without workes, *Abraham* might have beene so justified; but *Abraham* was justified by his workes, that is, by such a faith as had workes joyned with it. And not *Abraham* onely, but *Rahab* (that is another example) for it might be objected, *Abraham* indeed beleeved, and was justified by workes, but *Rahab* had no workes, she was a wicked woman, and therefore was justified by faith. 4 None were ever justified without works.

To this therefore he answereth, that she had works, or else she could not have been saved, unlesse she had such a worke as that in sending away the Messengers, her faith could not have justified her. Indeed that was a great worke, for she adventured her life in it.

And lastly, saith hee, *as the body without the soule is a dead body*, a stinking carrion, there is no preciousnesse, nor no excellency in it: *so faith without workes is dead.* Therefore look to your faith, doe not think that a faith that meerly taketh *Christ*, and beleeveth in him, that it is a faith that shall justifie you. Let all these arguments perswade you, that if it be not a working faith, it shal do you no good. Therfore let this be the first use, to consider whether it be effectuall or no, by the working of it. 5 It is a dead faith.

The second use that wee may make of it, is this: Hence we should learn to judge of our estates and conditions:

ditions, by the efficacy of our faith: for if no faith be received, but that which is effectuall, then it behooves us to looke to the working of our faith.

Not to beleeve all that say they have faith, nor all that say they have none.

Againe, if *God* accept no faith but that which is effectuall, hence we may learne also not to beleeve all that say they have faith, nor to beleeve all those that say they have none. As for those that say they have no faith, yet if we see the fruits of faith in them, that they have those things that faith brings forth: If you see a man that complaineth he beleeveth not, yet if he love the Saints, if he endevour to keepe *Gods* commandements, if he continue not in any knowne sinne, if he do not dare to omit holy duties, nor to sleight them, certainly this man hath faith, for we finde the effects of it there: although hee have lost one act of his faith, which is the comfortable assurance of a good estate; yet if the first act, by which hee resteth upon *Christ*, and by which he taketh *Christ* to himselfe, be there, we may conclude there is faith. When we see smoake, and feele heat, we say there is fire, though wee see no flame: so when we see these fruits in a man, wee may boldly say, he hath faith, though hee hath not such a reflect act, as to know himselfe that hee hath it, and so to have a comfortable assurance of his condition.

Act of faith double.

Simile.

A man may have faith, though he want feeling.

Of those that say they have faith, and have none.

On the other side, if a man saith he knoweth and is perswaded, that his sinnes are forgiven, his conscience is at rest, and yet for all this we finde no workes, I say this man hath not faith, for there wants the efficacy of it: So that as the two sonnes in the Gospel, one said he would goe into the Vineyard, and did not; the other said he would not goe, yet afterwards he repented and went:

went: so it is with these two; the one saith he hath no faith, and yet for all that we see he doth the things that faith requireth, we see the efficacy of faith in him. Againe, the other saith he hath faith, and yet doth not bring forth the fruits of faith, hee doth not shew the efficacy of faith in his life: the one shall be justified, the other shall be condemned.

As when we take two drugges, or two pearles, &c. the one hath lost his colour, seemeth withered and dead, so that to the outward view it hath lost all, yet it hath its efficacy still, that such a thing should have; the other lookes very faire, and hath a right colour and smell, but it hath no efficacy in it: we say, one is a lively drugge and a good one, and the other a counterfeit: so when one man complaines that hee hath no grace, that he is an hypocrite, and yet hee brings forth fruit worthy amendment of life, and we see the working of his faith; I say this is true faith. On the other side, he that makes a shew of faith, and yet wants the efficacy of it, he hath no faith. We should learn thus to judge when men professe they have faith, and we finde it not by their workes. It should teach both civill men and hypocrites to know their estates, for it discovereth both. For when the civill man commeth, and seeth that he doth much of the second Table, and little of the first; and the hypocrite againe doth much of the first and little of the second; let them consider that faith enableth a man to *have respect to all Gods Commandements*: it works a generall change. And as this is true for the substance, so it is also for degrees: for if *God* accepts onely effectuall faith, then so much efficacy, and

Simile.

Psal. 119. 7.

and so much working as you finde in any man, so much faith there is. If there be no workes, there is no faith; if the workes be few, the faith is a languishing faith; if the workes be many, the faith is great and strong. That is the second use we should make, to learne to judge aright of our selves and others.

Use 3. To justifie the Doctrine of good works against the Papists slanders.

Thirdly, if it be onely an effectuall faith which *God* accepteth, then this justifieth our Doctrine against the Papists, that say, we teach that onely faith justifieth, and require no good workes. I say, wee teach that not a naked, but an effectuall faith doth it. So that all the difference betweene them and us is this, we agree both in this, that workes are necessarily required to salvation, *that no man shall see God* without them, *without purenesse of heart*, and integrity of life. Wee say, except men *mortifie the deeds of the body by the spirit, they shall dye*; and *there is no condemnation to them that walke not after the flesh, but after the Spirit*: That is, there is a necessity put upon men to walke after the Spirit, in this wee agree: but here is the difference: They say that faith and workes both are required to justifie; wee say, that nothing is required but faith, and that workes follow faith: we say, faith indeed is working, and produceth such effects; so that whereas they say faith and workes, wee say faith onely, but it must be an effectuall faith, a working faith.

Difference between us and Papists in the Doctrine of justification.

Ob. If they object that place of S. *James*, *Wee are not justified by faith, but by workes.*

Ans. I answer, that there is a double justification; there is a justification of the person: so was *Abraham* justified by faith, as Saint *Paul* expresseth it, *Rom.* 4.

Justification double.

But

But then there is a second justification, a justification of the faith that *Abraham* had, he justified his faith by his workes, he shewed that hee had not a dead faith, a livelesse faith, a faith without workes, but that he had a lively effectuall faith: for hee added workes to his faith, his workes wrought together with his faith. So that if the question be, Whether *Abraham* was an hypocrite? His workes justified him that hee was none. If the question be, Whether *Abraham* was a sinner? His faith justifieth him, and shewes that he was made righteous through faith. So there is a justification of the person, and a justification of the faith of the person: as when a man is said to justifie such an action, or such a cause, the meaning is not, that he will make that just which was unjust before, but he will make it appeare to be just: so *Abraham* was declared to have a justifying faith, by that power and efficacie it wrought in him, in offering up his son. Note. Simile.

Ob. Againe, it is objected out of that place, that *by workes faith is made perfect*; therefore it seemes that faith is nothing alone, if workes bee not joyned with it.

Ans. I answer, that when it is said that faith is made perfect by workes, the meaning is, that faith is made good by works; the perfection of faith is declared by workes. As one that professeth that hee hath an Art, and that he is able to doe this and that; if hee doe the worke wherein his Art is shewed, if he make any artificiall worke, by that he maketh good his Art. Or, as when we say these Trees are good, because they have sappe in them, they are not dead Trees. Now the Faith made perfect by workes, what. Simile.

Tree is made perfect by the fruit; so faith by workes is made perfect. Not that workes put life into faith; the sappe must be first in the Tree, and then it bringeth forth fruit: so there must first be a life in faith, and then it bringeth forth workes. So that when we say that faith is made perfect by workes, the meaning is, that workes declare faith to be right, as the fruit doth declare the Tree to have sap.

Againe, if it be objected (as it is by them) that works and love, &c. are to faith, as the soule is to the body: *for as the body without the soule is dead, so faith without workes is dead:* Hence they gather that faith is as the body, and that love and workes are as the soule: therefore faith justifieth not, but workes.

What meant by these words *Faith without works is dead.*

Ans. To this I answer, they take the comparison amisse: for the scope of it is this; as a soulelesse body is nothing worth, it is dead, and no man regardeth it; so is a worklesse faith: The meaning is not, that workes are as the soule, and faith as the body: but, as a man, when he lookes upon a carcasse, and seeth no life in it, no pulse, no motion, no sense, such a body is nothing worth: so when wee see a faith without motion, that hath no pulses, that hath no expression of life in it, such a faith is of no worth.

Ob. But you will say, If wee bee not justified by workes, to what end are good workes required?

Why good workes are required, seeing they justifie not.

Ans. I answer, there is end enough, there are motives enow: Is not love a ground strong enough to bring forth good workes? When this objection was made to S. *Paul, Rom.6.* If Grace abound, why may we not sinne the more? for Grace aboundeth as sinne aboundeth:

deth: hee might easily have answered; Except you doe you good workes, you cannot be saved: but hee saith, *How can we that are dead to sinne, live any longer therein?* That is, when a man is once in *Christ*, there will be such a change wrought in him, that he shall find *Christ* killing sinne in him, and he shall be raised againe to newnesse of life, in so much that he must of necessity doe it; there will be love in his heart, that will set him a worke, that will constraine him: therefore saith he, are you not baptized into *Christs* death? That is, when a man is in *Christ*, he is dead to sinne, as *Christ* died for him: so that though there be no such motives, as for a man to get heaven by his workes; yet upon the taking of *Christ*, there is a love planted in the heart, there is a change wrought in the heart, so that there is an aptnesse in it to doe good workes; so that now a man *delighteth in the Law of God concerning his inward man:* he desires nothing more than to be imploied in it; *it is his meat and drink to doe the will of God.* Is not this enough to move us?

1. They evidence our right in Christ.

Againe, though good workes be not required for Justification, yet this may be a motive: *God* rewards us, he chastens and afflicts us according to our workes: 1 *Pet.*1.15. *Wee call him Father, that judgeth every one according to his workes:* That is, if our workes be good, hee is ready to reward us; if wee faile, hee is ready to chastise us, as a Father doth his children: therefore let us *passe the time of our dwelling here with feare.* So that the Saints, after they are in the state of grace, they may contract a kinde of guiltinesse unto them, so that they may make their Father angry, they

2. God rewards according to our works.

may feele many effects of his displeasure, though they shall not lose his favour for ever: and the more our good works are, the greater is our reward.

3. Good workes necessary, though not to justification.

Againe, we require good workes of necessity as well as the Papists: we say, you must have good works, or else you cannot bee saved; so that except you have repented, except you have love as well as faith, except there be a change of heart, *Christ* is not in you.

Different rise of good workes in Papists and us.

We require good workes with the same necessity, onely they have a different rise, they rise from different grounds. When the Papists are asked, What should move a man to doe good workes? They say, it is by way of merit, to get heaven; and that is it that maketh all their workes to bee of no worth. For take any naturall man, he that hath the most impure heart, may not hee, to escape Hell and to get Heaven, doe all the workes the Papists require, and for the same end that they require them? May hee not give almes, &c? But to doe it out of love, that is a thing that no hypocrite is able to reach unto: And therefore wee say, that the meanest worke, even the *giving of a Cup of cold water*, is a good worke, if it proceed from love: whereas, take the fairest worke, that hath the greatest glory and splendour, though it bee a Martyrdome, if it come not from love, if it be not a fruit of faith, *If a man give his body to be burned, & give all that he hath to feed the poore*, 2 *Cor*. 13. 1. if it come not from love, *God* accepts it not. So much for the third use.

An hypocrite cannot doe things out of love to God.

Use 4. To labour to grow in faith and assurance.

The fourth use that we should make of it, is this: If nothing bee accepted, but that faith that is effectuall, wee should learne hence, that if we will grow in in ability to worke, if we will grow in obedience, we must grow in faith: for all efficacy must come from faith, for it is onely the effectualnesse of faith that *God* requires. That is, if there bee any effectualnesse in man, that comes not from faith, *God* requires it not: for it is the efficacy of faith which *God* requires. Therfore if we will be enabled to doe the duties of new obedience, labour to grow in faith, that must enable us to doe what we doe: if wee have not the ground, all that we doe is in vaine. Therefore when we finde any coldnesse, any weaknesse in the graces wee have, any languishing; increase faith, and all other graces will grow. If you finde you cannot pray, when you finde your hands weak, and your knees feeble, that you can not run the wayes of *Gods* Commandements, strengthen your faith, labour to encrease your assurce. When the branches are weak and withered, we use to dung the root; so in this case, labour to strengthen your faith: for that will enable you to doe much, it is all in all.

What course to take in weaknesse of grace.

This will be of much use to us in many cases. When a sin is committed, wee should labour now to recover our selves out of that relapse. What is the way? By labouring to get assurance of the forgivenesse of it. Goe to *God* to strengthen thy faith, that is the way to get out of sin.

Labouring to strengthen faith, of much use.

1. In getting assurance of pardon after sinne is committed.

If there bee a strong lust that thou art to grapple withall, and which thou canst not get the victory over, the way is to go and encrease faith, to increase assurance: for the more faith is encreased, the more love, the more the heart is inclined to *God*: for faith turnes the bent of the heart from pleasures, and profits, from a desire of

2. In conflict with strong lusts.

 the

the praiſe of men, to *God:* So that the more faith, the more ability there is to ſtrive againſt the corruption that is in you.

3. In want of graces.

Againe, if a man finde he wants patience, he wants thankfulneſſe, the way is not to looke on the Vertues, to read morall Writers, but go & ſtrengthen thy faith, and that ſhall enable thee to doe wonders: otherwiſe we water the branches, and let the root alone.

How Miniſters ſhould build.

Thus ſhould we Miniſters doe, lay this maine foundation, to build up our hearers in this, and the reſt will follow. This S. *Paul* did, that was the great Maſter-builder, he layes down in all his Epiſtles the foundation of Faith: in his Epiſtles to the *Romanes*, to the *Epheſians*, to the *Coloſsians*, to the *Galatians*; and after that he deduceth particulars, and buildeth on it: So your maine buſineſſe is to conſider whether you have faith, to get aſſurance of that, and when you have that, then ſtrive againſt particular vices, and adorne your ſelves with particular graces: For, becauſe you labour not to have this maine grace, this root and foundation of all the reſt; I ſay, this is the reaſon why thoſe good motions that you have put into you by the Holy Ghoſt, thoſe motions that you have in the hearing of the Word, and the good purpoſes that you take to your ſelves, come to nothing, becauſe they have not faith for their ground.

Why good purpoſes in many come to nothing.

That generall of faith muſt goe before theſe particulars: Though the Plants be good, yet if the ground be not good, and connaturall, where they are planted, they will not grow. Therefore we finde it ordinarily, that when men have reſolutions to give over ſuch and ſuch ſinnes, to leave ſuch and ſuch vices, their wicked company, drinking, gaming, and the like; it may bee it holds for a day or two, yet it comes to nothing, becauſe the maine foundation is not laid, they goe to worke without faith: when the ground is fleſh, and the worke ſpirituall, how can it live? for every thing lives in its owne element; and theſe motions in them, are as the fiſh is out of the water: and as the fire, when it is out of his place dyes and is extinguiſhed, ſo theſe good purpoſes, when they are not particulars that ariſe from that generall of faith, they are in the heart as a thing out of its owne element, and therefore they periſh. Therefore when you have theſe purpoſes, know that they will come to nothing, if you take not the right courſe. Therefore labour to beleeve the promiſes, to be aſſured of ſalvation, that you are tranſlated from death to life by an effectuall faith: when this is done, you ſhall finde that your purpoſes will hold, and till then they are in vaine.

To look to faith in our ſearch.

And ſo againe, this ſhould teach us, ſeeing all depends upon faith, when wee come to ſearch, to conſider what aſſurance we have, that ſo wee may goe the right way to worke. For commonly, when we conſider our eſtates, we look what fruits we have, what ſincerity hath appeared in our life, and if wee finde that weake, we commonly conclude that our faith is weake alſo; and ſo the weakneſſe of our ſanctification weakeneth our aſſurance; but we ſhould goe another way to worke: When we finde a weakneſſe, we ſhould goe to the promiſes, and ſtrengthen our aſſurance: for there be two wayes to encreaſe aſſurance.

Two waies to increaſe aſſurance.

One is by the promiſes, the ſure word on which faith is built.

The ſecond is by the fruits of ſanctification in our ſelves.

Now when we finde theſe languiſhing, we ſhould goe to the firſt, and the other will be encreaſed by it. Faith worketh in you ſanctification, and maketh you to beleeve the promiſe. As exerciſe begets health, and we are made fit by health for exerciſe: or as acts beget habits, and habits are meanes to exerciſe thoſe acts, ſo aſſurance grounded npon the promiſe, it enableth, and inlargeth, and encreaſeth ſanctification, and ſanctification encreaſeth aſſurance: but firſt ſee faith, and then the other as fruits of it: If you finde a weakneſſe in ſanctification, labour to ſtrengthen your faith, and that will increaſe it: for that is the ground of all.

FINIS.

OF EFFECTUALL FAITH.

The third Sermon.

1 Thess. 1.3.

Remembring your effectuall Faith,&c.

IN the fifth place; If nothing pleaſe GOD, if he accepts of nothing but what comes from effectuall faith; then wee ſhould learne hence to judge aright of our works: for what workes ſoever we doe, they pleaſe GOD no further than hee ſeeth and findeth ſome faith in them. The Uſe before ſhewed us how to judge aright of our faith; this teacheth you how to judge

Uſe 5. To learne to judge aright of our workes.

judge aright of all the workes you doe, that you do not mistake in them. For men are very apt to judge amisse of what they doe in this case.

There be many workes that have a specious and faire shew in the view of men, and perhaps in your owne opinion: But if there bee not faith in those workes, *God* regards them not: as *James* 2.22. when *Abraham* did that great worke, in offering his sonne (which was the greatest worke that ever hee did, and the greatest worke that is recorded in all the Booke of *GOD*) yet, saith the Apostle there, *Doe ye not observe how faith wrought with his workes?* That is to say, if faith had not set him on worke to doe this, if faith had not beene the Spring to set this wheele on going, *God* had not accepted this. So doe whatsoever you will, further than faith workes with you in all that you doe, *God* regards it not.

God accepts our workes no further than he finds faith in them.

Therefore you shall observe in *CHRISTS* answer to the Woman of *Canaan*, in her earnest prayer, in her comming to *CHRIST*, her fighting and striving against the Divell, her tendernesse to her daughter, her holding out so long as shee did; all this *CHRIST* lookes over: But when he comes to give his censure of her worke, of her carriage; *Oh woman, great is thy faith*, saith hee. That was it that set a great price upon her worke: *Matth.* 15. 26,27. So take the most excellent, the greatest workes that can be performed, *GOD* sets them at no higher a price than hee findes faith in them: hee weighes by that: so much faith as is in them,

so

ſo farre hee accepts them, ſo farre hee regards them. Looke in *Heb*.11. you ſhall finde many glorious workes ſet downe. All the great workes that *Sampſon* did, all the workes that *David* did, the workes that *Gedeon* did, the workes that *Baruch* did, the workes that *Moſes* did, and ſo along; you ſhall ſee there, that there was nothing in all theſe workes that was regarded, but their faith: all is imputed to faith. And therefore, when you goe about any thing, labour to ſee faith ſet you aworke; and know, that as much faith as there is in any worke, ſo much GOD regards it, and no further. *Jacob* had done many good things that pleaſed GOD, yet GOD, when hee would put a marke of his favour upon him, when hee would call him *Iſrael*, when hee would change his name, it was for that great worke of faith, when hee prayed all night, when hee would not give over, when hee would not let him goe, when hee prevailed with GOD by faith; now, ſaith GOD, *Thy name ſhall bee called Iſrael.* (As if he ſhould ſay) Now I will put a name of honour upon thee: Why ſo? Not becauſe there was more in that worke, ſimply conſidered, as it was a worke; but becauſe there was more faith in it. And it muſt needs be ſo: for *God* doth not as men doe, who accept the giver for the gift. If a man come to you with a great gift, you will accept his perſon for it: But GOD accepts the gift for the givers ſake: though the gift be never ſo ſmall, if the giver be ſuch as beleeves in him, if his affections be right, if hee doe it out of a right ground;

God accepts the gift for the giver.

ground; that is, if hee doe it out of a ground of faith, hee is accepted whatsoever it bee. Indeed otherwise whatsoever we doe we may call it by our owne name; wee may say, hee is a patient man, or hee is a temperate man, or these are workes of justice, or workes of temperance: But wee can never call it godlinesse except it rise from faith, except it come from this ground; because indeed it is not done to *GOD*. (Marke it) I say, further than a man doth a thing out of faith hee doth it not to *God*. For to doe a thing out of faith, is nothing else, but when out of perswasion of *Gods* love to me I do this thing, meerly for his sake whom I have chosen, to whom I give my selfe; one that I know loves mee; and therefore, though there were no reward for it I would serve him. This is a worke of faith. Now, I say, this is properly godlinesse. And therefore in 2 *Pet.* 1. when the Apostle had named *Patience* and *Temperance*, lest wee should mistake (as if he should say, There be many vertues of this nature among men, that belong not to *GOD*) Therefore, saith hee, *Adde godlinesse*, that is, Let it bee such as becomes a godly man to doe. Godlinesse is that which is done to *GOD*; such things, and such qualities as have an eye and respect to him, such things please him. What if a man should doe never so much? if it please not *God* it is lost labour. It is said *Heb.* 11. 6. that *Henoch pleased God*. Marke how the Apostle reasons: (saith he) *without faith it is impossible to please God*: therefore, in that he is said

To doe a thing by faith, what.

Godlinesse what.

ſaid to pleaſe GOD, it muſt needs bee through faith. You know it is ſaid *Rom.*13. *Whatſoever a man doth, if it be not of faith*, and love, *God* lookes not to it; you know there can bee no love without faith.

Conſider but how it is with your ſelves; If a man ſhould doe any thing for you, you know he may have many other ends, he may doe you many a great good turne; yet if you bee perſwaded this comes not out of love to me, nor of true reſpect to mee, you regard it not whatſoever it bee. If it be but a ſmall thing, if it be done out of love, you reſpect it. So it is with *God*, workes that come from faith and love (for thoſe I reckon to be all one) thoſe he reſpects wondrouſly. Therefore we ſhould learne to judge aright of our works, it will help us againſt that poſition of the Papiſts, and alſo againſt the common opinion of men.

Every man thinkes that Almes-deeds, doing good to the poore, and doing glorious things, &c. that theſe are good workes, when as common actions they exclude, as if they were not good workes: But it is not ſo; we may doe the greateſt workes of this nature, and yet they may have no excellency in them at all.

We muſt reckon common actions in our callings to be good workes.

Againe, the very ordinary workes of our Calling, ordinary things to men, ordinary ſervice from day to day, if it come from faith, if it bee done as to the LORD, he accepts them, and they are good workes indeed. This uſe wee ought to make of it: If GOD regard not any thing but faith,

faith, we ſhould not be deceived in our works which we doe.

Uſe 6. To try if we have faith.

Againe, if faith bee ſuch a thing, that no works are accepted without it, that no branch will grow, except it come from this root; if there bee no ſalvation without it, if it be a thing that is moſt profitable for us; if thou ſaiſt now, How may I know whether I have faith or no? I may be deceived in it. When we hang ſo much upon this peg, we had need be ſure that it be ſtrong, and that it will hold us. I will therefore make this preſent uſe, in ſhewing what the ſignes of this faith, and what the characters of it are, that you may learne to judge aright, whether that faith that ſets all the price upon your works be a right faith, or no: you may know it by this.

1. Triall. A ſecret perſwaſion of the Spirit.

Where there is a true faith, there is a ſecret perſwaſion wrought in the heart, whereby *God* aſſures you that hee is yours, and you are his; as you have it *Rev.2.17. To him that overcommeth, will I give that hidden Mannah, and a white ſtone, with a new Name written in it, that hee onely knowes that receives it:* (that is) That is one thing by which yee ſhall know whether you have true faith or no. Have you ever had any of that hidden *Mannah?* (that is) Have you had ſuch a ſecret perſwaſion, which hath beene as ſweet as *Mannah* to you, which you have fed on, as they fed on *Mannah*; which gives you life, as *Mannah* gave life to them? Onely he ſayes it is a hidden *Mannah*, it lyes not abroad, others ſee it not, but it is

Hidden Mannah.

Mannah

Mannah that your hearts secretly feed on. So that wouldest thou know whether thou have faith? Hath *God* given thee such a stone with a new name written in it? that is, the stone of absolution: as the manner was among the *Athenians*, among the old *Grecians*; that the sentence of absolution was given by white stones, as the sentence of condemnation was by blacke stones: So (saith he) *God* will give him such a secret testimony that hee is acquitted, that when hee is called in question (as they were, that they knew not whether they should dye or live; in that case if they had the white stone, such a man was absolved: So I say) Hath *God* given thee such a stone, with thy name upon it? Hath hee given you such a stone as you know in the secret of your heart, such as none knowes but *God* and your selves? (that is) Hath he ever opened the clouds? hath hee ever shewed himselfe to you? hath hee cast a good looke upon you? hath hee *made your hearts glad with the light of his countenance in his Beloved?* (for such a secret work there is of the Spirit, by which *God* cheereth and comforteth the heart of a man:) that is his manner in working faith.

White stone what it signifieth.

After the Law hath beene a Schoole-master to a man, after there hath beene such an inditement, that hee hath beene brought in question of his life, when there hath beene a great storme, then hee comes into the heart, as hee did into the Shippe, and all is quiet. I say, that is his manner, hee comes into the heart after such a manner,

Gods manner of working faith.

manner, and ſpeakes peace to a man. Have you ever found this worke in your ſelves, that after much trouble and diſquiet within, *GOD* hath ſpoken peace to you, that hee hath ſaid to your ſoules, *I am your ſalvation?* Not that that is abſolutely required, that there ſhould be ſuch a trouble going before: For although it be true, that hee never ſpeakes peace, but when there hath gone ſome trouble, but when there hath gone ſome convincing of the ſpirit before, which convinceth a man of ſinne; yet this you muſt know, that ſtill the promiſe is made to the comming, and not to the preparation. And therefore if a man bee at his journies end, it is no matter how hee came there: If a man finde that hee bee in *CHRIST*, and hath had ſuch a teſtimony from his Spirit, though hee have not had ſuch a worke of humiliation, as perhaps hee expects, yet know that the promiſe is made to that. And if you have that which the promiſe is made unto, is not that ſufficient? It is true, as I ſaid, you muſt have it really, you muſt have it in good earneſt, there muſt goe alwayes a worke of humiliation before the teſtimony of the Spirit. But miſtake not: that turbulent ſorrow, that violent diſquiet of the minde goes not alwayes before. For example; Take two men, the one is arreſted and condemned, and brought to the point of death, hee makes account of nothing elſe: A Pardon comes to this man, and hee is ſaved; there was great trouble went before, and hee was wondrouſly affected when the Pardon came: But now

A like trouble of Spirit in converſion not neceſſary to all.

now there is another man that is guilty of the ſame offence, and he knowes certainly that he ſhall be called in queſtion,and he is ſure to loſe his life, unleſſe his peace be made. Now before this be acted,before that indeed he be put in priſon, before that indeed he be condemned, and before his head be brought to the block, he is certified that a Pardon is come out for him. This man knows his eſtate as well as the other,and he knowes that he had periſhed without a Pardon, as well as the other; and he makes as much account of his Pardon as the other,and will not let it goe for his life as well as the other.

Now,both theſe are pardoned,both are ſure of life: but there is a different manner of doing it. The one man was affected and much ſtirred before,he was put into a wondrous affright before: The other man is convinced of the danger hee is in, as well as hee, although hee be not put to that extremity of ſorrow, though he be not brought to ſo neere an exigent as the other: So if a man be convinced of ſinne,if a man know in good earneſt,throughly,what the danger is, that he muſt periſh,if he have not his Pardon: Now, I ſay, if thou have ſuch a teſtimony, build upon it: For it is true, that *God* before he comes in the ſoft voyce,he ſends a Wind before, that rends the Rocks downe, that brings downe the Mountaines there, ſo much as makes the way plaine, before he can come in the ſoft voyce. I ſay,if the Mountaines be broken down(after what manner ſoever it be)that is enough; doe not ſtand on that; Be ſure of this, that if there come a ſoft voyce, thou haſt reaſon to beleeve that, whatsoever preparations were before, which are divers: for *God* workes sometimes after one manner, sometimes after another.

Soft voice, what.

But now, what is this soft voyce? that I may a little further come to explaine that: for certainly, if he come in the soft voyce, that is, the voyce of the Gospell, you are sure. But what is it?

1. Part of the soft voice, a clearing of the promise.

I take it to be this. One thing is, when there is a clearing of the promise, (for the voyce is the very Gospel it selfe:) Now when we preach the Gospel to men, and open the promises of salvation, and of life, if *God* doe not joyne with us now, and cleare them to you, by kindling a light within, that you see the meaning of them; except he, I say, doe thus joyne with us, you shall not be able to build upon these promises. Therefore, that is one thing that *God* must doe: For though it be true, the Word is neare you, that you need not goe up to heaven, nor down to hell to fetch it, (for saith *Moses*, *the word is neere you*, the promises are neere, *in your mouthes*, in the middest of you) yet, except *God* do shew them, as cleere as they be, you cannot see them. As when *Iesus* stood by *Mary Magdalen*, he was neere enough, but till her eyes were opened, she saw him not. So *Hagar*, the Well was neere enough to her, but till her eyes were opened, she could not see it. So, when we preach these promises, when we lay them open as neere as we can, as neere as may be, yet it must be the worke of the Spirit, to see the promises, to see them so as to beleeve them, and to rest on them. Therefore that is one part of this soft voyce, to open the Gospel unto you.

Though the promises are neere, unles *God* cleare thē, we see thē not.

Luke 24.

There

There is another, which is the immediate teſtimony of the Spirit, ſpoken of in *Rom.* 8. *This Spirit beareth witneſſe with our ſpirits*: when *God* comes, and by a ſecret teſtimony of the Spirit, worketh ſuch a perſwaſion in the heart, that hee is a Father, that hee is a friend, that he is reconciled to us.

2. Part of the ſoft voice, the immediate teſtimony of *Gods* Spirit.

Object. But you will ſay, this may be a deluſion.

Anſw. Therefore you muſt have both together: know that they are never diſ-joyned: *God* never gives the ſecret witneſſe of his Spirit, he never workes ſuch a perſuaſion, ſuch an immediate teſtimony, but it hath alwayes the teſtimony of the Word going with it; be ſure to joyne them, be ſure thou do not ſever them one from the other. So that, if you would know now whether you have faith or no, conſider whether ever *God* hath ſpoken this to you, or no, whether ever hee hath wrought this worke in you. For faith, you muſt know, is wrought in this manner: The Spirit comes, and ſhewes *Chriſt* to you, and not onely ſhewes you his merits, not onely tels you that hee will be a Saviour, not onely tels you of a Kingdome that you ſhall have by him; but ſhewes you the beauty and excellency of *Chriſt*, it ſhewes you what grace is, and makes you love it, and then he ſhews you mercy: Out of this you come to long after *Chriſt*, and to ſay, I would I had him: a man comes to love him as the Spouſe loves her Husband.

How to know the teſtimony of the Spirit from a deluſion.

How faith is wrought.

Whence longing after *Chriſt* comes.

Now to this work he addes a ſecond: *Chriſt* comes and tels a man, I will have thee, he comes and ſhewes himſelfe; he diſcovers himſelfe to a man, and ſpeaks plainly, (as in that place we have often mentioned,

Ioh. 19.) and saith to him; I am willing to marry thee. When this is done on the holy Ghosts part, & we on our part come to resolve to take him, now the match is made betweene us, and this is faith indeed; when this worke is done, a man may truely say, *This day is salvation come* to me. Now thou art sure that all thy sinnes are forgiven, now faith is wrought in thy heart. Therefore if thou wouldst know whether thou have faith or no, look backe, reflect upon thine owne heart, consider what actions have passed thorow there: for that is the next way to know what faith is; to looke what actions have passed thorow a mans heart: a man may know what the actions of his soule are, for that is the benefit of a reasonable soule, that it is able to returne upon it selfe, to see what it hath done, which the soule of a beast cannot doe.

How to know whether faith be wroght in us.

A beast cannot reflect upon his actions as a man can.

Now let a man consider whether such a thing have passed or no; that is, (marke it) whether on *Christs* part there hath beene such a cleering of the promise, that thou art so built, that, if an Angell from heaven should come and preach another Gospell, if Saint *Paul* himselfe should be living on the earth, and should preach the contrary, thou wouldest not beleeve him. Dost thou see the word so clearely, art thou so set upon the Rock (as it were) that thou canst say in good earnest, as the Apostle said in *Rom.* 8. *I know that neither principalities, nor powers, nor things present, nor things to come, nor any thing in the world, shall ever separate me from the love of God in Christ*, and that because I have his sure Word?

How to know that the promise is cleared to us.

Again when thou hast such a secret impression of assurance

assurance from his Spirit, which will not fail thee, when thou findest this on *Gods* part, and againe when thou findest this act on thy owne part; when thou sayst, I have resolved to take him, (for a man may know what he hath done) I have resolved to take him for my husband, I have resolved to preferre him before all things in the world, to be divorced from all things in the world, and to cleave to him: This I know, these acts have passed on *Gods* part, and this I have done on my part; when thou findest this wrought in thy selfe, be assured there is faith wrought in thee: when the Law hath bin a Schoole-master to thee, and when *Christ* hath spoken peace, & when thou art built upon him againe; consider if this hath bin wrought.

The match betweene Christ and the soule reciprocal.

This is the first meanes to try thy faith: but because this may be an ambiguous means, a man may be deceived in it, therefore faith doth shew it selfe by many other effects. And therefore we will adde to this (which is the very thing wherein faith consists) other signes; and they are five in number.

Five signes of effectual faith.

First, a man must know that there may bee many delusions in this kind, many Hypocrites may have great raptures, they may have great joy, as if they were lift up into the 3d. heaven, they may have a great and strong perswasion that their estate is good. Satan is very apt to delude us in this kind, to put a counterfeit upon us instead of true faith; therefore wee will not content our selves with this, but give other marks, that will not deceive. At this time you are to consider, you that come to the Sacrament, Is it not a maine thing to consider whether you have faith or

1. Hypocrites may have great joy and strong perswasion that they are forgiven.

no? What doe you here elſe? you have nothing to doe with *Chriſt*, you have no intereſt in him; and if you have no intereſt in him, what doe you with the Elements which repreſent his body and his bloud? And therefore you have cauſe to attend to it. Firſt therefore, if thou find ſuch a worke in thy heart, (for if thou conclude that there is no ſuch work, thou needeſt not examine further, thou maiſt be ſure that thou haſt not faith, but if thou haſt ſuch a work) if thou wouldſt know whether it be really and truely, or whether it be a fancy, or deluſion, conſider:

1. Signe. True faith purifieth the heart.

Firſt, if it be true, it purifies the heart: in *Act*. 15. 9. ſaith the Apoſtle *Peter* there, *God hath put no difference between us and them, after that by faith he had purified their hearts*. So in *Act* 26. 18. *And thou ſhalt preach forgivenes of ſinnes to thoſe that are ſanctified by faith.* So that this you muſt take as a ſure rule: if thy faith bee true, it purifies thy heart, it ſanctifies thee. And therfore you ſee faith and repentance are alwayes put together. Repent and beleeve: for they are never disjoyned. If thou find the worke of repentance bee not wrought throughly and ſoundly in thee, if thou finde thy heart not purified, if thou be not ſanctified, if there be not a ſanctified diſpoſition in thee, be ſure it is a deluſion, it is not faith: or if faith be (as you have heard heretofore) a taking of *Chriſt*, not as a Saviour onely, but as a Prieſt, and not as a Prieſt only, but as a king too, it muſt needs be that there muſt bee reall obedience, or elſe it is not faith, thou haſt not taken him: If there be nothing but a meer aſſent, as the Papiſts affirm in another caſe; For faith is a taking of *Chriſt*, and

Faith and repentance put together in the Scripture, why.

True faith hath repentance.

Faith, what it is.

2. Obedience.

a

a giving of our ſelves to him againe, ſo that there is a match, there is a bargaine, a Covenant between us, as he ſaith in *Heb.* 8.8. *I wil make a new Covenant with them.* Now a Covenant hath two parts: If *God* doe this for you, you muſt doe ſomewhat on your part, you muſt love him and obey him. As in a marriage, the Huſband doth not onely take the Wife, but the Wife alſo takes the Husband. If faith bee ſuch a thing as this, there muſt needs be a general reformation of the life, or elſe it is certaine thou haſt not taken him.

A Covenant, what.

3. Generall reformation.

Therefore know that as there is a *lively hope*, ſo there is a lively faith: & when it is ſaid to be a lively faith, it intimates, that there is another, that is a dead faith; that is, there is a kind of beleeving, a kind of taking *Chriſt*, a kind of giving a mans ſelfe to him: but yet, (marke it) ſaith he, it is ſuch an one as breeds no life in thee. Marke if thy faith bee ſuch a faith as hath brought *Chriſt* to dwell in thy heart, ſo as the ſoule dwels in the body, if it bee ſuch a dwelling in thy heart, that there be life in thee, for *Chriſt*, when hee dwels in us, he acts the ſoule, as the ſoule acts the body: As the body now, when the ſoule is there, is able to move, to ſtirre, to do any thing: So the ſoule of a man, it fals to the duties of godlineſſe, and new obedience, to all good workes; it is *ready* (as the Apoſtle ſaith) *to every good work*; it is nimble and ready to go about them, you are *alive to righteouſneſſe*. Hath faith ſo brought *Chriſt* into thy heart, that he lives in thee, as hee did in *Paul*, that thou canſt find and ſay truly, I am *dead to ſin, and live to righteouſneſſe*? That thou haſt *mortified the deeds of the body by the ſpirit*? that thou findeſt

Chriſt dwels in the heart as the ſoule in the body.

Gal. 2. 20

findest another life working in thee? except thou canst find this, it is not true faith: for true faith is such as brings *Christ* to dwell in thy heart, and hee dwels there when he revives thy spirit; as it is *Isa.* 57.13.14. *I dwell in the high heavens, and with him also that is of a contrite spirit, to revive the spirit of the humble*; that is, hee never dwels, but he gives life. And if thou find not such a life in thy selfe, conclude that thy faith is not good. And this you ought the more to mark, because many thousands seem to take *Christ*, and to do much, and yet for all this, they have not life all the while.

Simile.

Take two grafts, it may be there is incision made in both, both may bee planted, as you often see in plants, after they be planted, if you would know whether the grafting be true or no, if you come a while after, & see one of the grafts dead and withered, you say this grafting was not good, or the stock was not good, somewhat was amisse: and if you find it to bud, and that there be life in it, then you say it was grafted indeed, the grafting was good and right. So when a man coms and takes *Christ*, if thou see thou be grafted, if thou find thy life to be the same, if thou find thou art no more able to pray, nor no more able to do any duty than thou wast before, that thou livest in thy lusts as much as ever thou didst, thou hast not that new heart, that new spirit, and that new affection which the Scriptures speak of; be sure then that thou art not grafted: for if thou wert grafted aright by faith, (for it is that which grafteth) there would be life.

How to know if Christ dwell in the heart.

Faith grafteth us into Christ.

When as the graft is taken out of the former Tree, it

it beares no more that fruit, but it lives, and beares another fruit: Therefore consider if this be so or no; and that is the reason of that answer of *Philip* to the Eunuch, in the 8. of the *Acts*, ver. 37. The Eunuch professed to beleeve, and would have been baptized: Saith S. *Philip*, thou mayest, *if thou beleeve with all thine heart.* Thou maist thinke it is nothing; but it is a resolving from time to time to give up thy selfe to be *Christs* servant, to take his yoke, to weare his Livery and his Badge. Now Baptisme is but a seale to confirme and testifie this to thy selfe, and to the World, that thou hast given thy selfe to *Christ:* saith S. *Philip*, take heed to thy selfe; if it be a false taking, thou maist not have him; but if thou beleeve withall thy heart, thou maist be baptized. So I say to men, there is a kind of taking *Christ:* when a man takes him with some part of his heart, when he resolveth, I confesse it is good, I have a present disposition to it, it will serve me for such a turne; I am affraid of Hell, it will deliver me from that; in such an exigent, in such a crosse, in such a trouble that will come upon me; it will free me from that: but this is not enough; but if thou beleeve with all thy heart; that is, when thou hast summed and reckoned all together, all reasons, and all objections to and fro, thou resolvest altogether to take him in all respects.

Baptisme, what.

Taking *Christ* deceitfully.

Againe, when all thy heart shall come in; that is, when the understanding of a man is fully perswaded of these promises, that they are true, and that it is best for him to take *Christ*; if the perswasion be good, and the will follow: for that you may take for a sure rule,

To take *Christ* with the whole heart, what

there

there is no man that is fully perswaded, and convinced every way, that such a thing is best, but the Will will follow. If the mind be right, the Will will follow; and if the Will follow, be sure the affections will follow. For, if a man wils a thing in good earnest, and resolve, I would have it indeed, then his desires will come and be earnest; and if he be in doubt, feare will come; and if any thing hinder, anger will come and thrust away the impediments; and if hee get the thing, there will be rejoycing; and so all the affections will follow; and then certainly action and endeavour will follow. There is no man that desires a thing earnestly, but where the affections are strong and busie, action and endeavour will be answerable. Now, if thou take *Christ* with all thy heart, that there is no reservation, that it is not done by halves, then thou maist have him, and the fruits, and all the priviledges by him, so as thou shalt be saved by him. Consider whether this be done or no.

When the understanding is throughly convinced, the will & affections follow.

When we preach faith, you may see what it is in *Acts* 26. 17, 18. Marke what the message was that *Christ* sends to S. *Paul*, nothing but to preach faith; but what was that? Saith he, *to turne from men, from the power of Satan, to God, to turne men from darknesse to light:* That is, to cause them to forsake their former wayes of darknesse, that they have beene led into by the Devill, and to turne them to *God*, to seek him. So that then a man is said truly to beleeve, when his heart is turned to *God*; that is, when a man before was given to this pleasure or to that pleasure and commodity, his heart was wedded to it, hee would have

To turne to *God*, what.

have an estate in this world, and he would have credit in the world, and he would have place with men, and he would be some-body in the flesh; his heart was set on these things, hee would follow them.

Now faith is nothing but this, we come and tell you that *Christ* is offered; if you will be content to let all these things goe, and to turne your hearts to him, that the whole bent of a mans mind is turned the contrary way, and set upon *Christ*, this is such faith indeed, when there is this generall turning of a mans mind from these things. Therefore know, that faith in *Christ* and covetousnesse, cannot stand together. When thy minde goeth a whoring after thy wealth, what hast thou to doe with *Christ*? That is not to take *Christ*. For to take *Christ*, is to turne the mind from these things to seeke him.

Againe, if thou wilt have praise with men, thou canst not beleeve and have that too; it is impossible. And so for any pleasure, for any lust, dost thou thinke to follow thy pleasure, to seeke that, to satisfie thy flesh, and to have *Christ*? No, it is another kind of taking; & this is not done with that sleightnesse as they did, *Ierem.* 3. *You turned to me* (saith the *Lord*) *fainedly, and not with all your hearts*: but it is to turne in good earnest, to turne to *God* upon sound ground. Therefore now let us come to the examination of this.

Faith, and the desire of satisfying lusts, cannot stand together.

Now, if we vvere not mistaken in it, there would be no question of this: we think that faith is nothing but a perswasion that our sinnes are forgiven, a perswasion that the promises are true, a perswasion that the

Men deceived in the definition of faith.

the Scripture is true, a perswasion that *Christ* dyed for our sinnes: And thence it is, that men are apt to be deceived in it: if they took faith as it is in it selfe, a marrying of our selves to *Christ*, with all our heart and affections, when he hath given himselfe to us, as in marriage, and we are given to him, in doing this we should never be deceived.

Try faith as we doe other things. *Similies.*

If thou wouldst know now if thy faith be right, examine it as thou wouldst examine another thing.

If you take Wine, if you would know whether it be good Wine, if you find it flat and dead, if you drinke it, and it heates you not, it warmes you not at the heart, it quickens you not, it revives not your spirits; you will say it is naught, if it were good Wine, it would doe this.

If you come to looke on Plants, if you find there no fruit, nor no leaves, you say, this Plant is dead.

So take a Jewell, and when it comes to the Touchstone, or any way that you try it, you say, it is a faire, but it is a counterfeit Jewell, it is a false Diamond, or whatsoever it be.

If you come to take a dramme of Physicke, if you take a Drugge, if it do not worke. Take Leven and put into your Dough, if it sowre not the lump, you say, it is dead Leven, it is a counterfeit thing.

So I say, if thou find not in faith this effect, this operation upon thy heart, that it works not this generall change in thee, that it fires not thy soule with love to *Christ*, if thou find not life in it, and that it bring forth such fruits, if thou finde it not grow, that it put another taste upon the whole soule, that it it leavens it throughout; know that thou art deceived, rest not in it, cast it away, get a right faith, such as will not deceive thee. But I cannot stand upon this. This is the first signe of effectuall faith.

Before I come to the second thing, know this, (by the way) you that receive the Sacrament, That if you be unworthy receivers, you cannot doe your selves a worse turne, than to offer to come to the Sacrament without faith, to provoke *God* more, *to eate and drinke your owne damnation*. Now examine your selves by such rules as this: If you have changed your life; if you have received it hertofore, and continue still in your sinnes. If you say, it is true, I have done it, I have returned againe to my gaming, I have returned againe to my swearing, to my loosenesse, to my company-keeping; but yet I had a good meaning, I intended it at that time: well, that is not enough. If thou hadst faith, thou wouldst doe it indeed: doe not say, I had a good meaning; for, if thou hadst faith, it would not onely worke a good meaning in thee, but it would worke power in thee, to doe this, that thou wouldst be able to mortifie these affections, it would make a reall and an effectuall change in thee. Consider, how faith doth it: faith takes *Christ*; when you have taken *Christ*, as soone as ever you have him, he sends his Spirit into your hearts, and the Spirit is able to doe all this, and doth, as Saint *Paul* saith, when he had *Christ* once, *I am able to do all things through Christ that strengthens me*. So certainly, when thou hast *Christ*, as thou commest to take the elements of Bread and Wine, if thou

Digressiō for application to the Sacrament.

Rules of examination before and after the Sacramēt.

Where *Christ* dwels indeed, he gives power against sin.

Phil. 4. 12.

thou hadest taken him indeed, thou wouldst be strengthened to do all things, thou wouldst find thy heart able to doe this, thou shouldst find a change in thy heart, that thou wouldst doe it without difficulty, thou wouldst finde thy selfe turned and changed, thou wouldst have new affections, and a new life. And if thou doe not find this, know that thou hast nothing to doe with the Sacrament, know it before hand, and know that thou hast had warning given thee, that thou receivest unworthily and art *guilty of the body and blood of Christ*; that is, thou committest such a sin as those did that killed *Christ*.

To be guilty of the body and blood of *Christ* what,

Quest. What was their sin that killed him?

Answ. They despised him, they mocked him, they knew him not to be *Christ*, they made no account of him; their greatest worke in killing him, was, they despised him, they mocked him: So thou commest and art bold with him here; it is a despising of *Christ*: if thou didst reverence him, if thou didst feare him, if thou didst tremble at him, if thou didst know him to be such a one as he is, thou wouldst not be bold to doe it. And therefore, if thou wilt venture upon small grounds to goe on in sin, and yet come and receive the Sacrament, the Apostle saith, *Thou art guilty of the body and blood of Christ*: that is, thou committest a sin of that nature, and therefore looke to it.

What was the great sin in killing *Christ*?

2. Signe. A Spirit of prayer.

Secondly, if thou wouldst know whether thy faith be true or no, consider whether thou hast this consequent of it, the Spirit of Prayer: for wheresoever there is a Spirit of faith, there is also a Spirit of Prayer: that is, (marke it, and you shall see the reason why

why I deliver this to be a ſigne of faith) Faith, you know, is wrought in us by the Spirit of adoption. Now what is the Spirit of Adoption, but the Spirit that tels you that ye are ſonnes? as in *Gal.* 4. 6. *So many as are ſonnes, receive the Spirit of ſonnes.* Now whenſoever the Spirit tels a man he is a ſon; that is, works faith in his heart, the ſecond thing that the Spirit doth, it teacheth him to pray: and therefore thoſe words are added, that you cry *Abba Father:* that is, the Spirit never doth the one, but it doth the other; if it be the teſtimony of the Spirit. And therefore this is the ſecond ſigne: If thou have ſuch a perſwaſion that the Spirit have ſpoken to thee, if thou wouldſt know whether this be a deluſion or no, thou ſhalt know it by this: If thou have the Spirit, it will make thee able to cry *Abba Father*, it will make thee able to doe two things.

Spirit of Adoption, what.

The Spirit of Adoption maketh us.

First, it will make thee able to cry; that they ſhall be earneſt prayers which thou makeſt; thy prayers ſhall be fervent; they were cold before, thou cameſt to performe lip-labour, thou cameſt to do thy duty, to performe it, perhaps, every day; but alas what prayer was it? This ſhall make thee cry.

1. Earneſt in Prayer.

But againe, which is the maine, not onely ſo, but thou ſhalt ſpeake to him, as to a Father: that is, thou ſhalt goe to *God*, and looke upon him as one doth upon a Father, as one looks upon one whoſe love he is ſure of, of whoſe favour he doubts not, one that he knowes is ready to heare his requeſts. It may be thou haſt prayed before, but not to him as to a Father all the while; that is the worke of the Spirit; if it ever give

2. Bold & confident.

give the testimony of thy sonship, it will make thee pray fervently, and it will make thee pray to *God* as to a Father: that is to be made able to pray.

Object. But, you will say, every body can pray: Is that such a signe, is that such a distinguishing marke and character, to be able to pray?

Answ. My brethren, bee not deceived in it: you must know, that prayer is not a worke of the memorie, or or a worke of the wit. A man that hath a good wit, or a ready invention, or a voluble tongue, may make an excellent prayer, in his owne esteeme, and in the esteeme of others, but this is not to pray. Prayer is the worke of a sanctified heart, it is the worke of *Gods* Spirit. There is a double prayer, *Rom.* 8. there is one prayer which is the voyce of our owne spirit: there is a second prayer, which is the voice of *Gods* spirit in us: that is, when the holy ghost hath so sanctified the heart, when he hath put it into such a whol frame of grace, that the heart comes to speak as it is quickned, as it is actuated and moved from *Gods* spirit. Now, saith the text there, *God knowes the voyce of his owne Spirit: for that makes requests according to his will*, he hears that prayer: But now the prayers which are made by the voice of our owne spirit, he knowes not the meaning of them: that is, hee heares them not, he hearkens not to them: consider whether thy prayer be such, or no; consider whether thy prayer bee the voice of *Gods* spirit in thee.

True prayer, what. Prayer double.

The voice of *Gods* Spirit, what.

Quest. But thou wilt say, How should I know that?

Answ. Thou shalt know it by this, as I said before, Doest thou come to him as to a Father? Another man

prayes

prayes to God, it may be, all his life, but he comes to him as to a stranger; yea, sometimes he may bee very earnest, when it is no prayer, but when he is put an exigent, he may be earnest, as a Theefe is earnest with the Judge to spare him: there may bee much earnestnesse, although this may be far off from prayer. But canst thou come to *God* as to a friend? Canst thou come to him as to one whose favour thou art assured of? Canst thou come to him as to a Father? Except thou canst doe this, know that he regardeth not thy prayers.

How to know the voyce of Gods Spirit in our prayers. Wicked men come to God, as to a stranger, the Saints as to a friend.

And this me thinkes now, when we consider, wee should not defer our repentance, and think with our selves, I will repent when I am sicke, I will go to *God* in the time of extremity. Well, it may be thou maist doe it; but alas, canst thou come to speake to God now as a friend, when as thou hast beene a stranger to him, and he to thee, all thy life? Certainly thou canst not. And when thou commest and prayest earnestly, when some great crosse is on thee, in some great exigent, in the day of death, in the time of thy sicknesse; know, that though thou pray never so fervently, although thou adde fasting to quicken it, yet it is doubtfull whether it be acceptable prayer at all in that exigent. The Scripture gives it another terme, in *Ho*.7. saith he, *You prayed not to me with your hearts, but you howled upon your beds:* it came not out of any love to me, nor from any change of heart, it came not out of a holy disposition in you. Therefore you prayed not to me, when you howled upon your beds: that is, as if he should say, they were no more but howlings.

One motive not to defer repentance.

Hos. 7.14. opened.

P Will

Will not a Dog, or a beast, or any other unreasonable creature, when they are pinched, when they are in extremity, will they not cry, will they not mone for helpe? Your Prayers were no more, they were but howlings upon your beds. And what were they for? They were to be delivered from the present affliction, they were to have Wine and Oyle in that great dearth that was upon them: And so in those cases, your earnest prayers are but howlings upon your bed. And therfore think not that this is prayer, be not deceived in it. And therefore it is the manner of the Saints, if you would know it; when they come to pray, they come boldly to *God*, they come boldly to the Throne of Grace, as the Apostle saith, *Eph.* 3.7. *By faith we have boldnesse, and entrance with confidence.* Another man he prayes earnestly, bur examine his heart and he must needs say, Indeed *God* is a stranger to me, I cannot be confident; it may be he heares me, it may be he heares me not. Whereas we are required to *lift up pure hands in every place, without wrath or doubting*; we are required to come with boldnesse. And know this, that if otherwise thou pray morning & night, if thou make never so many prayers from day to day, if thou be never so constant in them, *God* regards them not, he takes them by weight, and not by number, not by number, nor by labour, not by earnestnesse, which is a thing that may come from the flesh. If thy prayer come from his Spirit, he accepts of it, if not, be sure it is no prayer, and if there be no prayer, there is no faith.

Prayers of the wicked howlings.

Note.

3. Signe of faith: peace.

Thirdly, if thou wouldst know whether thou hast faith

faith or no, consider whether thou have peace: for faith pacifies the heart as well as purifies it, as the Apostle saith, *Rom.* 5. 1. *Being justified by faith, we have peace with God.* Now if thou wouldst know whether thy faith which thou hast be right or no, consider if there be peace there: Hast thou that peace that passeth all understanding? You know now, if a man were in debt, and were ready to be cast into prison, and saw not how he should escape, and one should promise him an hundred pounds, which would deliver him; if he beleeve this friend, he is full of peace and quiet: if thou beleeve thy pardon to be good, there will be peace.

But you will say to me, there is many a man hath peace who hath no faith. *Object.*

It is true: But I would aske this question concerning this peace: Is it a peace that comes after War? Hast thou knowledge of that enmity betweene *God* and thee? Hast thou had the sense of it, and after this hast thou beene reconciled againe? Is it such a calme as followed after a storme going before? As I said before, when it hath beene alwaies so with thee, when thou hast had peace, and there hath beene no difference with thee, certainly this is not peace; this is a blind peace, when a man is at peace, not because he hath escaped the danger, but because hee never saw the danger, because hee saw not what danger there was. Hence it is, that many men, yea, many thousands of men, live peaceably all their lives, and dye peaceably. Alas, the reason is, because they were never acquainted with the Doctrine of Justifi-

Answ. True peace is that that commeth after War.

Why many in an evill estate live and dye peaceably.

 cation,

cation, and of Sanctification, they are strangers to it; and hence it is that they dye with as much confidence as the best Christians, they have no more trouble than holy men: for this is all one, to be sure that I am free from a danger, and not to know it; both breed a like confidence.

Note.

Againe, know that there may be peace built on fancy, such contentments as a man may finde in a pleasant dreame, he is as strongly perswaded as the waking man: So, many Hypocrites that have had some trouble before, and come to have some peace after, they thinke it sure, when it is built upon a false ground, and not upon the sure Word. Therefore consider whether it be such a peace as is well built, whether it be such a peace indeed that casts out Satan, and thou findest some assaults made by him againe. For, be thou assured, if it be true peace, if Satan be cast out, he will not let thee alone, thou shalt be sure to have thy peace troubled, hee will make many rebellions against thee by the flesh and the world: And therefore if thou find all quiet, that there are no such assaults in thee, that there are no troubles or attempts made on thee, be thou assured it is counterfeited peace; But still keep this, that if there be faith, there will be peace; that is, the heart will bee at rest, it will be quiet, there will be a certaine security in *God*.

Vnsound peace built on fancy.

True peace is assaulted by Satan.

Instances.

See it in other things. Take faith in any thing else, and you shall see so much faith, so much quiet in you. For example, *Hannah*, in 1 *Sam*. 1. 18. when her petition was granted, that she beleeved it; saith the

Text,

Text, shee went away, and tooke meate, and *looked no more sad*. That was an Argument that she beleeved, she tooke meat, and looked no more sad. Take *Moses* at the Red Sea, *Exod.* 14. you find that the people were all troubled and disquieted, and that they knew not what to doe: But (marke how *Moses* carrieth himselfe) *Moses* was quiet, and stood still; he was not troubled: And why? Because he beleeved, and they did not; if they had beleeved as well as hee, they would have beene at rest as well as he. (Marke what he saith) *Stand still, and see the salvation of the Lord*: and, the *Lord* will fight for you; and therefore feare not: As if hee should say, If you did but beleeve, you would be at quiet, you would stand still, you would not feare, you would not have your soules troubled. So, I say, so much faith, so much quiet. Looke upon *David*, in *Psal.* 3. when he fled before *Absalom*; saith he, *Thou art my Buckler,&c*, and therefore *I layd me downe to rest and sleep*: that is, I was as a man that sleeps quietly. One would think that that was a matter that would breake a mans sleepe, when he lay in that danger, that if *Achitophels* counsell had taken effect, he had beene destroyed: and yet now, saith he, I layd me downe and slept: as if hee should say, This is an argument of my faith, my heart is at rest and quiet, so that I can sleepe quietly without stirring: and so S. *Paul*, see how hee accounts it, how hee behaved himselfe, when *God* told him that hee should appeare at *Rome* before *Cæsar*, hee knew that hee should be delivered from ship-wrack: and though forty men had bound themselves with a curse, that they would destroy him, and hee was told of it, yet hee made no great matter of it, but said, *Goe and carry this young man to the Captaine.* So consider whether thy heart be quiet, and rest upon *God* or no: for so much faith, so much peace. As in particular, so in generall, for matter of assurance, know, that there is a double peace or assurance: One peace that ariseth from the confidence in the creature, when a man thinkes he is strong in his wealth, when he thinkes he is at rest. The other is from assurance in *God*; I know that he will be as good as his word; *I know whom I have trusted:* Let security be built on this ground, and the more security, the more faith. Therefore examine thy faith by peace. I should adde somewhat more in this, and some other signes, which I must reserve untill the next time.

2 A two foldpeace.

FINIS.

OF

OF EFFECTVALL FAITH.

The fourth Sermon.

1 THES. 1. 3.
Remembring your effectuall Faith, &c.

THE third character of Faith, which I named in the morning, but did not fully finish, is this; If we have justifying faith, then we have peace. In this we should take heed. As it is a great mercy to have a true and sound peace; so to have a peace not well bottomed, is the greatest judgement in the world; when *God* gives up a man, that he shall be secure and at rest, that he shall not have his mind occupied about sinne, or about matters of salvation; I say, it is a signe that such an one *God* hates, if it continue so with him, it is a signe *God* will destroy him. But yet peace of conscience, upon a good ground, is a signe of faith; as I shewed in *Moses*,

The third marke of faith, it brings peace.

Vnsound peace a great judgemét.

Hannah, David, and the rest. So farre we went in the morning.

Now you must know, that all those instances that we brought you, that where faith is, there is peace & quiet; they were not onely for resemblance, to shew you, that as it is in those other things wherein we beleeve, so it is in the maine; (as you do not beleeve any particular promise, except you have some quiet in your mind after it;) but likewise to shew you whether that peace be good or no, whether that faith be sure or no. For if you believe the main, certainly you will believe the lesse. Thersore consider with your selves, (to enlarge this signe so far:) If thou wouldest know whether thy faith be good or no, whether thou have peace indeed concerning the maine; consider with thy selfe, whether thou art able to beleeve those promises which concerne those particular things which thou hast daily use of. For there are many promises which thou hast use of continually in thy course: thou hast every day some occasion or other of trusting *God*: See in these how thou dost beleeve, whether thou hast peace; and know, that if thou have not peace in these, it is a signe thou hast not peace in the maine. I will name but one place for it: Looke in *Phil.* 4. 6. *In nothing be carefull, but in all things let your requests be made unto God*: *And* then, saith he, *the peace of God which passeth all understanding, shall preserve your hearts and minds in Christ Iesus*. Marke the opposition: saith he, *In nothing be carefull*; when matters of trouble come, when crosses come, when great businesses come, wherein thou knowest not which way to turne thee

How to try our faith and peace in the maine promises.

Phil. 4 6. opened.

thee, (saith he) in such a case be not thou carefull ; doe the thing. Thou must have so much care as to set thy head aworke, as to devise what to doe, and to set thy hand aworke to act it ; but let there be no solicitude to disturbe and disquiet thy affections within. *Let thy request be made knowne to God* ; then, *the peace of God which passeth all understanding, shall keepe thy heart and mind in Christ Iesus.* As if he should say, If thou be not able to doe this, it is an interruption of that peace, it is a contradiction to that peace which passeth all understanding, that keeps thy heart in communion with *Christ* : if thou be not able to cast thy care on him for other things, that peace belongs not to thee. Where there is a secret intimation, Not but that men may have this peace, and be inordinately carefull; but ordinarily it is not so. He speaks not of such infirmities as the Saints are subject unto by distemper, but of an ordinary course.

What care required and forbidden.

Consider now, what thou dost for the things of this life : saith *Christ*, *Math. 6. Oh you of little faith* ! Why so? What was the signe of a little faith? Saith *Christ*, Dost thou thinke that he will *cloath the grasse of the field, which to day is, and to morrow is cast into the Oven?* Doest thou thinke that he will provide for the *young Ravens that call upon him*, & wilt thou not beleeve that he will doe so for thee ? If thou doe not beleeve this, thy faith is nothing. If thou beleeve little, thy faith is little. Consider that, consider how you carry your selves for the things of this life: do you think that *God* will doe the maine, and will not doe the lesse ? Doe you thinke that hee will give you *Christ*,

and

and will he not give you other things? The same faith that takes hold of the maine promise, is it not ready to take hold of the lesse, and to depend upon it? *God* is able to doe the greatest, and is he not able to doe the lesse? Therefore, I say, in such a case, as *Christ* saith, *Iohn* 3.12. to *Nicodemus*, *If* (saith he) *I come and tell you of earthly things, and you beleeve me not, how would you beleeve, if I should tell you of heavenly things?* So I say, if you will not beleeve *God* concerning earthly things, when hee promiseth these, how will you beleeve him for the greatest matters of salvation? How will you beleeve in him for the giving of *Christ*? How will you beleeve in him for the raising of you up at the last day? Therefore, consider whether you be able to doe this or no: and know, that if there be faith, if you have faith for the maine, you will have faith in particular cases.

He that trusts not *God* for earthly things, cannot trust him for matters of salvation.

Instances of trusting *God* in particular cases.

As for example, to give you some instance: *Gen.* 24.7. when *Abraham* had a particular occasion to send his servant to get a wife for *Isaac*; saith the servant, *Suppose the woman will not come with me*: See now what *Abrahams* answer was: *That God which tooke me from my Fathers, and hath made me many promises before,* (that is, *God* that hath done the greatest matters for me, that hath promised me the blessed seed, in which all the Nations of the World shall be blessed; dost thou thinke hee will not helpe me in such a particular?) *hee will send his Angel before thee, and will certainly give thee good successe.*

Consider what you do in such cases as these: these are things which you have continuall use of; you are

put

put many times to such exigents that you shall have somwhat to trust *God* for, and you will be tryed init.

So likewise S. *Peter*, that trusted *God* for the main, when it comes to the particular case, that he is bid to *lanch ou into the de pe*, when he is commanded to draw out the Ship and to goe a fishing; although he had no hope to doe it, he trusted in those particulars, that *Christ* would not faile him: When hee bade him go upon the water, he trusted that hee would support him. Take *David*, see how he trusted in *God*, how many occasions had he to trust on him? As it is true for the maine; so for the particulars. So S. *Paul*, did not he trust *God* for his maintenance? See in his Epistles, how carelesse he was that way. So it is with all the Saints. Consider what you doe in these things: See whether your hearts be at peace in these things, whether you trust in *God*, or no; so that your hearts are at rest, that you can sit stil & commit your care to *God*; if so, it is a good argument that you rest in him for the maine. So much for that.

4. Signe of effectuall faith. To hold out incleaving to *Christ*.

The fourth signe or Character of faith is, To hold out: and that you shall see in these three branches.

To hold out, implieth three things.

First, when it shall cleave to *Christ* constantly.

Secondly, when it will take no denyall.

Thirdly, when it is content to wait in prayer, and not be weary and give over.

1. To cleave constantly to *Christ*: which none can doe that take *Christ* amisse, as,

I say if you would know whether your faith be effectuall, you shall know it by your holding out, whether it cleave constantly to *Christ*. If thy faith be ineffectuall, (as you have heard the last day) it comes either from mis-information, (you know not what

Christ

Christ is, nor what it is to take him ; you looke for other things from him: when you see what it is, if your faith be not effectuall, you will goe back :) or else you take him out of feare, or out of love to his, and not to him ; or else out of false and slender grounds. Now if you would know whether your faith be such a faith or no, consider if it hold out, if it cleave to him.

1. Out of misinformation.

If thy faith come of mis-information; when thou hast experience of *Christ*, when thou seest what he requires at thy hands, when thou considerest and understandest what he puts thee to, there is an end, thou givest over.

2. Out of feare.

If thy faith come of feare ; as soone as the storm is over, as soone as those troubles in mind, those disquiets in conscience are past, there is an end, thy faith cleaves to *Christ* no longer.

3. Out of love to his, and not to him.

If faith come out of love to his, of love to a kingdome, nothing but hel and heaven, and some present commodities that move thee; when better things are offered, that are more present commodities, there is an end of it.

4. Out of slender & slight grounds.

Againe, if it be out of false, slender and slight grounds ; when stronger reasons and objections come, that faith ceaseth likewise. But now then, when thou findest that thy faith holds out, when all these are past, when all these are taken away, when the feare is gone, when such an offer is made, when all the objections are made that can be, this argues that faith is sound and good. Consider therefore whether thy faith cleave fast and constantly to *Christ*, or no ; whether

whether it hold out, when those flashes and good moods will not; whether it overcome, when it is assaulted by the gates of hel comming against it. That is, when a mans faith is good, it is built upon the Rocke, upon such a Rocke, that if the Devill himself and Principalities and Powers come, with all their strength, and all their wit, with al their temptations, and devises, if faith be sound, it will hould out, *the gates of Hell shall not prevaile against it*. The Woman of *Canaan* had a shrewd tryall, when *Christ* tels her she was a dog, in plaine termes, and when it came from *Christ* himself; and yet when her faith was good indeed, she could not chuse but she must cleave to him, she would not give over, there was a strong faith that did knit her heart secretly unto *Christ*? there was the ground, that she held out, notwithstanding all objections; although, it may be, she knew not how to answer them, yet she let not goe, and that was a sign her faith was good: So, consider whether thy faith hold out when thou art put to such tryals as these.

Againe, consider whether thou wilt receive no denyall when thou commest and seekest to him; when thou commest to seeke favour at *Gods* hands, when thou commest to seek forgivenesse of sinnes; consider whether thou art able to hold out, though he deferre long before he grant it. There is no grace that *God* gives, but he hath tryals for it afterward; Hee gives thee the grace of Patience, he will put thee to it, thou shalt have some crosse, some affliction or other. 2 To take no denial.

If he give thee love, he wil do as he did with *David*, hee

he will see whether thou wilt forsake him or no; he willmake thee an offer of preferment, an offer, of wealth, of praise, of somewhat or other, to see if thou wilt part with that for his sake, or no.

If he gives us faith, he often tryes us in this case, he denyes us long, he wrestleth with us, as he did with *Iacob*, he makes many shewes of going away. Thus, we know he dealt with *Daniel*, as soon as hee began to pray, the answer comes, that his request was granted; but *God* would not let him know so much; hee lets him goe thorough with the worke, hee lets him seek earnestly, and then he reveales and makes it known unto him. So perhaps *God* intends thee good, but he will put thee to the tryall, consider therefore if thy faith hold out in such a case.

3. To be content to wait. Instances of waiting.

Again, when thou hast gotten an answer, perhaps after thou hast gotten thine answer, thou must wait long before the thing it selfe be given thee: Therfore consider if thou be content to wait for it, for that's the property of faith, to be willing to wait, as *David* often repeats it, *I waited upon the Lord*. You know, *Abraham*, how *God* tryed him that way; when hee made him a promise of a seed, of a sonne, you know hovv long he vvaited for the performance. So *Isaac*, he vvaited long before he had those tvvo sonnes, *Iacob* and *Esau*. So *God* vvill put thee to it, to vvait it may bee for matter of Iustification, that is, he vvill not shevv himselfe, hee vvill not speake peace unto thee, hee vvill not give thee a good looke, but yet hee gives thee a secret strength that thou shalt vvait, thou shalt not give over, thou shalt stay til he speak peace, that

God puts his children to wait.

In Iustification.

that is, til thou have comfortable assurance, till thou have the full testimony of the Spirit, as thou hast a secret testimony of the first working of faith. And so for matter of sanctification; It may be, *God* will suffer some strong lust to wrestle with thee, to contend with thee, as he suffered in S. *Paul*: he will put thee to wait, before he will give thee victory over it. If thy faith be good now, thou wilt consider that he hath sworne, he hath made an absolute promise, that hee will give the Holy Ghost to those that are in *Christ*, that no sin shall overcome them, or have dominion over them. If once thou come under grace, if thou have faith, thou wilt never give over, but wilt be content to wait and continue, still striving and wrestling with it, thou wilt never lay downe the wasters, as a man that is overcome, as a man that is discouraged, as a man that is weary of the fight.

In Sanctification.

For deliverance.

And so for matter of deliverance; perhaps *God* will let a crosse lye long upon thee: if thou have faith, thou wilt not make haste, thou wilt be content to wait. *Hab.* 2. *The vision is for an appointed time, it will not lye:* Therefore, saith he, *wait*, *it will come*, *it will not stay*. That is, there is a certaine time that *God* hath appointed for thy deliverance, before hee will give thee such a particular mercy; consider whether thou be able to wait in such a case: for, if there be faith, (marke it) a man will be sure to wait, and not to give over: as in *Iam.* 1. it is given there as a signe that faith is unsound; they had so much faith as to come to *Christ*, but that was a signe that their faith was faulty, and unsound faith, that it was not able to wait to the end, but gave over. If

Simile.

If a man were ſure now, that ſuch a man were in the houſe that he muſt ſpeake withall, he will wait till he come out, if he be ſure he be there. If thou be ſure of *God*, if thy faith be ſound, though he doe not anſwer thee preſently, in many particulars, yet thou wilt be content to wait upon him. Therefore this will ſhew that many a mans faith is unſound, ſleight, and uneffectuall, that they have ſo ſoone done, that they are ready to doe much in flaſhes, in ſome good moods, on a Sacrament day, it may be, or in the time of ſickneſſe, or when they are affected with ſome Sermon, or upon ſuch an occaſion; but if thy faith were right it would hold out, it would cleave to *Chriſt*, it would goe thorow with all tryals, thou wouldeſt receive no denyall, it would continue waiting upon him. This is the fourth ſigne.

5 Signe of effectuall faith, the concomitants of it, which are foure.
1. Love.

Laſt of all, you ſhall know faith by the concomitants of it; and they are foure; Love, Hope, Joy, and Humility. If there be Faith, if thy Faith bee good, it will alwaies have Love joyned with it, as the Apoſtle S. *Peter* ſaith, in 1 *Pet.* 1.18. *Whom though you have not ſeen, yet you love him.* And you know the place in *Galath.* 5. *Faith which worketh by love:* That is, Faith which begets Love; and ſuch a love as ſets a man on worke. But it is a thing that needeth no proving: you cannot deny it: you know how they are joyned together in the firſt to the *Corinthians*, Chap. 13. *Faith, Hope, and Love:* And it muſt needs be ſo, that if thy faith, be good, it will have love joyned with it. For, if thy faith be right, thou lookeſt on *God* as upon a friend, as upon a Father; now thou lookeſt upon

Chriſt

Christ, as on one that is married to thee; thou lookest on him as upon one that loves thee, and hath given himselfe for thee. Now if thou see this, and art perswaded of this indeed, if thou thinke, and art perswaded indeed that hee loves thee, love will beget love, as fire begets fire. Therefore, if thou wouldst know whether thou hast taken *Christ* indeed, consider whether thou love him or no.

Object. But you will say, you love *Christ*, I hope there is no great question of that.

Answ. *Salomon* saith, Every man will make shew for fashions sake, of goodnesse, *but where can you find a faithfull man?* So may I say of Love: Every man saith he loves, but where shall one find one that doth love indeed? Therefore consider, doest thou love in good earnest?

Quest. You will say, How shall I know it?

Answ. It is not a place now to stand to give notes of Love: wee will onely shew at present, that Love is a sure companion of Faith, and that Faith is not good, if Love be not there: But yet I say, if thou love him, thou shalt find that in thine owne heart, thou needest not goe farre for a tryall of that. Tryals of love.

1. By the quicknes. Love is the most sensible, the most quick, & most active affection of al others. Consider if thou love any creature, or any thing, any man or woman, dost thou not feele thy affections stirring in thee? doest thou not finde thy heart thus longing after them whom thou affectest? thou delightest to be in their company, in their presence, thou desirest to be with them. So that, if a strangenes grow between you at any time,

thy heart is not at ease till all be right again between you: So, doest thou love the *Lord Iesus?* Dost thou keepe his Commandments? Doth a manprofesse to love *God*, and cares not to vex him, and anger him?

2. By hating sinne.

Againe, Dost thou hate sinne? Dost thou thinke to love *God*, and not to hate that which he hateth? If a man love *God*, he is holy and pure; and there is no man that loves the one contrary, but he must needs hate the other. There is no man that loves light, but he must take hate darknesse. If thou love *God* in his person, in his purity, in his holinesse, thou must hate sinne: and this hatred is generall; thou wilt hate all sinne, if thou hate any, and hatred will breed the destruction of a thing.

3. By doing.

Againe, Doest thou love *God?* art thou willing to do any thing for his sake? Dost thou reckon matters of greatest difficulty, easie to doe; as *Iacob* did make it a matter of ease because of love?

4. By love to the Saints.

It is easier to love holinesse in the Saints than in *God.*

Againe, Dost thou love the Saints, those that are like him, those that are of such a disposition as *God* is of? Shall a man say hee loves the purity and the holines of *God*; which he hath not seen, which is hidden from his eyes, when he doth not love the holines and the purity that hee sees in his Saints? For there it is taught in a visible manner in the creature, where you may see it more proportionable to you. It is a hundred times more easie, to love godlinesse in the Saints, than in *God* himselfe, because he is remote farre from us, and they are amongst, us, and are visibly seene. Therefore except thou love the Saints, which thou seest holinesse in; except thou seest thy heart

heart inwardly, to love them with a naturall affection, as it were, that that thou lovest them whether thou wilt or no, thou dost but pretend.

Againe, Dost thou love *Christ*? Art thou willing to part with any thing for his sake? *Love is bountifull:* Thou sayest thou lovest *God:* What if hee will have some of thy wealth? What if hee will have thy credit? What if he will have thy liberty for his sake? If thou love him, thou wilt be content to doe it. Therefore, consider if faith hath begotten such a love in thee, so that thou canst truly say, *though thou hast not seene him, yet thou lovest him.* 5. By the bounty of it.

The second concomitant of Faith, is Hope: If thou hast Faith, thou hast Hope. And this distinguisheth a Christians faith from the faith of Reprobates, from the faith of Devils, from the temporary faith that others are capable of: You know the Devils beleeve and tremble: He saith not, The Devils beleeve and hope; for that they doe not. Hope is a property of Faith, where there is Faith there is Hope. Now you must know, that a man hath never faith to beleeve; but he hath hope which makes him expect what he beleeves. If a man have a promise of so much mony which he needs, he hopes for the performance of it, and quiets himselfe; when hee casts his thoughts upon it, he is at rest: when a man beleeves it, he hopes for it. Take an Heire that hath such possessions, which is yet a Ward, and is young, he hath not the Land in possession, but (marke) what hope he hath; it is not a vaine hope, but such a hope as puts other conceits in him than other men have, 2. Hope. Hope distinguisheth the faith of Christians from the faith of devils and reprobates.

puts another fashion upon his actions, it makes him neglect many good things he would doe; hee will not be of such a calling, he will not be diligent: for he hopes, hee makes account of it: See how such things worke upon a man, which he is not to have in seven or eight yeeres after, perhaps. So thou hopest for Heaven, it is not a vaine hope, but by it thou shalt carry thy selfe after another fashion, and be so minded, that thou wilt have an eye to it: and every man that lookes on thee, may see that thou hast an eye to it: So that Faith is accompanied by Hope. But now you must not say, that if a man hope, therefore there is no feare mingled with it: for you must know, that a man may have Hope that is true and good, yet may have feare mingled with it. For this you must know, that if there be nothing but hope, it is a signe that that Hope is not good. And therefore thou hast so little reason to be discouraged, because thou hast some feare mingled with thy hope, that thou hast the more cause to hope, & to think that thy hope is good, because there is feare mingled with it: for know that there is a certain sort of men, that have neither faith, hope nor feare; as Atheists, that have some hope but no feare, as Devils and desperate men, that have some feare but no hope; as presumptuous men, which have but a shadow of faith: But those that have hope, and feare mingled with it, those may rather hope that that hope which they have, is good; they may be so much the more confirmed in it, because they have some feare mingled with it.

Hope may be mingled with feare.

Note.

Therefore consider whether thou have hope or no:

Consider

Consider in what manner it is joyned with faith. When thou beleevest that *Christ* is thine, that Heaven is thine, that thy sinnes are forgiven, and thou art a sonne of *God*: but these things thou hast not yet, thou art as any other man, there is no difference betweene thee and them, thou hast no more in possession than other men that walke with thee; now comes in hope, and that expecteth that which is to come, that holds up thy head, as it were, that though you have nothing at all for the present, yet that hope will comfort you, that though you have troubles, and crosses, and a thousand things more, to obscure and blot your faith, and the waves goe over your head, that you are ready to be drowned, this hope holds you above the water, and makes you expect with comfort that which is to come: and not so onely, but, I say, it is a *lively hope*, a hope that sets a man a-worke, a hope that purgeth him. For, you know, that which a man hopes for, hee will endevour to bring it to passe, it is such a hope as will not faile you, but will continue as well as faith it selfe.

The property of hope.

Thirdly, the third concomitant of faith is Joy: *Romanes* 15.13. *The God of hope fill you with ioy, through beleeving.* If you have beleeved, you have Joy. So in the first of *Peter*. chap. 1. verse 8. *In whom you have beleeved:* (saith he) *whom, though you have not seene, yet you beleeved in him, and ioy with ioy unspeakable and glorious.* (As if he should say) If you beleeve in him, you shal know it by this, Whether doe you rejoyce in him, or no? Consider, that where there is Faith, there is ioy. And it must needs be so: As you know, hee that had

3. Ioy.

the Pearle, *went away reioycing*; and *the kingdome of God consisteth in Ioy, and Peace, and Righteousnesse*. And therefore, where there is faith, there certainly is Ioy. And therefore consider, and examine thine own case: Hast thou this rejoycing in *Christ*? this reioycing in the doctrine of Iustification, and forgivenesse of sinnes? If we should examine mens faith by this, wee should find that there is but a little Faith in the World. Examine your selves, you that now heare me, that heare this Doctrine of Faith; it may be it hath bin burthensome unto you; it may bee it is a thing you care not for; to heare of Justification and forgivenesse of sins, they are things, at the least, that it may bee, you take no great paines for, you doe not study them, you doe not prize them much: but, if you were forgiven indeede, you would preferre it before all other joy, it would comfort you above any thing. If you would say, what you would heare above all things else, you would heare of matter of forgivenesse. A man now that hath known the bitternesse of sin, and afterwards comes to the assurance of forgivenesse, (that is) to have faith indeed, I say, hee will reioyce in it above all things else: all worldly joy would bee nothing to it. Therefore consider whether thou have such a faith or no; if thou have not, certainly thou hast not faith; and it is a sure signe that will not deceive you; there is no man that hath it, that hath not Faith; and wheresoever there is faith indeed, there is extraordinary great rejoycing in *Christ*.

But you will say, Many a man may have Ioy; the second ground *received the Word with Ioy*, and those that

that followed *Iohn* the Baptist, *reioyced in his light*: and in *Heb*.6.the Apostle saith, *They have tasted of the good word of God*, they have tasted with sweetnesse; that is, they have had Ioy in it.

Answ.

It is true, we confesse there is a false joy: and therefore, if thou wouldst know whether the joy which thou hast be good or no consider these three things.

Tryals of joy.

1. It holds out in tribulation.

First, consider whether thy joy hold out in tribulation or no. Therefore the Apostle addes, *Rom*. 5. 3. *Not onely so, but we rejoyce also in tribulation*. As if he should say, Those that are hypocrites, those that have a false faith, there may be much rejoycing in them for a while, but we rejoyce in tribulations; yea, we not onely rejoyce in tribulations, but our joy is encreased by them, they are as fuell, they adde to our joy: as in *Act*, 5. *The disciples went away rejoycing, because they were accounted worthy to suffer for Christ*. Whereas the second ground, when persecution comes, there is an end of their joy. Therefore consider whether thy joy will hold out or no.

2. It is great.

Againe, consider the greatnesse thereof: you know those words are added, 1. *Pet*.1. 8. *Rejoycing with joy unspeakeable and glorious*. If it be right joy, it will be such a great joy, it will exceed all other, it will be like to that *joy in Harvest*, as *Esay* speakes, it will be a joy unspeakeable for the greatnesse of it; such a joy, that at the least is so great, that whatsoever comes, yet it exceeds it. The other temporary Christian may have joy, but it is not so great, but some other joy wil come and overcom it, and drown it, and put it out.

Therefore, in the second ground, as their humiliation was sleight, so was their faith, they had a little humiliation for their sinnes, and they tooke *Christ* in a more remisse manner. And as their Faith was, so was their joy, all sleight. But now, when faith is sound and good, that joy is accordingly great, it is a great joy, that at the least overcomes all other; that, take what joy you wil, if a man could have an earthly kingdome here, if a man could have as great pleasure here, as mans nature is capable of, if he had never so much praise and glory of men, (these things we naturally rejoyce in) a right Christian, that hath faith indeed, will not so rejoyce in these, but that he will rejoyce in *Christ* above them. If thy joy therefore be so great, that it overcome & exceed all other, be sure that joy is good. But yet we must have one thing more in joy. In whō though you have not seen, yet you joy with joy unspeakeable and glorious: That is, if it be such a joy as is right indeed, which is a testimonie of faith, that it is a signe thou beleevest, if a joy that is glorious, it is a joy that is glorious and spirituall. Now an hypocrite may rejoyce, he may rejoyce in *Christ*, he may rejoyce in the Kingdome of God, and the assurance he hath of it, and he may rejoyce in the hope that he hath that his sins are forgiven; but all this while he rejoyceth after a carnall manner, as, you know, a man may rejoyce in spirituall things after a carnall manner, as a man may rejoyce in a carnall thing after a spirituall manner. Therefore the joy of hypocrites, when it is at the best, it is but a carnall joy; there is something there that his flesh is able to rejoyce in, it may be he had some

Note.

3. It is spirituall.

Hypocrits joy is carnall.

ſome feare and terrour in his conſcience, & after this comes a perſwaſion perhaps that his ſins are forgiven him, and that he is in a good eſtate; that ſame fleſhly feare and griefe before, that worldly feare & griefe will have a joy anſwerable to it, a naturall joy; & yet it may be great, it may be a great flaſh of joy; that may be as a Land-flood, make a great ſhew, which becauſe it hath no ſpring, is ſoon dried up; but it maks a great flaſh: & therfore in that, *Heb.6. They taſted, &c.* I take this to be the meaning of it, That an hypocrite may taſte of the good Word of *God*, and of ſpirituall priviledges, he may taſte of them, but not drink deepe of them, for this is certainly the meaning of the place, They taſted ſome things in the good Word of *God*, which was ſweet to them. Now in ſuch men there is nothing but fleſh. (Marke) If a temporary Chriſtian beleeves for a time, hee hath ineffectuall faith, in ſuch a man there is nothing but fleſh. That concluſion muſt be ſet downe: and if there be nothing but fleſh, there is nothing can taſte but fleſh; for there is nothing elſe to do it, and the fleſh taſtes nothing but objects that ſuite with it ſelfe. What ſhall we ſay then? There is ſomewhat in him that picks out, that in theſe ſpirituall comforts, that in theſe ſpirituall bleſſings, in this good Word of *God*, hee pickes out that which ſuits with his fleſh: That is, ſuch a carnall man may bee able to rejoyce in the Word. Doe you not thinke, that ſuch a good Word of *God* may make carnall men rejoyce in it? May he not taſte ſuch ſweetneſſe, as to take upon him the profeſſion of Religion, and to

Simile.

Heb. 6. opened.

What meant by taſting the powers of the world to come. Heb. 6.

to bring forth fruit, and to hold out long? No doubt there is. Are there not ſuch things in that which wee propound in the Goſpell? To tell men of a Kingdome of ſalvation, of the Love of *God*, of the precious promiſes, of an inheritance, of eſcaping of Hell; may not a fleſhly man, a man unregenerate, may he not ſee and rejoyce in theſe? He may; and hath ſuch a taſte as is there expreſſed.

Conſider now therefore if thy Joy be right; If it be a ſigne of faith, if it be good and ſound, if it be a Joy that is ſpirituall and unſpeakeable; that is, if it be a Joy that is ſo great, as that it exceeds all other joyes; if this Joy doe but hold out in tribulation, it is a certaine ſigne thy faith is good.

4. Humility.

Now, laſt of all, the laſt concomitant of faith is Humility. If thy faith be right, it will bring that with it, to make thee humble and vile in thine owne eyes: For what is true Faith? It is that which brings *Chriſt* into the heart, as you have heard oftentimes; that which knits *Chriſt* and the ſoule together, it is that which cauſeth him to come & dwell with thee. Now whereſoever *Chriſt* comes to dwell, hee comes with a light, he ſhewes the creature his vileneſſe, he makes a man ſee his ſinne, hee makes him ſee what creature he is; whereas another that hath great hope, and profeſſeth that hee hath much aſſurance, his heart is lifted up, and not caſt downe. Such are not men which thinke themſelves vile, and naked, and miſerable, but they thinke themſelves better than other men, they are forwarder than others in any thing, they thinke other men are not like them. And there-

therefore they are ready to be more bold and venturous in any thing, they are ready to take up opinions they are ready to strike out this way or that way. But now a true Christian is humbled with it, because when *Christ* comes into the heart, he makes a man to see his vilenesse. As you know, when *God* drew neere to *Iob*, when he came neere indeed, then *abhorred himselfe in dust and ashes*, then he saw what a one he was, he saw not before, he thought the contrary, but when *God* drew neere indeed, that made him manifest.

When *Christ* comes into the heart, a man is vile in his own eyes.

So it was with *Isay*, when he saw *God* upon his Throne, and the Angels about him, when he saw his holinesse then, *woe is me, I am undone, because I am a man of polluted lips*: He was so before, but when he drew neere to *God*, he saw it.

Isay 6.

So *Peter* said, *Depart from me, I am a sinfull man*, when he saw *Christ*, when *Christ* came neere him, when he manifested himselfe in his Divinitie, that he saw *God* in him; for so he did by that miracle that amazed *Peter*, and cast him downe, and made him see what he was. So *David*, when *God* drew neere to him, and promised to *build him an House*, to give him an House that should be eternall, to give him the *Messiah*, whose Kingdome should never end, (for that is included in the giving him a Kingdome for ever, and an House that should have no end:) when *God* vouchsafed him so great a favour, we see, *David* was never so cast down as then in the sight of his own vilenesse, he was never so little in his own eies, he never said so much as he said then. Now, (saith he) what is *David? what am I, or what is my Fathers House, that thou shouldst regard me*

thus,

thus, that thou shouldst bring me hitherto? This is *Gods* manner, when he comes into a mans heart, when he speakes peace indeed, when faith is a right faith, that brings *Christ* to dwell there; I say, it makes a man exceeding humble. Therefore the Spirit of Christians is a meeke spirit, they are humble and gentle, they are little in their own eies. Consider whether thou hast such a disposition bred in thee, or no: it is a signe thy faith is good, if there be; if there be not, it is a signe thy faith is not true. So much for the signes of faith. I make haste, because I have one use more to adde.

Use 7. To act and exercise faith, or to set it on work.

If nothing be regarded of *God* but effectuall faith; that is, if that be the vertue of faith to be effectuall, or els it is nothing worth, then we should learn hence not to let that be wanting to our faith, which is the excellencie of it, which is the vertue of it, which is the proper quality of it. As, if it be the vertue of a Horse to go well; If it be the vertue of a Knife to cut well; If it be the vertue of a Souldier to fight well; or whatsoever you will instance in, whatsoever vertue it be, or whatsoever thing, you labor to find that in it, whatsoever be wanting; (for every thing hath some proper excellency, some special vertue wherein the thing consists.) Now to be effectuall, to be working, to be operative, if this be the vertue of faith, (as it were) if this be the character & excellency of faith; Let not this therfore be wanting in faith. What is that then thou shouldst do? Use thy faith, set faith a work, live by it.

Object. You wil say, This is more than I can do, this is *Gods* action, he must set faith a work, and work this in me.

Answ. I say, thou art able to doe this of thy selfe, when thou

thou hast faith once. I speake to those that have it: and this exhortation is to you. If you have faith, use it: many have it, that doe not use it. This is a thing that you are able to do: For though *God* work in you all the worke of faith, as it is received; yet know, he doth not worke in you only but by you; hee makes you instruments: you are not as dead instruments, but as living instruments, to move of your selves. It is true, that before you have faith you are able to doe nothing; but when you have it once, then you are able to use it. Before a man hath life, he is not able to stirre, but when he hath life once, then he is able to move and stir himselfe, for there is life there. When the Lamp is once lighted, you know you may feed it with the oyle, and if you put more oyle to it, you shall have the greater flame: There is light, and you may increase it; indeed the difficulty is to light it; & that is *Gods* work; he kindles the first fire, he works faith in the heart: But now, when thou hast it, learne to use it. Dost thou think a necessity lyes upon us to use other Talents that *God* hath put into our hands, and will hee not require that thou shouldest use the Talent of Faith? Wilt thou wrap that in a Napkin, and let it lye dead by thee? Will not he call thee to an account for it? What folly is it, (my brethren) you have faith, which is so excellent a Grace, able to doe so great things as it is, and yet you will not use it. There are many Christians that have faith indeed, and yet will not set it on worke. How great things would it doe, what a reward would it bring? As *Aristotle* saith of habits, That if a man have no more but a habit

Those that have faith are able to use it.

Similie.

Similie.

Motives to set faith on worke.

Habits are for action.

a habit, and uſe it not, there is no difference between the wiſeſt man and a foole; for what are habits for, but for action? what is the Tree for, but for fruit? The habit ſerves but for the act; and this is according to the judgement of Scripture, in *Rom.* 2. *God* rewards not men according to the habits they have, but according to their works. Therefore thinke not that thou ſhalt be rewarded according to thy habits of faith which thou haſt, though it be true, that that ſanctifies thee, but *God* doth reward us according to the uſe of our faith, according to the works that our faith doth bring forth, according to the efficacy of our faith. It is true, the taking of *Chriſt* is one worke of faith, thou ſhouldſt ſet it aworke to doe that; and beſides that, all the workes of ſanctification are all workes of faith; all thy life long, every houre thou haſt ſomewhat for faith to do. Set thy faith a work, and thy reward ſhall be accordingly.

God rewards not according to workes.

And againe, if thou uſe not faith, thou ſhalt have little enough of it; the uſing of it, is that which ſtrengthens faith. It is *Gods* uſuall manner, when he gives faith to a man, to give him exerciſe, to keepe Faith breathing, as it were; hee will be ſure to have ſomewhat wherein he will put him to it, ſome tribulation, he will put fire to it, to cleanſe it. And therefore we ſhould learne to make uſe of Faith, to ſet it on worke.

Want of uſing faith makes it weake.

It is a generall Rule in all things, and as true in this, If a man have an eſtate, what is he the better to have it, if he doe not uſe it? To have a friend, what is a man the better if he doe not uſe him? Shall a man be a

Faith gives us intereſt to all that *God* hath.

Favorite

Favorite of a Prince, and get nothing by it? Faith makes a man a Favorite of *God*, a friend to *God*; and will you make no use of *God*? It is that which he expects at your hands; will you have *God* in vaine? Shall he be your *God*, & will you make no use of his power, of his wisedome, of his ability to hold you up, to helpe you upon all occasions? You make use of him; all that is his, is yours, if you make use of it by faith.

Againe, shall men have such priviledges as we have by faith, and shall not wee comfort our selves by them? What is it for a man to have great estates, great Titles of Honour, and Houses, and Lands, if a man doe not thinke upon them, that these considerations may cheere him? We should do so with faith, this is the use of faith.

Againe, if faith be used, it is able to doe much for us; if it lye still, it will doe nothing. You know what they did *Heb.* 11. They having faith, it made them doe that, it was but the use of their faith: So it is with us; Looke how much thou usest thy faith, so much thou shalt be able to doe. Therefore *Christ* saith, *Be it according to thy faith*: that is, not according to the habit of thy faith, that lies dead, as a Talent wrapped up there; but, be it unto thee according to the use of thy faith. If thou set faith on worke, it will be able to do great things, it will be able to do wonders, it will be able to overcome the world, it is able to worke righteousnes it is able to prevaile with *God* & men, it is able to go through the greatest matters. Faith enables to do much.

But, you will say, How shall I use it? *Quest.*

That is the thing indeed which I purposed now to have *Answ.*

have ſhewed, how faith muſt be uſed, how wee muſt live by faith: I ſhould have ſhewed how you ſhould uſe it.

How to uſe Faith.

1. In comforting our ſelves.

Firſt, in comforting our ſelves; for that is one uſe of faith: thou ſhouldſt ſet it aworke to fill thy heart with joy, out of the aſſurance of the forgiveneſſe of ſin, and of the priviledges which thou haſt by *Chriſt*. When a man hath faith, and finds his heart no more affected than other mens, 'he finds no rejoycing there more' than ordinary; Now ſet faith on worke, learne to beleeve, and that throughly.

Gal. 3. opened.

First, ſet faith on worke to beleeve, to *truſt perfectly*, as the Apoſtle ſpeakes, *Gal.* 3. *in the grace revealed by Ieſus Chriſt:* truſt perfectly; that is, thou ſhouldeſt beleeve the full forgiveneſſe of thy ſins: thou muſt not beleeve it by halves, ſo that there ſhould be a diſtance, as it were, betweene *God* and thee, ſome odde ſcores unacquitted, uncroſt; but thou ſhouldeſt beleeve ſo, *that thy joy may be full*, thou ſhouldſt beleeve throughly that thy ſins are forgiven, that all are acquitted, thou muſt not limit *God* in his mercy at all, as thou ſhouldſt not limit him in his power. Thus a man ſhould ſet faith on worke, that he may be able to ſay, *My beloved is mine, and I am his.* I know there is a Match made betweene us. For unleſſe you lay this ground, a man ſhall not rejoyce. This is all, therefore now uſe thy faith. If Satan now come, and tell thee of ſome ſins, and of ſome circumſtances of thoſe ſins, and of ſome wants in thy repentance and humiliation, what ſerves faith for now? What ſerves all this for that you have learned here concerning the

Iohn 16.

Doctrine

Doctrine of Faith, but to teach you that these should be no scruples, you should beleeve, and that perfectly? When this is done, that you see there is a Match, a Covenant made betweene *God* and you, now you must know, that all that *Christ* hath is yours; whatsoever he hath by Nature, you have it by Grace. If he be a Son, ye are sons; If he be an Heire, ye are heires; and when ye have done this, then consider all the particulars of the wealth of a Christian, that all is yours, *whether it be Paul, or Apollos, or the world, &c.* These things wee have often spoken of, you should run through and consider of them: If a man will consider that he is a King, that the world is his, that whatsoever is in *Christ* belongs to him, and oweth him a good turne, and will doe it at one time or other; when he considers all the precious promises. A man reckons his wealth not only by his money which he hath lying in his Coffers, that he hath present, but by Bils, and Bonds, and Leases, &c. See how many promises thou hast, there is not a promise in the Booke of *God*, but it is thine; set thy faith on worke to consider this, and to rejoyce in it; set faith on worke so to see them that thou mayest rejoyce in them, and weane thee from the things of this world, not to regard them; for they are small things of no hold. Shall a King regard Cottages and trifles? No, if thou thinke in good earnest that thou art such a man, why dost thou regard trifles? Thou shouldst do this; when other men reckon their Lands, and their Houses, and their Friends, a Christian reckons hee hath *God*, hee hath many good works in store, he hath so many *pre-*

Similie.

Faith makes a man regardlesse of earthly things.

cious promises laid up *in the La d of the living*. Set thy faith on work thus, not only to rejoyce, but to bring in a holy magnanimity, answerable to such a condition; and let not Faith give over till it have brought thee to this. Certainely, a man that beleeves he is a King, he will have another spirit: for there is no other reason wherefore it is said *Saul* had another spirit, but that when he came to be a King, he had a spirit answerable. When thou beleevest these priviledges, when thou settest thy Faith on worke to beleeve indeed, to beleeve them to be reall things, and not fancies, and notions, there will be bred a disposition answerable, a carriage and spirit sutable; thou wilt not admit of things that are unfit for such a person, thou canst not doe it; but as one that is a Prince, that hath those hopes actually, hee cannot admit of thoughts that other men have; no more can a Christian, when he is borne from above by the *immortall seed*, there is such a disposition wrought in him, that, if hee will set his faith on worke to beleeve these things, hee shall not be able to admit of those base things which he did before, and which others doe.

Againe, if a man set his faith aworke to beleeve these things, he would be able to use the World as if he used it not, he would not care for losses and crosses, he would not grieve for them, as one that is not able to beare them, Thus wee should learne to set faith on worke, in beleeving these priviledges, that we may be able to walke with *God*, as *Henoch* did, and as S. *Paul* & *Moses* did; to walke with him in the upper Region, above the storms. There is much variety of weather when a man is below here, now it is faire, and then it is foule; if a man were above these, there is a continuall serenity; So a man that hath his heart in Heaven, a man that walkes with *God*, that hath his heart raised above others: if you would doe this, if you would use Faith, if thou wouldst consider this, it would set thee aloft above these things; thou wouldst soare aloft as the Eagle, thou wouldst care no more for these things, than the Eagle cares for the chirping of Sparrowes: they are trifles, thou wouldst over-looke them all. If we did consider this seriously, how would it alter our course? It would work another disposition, another affection in us. A man would consider, that if *God* be sure, what matter is it if a friend dye? If I have *God*, what is the losse of any creature? And so, if a man suffer wrong in his name, what is it, if he have *praise of God?* If thou beleeve, and see *God* in his greatnesse, to have praise of such a one as he, will make thee to contemne the rest. And so for wealth: What is poverty? What account did S. *Paul* make of it? It is nothing to one that hath Treasure in heaven, to one that beleeves indeed, to one that seeth he hath all *Gods* Treasnres opened to him. Thou shouldst learne to do this in good earnest. If a man would set his Faith aworke to beleeve it, his heart would be fixed, he would *be affraid of no evill tydings*, he would say with himselfe, if there be no ill tydings from heaven, it is no matter from whence they come on earrh. If a man would build, through faith, upon the promise, and consider it really. This is the use of Faith: thus a mans heart should

Faith makes afflictions easie.

be filled with joy, and a man would be able to goe *through ill report and good report, through want and through abundance*, without being much troubled with either; the one would not much puffe him up, nor the other would not deject him, but he would goe as a Gyant, and march through the variety of conditions; hee would passe through them, that neither the one hand nor the other, the good successe nor the ill successe should worke upon him much. This is a strong man: and this Faith will make thee to doe, if thou use Faith, and set it aworke. But I am sorry the time hath cut me off: this is but an entrance, I give you but a little taste: There are many things wherein Faith stands us in much stead, wherein if we did use Faith how much service would it do us? But for that which remaines in this Doctrine of Faith, I had thought to have shut it up at this time, to shew you how to use it, how to make it effectuall, how to set it aworke, how to walke by it; how to husband and improve this Talent for *Gods* advantage and your owne. But I cannot stand on it. So much for this time.

FINIS.

OF EFFECTVALL FAITH.

The fifth Sermon.

1 THES. 1. 3.
Remembring your effectuall Faith, &c.

THE first thing wherein thou shouldst use faith, is to comfort thy selfe by it. Therefore consider, you that doubt of this, you that make question, (I speake to those that have the worke wrought, whom the *Holy Ghost* hath made to desire *Christ* above all things, I say) remember that *God justifieth the ungodly*, and that you have nothing to doe, but to take him.

Considerations to help faith in comforting the Soule.

1. *God* justifieth the ungodly.

2. Remember that *Christ* is *made righteousnesse to us*, that no flesh might rejoyce in his sight, but he that rejoyceth, might rejoyce in the *Lord*.

2. Christ is our righteousnes.

3. The pardon is generall.

3. Remember that the pardon is generall. Looke to the promises of the Gospell; you shall finde them without all exception. To us a Saviour is borne, to take away the sinnes of his people; hee came to take away sinnes of all sorts, Now, when *God* hath made no exception, why should we make any?

4. God delights in shewing mercy.

4. Consider that we have to doe with a *God*, who delights to shew mercy, it is a thing that he is not weary of, it is naturall to him: And therefore as the eye is not weary of seeing, nor the eare of hearing, because it is naturall to them, no more is *God* weary of shewing mercy. Nay, he delights in it, *Mich*. 7. 8. *Who is a God like unto thee, taking away iniquities, delighting to shew mercy? &c.* Why so? *Because mercy pleaseth him.* That is, there is no worke that he so much pleased in, as in shewing mercy.

5. His mercy is infinite.

5. Consider, thou art in such a case, consider that his mercy is as large as any other attribute. Every man thinkes that this is no newes; what need you tell us that *God* is infinite in mercy? I say, this is a thing that thou doest not consider: if thou diddest, thou wouldest not sticke upon it as thou doest. If thou diddest beleeve that *God* were as mercifull as hee is; but wee scant *God* according to our measure; we square *Gods* mercy according to our owne thoughts. Every man measures *Gods* mercy according to that which he can conceive. He thinks with himselfe, If a man commit one sinne, it might be forgiven, but when his sinnes exceed, when they grow out of measure sinfull, when they are sinnes so circumstan-

cumſtantiated, as we ſay, that they are out of meaſure ſinnefull, here a man ſtands at a ſtay: What is the reaſon of this? Becauſe wee draw a ſcantling of *Gods* mercy, according to our own conceits. Whereas, if we conſidered that his mercy were as large as any other attribute, then wee would conſider that it hath no limits: and if it have no limits, then whatſoever thy ſinnes are, it is all one.

6. Chriſt came to pardon the greateſt ſins.

6. Doſt thou thinke that *Chriſt* came from heaven, and tooke fleſh, and ſuffered death, to forgive ſmall ſinnes? No, it was to forgive the greateſt: the worke is large enough to match with the greateſt ſinnes. Theſe and ſuch like reaſons thou ſhouldeſt labour to bring to heart, that thou mayſt beleeve perfectly and throughly; and give not over till thou have done it. Let not thy faith truſt in *Chriſt* by halves, but truſt throughly. Thou ſhouldeſt come to this diſ-junction: If I be out of the Covenant, why doe I beleeve at all? why doe I receive any comfort? If I be in the Covenant, why do I not beleeve perfectly? I ſay, give not over till thou have brought thy heart to a full aſſurance. Thus a man ſhould do that yet doubts whether his eſtate be good, whether *Chriſt* be his, when he is his. For when a man is once in the Covenant, that the match is made betweene him and thee, why doeſt thou doubt? If thou be in the Covenant once, doubt not then that a ſinne or two, or daily failings ſhall breake the Covenant betweene *God* and thee, it is impoſſible. Thou muſt know, that thou often breakeſt the Covenant; but except there be a quite turning backe, except thou

Note.

Daily failings break not the Covenant

thou altogether forsake *God*, except thou leave *God*, and chuse thee a new Master, (this indeed breaketh the Covenant) otherwise, if it be but a failing, if it be but a sinne of infirmitie, from day to day, when as yet thou keepest *God* in thy heart, thou cleavest fast to him, thou intendest to serve him, and not to forsake him and give him over; thinke not that those sinnes, although they be great, breake the Covenant. And therefore, *Psal.* 41.7. said the people of *God* there: *Although these things be befalne us, yet have we not forgotten thee, nor dealt falsely concerning thy Covenant.* Why? *we have not turned backe*; although wee have failed and done many things amisse, yet have we not dealt falsely concerning thy Covenant. That is, wee are not Hypocrites, our hearts are sincere.

Quest. How prove they that?

Answ. We have not turned back from thee, our feet have not gone out of thy wayes. That is, we have not quite given over, as many men do that make their pleasure their *God*; when they make their profit their *God*, when they divorce themselves from *God*, then they breake the Covenant; but else it is not a breaking of the Covenant; Know therefore for thy comfort, when thou considerest this, summe them up together, and see now whether thou hast *put thy seale to the* truth of *God, that he is true*; that is, whether thou beleeve the promise, whether thou take & receive *Christ*: for that is to put thy seale to the truth of *God*: when thou canst conclude that thou hast done that, then see if *God* hath put his seale to thee. There is a double seale.

One is, thou art sealed by the Spirit; that is, there is a secret witnesse of the Spirit, *the sealing of the Spirit to the day of Redemption*; the hidden *Mannah*, the secret witnesse that *God* gives to every mans heart, as a privie Seale that *GOD* sets on thee, *Grieve not the Spirit, by which yee are sealed to the day of Redemption.* Now there is another seale, which is more manifest than this; as in 2 *Tim.* 2.19. *The foundation of GOD remaineth sure, and hath this seale, The Lord knoweth who are his, and let every one that calleth upon the Name of the Lord depart from iniquity.* That is, there is another seale that *GOD* sets upon you, whereby he enables you to depart from iniquity: This is a more open seale than the other. If thou finde that thou have put thy seale to *God*, to his promise, that thou findest againe that he hath sealed thee by the inward witnesse of his Spirit, and hath sealed thee likewise by the fruit of amendment of life, with enabling thee to depart from iniquity; now, what shouldest thou doe then? Make no more question, take it for granted, that *Christ* belongs to thee, and thou to him; *Trust perfectly to the grace revealed through Iesus Christ:* A place that I have often named, 2 *Pet.* 1.13 Trust perfectly in the favour; that is, in the free favour, in the free promise revealed through *Iesus Christ*; that is, Doe not mince the matter, and say, it may be *God* will forgive mee, or it may be he will not; but doe it perfectly, let nothing be wanting, doe it perfectly, that thy joy may be full; if thou doe it by halves, if thou doe it but in part, thou shalt have but imperfect joy.

Seale double 1. Secret.

Eph. 4.

2. Open.

The use now that thou shouldst make of Faith, is to see thy joy may be full: if thou be not certainly perswaded, thou dost not use thy Faith as thou oughtest. When thou hast done this once, when thou hast setled upon this conclusion, to say certainly *Christ* is mine, my sinnes are forgiven; now come to the priviledges, consider them, and goe through them all: (I have named them heretofore upon another occasion:) and labour to comfort thy selfe with them; labour to have thy heart filled with joy; at the least, get so much comfort as may overvalue any affliction in the World, that there may be a greater weight in the other Balance, that though great afflictions doe befall thee, yet thou art not drowned, thou art not swallowed up of affliction, that thy heart faints not; but set thy faith aworke that thou maiest have so much joy, as that thou mayest goe through it. And againe, get so much joy, as at least may overtoppe any prosperity outward, any comfort that thou mayest take in thy friends, or in thy wealth, or in those things that thou findest thy heart too much to cleave unto, that thou settest them at too high a rate; set thy Faith on worke, that thy joy may be full, that thou mayst not prize those so much, but that thou mayest look upon them as trifles, as matters of nothing in comparison of the joy that is prepared for thee in heaven. Thus a man should use faith; that is, in any affliction, that he doe not over-grieve; and that no outward comforts whatsoever befall him, take not up his joy too much.

Thus our faith should passe through all conditions,

ons, to use the World as if wee used it not: So, I say, set thy faith on worke. This is the first worke that Faith should doe, to comfort a mans heart.

The second use wee should make of Faith, should be to guide and direct our lives; that is, we should use Faith to be as the Rudder to the Ship, to turne our courses the right way upon all occasions in our conversation: For that is the office of Faith, to guide a mans life. For as it is in a way, so it is in our life, there are many turnings, it is not onely a strait way, but there are many turnings, and when a man comes to a place where there are two wayes to turne to, that he knowes not which way to goe, now Faith comes and teacheth thee what thou shouldest doe. That is, there are many difficult cases, wherein a man knowes not what to doe, he is amazed at them; It may be *God* will lead thee through the way of the *Philistims*, through great persecutions, and troubles, which thou must wrestle with: Now set thy faith on worke, *fight the good fight of faith*; that is, thou must now overcome, thou must not balke the way of Religion, because of the troubles thou meetest withall, but passe through the troubles, that thou mayest keepe thy way.

2. Use of faith to guide and order our lives.

Simile.

The use of faith in the severall turnings of our life.

Againe, it may be *God* will leade thee through pleasant waies, and not through the way of the *Philistims*, (as when the people came out of *Egypt*, the *Lord* led them not by the way of the *Philistims*.) If GOD give thee peace and prosperity, now set Faith on worke, that this peace and prosperity that thou hast, that it soften not, that it loosen not the sinewes of thy minde, that it dissolve not thy strength: but keepe thy faith, and hold thy strength, that thou be not drawne to sinne against GOD by such a condition. In all the turnings of a mans life, to be kept straight, a man must set his faith on worke. It may be GOD will giue thee peace for a time, take heed thou sit not downe now, and forget thy journey. As thou must not turne to the left hand, so thou must not turne to the right hand, but passe through all, that thou mayest *approve thy selfe the servant of Christ in straits, in necessity, in tribulation, by the Armour of righteousnesse on the right hand and on the left; through honour and dishonour, by ill report and good report*: That is, set Faith on worke in all the variety of conditions, to keepe thee in the right way, that thou turne not out of it. It is faith that must doe it: For example, Put the case thou commest to *Hesters* condition; there was a turning of her minde, shee had peace before, but when it comes to that, that shee must venture her life for the Church, here she had use of Faith. And so for *Abraham*, GOD bade him offer his Sonne, he was at rest a great while before, but now *God* tryes him what he will doe; here is a turning of his life, here was an exigent, here was use of his faith, hee did it, faith turned him this way; Another man would have turned another way, that hath not faith. So when GOD calls *Moses*, hee was quiet before in *Pharaohs* Court: now hee must goe to *suffer affliction with the people of God*, then what must he doe in such a case? The Text saith, he did it by faith; by faith

Instances.

he

he forsooke the glory of *Pharaohs* Court, and chose rather to suffer afflictions with the people of *God, than to enjoy the pleasure of sinne for a season.* There be many hundreds of such cases that befall continually. I say, thou shouldst use thy faith now, that it should leade thee in the right way, in all these difficult cases: for this is the use of Faith. See now another man that hath not faith, take a false-hearted man, and say what you will to him; when any such exigent comes, you shall never draw him from his wealth, from his friends, from his worldly credit, because he makes that his maine, his heart secretly trusts in that, hee thinkes if that be gone, hee is undone; that is his god, therefore you shall never draw him from that, for he wants faith to make *God* his *GOD*. Come to another man, let him come into such an exigent, and you shall not pull him from *GOD*, hee is his trust, hee is his hope, and if he loseth *GODS* favour, he loseth life and all; and therefore that is the difference in all the passages of things in their conversation. this then is the second use wee should make of Faith, to guide and direct us in our lives. But because this is generall, it may be it will not be enough: I will come a little to instances.

Instances of faith guiding a man in difficult cases.

Suppose a man come to such a turning as those in *Iohn* 22.12. *Many of the chiefe Rulers beleeved in him, but they durst not confesse him, lest they should be cast out of the Synagogue.* Put the case that thou be in such a case, as that thou art brought now to such a tryall: Now, if thy faith bee such a faith as they had, that is a signe that thou wantest faith indeed.

1. Instance. In confessing of *Christ*.

Take two men, the one will be content to bee cast out, he will confesse *Christ*, come what will of it. Another man, when it comes to such a competition, that either hee must bee cast out of the Synagogue, or deny *Christ*, hee will rather leave that than the other, he will rather part with *Christ*, hee will rather forsake him, and the confession of him, than indure such trouble.

2. Instance. Praise with men.

So againe, come to a matter of praise of men, to a matter of credit, when a man sees that this is his condition in the place hee lives in, and considers, if I serve *GOD* indeed, if I goe through in my profession, I see I must be contemned, I must be despised, I must be trampled upon; I see, I must be hated of all men, as our Saviour *Christ* saith, (for to be hated of some men, a man might beare it well enough) but to have all mens hands against him, to bee excluded of all good company; (as they say) such a thing a man shall have much adoe to beare, to lose all his worldly credit, all his friends; but when it comes to such a case, one man is willing to beare these, because he trusts in *God: I know whom I have trusted*, saith S. *Paul*: Therefore he was willing to undergoe all shame, to endure imprisonment, to doe any thing: another man doth not trust in *GOD*, and therefore he will not endure, he will leave Religion, he will not doe the things that may breed this trouble, hee will mince the matter, hee will leave that, that hee may secure himselfe, and keepe his credit that he hath amongst men.

3. Instance. In case of profit.

So againe, come to matter of commodity: Let matters of profit, or advantage in the World for a mans estate bee offered, see the different condition now of a man that hath faith, and of a man that wants faith. See *Saul*, when hee saw the fat Cattell, he tooke them, his faith was nothing but a notion: If he had beleeved in *God*, hee would not have thought that the fat Cattell would have made him more happy, but because he saw them, and thought they would be advantage to him, he saw them present, that was the thing he felt, he beleeved not the other, therefore he did that.

And so for *Balaam*; when the case comes, that either he must curse the people, or else forsake *the wages of unrighteousnesse*, surely he will have respect to the wages of unrighteousnesse: that is, though *Balaam* made a faire shew hee would doe any thing rather than goe against *GODS* Commandements, yet he had an eye to the other all the while, and *God* saw that he secretly looked to himselfe. So it may bee thou makest profession, thou makest a faire shew, thou wilt doe much. Remember this, it may be, it is but a high flying: The Eagle, though shee flye high, yet shee hath an eye to the prey below all the while: So many men, although they doe much, yet they have a secret eye to the prey; that is, they want faith, and therefore they regard these things, too much. And when the time comes, that they must stoope to it, the time of tryall, when a man wants faith to magnifie other things, hee overvalueth those things, having nothing better to trust unto. In such a case, *Iudas* his thirty pence was a greater matter: *Gehazi's* change of rayment, and *Achans* wedge of Gold. I need name no more exam-

Hee that wants faith, highly values outward things.

ples. But take a man that hath faith, & this is no difficulty to him, he will not onely let goe that wealth which he hath inordinately gotten, as *Zacheus*, but he will suffer the spoyling of his goods with joy, because *hee beleeves God, that hee hath in heaven a more induring substance.* There is no Christian, no good man, but he would be content to gaine as well as thou; what is the reason he takes it not? Hee beleeves that by forsaking that, he shall have a more induring substance in heaven. There is no man would forsake any thing but for the better, and that is the reason we beleeve, and thou dost not.

The nature of good men takes content in outward things as well as others.

4. Instance. In case of safety and danger.

And so come to matter of safety and danger, and there you shall see what difference Faith makes betweene men, how it turnes their course, when they come to such an exigent. See it in *Saul*, you know he was commanded not to offer Sacrifice till *Samuel* came, GOD did put him to the tryall, the *Philistims* were upon him, the day of Battell drew neere, hee saw the people shrinke away, *Saul* was put to it now, whether he would trust *God* for his safety or no: If *Saul* had had faith now, and had thought with himselfe, If I keepe the Commandement, is not GOD able to helpe me? what though the people shrinke away? cannot GOD doe as much with a few, as with many? If he had beleeved, hee would have done otherwise: But if he did not beleeve, and therefore you see which way he turned.

The like we see in *Ioram*, *Ier.* 42. This was his case, he was the Captaine of those that were left behinde in Captivity; if he had stayed in *Ierusalem*,

lem, he had had nothing to defend him, there was poverty and want of all things; if hee went downe into *Egypt*, that was a safe Countrey, as farre as any one could see, it lay farre from all danger of War, there was plentie of all things, and he was a strong King, able to defend him. There comes Commandement from GOD, that hee should keepe himselfe still in *Ierusalem*, and should not goe downe into *Egypt*: It is a place worth the reading, *Ier*. 42. & 43. *Ioram*, in this case, beleeved not that GOD would keep him safe where he saw no meanes of safety. Therefore, in that turning you see what choice hee made, which was his utter undoing; he went downe into *Egypt*, and there the Sword and the Famine followed him, that *God* might make him know, that it was not any outward condition that could keepe him safe, and that hee was able to keepe him safe in another place, where there seemed to be more danger.

On the other side, take those that trust in *God*, in any such case, when they are brought to any such difficulty, they are willing to venture to put themselves upon *God*, to goe any whither, as *Luther* went to *Wormes*, they care not for any danger before them.

But some will say, It is true, if I had a Prophet sent to me, to tell me in such a case that I should be safe, I should trust on him. *Object.*

Certainely, if thou hast not, yet if the cause be good, if it be a thing that *God* sets thee aworke on, if thou goe by a right rule, know, that in this case thou hast as true a promise of safety, that *God* will deale

Answ. In a good cause *God* hath promised good successe.

deale well with thee, as if thou haddest a Prophet sent immediately from *GOD*. Therefore I say to thee in such a case, as *Luther* said to *Melancthon*; which was a good reason when *Melancthon* began to faint: *Luther* being a farre off, wrote a Letter unto him, and tels him, saith he, if the Cause be not *Gods*, why doe not wee give over? why doe wee not shrinke? why doe we doe any thing? And if it be *Gods* Cause, why doe we shrinke? why goe wee not thorow? He needed no more but to know that it was *Gods* Cause: and after that, see how hee exposed himselfe from time to time: and as no man was bolder than he, so no man had more comfort. It is with us in this case as it was with *Ieremiah*, *Ierem.* 26. *God* bids him goe and speake his Word to the people, all his words, and tels him that the people would be ready to put him to death; and so they were, they said he should dye, but yet hee obeyed *GOD*, because the *Lord* sent him; and see what was the issue of it, *God* turned the matter and saved him. This is faith, when a man comes in that case to set his faith aworke, that it may set him the right way that he is to goe in, which way hee is to turne.

5. Instance. In great feares.

And so, put the case that *God* brings thee to such a case, that thou art in danger of prison, in danger of death, in danger of the greatest crosse, of the greatest persecution and trouble, now one man consults with flesh, the other consults with the spirit, he sets faith aworke to worke his worke for him: you see what *Stephen* did in such a case, and the reason of it, *Act.* 6. He was a man full of faith,

and

and therefore he feared not what they could doe to him. See what S. *Paul* did in such a case, you see what danger he was exposed unto, yet *hee consulted not with flesh and bloud*, but what did hee? He set faith on worke, that it might guide him in all the way that he went, in all the turnings of his life.

And so, on the other side, for pleasure, there are two men that have pleasures propounded, the holiest man hath the same nature that others have, they would take the same delight that others doe, as far as they are naturall. *6. Instance. In pleasures.*

What is the reason then they doe not? why doe such men turne from all sinfull delights, and runne another course? *Quest.*

It is nothing but faith that enableth them to doe it. By faith *Moses* left *Pharaohs* Court, and the pleasures of sinne for a season, and chose adversity with the people of *God*: that is as if hee should say, If you would know why *Moses* did this, it was faith that enabled him: that is, hee beleeved, that if hee had enjoyed those pleasures of sin, he should have beene a loser by them, hee should have fared the worse for them. Againe, he beleeved, that by his suffering adversity with the people of *God*, he should gaine; it was onely faith that made him doe this. If thou haddest faith, thou wouldest forsake thy pleasures, and live a more strict life, as the Saints doe. So that still you must keepe that conclusion, that you must set faith aworke in all the turnings and passages of your life, for that is it that guides you in the right way. *Answ. Why holy men forsake the pleasures of sinne.*

Againe, Take two men that have both children to *7. Instance.*

In case of provision for posterity.

to provide for, they have posterity to care for; the one man he reasons thus with himselfe; If I leave them not as good a stocke as I would, yet I shall leave them *Gods* blessing, which is able to make them prosper; and though I should leave them abundance, yet all that without *Gods* blessing, will not be able to doe it. Therefore such a man will be indifferent for matter of estate, he will leave a conveniencie for them, if he can, but he takes no great care, he had rather lay up faithfull prayers in heaven, he had rather see them *brought up in the feare of GOD*, for hee trusts *GOD*, and he thinkes that his blessing can doe it, without meanes; and hee knowes that great meanes, without *GODS* blessing, cannot doe it. But when another man is in this case, he lookes to that which is represented to his eyes: and therefore he will not have done till he have provided such a portion for such a childe, till hee have built him houses, till he have made them firme on every side, till he have added house to house; this is our want of faith, hee beleeves not: hence it is that these two runne a different course.

8. Instance. Imployment.

So againe, one man lookes to his businesse, hee will not spend time to examine his heart, hee will not spend time in prayer from day to day; he saith, my businesse will goe at sixe and sevens, my businesse will not be done: whenas another man, that hath chosen *Maries* portion, is content to lose somewhat, he is content that many things should goe amisse, he is content to lose somewhat of his estate, he is content to let his businesse lye undone, or not

to

to be so well done, because he thinkes to bee busie in good workes, in prayer, and to have the favour of GOD is greater advantage, he thinkes he hath chosen the better part. Now it is faith that workes this difference. What should I doe? Why should I name any more Instances? you may name more to your selves: as you have faith, so it will guide you, it will turne you this way and that way in the turnings and passages of your life.

Quest. But now, because I am farre in the point, (and I see the time runnes fast away) before I leave, I would not onely shew you what faith is able to do, but I would worke you to this a little.

Answ. You will say then, What is it to trust in *God?* For that is the reason of all the difference you see: Therefore, saith *Paul*, 1 *Tim*.4.10. *We labour, and suffer rebuke:* what is the reason? If you would know the cause why we lead such a life, why wee runne another course than others, why wee live a painfull life, in labour from day to day: (but if a man had good wages, he might well doe that:) we labour, and suffer, and are rebuked, and have nothing but persecution for our paines; but, saith he, we doe it *because we trust in the living God:* therefore we labour, and suffer, and are rebuked, because wee trust in the living GOD. I say, doe this, and thou shalt be able to doe the same that *Moses* did, thou shalt be able to doe the same that S. *Paul* did, the same that all the Saints have done. If I could but perswade you now to trust in *God*, to set your faith a worke thus farre; there is no man that heares mee this day, that is in any other course than in the

wayes

wayes of Religion and godlinesse, but hee would turne his course: and therefore I will labour in this a little.

Quest. You will aske me then, what it is to trust *God*?

Answ. I will shew you a little what it is, because every man is ready to say, trust in GOD, but I am not able to do this that you say, when I come to such a hard turning. Deceive not thy selfe, this is to trust in GOD, namely, to be unbottomed of thy selfe, and of every creature, and so to leane upon *God*, that if he faile thee, thou sinkest. There is many a man, that pretends hee trusts in *God*: but hee so trusts GOD, that withall he will provide for himselfe: such a man saith, GODS blessing is a good addition, but to have that for all, hee will not, hee will be sure he will bee strong, hee will make his Mountaine strong about him, and he will have the blessings of *God* too: for faith in the promises, hee makes them good notions; but for things to trust to, to rest on, it is a thing he will not be perswaded to. Now this is not to trust in GOD. But this is to trust in him, when thou dost so cast thy selfe on him, that if he should faile thee, thou wert undone by it.

To trust in *God*, what.

To exemplifie it to you: There was an action that *Alexander* the Great did, (I use it onely to expresse what I meane by trusting in GOD.) When he was sicke, there comes a friend that was alwayes close with him, that was a Physician, and hee prepared him a Potion; but before the same came to him, there was a Letter delivered to him, to signifie to him, that that very Potion was poyson:

Example of trust, in *Alexander*.

ſon: when his friend came with his Potion in his hand, he takes the Letter that was ſent to give him notice of the Treaſon, and drinkes off the Cup with one hand, and reaches the Letter with the other, ſo he dranke off the Cup before he ſhewed the Letter. Here *Alexander* truſted him; if he had failed him, he had loſt his life; hee did not firſt ſhew the Letter, and then heare his excuſe for himſelfe, but he ſhewed that he truſted him. In ſuch a caſe, if thou be able to truſt *God*, if thou canſt put thy ſelfe upon him, if he faile thee, thou art undone, in ſuch a caſe; this is to truſt in *God*.

To uſe another expreſſion, that you may know what it is.

There was a King of this Land, that ſent to his ſervant, a Generall of his Army, to ſpare a Citie: he had command under the Broad Seale, from the Counſell, and from the Kings owne hand, to doe it: and to diſobey this Warrant was death: But withall the King ſent him a ſecret meſſage that hee ſhould deſtroy the Citie, and to truſt him to ſave his life. The party did ſo: The Broad Seale and Commiſſion was to ſpare the City, to forbeare it; The ſecret charge was to deſtroy it: This hee did, and truſted the King for his life; if hee had failed him, he had beene deſtroyed. Theſe ſimilitudes ſhew what it is to truſt in *God*: If thou be brought to ſuch an exigent, if thou wilt truſt *GOD* in ſuch a caſe, as wherein if he faile thee, thou art undone; This is to truſt *God*, not to ſeeke his bleſſing ſo as to make that an addition, but to put all upon him. Therefore, that you may know that this is to truſt

in

in *God*, know, that except thou doe it thus, GOD is not ready to answer thee. Therefore commonly, he puts not forth his strength to deliver men, or to bestow upon them any great blessing, but when hee hath brought men to such an exigent. And because men will not trust in him commonly, while other props are taken away, (For we should trust in GOD in the middest of prosperity and happinesse, but because men will not doe it till then,) he strips them of all, that they may doe it; hee brings a man to such a case, that he shall have nothing else to trust unto.

Why *God* defers deliverance till extremity.

Quest. 2 Cor. 1.10 opened.

What is the reason that S. *Paul* saith, 2 *Cor.* 1.10. *Wee receive the sentence of death, that wee might learne, not to trust in our selves, but in* God *that raised the dead?*

Answ.

GOD meant to deliver him, when he saith, *he received the sentence of death*; that is, there was no help in the World, that he could see, in himselfe, or in any other creature; Now he was brought to trust in him, and then GOD answered him in his trust: so you shall find, *Zeph.* 3.12. *I will leave among you men that are humble and poore people, and they shall trust in the Name of the Lord.*

Quest.

Why did not these trust in the *Lord* while they were rich?

Answ. We trust not in *God* till other helps faile.

Our nature is so backward, and exceeding deceitfull, that we cannot till other helpes are gone. *I will leave among you a sort of poore people, and they shall trust in my Name.* (As if hee should say) When men are brought to that, that all other things are taken away, and till then they will not trust in him.

Indeed

Indeed till then it is not trusting. And therefore in 1 *Tim.* 1.5. *Shee that is a Widow, is left alone, and trusts in God.* Till she be left alone, till the other props bee taken away, a man cannot trust in *God*. Hence it is, that commonly when men are brought to the lowest, they are neerest to *God*, they have best accesse unto him; because when they are brought to such an exigent, then a man will pray best; and when he prayes best, then he speeds best, then faith is set on worke, and it workes best when it is alone, when it is stripped of all other helpes. And therefore you shall find in the Booke of *God*, when men were lowest, they had neerest accesse to *GOD*, *Asa*, when he was come against with many thousands, he trusted upon *God*, though hee went against them with halfe the number, and *God* delivered him, because he prayed and sought to *GOD*, and saw that hee was not able to doe any thing, he trusted in *GOD*. Another time when *Asa* had forgotten *God*, when he was strong, when he thought himselfe more able, when he was to deale with one that had a weaker Armie a great deale, the King of *Israel*, he was overthrowne, and shut up that hee could not stirre, because he sent to the King of *Aram* for helpe. It is *GODS* manner to deferre sending of helpe till a man be brought to the Mount, as he did with *Abraham*; he might have done it before; but, you know how he did with *Abraham*, he brought him to the last cast. And *David*, hee was brought to the very point of perishing by the hands of *Saul*, before he delivered him. And so hee did

2 Chro. 14 11.

Instances of *Gods* deferring to helpe.

with *Iacob*, *Esau* comes against him with foure hundred men, (with a full resolution to destroy him) before he would deliver him. It is *GODS* manner to doe thus. And so he did with *Iob*, and other servants of his; his fashion is to doe so: to bring men unto the very *brow of the hill*, till their feet be ready to slip, when they are even going, and then hee delights to appeare and deliver them. Therefore, in such cases, trust *God*, put all upon *God*; that is, when *GOD*, in any turning of thy life, brings thee to such an exigent, that thou seest all at the point to be lost, that thou art at the point to bee utterly undone, learne to trust in *God* in good earnest, and that shall guide thee, and turne thee the right way, when thy flesh is ready to goe another way.

Quest. What was the reason that *CHRIST*, when hee was on earth, would doe nothing except they beleeved in him?

Answ. Why God is ready to helpe, if we beleeve.

When thou hast any thing to doe, if thou beleevest in *GOD*, that will make him ready to helpe thee, because then it is an acknowledging, and an attributing to his power. If he should doe it in another case, he should lose his labour, hee should lose his glory, men would not be built up in him by that which hee did. Therefore make use of faith, set faith on worke as I said. I should come to this now, to move you to trust in *GOD* in all cases. If I could perswade this, men would turne the courses of their lives, and would trust in him: for know, if thou trust in *GOD*, hee never failes any that trusts in him, as *David* saith in *Psal.* 37. *I never*

saw

saw the righteous forsaken, &c. As if he should say, Aske all his servants, aske all men that ever have knowne him, all the men that have lived with him, that have finished their course with him, aske a servant of GOD, when he comes to dye, how GOD hath dealt with him, whether he hath failed him all his life; I am perswaded that there is not a servant of GOD but will say that he never failed him; and if he were to leave an exhortation behind him, hee would exhort others from experience of his trust; It cannot be that GOD should faile thee, if thou rest upon him. Thinkest thou that GOD can faile thee, when he saith himselfe so often, hee will never faile thee, nor those that trust in him? Will a man faile one that trusts in him? We use to say, Oh, I will not faile him, for he trusts in me; and dost thou thinke that GOD will faile thee in such a case? If *God* should faile men in such cases, there is no man that would seeke him. But that men should be encouraged to serve him, he hath promised, not only, not to faile thee, but he is abundant in truth, hee will be better than his word, he doth what he saith, and more too: If thou wouldst trust upon him in such a case, thou shouldest find that hee will answer thee.

Our trusting in *God* ingageth him to helpe us.

But thou wilt say, I see not how he will doe it, the case is such a hard and difficult case. *Object.*

Thou must know, that there are strange passages in GODS Providence, hee is able to bring things to passe, though thou know not how it should bee. See his Providence, 2 *Kings* 8. The Woman there, *Answ.* God can helpe in difficult cases.

the *Shunamite*, shee beleeved the word that the Prophet had said; that there should be seven yeares Famine, she left her Land and Countrey, this was an act of Faith, that made her doe this; See how this Woman beleeved now: shee followed the direction of the Prophet, shee did that which GOD appointed her to doe: see how GOD brought it to passe, that the servant of *Elisha*, *Gehezi*, should be there with the King, and that he should bee telling the King of *Israel* of the great acts of *Elisha*; That there should bee such a concurrence of all things, that she should come just at that time; and no other, when the man of *God* was there, yea, when he was telling of that very story, that then she should come in, and so she got her Land; or else it is likely, that the Woman, having lived away so many yeares, it is likely she had had a hard suit of it; but GODS Providence brought these things together.

So againe, looke on *Mordecai*; It is a strange case: It was concluded, that hee and all the Iewes should bee slaine: The Decree was gone out, there was nothing in the World, for ought hee saw, that could hinder it; the very night before *Hester* was to come to the King to make her request; if it had beene but a night longer, perhaps it had failed: but that there might be a concurrence of all this, it is said in *Hester 6. The King hee could not sleepe that night*, and when he could not sleepe, he might have called for another Booke than the Booke of the Chronicles; and when he had the Booke brought, he might have fallen upon another place, and not upon uponthat where *Mordecai's* act was recorded, but thatthere should be a concurrence of all this in that very time. Is not *God* the same *God?* why should not wee be ready to trust in him still? Doe wee not see the same daily? If his workes were recorded and observed in our remembrance, certainly wee should trust in *God*.

Object. But you will object, the *Lord* doth every thing by meanes, he doth not worke Wonders, he workes not Miracles now adayes: And, when I see no meanes, I hope you will not have me to expect Miracles at *Gods* hands to tempt him.

Answ. Concerning use of meanes. You must remember *Ahaz* his case: when *God* came to *Ahaz*, and told him by the Prophet *Esay*; Chapter 7. *That* Aram *and* Remaliah's *sonne, those two smoaking Fire-brands, should not have their wils*, should be disappointed, that hee would fight for him against them: Saith the Prophet to him, *Aske a signe of the Lord in the Heaven above, or in the Deepe below*. No, saith he, *Ahaz will not tempt* GOD. What is the meaning of that? That is, I will provide for my selfe, I will not trust to his Word, I will looke unto my selfe, I will provide an Army. I will not tempt *GOD*; That is, I will not goe about it without meanes, I will looke about mee; And for such a signe, as resting on that promise, If I should doe this, I should tempt *God*. *Note.*

See, here is a faire excuse: Take heed of such excuses; say not, I shall tempt *God*: and know, that though there be not Miracles, yet *God* hee workes wonders now adayes, as well as then, his hand is not ſhortned, now hee is the ſame *God,* hee is as powerfull as he was. It is true now as it was in *Davids* time, that wonderfull are thy workes. And *Chriſt* now in the time of the Goſpell, his Name is wonderfull. In *Iſa.*9. *The government is upon his ſhoulders, and his Name ſhall bee called wonderfull*; in the government of his Church he doth wonderfull things; that is, when a thing ſeemes to be never ſo ſtrong and well built, when the ſtrength of the Enemy ſeemes to be never ſo great and invincible, he is wonderfull to diſappoint them.

Though *God* worke not miracles now, yet hee workes wonders.

Againe, when the ſtrength of the Church ſeemes to be little, he can make that effectuall to doe great matters, it ſhall doe wonders: and therefore, I ſay, *GOD* is able to doe wonderfull things now.

Now thoſe very things which ſeeme wonders to men, are not Miracles, though they may bee great workes.

Wonders wrought after an ordinary manner.

That Wonder that *Eliſha* ſaid, that the next day things ſhould be ſo cheape, you ſee, that was reckoned ſo great a matter, yet it was done after an ordinary manner: There was but a falſe feare ſcattered in the Army, and it was done. Therefore hee that wrought wonders then, he can doe the ſame now.

That deliverance which the Iewes had, it was a thing that may be done now.

So thoſe wonders, thoſe great acts which *God* did when men truſted in him, they are things which he doth daily now.

Therefore to anſwer punctually, becauſe men doe deceive themſelves in that, when wee exhort

them

them to trust in *God*, they say still, we must use the meanes, I will give a threefold answer to it.

It is true, that *God* useth meanes, but they are meanes of his owne providing, and not the meanes, many times, that thou pitchest upon. For thus farre it is true, *God* doth it not but by meanes; that is, hee doth things by second causes, he doth them not by an immediate hand of his owne, though hee be able to doe it: But now what those causes are, thou knowest not. Therefore this set downe, that *God* doth it by meanes of his owne, and not by those meanes thou seest. It may be thou pitchest upon some particular meanes, and thinkest surely it must be done by this: and because thou seest no other, thou thinkest if that faile, all is spoyled: But it is not so; *God* will not doe it by these, nay, *God* is so farre from doing it by them, that his usuall course is, when men have pitched upon particular meanes, and thinke surely the businesse must bee brought to passe by this, or else all will faile; *God* many times useth not that, but a meanes which thou never thoughtest of.

Answ. 2. Consisting of three parts. 1. We must use *Gods* meanes.

We must not pitch upon particular meanes.

In such a case, it fares with us as it did with *Naaman* the *Assyrian*, when hee comes to the Prophet of *GOD*, hee thought before-hand, that the Prophet would have spoken some words, and have healed him, but he bids him goe and wash, which was a thing that he never thought of: So thou many times thinkest of these meanes, thou pre conceivest things in thine owne heart, thou thinkest thou art right, thou thinkest it must needs be done this

 way,

way, thou seest no other meanes; but, it may be, *GOD* will not doe it this way, but he will doe it a way that thou thinkest not of.

So *Ioseph*, when he was in favour with *Pharaoh* his Steward, one would thinke, that this should have beene the meanes of *Iosephs* advancement, and of bringing to passe that promise; but this was not the meanes that *God* used.

Againe, when that *Pharaoh* his chiefe Butler was delivered, one would thinke that that should have beene the meanes to have wrought his exaltation; but yet these were not, there fell a meanes that *Ioseph* thought not on; and so *GOD* doth daily.

Many times the thing that wee most trust unto, and put most confidence in, doth faile and deceive us, *God* dasheth in pieces such meanes, and useth other meanes to helpe, that never came into our hearts to thinke of. Doe wee not see it oftentimes?

Againe, that meanes which wee thinke will not doe, oftentimes doth it. Therefore say not, I trust in *God*, that he will doe it by meanes; for *God* delighteth to doe it by meanes.

Men are ready to say, Oh, if I had such a Physician, or if I had such ayre or such meanes, I should doe well enough: How dost thou know that? It may be *God* will not use that.

So, those that are in distresse; Oh, if I had such a man to comfort mee! Why thou knowest not whether that be the meanes that *God* will use or no. Therefore say not, because I see not meanes, therefore

fore I will not trust in *God*. I say, *God* will doe it by meanes, but he useth meanes of his owne providing, and not of thy seeking. This is the first answer to it.

The second answer: If thou say that *God* doth it by meanes; yet remember that it is his blessing or his curse, which makes those meanes on which thou art fixed, effectuall or in-effectuall. The greatest meanes, the fairest, the most specious, and most probable to bring things to passe; remember, that if *God* doe but say to that meanes, prosper not, (for that is the curse, when he bids a thing wither) thou shalt not doe it.

2. *Gods* blessing maketh the meanes effectuall.

Againe, if it bee weaker, if *GOD* say to such a thing, goe and doe this businesse, it shall be able to bring it to passe: this is his blessing and his curse; you should learne to have these words, not onely in your mouthes, but to know the meaning of them; and not onely so, but to come to the practice; to say with your selves, when things are faire and probable, except *God* bid this doe it, it shall not be effectuall; if he curse it, it shall wither.

Thirdly, remember this, That his blessing is dispensed, not according to thy meanes, but according to the uprightnesse of thy heart, according to thy workes. One would thinke, when hee hath riches, then he should bring it to passe: but, saith the Prophet, *Psal. 62. Riches belong to the Lord, they come neither from the North nor from the South:* And, *when riches increase, set not your heart upon them.* Saith hee, it is not riches that makes men happy;

3. *God* gives his blessing not to our meanes, but our uprightnesse.

happy; for that Objection will come in;

Object. If I had riches, I should bee able to doe this or that; they are the meanes to make a man happy, though happinesse consists not in them.

Answ. Riches make not happy.

No, (saith he) *when riches increase, set not your heart upon them.* As if hee should say, If wealth would doe you good, I would give you leave to set your hearts upon it: but it is not in wealth or riches to make a man poore or rich, but that comes of the *Lord.* But now comes in the Objection:

Object. Yea, but *God* doth it by meanes, the *Lord* doth it by riches.

Answ. God rewards not according to wealth, but works.

No, *God rewards men according to their workes, not according to their wealth.* So that, when thou trustest to the meanes, know that *God* blesseth thee according to thy workes, not according to the outward condition thou art in. Thus we should learne to doe; when we say *GOD* doth things by meanes, when thou seest the fairest meanes, yet, if thou find that thou hast not prayed, thou hast not sought to *GOD*, thou hast no secret assurance of his blessing, thinke not that such a businesse will be done.

Againe, when the meanes are low, meane, and weake, yet, if thou have sought him earnestly, if thou hast had a secret assurance of him, that hee will bee with thee, let not thy heart bee discouraged; doe in this case as *David* did, *Psal.* 31. (saith he) *I heard the speaking against of great men, they sate and conspired against mee, but I trusted in thee, I said, my times are in thy hands.* (Marke) When *David* saw the greatest meanes used against him as might

might be, They were great men set against him, and many of them, they joyned together, they tooke counsell against him, he was not discouraged, but saith, *My times are in thy hands*. If my times were in their hands, they might make mee miserable, I had reason to be discouraged at that; but my times are in thy hands: See if thou canst say this on both sides. When great men joyne for thy wealth, say not now, I shall be made a great man in the World: but say, my time is in *GODS* hand, it is not in their power to doe it.

Our times in *Gods* hands.

Againe, when great men seeke and consult against thee, say not now, I shall bee miserable, but consider thy times are in *Gods* hands, it is not in their hands to doe it.

FINIS.

OF EFFECTVALL FAITH.

The sixth Sermon.

1 Thes. 1.3.
Remembring your effectuall Faith,&c.

WEE have already answered one Objection, that *God* workes by meanes; we shewed after what manner: Well, Use. if these bee so, (before wee leave the point) take heed you deceive not your selves; you commonly say, GOD workes things by meanes: the saying is true, if thy heart bee not false: for it is true, hee workes things by meanes; but if such meanes come in competition, (as *God* hath not appointed that which is unlawfull for thee to doe) if it come in competition with that which

which GOD hath set apart, in such a case thou must let such meanes goe, else thou mayest use that meanes, but it is the meanes alone, thou shalt have no encouragement in the use of them. If thou hast meanes, encourage not thy selfe so much because of them, but because thou hast *God* for thy friend; *Let not the rich man rejoyce in his riches, nor the strong man glory in his strength,* or the wise man joy in his wisedome, *Ier.* 10. *but let him that* glorieth and *rejoyceth, rejoyce in the Lord.* If they could doe a man good, we might rejoyce in them. The *Lord* requires nothing but that which is reasonable: I dare be bold to declare it, that if the confidence in the strength of a man were able to doe him good, hee might rejoyce in it. Therefore we see in that place, hee saith, it comes of the *Lord.* As if he should say, Wee see by experience, when GOD will use them as instruments, it is otherwise, then they doe that which of themselves they cannot; they doe it no farther than GOD blesseth them, for else they hurt, and doe no good to a man. Take heed therefore thy heart be not false, and deceive not thy selfe, that thou mingle by-respects in the businesse; but use the meanes, and depend and trust in GOD for the bringing it to passe; which thou shalt know by this, if thou draw neere to *God*; for that is a tryall, *Ier.* 17. *Cursed is hee that maketh flesh his arme:* this drawes the heart from GOD; you shall find that noted in 1 *Tim.* 1.6. *The Widow that trusts in God prayeth day and night.* Therefore when thou hast the best meanes, if thou bee not slacke in prayer,

Caution in using meanes.

How to know that we trust *God* in the use of meanes.

prayer, it argues thy trust in *God*; when thou goest to *God*, and strivest with him by prayer, and seekest not to the creature, to say thy wealth, or riches, or the like, shall helpe thee. So much for the answer to the first Objection.

Object. 1. Concerning evils feared.

Another thing that wee are ready to object, is, But what if such a thing should come to passe? what if the evill that I feare should fall upon mee? what if the businesse I goe about proceed not, which is of that moment, I am undone, if it be not done?

Answ. 1. Wee thinke the evill worse than it is.

Herein the heart of a man must be quiet.

First, it may bee thou art too hasty in this kinde; many times thou thinkest in such cases, that thou art without helpe, and without hope, when it is not so: Know therefore, that a man may bee under water and rise againe, hee may sinke twice or thrice before he be drowned; thou mayest receive many foyles, many blowes, and yet not lose the victory. The best Saints have been under the cloud for a great while, but they were not destroyed, they perished not: So was *Ioseph*, so was *David*, so were all. Therefore put the case that thou fall into the particular ill, that the evill which thou fearest, fall upon thee, *cast not away thy confidence*, *God* may helpe thee, hee may come betweene the cup and the lip, as often it is seene: It is his usuall manner to appeare in the Mount, and not before: It was a Proverbe in *Israel*, *The Lord will bee seene in the Mount*; not so much because it was a common speech, but because it was commonly done, it was a thing that

GOD

GOD used to doe. Therefore be not discouraged too soone, *God* may helpe thee, as low as thou art. Suppose this doth come to passe, as a mans heart will never be at rest, till he suppose that which hee would not bee content should bee so: and hence comes disquiet in a mans heart; if it doe come, hee hath not resolution to beare the perplexity. Therefore in such a case, if thou suppose it will be so, doe as *Hester* did; resolve *If I perish, I perish*. The meaning is, if I perish, I shall not perish: when she saith, If I perish, I perish, she meanes not such a matter as we say in our common speech; but, if it will come to passe, let it come to passe: so *Hester*, If I perish, I perish: Shee know that it was a good worke that shee went about, and shee knew shee should have a reward for it. It is not such a thing to lose the life, as men thinke it is: If wee looke upon it with the eye of faith, it is no such matter. And so the three Children, they care not what should become of them; they knew not whether *God* would deliver them, or no; but if he would not, they resolved to beare it, and so should we doe.

But, you will say, A man is not able to doe this. *Object.*

If thou diddest know the reason, it would move thee: Therefore labour to worke thy heart to consider, that all these worst things that befall thee, may be good enough; and if thou have not learned before, learne now: Marke what S. *Paul* saith, *Wee are afflicted, but not overcome; persecuted, but not forsaken; cast downe, but wee perish not; ever dying, but yet behold wee live; sorry, and yet wee rejoyce.* *Answ.* There may be good in that evill we suffer.

That

That is, there is somewhat that sustaines us in the worst dangers, somwhat that keeps us from sinking: And *Paul*, he is as good as his word; what he saith there, we see by his carriage; we see in what a manner he went thorow all, all was nothing, persecution was nothing, but what he did in such a case, he had *God* stood actually by him, and said, Feare not *Paul*, I have much people there, when he sent him into *Macedonia*.

Object. But thou sayest, thou hast nothing to beare it.

Answ. Consider, whatsoever thy case be, If the thing doe so fall out, thou shouldst be ready to say, this is not so desperate, but it may be helped; it is not so heavie, but it may be borne; it is not so miserable a case, but it may be happy; and lastly, it is not so bad, but it may be good for me.

1. No case so desperate, but there is help. Good name like glasse.

First, There is no case so desperate, but it may be helped: Put the case thy name, which is so tender a thing, which is like unto glasse, which if it bee broke, cannot bee made up againe: Suppose it bee broken all in pieces in the World, *GOD* shall make it up. *Ioseph* his name could not be made up againe, and he cleared as innocent of all; but *God* cleared him. *David* now by his great sins, he brake his good name, so that now it was not an easie thing to heale *Davids* name; yet *God* did it abundantly, *and he died full of riches and honour:* It was forgotten as a thing that had never been; when hee had gotten credit with *God*, he got credit with men.

And so for poverty: It is not easie for a man to be rich, *riches have wings*. It is true, riches have wings

to

to fly to a man, if *God* bid them come, as well as they have wings to fly from a man, if *God* bid them leave him.

Againe, what if such a man bee thine enemy? There is no man that is such an enemy, but GOD can soone make him a friend, as we see in *Iacob* and *Esau*. Let the case be what it will: you know *Iobs* case, there was all extremity of misery upon him, that, if a man should looke upon him, hee would thinke it impossible to helpe him, yet you see what *God* did.

Againe, I say, it is not so heavie but it may bee borne: we see how *Paul* did beare all his afflictions, (we see it in other instances, which before wee reckoned up:) in 2 *Cor*. 11 See how he was stoned, how he was scourged, and imprisoned, the troubles that he had within him: *the care of all the Churches was upon him*, and who was afflicted, and hee did not burne? it was to him, as a fire to a man, it scorched him, and yet you shall see, that he did beare them in such a mãner, that if a man were to chuse *S. Pauls* comforts with his afflictions, hee should make a good choice to take the one with the other. *S. Paul*, in the presence of *Nero*, is not daunted, who was a wicked Tyrant. So *David*, hee was in a miserable case at *Ziglag*, he had lost his Wives, and all that he had, he had no helpe, but a few (600.) men, and yet they would have stoned him too: this was nothing to him, when *God* had settled his spirit with comfort, *he comforted himselfe in the Lord*. So in any case, if *God* keep a whole *spirit* in thee, it is no matter.

2. It is not unsupportable.

Similies. A sound spirit will beare any affliction.

Take a plaster that is sharpe, if you lay it to a sore place, it will smart and grieve it, but lay it to the whole flesh, it is nothing: So it is with afflictions, when thy soule is whole, it is like a whole shoulder; lay a heavie burthen upon a whole shoulder, and it goes away with it well enough: But if the soule and spirit be broken, it is not fit to beare a crosse. If *God* enable a man, it is another thing; then disease is nothing, imprisonment is nothing, and disgrace is nothing; when GOD enables a man to beare it, it is nothing: therefore it is not so heavie but it may be borne.

3. A Christian happy in affliction.

Againe, it is not so miserable, but thou mayest be happy in it. Why? The reason is in *Rom.* 8. Because, whatsoever it be, *it shall not separate us from the love of God in Christ: neither principalities, nor powers, nor things present, nor things to come*, neither men, nor divels: In such a case, the Divell, with all his forces set against thee, shall not bee able to make thee miserable, thou art a happy man notwithstanding, he shall not be able to hurt thee, GOD loves thee still, and loves thee tenderly, thou art deare to him at all times. Therefore whatsoever it is, it shall not separate thee from the love of GOD in *Christ*: and when he could name no more, he names in generall; saith he, neither men, nor divels, nor *any thing* shall doe it.

God loves us in affliction.

Againe, it is not so bad, (I say) but it may bee best for thee, it may doe thee good: for our nature is so rebellious, and so set upon things of this World, that except GOD should take this course, to

4. Afflictions may be good for us.

to worke a wearinesse in the World, to mortifie our lusts, if *God* should not take such courses, our nature would be ready to rebell: therefore *God* dealeth so with men. Sometimes hee afflicts thee with sicknesse, sharpe sicknesse, which is irkesome to thee; but know, that if that disease were taken from thee, thou knowest not, what thy heart would doe. Some men be afflicted with enmity of others; thou knowest not, if thou wert friends with all men, how thou shouldest be. Thou art afflicted in the World, in thy wife, in thy children, in thy neighbours, in thy name, in thy estate, and though thou thinke with thy selfe, If I were free from this, I should be happy, I should be humble, I should serve *God* the better; I say unto thee, thou knowest not what thou shouldest be: A mans minde doth not know what it would bee in another estate, onely he knowes the present. If thou hadst such and such circumstances, if thou haddest wealth, if thou hadst such crosses removed, if all things should goe well with thee, Oh then thou wouldest bee happy: but thou knowest not what thou shouldest bee. You know what the Prophet said to *Hazael*: (saith he) *Doest thou know what thou shalt be when thou art King of Aram?* Thou knowest how thou art affected now, but thou knowest not how thou shalt be then, when thou art a King, then thou wilt bee answerable to thy state and condition. So much for the second Objection.

Note.

Thirdly, it will be objected; It is true, if *God* did heare my prayers, or if he did usually heare the

Object. 3. Concerning *Gods*

prayers that the Saints make, that it were no more but seeke and have, we would trust in *GOD* in difficult cases: But I find by experience, that I pray, and he doth not answer me: and it is not my experience only, but it is the experience of others likewise; they pray, and *GOD* doth not heare their prayers; what should sustaine me therefore now?

hearing our prayers.

Answ. To this I answer; It is certaine that *GOD* alwayes heares thy prayers, there is no doubt to bee made of that; he is a *God* hearing prayers, and hath made a promise, that when they come, hee will heare them: Be assured therefore that hee heares. But now to answer thee.

Why *God* heares not sometimes.

First, there are many cases wherein *God* heares not: as first, it may be thou askest amisse.

Object. But thou wilt say, My heart is right; and therefore I hope I aske not amisse.

Answ. 1. When we aske amisse.

Yes, though thy heart be right, thou mayest aske amisse out of mistake, out of want of judgement; thou must not thinke with thy selfe, because thy affection is strong to such a thing, therefore it is lawfull for thee, and meete for thee to have it. There are many things which a little child asketh, which are not meete for him, a wise father will not second his child in all that hee affects and desires, thou must thinke that *God* will not doe it in these cases. And therefore learne in such a case when thou commest to *GOD* for outward things, or for the measure of grace, or for the present use of grace (as you shall heare hereafter) it may be he answers thee not; yet thou must acknowledge *God* to bee onely

onely wise. If we could remember that in 1 *Tim*.1. 19. *To the King only wise, be glory and immortality*: we thinke our selves wise too, wee thinke that wee have some part of wisdome; but if we did beleeve that hee were onely wise, that is, if thou diddest beleeve that none were wise but hee, thou wouldest be content to resigne thy selfe unto him, let him do with thee what hee will, although thou see no reason, yet thou wouldest bee content. Therefore when thou commest to aske at *Gods* hands, thou shouldest be ready to say thus; *LORD*, I see no reason why this should not be good, and yet I may be deceived, I may be mistaken: Therefore I will not aske it absolutely; It may be the want of it is better for me than the enjoying of it; it may bee to be crossed in it, is better for me than to have successe in it: thou art onely wise, I am not able to judge: and therefore when wee come to aske any thing of *GOD*, thus we should doe. S.*Paul*, when he comes to aske the mortification of his fleshly lusts, 2 *Cor*.12. one would thinke hee might have asked that absolutely, wee cannot see how *God* should not heare that prayer, and yet in that case S.*Paul* was mistaken, *GOD* saw it was best to suffer that lust to continue upon him, and to contend with him; thou shalt not bee free from this strong temptation; for, saith hee, by this I will humble thee, thou shalt have a better grace than thou shouldest have, if that lust were taken away: when Saint *Paul* saw that the continuance of that upon him humbled him more, that it brought more glory to

A man may aske amisse, though his intention be right.

God, that it shewed GODS power in his weaknesse, he was content, he saw that hee was deceived before: I say, in such a case a man may bee deceived, much more in outward things. You know, the Disciples, when they came to aske fire to come downe from heaven, they thought it was a zealous request; but *Christ* tels them that they were deceived, they knew not from what Spirit that request did come, If it had come from GODS Spirit, he would have heard it, but they were deceived: So, if thou wouldest have GOD heare thy prayers, know whether they come from GODS Spirit, whether thy prayers be the voyce of thine owne spirit, or of *Gods* Spirit; if it be the voyce of GODS Spirit, he heares it alwayes, because it askes according to his will; our spirits may aske that which is good, but not that which is fit at this time.

2. When we are not fitted for mercies.

Secondly, he will heare thee, but it may be, thou art not yet fit for the mercy: not because hee doth not heare thy prayer, and tender thee in that case thou art in, but thou art not yet fit. Herein *God* deales with us as the Physician deales with his Patient; The Patient earnestly desires such and such things; The Physician wants not will to give them him, but he resolves to give them as soon as he is fit: and therefore he makes him stay till he have purged him and made him fit for it, till hee be fit for such a Cordiall, for such a Medicine, that it may not hurt him: it may be *God* staies thee for this end. So the men of *Benjamin*, they were fitted when they had fasted and prayed three times; when they had

Simile.

Instances

fasted

fasted once and twice, they adventured, and prevailed not till the third time. So *God* deferres long: What if thou fast and pray, and *GOD* doe not heare thee? yet conclude with thy selfe, that thou art not yet fit. There is somewhat more that must be done. *David*, a man would thinke that hee had been fitted for the Kingdome before that time, but *God* deferred it untill *David* was humbled enough, till he was broken enough, till *God* had provided a kingdome, as he promised.

And so he did with *Ioseph*, and so with the people of *Israel*; they were kept long in bondage, they were long pressed, before they were fit to be delivered: *GOD* tendred his people then, hee had no delight in their afflictions. And so wee may see in the whole Booke of the *Iudges*, how *GOD* suffered his people to bee afflicted, to fit them for deliverance. So, thinke with thy selfe, thou art not fitted yet; and if thou wouldest goe by a rule, 1 *Pet*. 5. 6. *Humble your selves under his mighty hand, that hee may exalt you in due time.* Marke, whensoever *God* layes any affliction upon any man, his end is to humble him. And, if the worke be done, hee will performe that which he hath promised, assoone as thou art humbled, he will exalt thee: therefore that word is added, he will exalt you in due time, not when thou thinkest he will before-hand, for *God* is wise, and will doe it in due time, if he should defere it beyond the time when thou art fitted, hee should not doe it in due time, but beyond the time.

God delivers in due time.

Againe, if hee should send deliverance before

thou art fit, it were not in due time, it would come too soone: But assure thy selfe, when thy heart is humbled and weaned from the World, when thy lusts are mortified, and when thou art made spirituall and heavenly-minded by such afflictions; bee sure, *God* will not deferre one jot, hee will come in the exactnesse of time, that as it is said, *In the fulnesse of time* his Sonne came, so it is in the fulnesse of time before he will save thee, in the fittest time. Therefore I would say to thee, whosoever thou art, that suest to *GOD* for pleasure, for honour, it may be, to be releeved in thy state, for health, for life, or for comfort; I say, *God* hath made a promise, and it is impossible that hee should faile in the performance of it, as *Salomon* saith, *Prov.* 22.4. *Riches, and honour, and life shall he give*; but to whom? *to him that is humble, and that feareth the Lord.* You must put in both the conditions. Many men feare the *LORD*, which are not humbled; and some men are humbled, but they have some secret way of wickednesse, wherein they are indulgent to themselves, but they must goe both together. Let a man be holy, that he may have no way of wickednesse in himselfe, and let him be humbled, or else *GOD* may bestow wealth on thee, but if thy heart be not holy thou wilt forget *God* in it. And if he give thee health, if thy heart be not humbled, thou wilt bee ready to use it intemperately, thou knowest not thine owne heart: but be assured, when thou commest to *God*, he heares the requests that are made by his Spirit, that if thou be prepared, hee will not deny

Holinesse and humility.

deny thee; the promise is absolute, let the condition be fulfilled: for those are the words, *The reward of humility, and the feare of God, is riches, and honour, and life:* Expect not these, when there is not the precedent preparation: for it is not best for thee.

Thirdly, it may bee GOD doth it not, because there is a defect in thy prayer; hee will have thee pray more fervently, that condition is put in, *Iam.* 5. *The prayer of the righteous availeth much, if it be fervent.* Indeed *God* might bestow blessings upon us for the meere asking, if we did but *make our requests knowne*; yet he is pleased to require that condition, that our prayers be fervent, and he deferres the giving of the blessing untill we bee quickned: and therefore he deferres oft-times, to inhance, and to cause us to prize his blessings, (*lightly come, lightly gone,* as we use to say.) Things that come easily, we willingly part with, but *God* will have us prize them high: and therefore we must beg them earnestly: he holds them backe to affect our appetites, to make us contend with him in prayer; or else why did hee deferre to grant the Woman of *Canaans* request? why did he deferre, to give *Iacob* deliverance from his brother *Esau?* If hee had done it in the beginning, *Iacob* had not so wrastled, he had not done that excellent duty of prayer all night. When *Hannah* comes to aske a sonne of the *Lord*, (he hath given to many with lesse adoe, but) hee would not grant it her till her spirit was troubled, till shee prayed earnestly with contention and violence,

3. To make us pray fervently.

To prize his blessings.

lence, that *Eli* thought ſhe was drunke: No, ſaid ſhe, but *I am a woman troubled in ſpirit:* they muſt be earneſt, thoſe prayers that *GOD* will have at thy hands; and if thou bee not heard, goe and mend thy prayers, that thou mayeſt mend thy ſpeeding; quicken thy prayers, as thou laboureſt to make thy heart more righteous, that thou maiſt be fit. *The prayers of the righteous prevaile much, if they be fervent:* ſo pray more fervently.

4. When it croſſeth *Gods* providence otherwiſe.

Fourthly, it may bee *GOD* heares thee, but it croſſeth ſome other ſecret paſſage of his Providence. There are many things that *God*, the great Governour of the World, muſt bring together, and though you ſee no reaſon why hee ſhould not heare thee, yet it may be he will diſcover unto thee, that the ſumme of all things being put together, thou ſhalt ſee that it is not beſt for thee to be heard. *David* now, when he comes to aske a requeſt at *Gods* hands, that he might build him a Temple, it was a thing that he deſired, and he made no queſtion but that it was according to *Gods* will: and *Nathan* was of that opinion too, *Goe,* ſaith he, *and doe all that is in thine heart: David* did not know what belonged to that buſineſſe, becauſe no man can judge of thoſe things that *God* hath appointed to bring to paſſe, a man cannot ſee round about all the corners of *Gods* Providence, no man is able to ſee it: we ſee not the concurrence of things, how one thing ſtands with another. And therefore wee ought not to looke in ſuch caſes to be heard; as the Wiſemen, they thought it fit to have returned by the

the way they came, but *God* saw a reason to turne them another way. Therefore be not hasty in thy requests, but know, that *God* is wise, and will worke all for the best, his glory must goe in all, and one thing must be done, that his end may be brought to passe in all.

Againe, it may be *God* will grant thy request; but for the manner and the meanes by which hee will doe it, and for the time, it is in his owne power. But because these things are knowne, I will not stand to presse them further: but now I come to the last Objection.

Object. 4. About the prosperity of wicked men, and the Saints afflictions.

Last of all, you will be ready to say, It is true, I would trust in *God*, if he did alway shew mercy for my sake; If I saw the Saints alwayes bring their enterprizes to passe; If I did see it still well with them that trust in him: but I find it contrary for the most part: It is ill with them that trust in the *Lord*, and evill men prosper; and therefore what encouragement have I to trust in *GOD*, in this manner as you exhort me to doe, when I am brought to such an exigent, to such a case, that my life or my goods are in hazzard, or my name; it is not my best way so to doe: I see by experience, that those that are wise men, politicke men, and those that have the greatest meanes, they prosper, when as other men that feare *God*, doe not bring their devices to passe.

Answ.

I will answer this, and so will have done with the point.

Evill men may prosper, and

First, I answer, it is true, that ill men oftentimes doe prosper, and that good men many times doe not good men may be crossed.

not succeed; I say, we will not deny it: for we see the Scripture is plentifull, *Psal.* 37. *Feare not the man that bringeth his enterprizes to passe:* where it is supposed that they doe so. In *Ier.* 12.1. *Why doe the wicked prosper?* where the Prophet sets out in particular how they prosper; he saith, *they grow and take root, they spring and bring forth fruit.* And you know what *Salomon* saith, who was a wise man, and looked through many events that fall out under the Sunne: *Eccl.* 8.14. *I have seene this vanity,* (saith he) *that where should have beene Iustice, there hath beene wickednesse, and it hath come unto the just, as unto the wicked: I have seene the Battell hath not beene to the strong, nor bread to the wise.* And so he goes along, as you know well. He sets out in that Booke plentifully, that evil men may prosper long, & may exceedingly bring their enterprizes to passe.

Againe, on the other side, the Saints may not prosper, and that in those things which they doe according to GODS will. When *Christ* sent his Disciples over the Water, and bade them goe to the other side, yet they rowed all night, there was a great storme, that they could not doe good, so that they were in great jeopardy and danger, and yet it was his owne appointment: So, I say, thou mayest goe about a businesse, and yet finde such stormes, such contrary windes and waves, such streames running against thee, that thou mayest bee exceedingly hazzarded, though *God* himselfe set thee on worke. When S. *Paul* went to *Macedonia*, you see *God* called him from another place, and he bade

A man may find crosses in the worke that *God* sets him on.

bade him goe thither: you ſhall not find that S. *Paul* was the better uſed; nay, you ſhall find, that for the time, he ſeemed to doe least good there of any place, there were few that beleeved in *God*. And *Peter*, when he came to *Chriſt* on the water, he had a warrant for it, he did that which was a fruit of his faith, yet for all that hee ſunke, he began to ſinke, till *Chriſt* put forth his hand, and was faine to helpe him. Therefore I ſay, you may goe about *Gods* buſineſſe, and yet it may not proſper. Therefore we muſt ſet downe that concluſion, it is a great light to know that it is ſo. The Wiſeman gives the reaſon of it, *Eccl*.7.14. (Saith he) *Thou ſhalt finde great variety, thou ſhalt find ſometimes, good times: and in the day of wealth, when thou haſt it, rejoyce.*

Againe, another time afflictions will come; know that *God* hath done it for ſome purpoſe: *Hee hath made this contrary to that, that thou ſhouldeſt find nothing after him:* That is, that all the world may ſee that *his wayes* and his actions *are paſt finding out.* If *God* ſhould deale alwayes after this manner, you might know where to have him in his wayes: If he ſhould alwayes give affliction to ſinners, a man might ſay, ſurely *God* will doe this: but it is not ſo, he hath made this contrary to the other; that is, he takes different courſes with men, he hath made this contrary to that, that men ſhould not find the print of his footſteps: to ſay that GOD will certainely doe this another time. Therefore he addeth thoſe words, which doe immediately follow, that none might find out any thing after him: *I have ſeene the*

Why the Lord dealeth promiſcuouſly with good and bad in outward things.

the just perish in his justice, and I have seene a wicked man goe on long in his malice. This *GOD* hath done, that men might know to feare before him, that men might learne to cry out with S. *Paul, Oh the depth of his wisdome and understanding, and his wayes are past finding out*; that men might tremble before *GOD*, and acknowledge his wisdome. But I come now to a particular answer: for it is a point worthy the answering, it is a point that will stand us in much stead, when we meet with many such objections as mans heart will have in that case. Therefore I answer particularly and briefly.

Answ. 1. Wee must not judge by *Gods* outward proceedings.

First, though *GOD* doe so, yet remember that thou must not judge any thing, till thou see he hath finished the worke: thou wilt not judge a mans worke till he hath done it: If a man goe about to build, judge not his worke till it bee done, because thou seest not for what end many things are framed and made, wilt thou therefore say that he is an unskilfull builder? it were folly to doe so; but stay till he hath finished his worke, and then see how one part answers with another, and in what proportion. So in all the workes of *God*, if thou see it goe well with those that are ill, and those that are good are afflicted, stay till thou see *God* have finished his worke.

And therefore I say to thee in this case, as S. *James* saith; *Know yee not what end the Lord made with* Iob? So marke what end the *Lord* makes, as with *Iob*, so with all the Saints; know what is their ends. And otherwise take all the evill men, as *Iero-boam*

boam and *Saul*, and see what end the *Lord* made with them; their prosperity was as a pleasant dreame, which was soone gone; as the flower of the grasse upon the house top, which withereth: Looke to the end of things. I cannot stand on it.

Secondly, though the wicked prosper, yet their prosperity hurts them as much as affliction and adversity doth good to the godly, their prosperity slayeth them, whereas the afflictions of the other benefit them: if thou find this to be thy case, that thou prosper, and that thou seest thou goest on in sinne, thou hast no cause to rejoyce in this; or if thou seest other men prosper, thinke them not happy for this, it is out of mistake. It is the miserablest condition in the world; you know what *God* did to *Hophni* and *Phineas*, he did not afflict them, hee let them goe long, he sent them no disease, hee interrupted not their course: What was the reason? He had a purpose to destroy them.

Answ. 2. Prosperity hurts evill men.

To prosper in sin, a miserable estate.

So againe, when thou dost not succeed in thy matters, but art crossed, yet so long as that will doe thee good, what needest thou care?

But, you will object, My afflictions are great, and many, and therefore how shall I beare them?

Object.

I will instruct thee; I say, thou hast need of strong afflictions. Some Colts are so untamed, they must needs be broken: so some corruptions are so unruly, that they will not be wrought out without great afflictions.

Answ. We have need of strong and long afflictions.

Againe, thou needest many afflictions, because the corruptions of thy heart are of divers sorts, and

if

if there were but one affliction, it would not serve the turne.

Againe, thou hast need that afflictions should continue long, because sinne is very naturall, some are hidden, and long a breeding, and cannot easily be removed. Therefore what though thy afflictions be so, as it is said, *Dan.* 11.7. *They shall fall by the Sword, by the Famine, by Captivity many dayes?* These were men of understanding, holy men, yet they had great afflictions of divers sorts, Sword and famine, such as S. *Iames* speakes of, and long afflictions for many dayes. Now all this was to doe them good, to try them, *to purge them, to make them white.* So, when those afflictions are to doe thee good, and their prosperity for their hurt, let this satisfie thee.

Answ. 3. Afflictions of the godly better than the prosperity of the wicked.

Thirdly, consider, that though they doe prosper, and godly men doe not so, yet their low estate, their imprisonment, their poverty, their obscurity, the disgrace which they are under; this is better to them than the honour, and the pompe, the titles and the riches that evill men have. I can but name these things, *Psal.* 37. *A little that the righteous hath, is better than the riches of many wicked.* What is the meaning of that? That is, they have more comfort in that little, than the other have in their faire Palaces, in their great estates; thou mayest have more comfort in a little, than they have in their abundance; thou mayest have more comfort in obscurity, as S. *Paul* saith; *as not knowne*; though a man be obscure, yet if he be knowne to *God*, and to

mens

mens consciences, he is of greater eminencie than those that are in the highest place. So though thou have poore possessions in outward things, though thou be melancholike, and alwayes sorry, yet that little, that very condition is better to thee, than the outward condition is to the other.

Fourthly, in perillous times this is a great difference: for though a man have prosperity, yet certainly, a hard time will come, a time of sicknesse, and of temptation, and of death will befall us: *Psal.* 37. *In perillous times they shall be confounded:* here is the difference: and *they shall melt as fat:* that is, In such a time their hearts shall faint, and such men have nothing to sustaine them; they shall bee confounded in such a time, they shall not know what to doe.

Answ. 4. Evill men at last come to miserie.

But now you will say, What perillous time is that, when *God* will deale so with them? you will say, in those perillous times, for ought we see, the sword devoures one aswell as another; captivity, it sweepes away one aswell as another: Sicknesse, when it comes, it falls upon the just aswell as the unjust: And therefore in the perillous time, I see no difference betweene the godly and the wicked. I answer, there is difference when the same affliction falls upon both. Looke in *Ier.* 24. you shall find there, that both were carried away captives, good men and bad men, the whole Chapter is spent in it; it is but a short Chapter: See there, what difference there is in the same afflictions which fell to both: saith he, There were two Baskets, the one was full

Quest.

Answ. Difference betweene the saints and others in the same afflictions.

of good Figs, the other was full of bad, which *could not bee eaten for badnesse:* looke in the Text, you shall find that both were carried away captive, but here is the difference, they were carried both in an indifferent manner, (saith he) you shalbe carried captive aswell as the other, the good Figges in the Basket, but *I will know you, mine eyes shall bee upon you to doe you good, and I will bring you backe in due season, and I will plant you in captivity, and you shall grow; and I will build you, and you shall not be destroyed; and I will give you an heart to know me in that condition; and I will be your God, and you shall bee my people:* all this I will doe to you, although you be in the same affliction. And what will he doe to the other? They shall be carried in a basket into captivity; but saith the *Lord*, *I will make you a reproach, I will make you a curse, I will make you a common talke, I will destroy you when you come into captivity, with the sword, with famine, with pestilence, mine eyes shall bee on you for ill* in such a case. So I say, the same Besome of destruction may sweepe away both, the same sword may devoure both, the same disease may seaze upon both, there is no great difference outwardly in the same affliction; both may die, and is there no great difference in their death? both may be sicke, and is there not a great difference? In the one, his heart is made glad and light in *Gods* countenance, in his Beloved; when as the other hath nothing to hold him up: The one hath the cõsolation of the Spirit, the other wants it.

Though the same affliction befal both, yet *God* hath respect to his in it.

Againe, consider in affliction there is great difference,

2. The wicked are in

rence, as you shall find this difference betweene the condition of the Saints and others, although their outward condition seeme to bee alike; The evill man *stands in slippery places*, and his condition is uncertaine, and it is a great misery to bee uncertaine, for a mans condition to bee ready to bee blowne downe with such a wind, he knowes not how long he shall continue and stand; so they stand in slippery places. The other, those that are built on *Christ*, are like the house built on the Rocke, they are sure it shall be well with them.

slippery places.

Againe, afflictions that come to the wicked, they come suddenly. Therefore it is a thing proper to the wicked, *Pro. 1.27. Their desolation shall come suddenly, and their destruction as a whirl-wind*: Why, is it not so with the godly? do not they often perish by sudden death? doth it not fall on them ? do not sudden changes come to them as well as to the others? No: Things are sudden, not fro the suddennes, but from the want of the preparation of the person that they fall upon: therefore *God* will not send affliction upon his children till he have prepared them; he will prepare them, and then it is no matter if they come suddenly, it is no matter though he strike them suddenly before they be aware: when hee hath fitted them, it comes not suddenly, Death comes not upon them as *a snare*: that is to be taken in a snare properly, when the beast is taken in a snare by the Huntsman, or by the Fowler, who meanes their destruction; so afflictions come upon evil men as a snare, when as they are taken in an evill Net, Satan takes them there

3. Misery comes suddenly on the wicked.

In what respect things are said to be sudden.

Snare.

there to destroy them eternally.

4. Afflictions easie to the godly.

Againe, the afflictions of the godly are not so heavie to them, as the afflictions of the wicked are; *GOD* afflicts them in the branches, not in the root; they drinke of the Cup, but not of the dregs; but as for the wicked, he smites them so, as that hee smites them not the second time, that they roare for his wrath, *Psal.*31.24. The godly *though hee fall, yet shall he rise againe*, he shall not bee cast off, the *Lord* puts under his hand: That is, though the godly fall into affliction, yet he is not broken in the fall. *God* puts under his hand, he falls soft, he falls not so, as to breake his necke, to bee undone; so there is that difference. So that though *GOD* doe the same act to both, yet he doth it to the one for love, to the other he doth the same act for destruction. Like to a man that loppeth Trees, there is a certaine season in the yeare, when if he loppe his Trees, they will be the better for it, if they be lopped in due season, they are the better; loppe them at another time, and they will wither: So *God* comes to the wicked man in the unfittest time to him, *a time when they looke not for him*, a time that wicked men feare least, then hee comes just as a Theefe doth in the worst and most dangerous time of all for the owner of the house, then comes the Theefe, he picks out that time: So *God* comes upon the wicked, and afflicts them when they are in peace and prosperity: take heed that he loppe thee not at that time when thou shalt wither to destruction, when thou art not prepared. So the Scripture saith,

God meets with men in the unfittest time.

ſaith, ſudden deſtruction comes upon wicked men: So that ſuddenneſſe is, when men are not prepared. And ſo when *God* ſaith, he will free the godly from ſudden death, his meaning is, he will prepare him and fit him for death. Put all theſe together, That the wicked bring their enterpriſes to paſſe, that the godly are croſſed and afflicted, that *God* hath a ſpeciall end in this, that death, affliction, and ſickneſſe come ſuddenly upon none but wicked men, and it will give ſatisfaction to any man. I ſhould come now to preſſe the point, but the time is paſt, I cannot doe it. So much ſhall ſerve for the ſecond Uſe, for the anſwering of the Objections.

The third thing to ſet faith on worke in, is to ſanctifie you, to mortifie your luſts, to revive and ſtrengthen you, in the inward man, and to make it quicke in every good worke. This point I intended to handle at this time. Faith is exceeding effectuall to doe this. I will touch it but in one word. I will not hold you long. Set faith a worke to ſanctifie thy heart.

3. Faith muſt be improved to increaſe ſanctification.

You will aske me, how ſhall I doe it?

Queſt.

Anſw. How faith ſanctifies the heart.

Faith doth it divers wayes. I cannot goe through them: Set faith on worke to beleeve the forgiveneſſe of thy ſinnes, to beleeve the love of *God* towards thee, to beleeve the promiſes, and thou ſhalt find that theſe will ſanctifie thy heart, this act of faith will purifie thy heart. But how can that be? Becauſe this ſhall turne thy heart from thy ſins, to *God*: for there is no way to mortifie luſts, and to quicken thy heart, but by cauſing thee to delight in

 God.

The best way to mortifie lusts.

God. No man can have his heart weaned from sin, divorced from sin, which he hath beene wedded to all his life, except he find another husband, in whom he may delight more: Now the more thou beleevest that *God* is thine, the more thou beleevest that thy sins are forgiven, the more thou canst set faith on worke to doe this, the more victory thou shalt get over thy sins, that is the nature of mans disposition, that still it desires that object that is amiable and pleasant. Now if thou looke on *God* as a Iudge, that will turne thee away from him, that makes thee continue still in sin; but when thou lookest upon him as upon one that loves thee, as one that favoureth thee, as one that is thy friend, that accepts thee, that will winne thine heart, this will cause a mans heart to turne from sin, to turne from darknesse to light, it will make him to leave the wayes wherein he delighted before, it will divorce a mans heart from the sin wherein it hath taken pleasure a long time, so that it shall never get the victory over it. Therefore the best way in such a case, is to set faith on worke, to beleeve the forgivenesse of sinne; remember the promises of *God*, those promises you have heard often, that *God* will forgive thy sins, that he will pardon thee, take these promises, and apply them; see *God* ready to forgive, this will turne thy heart from sin, thou shalt find sinne die and wither in thee, and thy heart to grow and be quickned in grace: you know, that to get a loving heart, is to beleeve that *God* loves us, to beleeve that our sins are forgiven. Now I say, there

is

is nothing that weakneth ſin indeed, but to love *God*, whatſoever ſin is weakened by other meanes than by love to *God*, by turning the heart to him by repentance and mortification, that ſinne lyeth hid, though it ſeeme no way to increaſe: this increaſeth love, when we beleeve the promiſe of *God*, that he is ready to forgive; that is effectuall for this purpoſe. When *Chriſt* came to *Peter*, and ſaid unto him, *Loveſt thou me?* then, ſaith he, *feed my ſheepe.* So after this manner, when thou once beleeveſt that *GOD* loves thee, and canſt bring thy heart to love him againe; if now *Chriſt* ſhould come to thee, and ſay, *Loveſt thou mee, who loved thee, and gave my ſelfe for thee?* if thou doſt love me, diſdaine ſuch a thing which I hate, doe not ſuch things as will grieve me; *keepe my Commandements, keepe my Sabbaths:* if thou loveſt me, let not thy converſation be in wantonneſſe, *in ſtrife and envying*; if thou love me, labour to bring ſome glory to my Name, and to do ſome good to mankind; if thou love me, be diligent in thy Calling; if thou love me, honour me, doe good to others, doe good to thy ſelfe with it. Let a man goe thorow all the particulars of ſinne, and he would abſtaine from it, if he would ſet faith on worke this way, to ſanctifie his heart.

Nothing weakneth ſin but love to *God*.

Againe, faith doth it by overcomming the World; for when a man is drawne, one of theſe two things drawes him, Either ſome offer of ſome great benefit, or ſome great evill which he is put in feare of: now when he lookes, and ſeeth that *God* is able to keepe him, when men doe their worſt, and that

2. By overcomming the world.

he can give him a heavenly Kingdome : when hee lookes to the promise, he is above the World.

Againe, he not onely overcomes riches, but hee makes advantage of them ; he not only loves them as a slave, but he gets the victory over them, and he gets service from them. And so when men can make their recreations to serve their turns for better purposes, when a man not onely overcomes them, gets the victory of them, but makes them serviceable, so a man makes advantage of the World.

3. Because the more wee beleeve, the more the spirit of *God* dwelleth in us.

Againe, when thou wouldst have thy sanctification increased, increase thy faith. The more thou beleevest, the more the Spirit of *Christ* is conveyed into thy heart. The stronger thy faith is, the more the wind of grace, the sappe shall flow from *Christ* into thy heart. As old *Adams* corruption, it is with the grace of *Christ*, when thou commest neere, thou *art ingraft into the similitude of his death* ; that is, there comes a gift from him, he sends his Spirit into thy heart, that makes thee joy in him, that causeth thee to die to sin, and to live to righteousnesse. This I thought to have opened : But so much shall serve for this time, and for this Text.

FINIS.

OF LOVE

The first Sermon.

GALAT. 5.6.

For in Iesus Christ, neither circumcision availeth any thing, nor uncircumcision, but Faith which worketh by Love.

IN the fourth Verse of this chapter the Apostle affirmes, that there is no justification by the Law: for, saith hee, *If you bee justified by the Law, you are fallen from grace:* that is, you cannot be partakers of that Iustification which is by grace: because to have it by the Law, and to have it by Grace, are opposite. And he gives a reason for it, because (saith hee) *Through the Spirit we wait for the hope of that righteousnesse which is by Faith*, and not by the Law.

When

When he had expressed himselfe so farre, which is the righteousnesse received by faith, that is, that righteousnesse which is freely given by GOD, offered to us, wrought by *Christ*, but taken by faith on our parts: Thus, saith he, you must be justified. Now to confirme this, hee gives a reason in this verse that I have read: for, saith he, *In Christ Iesus*, (that is, to put a man into *Christ Iesus*, or to make him acceptable to GOD through *Christ Iesus*, to doe this) *neither circumcision availeth any thing, nor uncircumcision*: that is, neither the keeping of any part of the ceremoniall law, or the omission of it, nor the keeping of the morall law, or the breaking of it, will helpe to ingraffe a man into *Christ*, or to make him acceptable to GOD through *Christ*: What will doe it then? Nothing (saith hee) but onely faith. Now lest wee should be mistaken in this, as if he should require nothing at their hands but an empty idle faith, he addeth further, it must be such a faith as is effectuall, as is working: And that is not enough, but it must bee such a faith as *workes by love*. So that you have two parts in this Text: One is a removal or a negation of that which doth not ingraffe us into *Christ*, or that makes us not acceptable to GOD through *Christ*; it is not being circumcised or uncircumcised, or any thing of that nature. The other is the affirmative part; What is that doth it, that makes us in a glorious condition, that makes us sonnes of GOD? Saith he, it is onely faith and love, it is such a faith as is accompanied with love and good workes; so that you

Two parts in the Text.

you see he removes all workes of ours, all workes of the Ceremoniall Law, Circumcision is nothing, it is as good as if you were not circumcised, it is all one. And by the same reason that Circumcision is excluded, all other is. And not onely workes of the Ceremoniall Law, but all the workes of the Morall Law also, considered as the meanes of justification; because they are opposite to faith, they exclude faith, and faith excludes them, so as they are aswell to be shut out, as the workes of the Ceremoniall Law. None of these, saith the Apostle, will doe it. For you must know, the way to salvation is contrary to that of damnation. Looke how you lost the kingdome of *God*, so you must get it, looke what gate you went out at, by the same gate (as it were) you must come in at. What was it that lost all mankind the kingdome of heaven? You know it was not our particular breaches of the Morall Law; but it was the fall of *Adam*: and when the root was dead, you know, all the branches dyed with it. Well, what way is there then to regaine this losse? we must go in againe into Paradise by the same way that we went out, that is, by being borne of the second *Adam*, and by being made partakers of his righteousnesse: by being borne of him, or ingrafted into him. As you communicate of the sinne of the other, because you are his children, so you must partake of his righteousnesse. Againe, saith the Apostle, it is the *Lords* pleasure that you should bee saved after this manner, because hee would have it to be of grace. If you should have beene saved by any

any workes of your owne, you would have imputed it to your selves, and to your owne strength: But the *Lord* would have it to be of grace, of his free will, and therefore he would have it meerely of faith, by taking the righteousnesse of the second *Adam*, which he hath wrought for you. Againe, he would have it sure to all your seed: if it had beene by workes, it would never have been sure unto you, you could never have kept the Law so exactly. But since *Christ* hath wrought righteousnesse, and you have no more to doe but to take it, now it is sure, or else it would never have beene sure. Againe, if it had beene by workes, the flesh had had wherein to rejoyce, it might have something to boast of: But the *Lord* will have no man to rejoyce in the flesh; but *let him that rejoyceth, rejoyce in the Lord*. Now if it had beene by workes, if it had been by any inherent righteousnesse, by any ornament of grace that the *Lord* had beautified us with, we had rejoycing in our selves; but now that it is by the second *Adam*, by comming home to him, by taking him, by applying his righteousnesse: Now no flesh can rejoyce in it selfe, but now whosoever rejoyceth, rejoyceth in the *Lord*. Therefore saith the Apostle, you must know this truth, you can never be saved by doing these actions, no, nor you shall not lose salvation by omitting them, for this is not the way that the *Lord* hath appointed mankinde to be saved by: But the way by which mankinde must bee saved, is by receiving *Iesus Christ* and his righteousnesse. But you must remember, that you must take

him

him ſo as to love him. And it muſt be ſuch a love as is fruitfull in good workes, and not an empty and idle love, that is a love in ſhew only, but it muſt be a love in deed and in truth. Now in the handling of theſe words, wee will begin with the affirmative part, becauſe though the other be put firſt, yet the affirmation, you know, in order of nature, is before the negation: therefore I will begin with this, what it is that puts us into the happy eſtate of life and ſalvation, Faith. But *faith that workes by love.*

This is enough to to make this cleare to you, that theſe two great radicall vertues, Faith and Love, are the two pillars, as it were, upon which our ſalvation is built. The firſt of them we have handled at large, Faith and the efficacy of it, in the Text we handled of effectuall Faith: Now the other remaines, of Love; whence we will deliver this point to you, that,

Whoſoever loves not, whatſoever elſe he find in himſelfe; whoſoever loves not the Lord Ieſus, is not in Chriſt, and by conſequent, is in acurſed and damnable eſtate.

Doct. He that loves not, is not in Chriſt.

Becauſe this is neceſſarily required, that you have faith and love, or elſe you can have no ſalvation; or elſe you are not in *Chriſt*, and cannot be acceptable to *God* through *Chriſt*. So our buſineſſe will be to open unto you this grace of Love, that you may know what it is. And that you may know it, we muſt firſt declare unto you a little in generall what this affection of love is.

All affections, as you know, are nothing elſe but the

the divers motions and turnings of the will. As the will turnes it selfe this way or that way; so a man is said to be affected, to love or to hate, to grieve or to rejoyce. Now love is that act of the will, whereby it turnes it selfe to a thing, as hatred is that whereby it turnes it selfe from a thing: And that which is the object of this affection of love, is something that is good; for that which is true, and that which is beautifull, is not the proper object of love, that is the object of the intuitive understanding: but it is no further the object of love, than it is good. For, this take for a generall rule, we love nothing but as it is good; and a thing is said to be good, when it is sutable, proportionable, and agreeable to us, for that is the definition of a good thing. There may be many things that are excellent, that are not good to us; we say not that any thing is good, but that which sutes and is agreeable to us, and convenient for us. So that, if you take the definition of this affection of love in generall, *Love is nothing else, but a disposition of the will, whereby it cleaves or makes forwards to some good that is agreeable to it selfe:* I say, it is a disposition of the will, whereby it cleaves to, and makes forward to some good thing agreeable to it selfe. Which you must marke, for we shall have use of all this in the sequel of this tract.

Love what.

Definition of love in generall.

Now this love shewes it selfe by two effects: It would have the thing it loves to be preserved.

Two effects of love.

And secondly, a man that loves, would have it his, and therefore he drawes neare to it, or else hee drawes the thing neare to him. For I take it not to be be true, that is commonly taken for granted, that love is a desire of union. For we doe not alwayes desire that the thing should be united to us, that we love, (for a thing may be too neere us, as letters may be too neere the eye, as well as too farre off:) But we would have things in such a distance as is most agreeable to us. As wee love fire for our use, but it may be too neere us; and we love a knife for our use, but it may be too neere: So by the way, marke it, It is not alwayes a desire of union, but it is a desire to have the thing it loves, in such a distance as is most agreeable to us; but still remember this, that love shewes it selfe by these two effects: It desires the preservation of the thing: Secondly, he would that what he loves, might be his. As when a man loves an unreasonable creature, when hee loves a glasse, when he loves a horse, he preserves the glasse, hee keepes the horse strong and faire; and if he can, he would have them for his use. So a man that loves riches or honour, or that loves a good name, he preserves them, he would have them his: that is, hee would have them at his owne arbitrement, for his owne turne and service. So a man that loves his son or his friend, he desires the preservation of them, and withall he would have them his; that is, hee would have them so sure united to him, as may stand with his conveniencie. This is the nature of love. One thing more know of it, it is a commanding affection: Love and hatred are, as it were, the great Lords and Masters that divide the rest of the affections betweene them, as when a man loves, he desires,

he

Love a commanding affection.

he goes and makes forward towards the thing he loves; if he obtaine it, he rejoyceth in it; if he doe not obtaine it, yet, if there be probability, then hee hopes, if there be no probability, then he despaires; if there be any inconvenience and impediment that hinders him in his prosecution, he is angry with it, and desires to remove it: thus these affections hang on love. Againe, on the other side, as love desires the preservation of the thing in a neerenesse and union of it, so hatred desires the destruction of the thing, and the separation from it. And upon this affection likewise hang the others. When a man hates a thing, hee flies from it; if it overtakes him hee grieves; if it be likely it will overtake him, though it be not yet on him, hee feares; if hee thinke hee is strong enough to resist it, he is bold and confident. So these two affections (I say) divide the rest. Now I will adde but this further, that I may declare to you the generall nature of this affection, that is, the kindes of Love: And you shall find these kindes of Love: I will name them briefly.

Five kinds of love.

1. A love of pity.

First, there is a love of pity, as when you love a thing, you know, you desire the preservation of it; when you find any thing lye upon it that destroyes it, you pitie the thing you love, and desire to remove it: So a father pities his son when he is sicke, when he is vicious and untoward, he loves him now with a love of pitie, he desires to remove the thing that hurts him.

2. A love of concupiscence.

Secondly, there is a love of concupiscence, that is, when a man desires the thing that hee is said to love

love meerely for his uſe. As when you love an inanimate creature, or any other creature for your uſe, you are ſaid to love it with a love of concupiſcentiall deſire: and this is in common men, a ſutableneſſe betweene the object and the lower faculties.

Thirdly, there is a love of complacency, when a man is well pleaſed with the thing, that is, when the object is ſomewhat adequate to the higher faculties of the will and underſtanding; that there is ſome agreeableneſſe betweene the thing loved, and the frame of the ſoule, ſo that when he lookes on it, he is well pleaſed with it. So the maſter loves his ſcholler that is every way towardly: ſo the father loves his ſon, as one in whom he is well pleaſed. 3. A love of complacency.

Fourthly, there is a love of friendſhip that goes beyond this love of complacency, becauſe in the love of friendſhip there is a reciprocation of affections, when a man both loves and is beloved againe: So a man loves his friend, and is loved againe by his friend. 4. A love of friendſhip.

Laſtly, there is a love of dependence, when one loves one upon whom all his good depends, ſo wee are ſaid to love *GOD*, wee love him as one upon whom all our good and happineſſe, all our comfort and hope depends. Now, as you ſhall ſee after, with theſe three laſt loves, we are ſaid to love the *LORD*, we love him with the love of complacence, becauſe he is a full adequate object to the ſoule: and we love him with a love of friendſhip, becauſe there is a mutuall love, he loves us, and we love him; as the Spouſe ſaith, *My beloved is mine, and I am his.* 5. A love of dependence. Our love to *God* threefold.

Againe, we love him with a love of dependence, for we hang and relye upon him for all our happinesse and comfort. Now this love wherewith we love any object that is sutable to us, it hath degrees, and that love is stronger, as the object of that love is more adequate and full. Againe, as it is more free from mixture; for all things that wee love in this world, we know, there is some mixture of evill in them, and therefore our love is lesse.

Againe, as the thing we love is more high and supernaturall; as we hang and depend upon it more, so we love it more; all these you shall find in *GOD*. Now lay these generall principles, and wee will make use of it afterwards: Onely this observe more, before I passe from the generall description of it, That there is a naturall love that *GOD* hath placed in the heart of every man, and that love wherewith every man loves himselfe, such a love as every man hath to his children, such a love as wherewith a man loves his wealth, or any thing by nature that is good to him.

Three sorts of love.
1. Natural.

Now this naturall love hath two other loves hanging on both sides of it:

2. Sinfull.

One is a vicious and sinfull love, that carryes it the wrong way to love sinfull things.

3. Spirituall.

The second is a spirituall love, which sets limits to this naturall love, that sets bankes, as it were, to the streame of naturall affection, that suffers it not to runne over; and not so onely, but gives a higher rise to this naturall love, and pitcheth it on higher ends, it elevates naturall love, and makes it an holy love.

love. So that all naturall love is to bee subordinate to this, otherwise it is not good; for naturall love is but given us to helpe us to goe that way that spirituall love should carry us, even as the wind helpes the ship, whereas otherwise it should have beene driven with Oares: And therefore the *Lord*, to helpe up to love our selues, and to love our children, and to love those things that are sutable and convenient to us, he hath in mercy, and for an help to us, put a naturall affection into our hearts, which yet is to be guided by spirituall love, that wee are now to speake of.

Why *God* hath planted natural love in us.

So the next thing is, to shew what is this spirituall love, this love of *GOD*, this love of *Christ Iesus*.

And first we will shew how it is wrought, and withall, what it is. For you must know, that every man by nature hates *God*, by reason of that opposition and contrariety which is betweene *God* and every man by nature, for all love comes from similitude and agreeablenesse: And therefore where there are two of a contrary disposition, there must needs be hatred. Now the pure nature of *GOD* is contrary to us, and therefore every man by nature hates *GOD*. And therefore that love may bee wrought in the heart of man towards *GOD*, this sinfull nature of ours must be broken in pieces, and subdued. And againe, it must be new moulded and framed before that can ever bee fit to love *God*. Therefore if you would know how this love of *God* is wrought in us, it is done by these two things:

Why we hate *God* naturally.

Love of God wrought in us by two things.

1. Breaking our heart by the Law.

First, by breaking our nature in pieces, as it were; that is, by humiliation, and by the Law.

Againe, by moulding it anew, which is done by faith, and by the Gospell: for when wee come and propound *Christ* to men to be taken, and to bee received and loved by them, what is the answer wee have from them? Most men, either mind him not, or regard not all this invitation to come to *Christ*, but they deale with us as those that were invited to the marriage, saith the Text, they made light of it, they cared not for the invitation, it was a thing they looked not after: or againe, if they doe, yet they mind them not enough, because they doe not prize *Christ* enough. Therefore the first thing the *Lord* doth to prepare mens hearts to love him, is to send the Law to humble them, to discover to men what need they are in, to make an impression on their hearts, of that bond of damnation that they are subject unto when the Law is broken, that mens eyes may be opened to see their sins; then a man begins to looke towards *Christ*, to looke on him as the captive lookes on his Redeemer, as a condemned man lookes on him that brings him a Pardon, as a Widow that is miserable and poore, indebted and undone, lookes upon her husband that will make her rich and honourable, that will pay all her debts, I say, when a mans heart is thus humbled and broken by the Law, by sound humiliation, then he begins to looke towards *Iesus Christ*. But, I say, men doe faile, partly that they have no sense of their sinnes, or else they have a sense of their sinnes,

but

but not enough to bring them home to *Christ*; for that was the fault of the second and third ground; there was impression made in them, that they prized *Christ*, but there was not so deepe a preparation as to love *Christ* indeed, so as to preferre him above all things, so as to cleave to him, so as they will let him goe for nothing. And therefore this is required, that our natures be broken all in pieces, that is, that the humiliation be deepe enough, not a little light impression, a light hanging downe of the head, a little sense of sinne, but so farre as it may be to purpose, that he lookes to *Christ* as to the greatest good in the world, that he will rather undergoe any thing than misse of him, that he will rather part with all his pleasure, than he will goe without him. That is the first thing that must be done to prepare our hearts for this love, our hearts must bee humbled by the Law.

Now, when this is done, they must be made up againe, as I told you, they must be moulded anew, and that is done by the Gospell, and by Faith: For when the heart is thus prepared, now let the Gospel come and welcome: now a mans heart is fit to bee wrought on: Why? what doth the Gospell? The Gospel comes and tels you that the *Lord Iesus* is willing to be your Redeemer, is willing to be your *Lord*, he is content to be yours.

2. By making them up by the Gospel.

If you will take him, you shall have him and all his.

Now when a mans heart is broken, you cannot bring him better newes; Indeed till then you may goe and preach the Gospell long enough, you may propound *Christ* to men, they will not take him: But when we propound him thus to a heart prepared, thus to him that is poore in spirit, to him that hath his heart wounded in the sense of his sins and of *Gods* wrath, now I say, he is willing to come in, he is willing to take *Christ* as a Lord, as a Husband: when that is done, that *Christ* hath discovered his will to take them, and they resolve to take him, then there ariseth a holy, a constant conjugall love, wherein they are rooted and grounded. This is the love we are now to speake of. So that to prepare us to love *Christ*, we must come to looke on him, as upon that which is sutable and agreeable to us. And againe, as one that is willing to receive us: And that you must marke diligently. Therefore we will give you this definition of love out of that which hath been said: *It is an holy disposition of the heart, rising from faith, whereby wee cleave to the Lord, with a purpose of heart to serve him, and to please him in all things.*

The love of Christ what.

When these two things are joyned, that a man is humbled, and lookes on *Christ*, as one that is now fit for him: And secondly, hee is perswaded that *Christ* is willing to take him, when this is done, a man receives *Christ* by faith: and from this faith, this love issues. Whence this is specially to bee marked, and it is a matter of much moment, that to love the *Lord*, it is not onely required that you bee perswaded that hee is well affected to you, that he is willing to receive you, (for that men may have,

which

which ſay that *Chriſt* is mercifull and ready to forgive, and ſo they thinke; but yet they love him not: Therefore, I ſay, it is not onely required that you looke on *Chriſt* as upon one that is well affected and propitious to you) but alſo that you looke on him as one that is ſutable and agreeable to you, for both theſe muſt concurre to incline your hearts to love him: you muſt, I ſay, both looke on him as one that is fit for you, as a good that is agreeable to you; and alſo you muſt be perſwaded that he is willing to receive you. Now the firſt indeed is the maine. This ſecond, That *CHRIST* is willing to forgive you, and to receive you, though it be weake, it may be ſuch as is a true faith, and may beget love: when a man lookes on any other men that he loves, if he ſee ſo much excellency in them, as that hee longs after them and deſires them, though hee thinkes there be a backwardneſſe in them to love him, yet if there be ſome probability that they are likely to love him, he may come ſo farre as to embrace them in his affections, and have a deſire to them, though it be true, as that perſwaſion is ſtronger, ſo their love is more neere, for faith and love grow together: Indeed if there were an utter adverſeneſſe, if there were enmity, as it were impoſſible to remove it, then we could not love, but hate even as *Cain* and *Iudas* did. But I ſay, that is a thing you muſt eſpecially marke, that Faith doth not conſiſt in being perſwaded that *Chriſt*, or *God* through *Chriſt*, is willing to forgive you your ſinnes, or to receive you to mercy, but in this, your judgement muſt be rectified,

Two things make us love Chriſt.

Note.

rectified, that is, to know that you are to looke on *CHRIST* as one that is sutable and agreeable to you, as one to whom you have an inward inclination, as one that is fit for you. This is the maine thing, the other easily followes, to bee perswaded that he is willing to love us: therefore whereas, it may be, you have thought, that to beleeve that *GOD* is willing to forgive you your sins, is faith: I dare be bold to say, it is not full faith: you may have it, and yet not savingly beleeve, you may have it, and yet not bee true beleevers. This I make cleere by this argument: That which begets no love, is not faith. But you may be perswaded that *Christ* is willing to forgive you your sinnes, and yet not love him, as a prisoner may be perswaded that the Iudge is willing to pardon him, and yet for all this he may not love the Iudge: for love, as I told you, comes from some sutablenesse, some agreeablenesse betweene the partie that loves, and the party that is loved. Againe, you shall find this by experience: A man may be perswaded that hee is in a good estate, that he shall be saved, and that his sins are forgiuen him, and yet for all this, he may be an unregenerate man, hee may be a man that hath no life of grace in him: I say, we see oft in experience, many men applaud themselves in their good perswasion, and they die peaceably and quietly, and all is well, they thinke *GOD* hath forgiven them; and yet we find there is no love in them, nor no fruit of love. Againe, on the other side, a man that hath his heart broken with the sense of his sinnes, may hunger

Men may have a perswasion of forgivenesse, and yet not beleeve.

ger after righteousnesse and after Christ, hee may long after the *Lord* himselfe, that hee desires him more than any thing in the world; and yet there is but a weake perswasion that the *Lord* will receive him and forgive him his sinnes: I say, this man may be a true beleever; though hee be not so fully perswaded that *CHRIST* will forgive him, when the other is no true beleever, as I said to you before. As when one loves another man or woman, if hee looke on him as one that is sutable to him, if hee thinke it bee but by good probability and likelihood; I shall obtaine their love, though I have not yet a full assurance of it; I say, there may be an affection of love. And thence I confirme that which I said to you, that faith that hath beene joyned with it is true; and that faith that is disjoyned from love, it is not true. So I say, such a disposition of heart as lookes on Christ as one whom he longs after, he lookes on him as on a husband, as one whom hee is willing to match with, that he can say truely, This is the best husband for me in all the world, though yet I have not wooed him, though yet I have not a full assurance of his affection to me, as I would have; I say, this will certifie your judgement, and withall it will comfort you, that though your faith be weake, yet he belongs to you, it is a true faith. Againe, it shuts out those that have false hearts; although thou thinkest thy perswasion bee full, that *Christ* belongs to thee, yet if thy heart be not thus prepared to seeke him, and to esteeme him, thy faith is not true. I can stay no longer in the opening of

A true beleever may have but a weake perswasion of forgivenesse.

of this, so much shall serve to shew you what this love is: You see what love is in generall, and this love to the *Lord*, this love to *Christ*.

Now I come to prosecute the point, having gone thus farre in the explication of it; I say, this love is so necessary to salvation, as that he that hath it not, is in a cursed and damnable condition, he is not in *Christ*, if he doe not love, that, as the Apostle saith, *Hee that beleeves not shall be damned*, we may say as well of love, for there is a tye betweene all these, faith, repentance, and love. And therefore we find these words put promiscuously, sometimes he that beleeves not shall not be saved, sometimes hee that repents not shall not be saved, sometimes he that obeyes not, sometimes he that loves not shall not be saved: and therefore the Scripture is cleare in it, and there is good reason for it.

Reason 1. If a man loves not, there is a curse on him.

First, because if a man loves not, there is a curse, there is a woe due to him. For wheresoever there is not love, a man is an hypocrite, as our Saviour saith to the *Scribes* and *Pharisees*, *Woe bee to you Scribes and Pharisees, hypocrites*, that is, because you are hypocrites. Now wheresoever love is not, there is nothing but hypocrisie in such a mans heart. For what is hypocrisie? Hypocrisie is nothing but to doe the outward action without the inward sincerity; as we say it is counterfeit gold, when it hath the forme and colour of gold, but in the inside is base: as we say, he is a false *Hector*, when he acts the part of *Hector*, but is not so indeed: So hypocrisie is to doe the outward act without the inward sincerity.

Hypocisie, what.

Now

Now to doe them without inward ſincerity is to do them without love; for to doe a thing in love, is to doe it in ſincerity. And indeed there is no other definition of ſincerity, that is the beſt way to know it by: A man that doth much to *God*, and not out of love, all that he doth is out of hypocriſie, hee is an hypocrite, and there is a woe belongs to him. So that as we deale with counterfeit wares, wee breake them in pieces, or we ſet markes upon them, as wee doe with counterfeit pieces of gold and ſilver, wee bore holes in them, as condemned pieces; ſo the *Lord* propoſeth a woe to ſuch as love him not, for in that hypocriſie conſiſts, when a man doth much, and doth it not out of love.

Reaſ. 2. He breaks the Evangelicall Law.

Againe, he that breakes the Law, you know there is a curſe belongs to him: Now there is a double keeping of the Law, a ſtrict and exact keeping of it, and there is an evangelicall keeping of it, that is, when you deſire and endeavour to fulfill the Law in all things: and accordingly there is a double curſe, there is a curſe that followes the breach of the morall law that belongs to all mankind, till they be in *Chriſt*; there is beſides an Evangelicall curſe, that followes upon the Evangelicall breach of the Law. Now when a man loves not, hee breakes the whole Law: for as love is the keeping of the whole Law, ſo the want of Love is the breach of the whole Law; becauſe though he may doe many things of the Law, though he may keepe the Sabbath, though he may deale juſtly, though he may heare the Word, and doe many things, yet becauſe

because it is not out of love, he breakes the whole Law. When he breakes the law thus, there is a curse belongs to him, and it is the curse of the Gospell that cannot be repealed, it is more terrible than the curse of the Law. And therefore he that loves not, is in a cursed and damnable condition.

Reas. 3. He is an Adulterer.

Againe, you know, in the Law of *God*, an Adulterer ought to die. As in the law of tryall; when the woman was to drinke the cursed water, if shee were an Adulteresse, it was a curse to her, the *Lord* appointed it to be death to her. Now he that loves not the *LORD*, is an Adulterer, that is, hee is false to the *LORD* that should bee his husband. And when he loves not the *Lord*, hee doth love somewhat else: And doth it not deserve a curse to prefer pelfe before the *Lord*? That he should *love pleasures more than GOD*? That hee should *love the praise of men, more than the praise of GOD*? And this is the case of every man that loves not the *Lord*, he loves the world: and he that loves the world is an *Adulterer and an Adulteresse*, saith S. *Iames*.

Reas. 4. Because he slights *Gods* offer.

Lastly, when the *Lord* shall bee a Suitor to us, when *GOD* shall offer his owne Sonne to us in mariage, and we refuse him; when *Christ* shall come frome heaven to shew us the way to salvation, and to guide our feet into the way of peace, and wee shall either be carelesse or resist it, doe you not think the *Lord* will be filled with indignation against such a man? Will he not be angry with such a man? Is not the Sonne angry when he is not received? *Kisse the Sonne, lest he be angry*: Will he not lay *the Axe*

to

to the roote of the tree, and cut off ſuch a man,as men doe bryars and thornes, *whoſe end is damnation?* This is the caſe of all thoſe that love not, when they reject the *Lord*, and the *Lord* ſhall come to bee a Suitor to them, and they will have none of him. This is enough to cleare this to you, That whoſoever loves not, is in an evill condition, in a ſtate of damnation: he is not in *Chriſt*, he is a man without the Covenant. Wee come to make ſome uſe of this.

Uſe 1. To examine if we love *Chriſt*.

If it be of ſuch moment to love the *Lord*, then let every man looke to himſelfe, and conſider whether he have in his heart this love to the *Lord Ieſus*; for as it is with men, although you may doe them many kindneſſes, yet if it proceed not from love, they regard it not: ſo it is with the *Lord*, whatſoever you doe, though you may doe much, though you pray never ſo conſtantly, though you ſanctifie the Sabbath never ſo diligently, doe what you will, yet if you love him not, he regards it not: Neither circumcifion is any thing, nor uncircumciſion is any thing, but love. Indeed, when a man doth love him, the *Lord* beares with much; as you ſee he did with *David*, becauſe hee was one that loved him. But when you love him not, performe never ſo much, he rejects all, he heeds it not: As you ſee it was with *Amaſiah*, you know how much he did, yet it was not accepted, hee did it not with a perfect heart, that is, he did it not out of love. And therefore the *Lord* doth with us as wee doe with men, when men have falſe hearts, and we ſee they love us

not,

not, we say they doe but complement. So the *Lord Iesus* doth. This should helpe us to discover our selves, there is no way to discover hypocrisie, none so sure a signe of it, as where love is not.

And therefore learne by this to know your selves, and to judge of your condition: It may bee, when we confesse our sinnes, we have no thought of this, that we love not CHRIST, or at the least, wee have not considered what a sinne it is; but you may know what a sinne it is by the punishment of it: 1 *Cor.* 16.22. *Let him bee accursed that loves not the* Lord Iesus. You may know the greatnesse of the sinne, by the greatnesse of the punishment; for the punishment is the measure of the sinne: and (marke it) he doth not say, If you beleeve not in the *Lord Iesus*, or if you doe not obey him; but, If you love not the *Lord Iesus*: That is, if there be an omission but of this one thing, that you love not, let such a man be accursed, yea, *let him bee had in execration to the death.* Therefore consider this, how great a sinne it is, not to love the LORD. And when you consider your sinnes, and make a catalogue of them, looke on this, as that which discovers to us the vilenesse of our natures, as S. *Paul* saith of lust, *I knew not that it was sinne, but by the Law,* but when sinne began to live, he dyed: So I may say of this, it may be men take not this into consideration, this sinne, that they have not loved the LORD; and therefore learne to know it. When wee consider this, that he is accursed who loves not CHRIST, it may open a crevise of light unto us, to see what condition

condition we are in, how cursed our nature is, how hainous this sinne is, when a man sees that there is a cursed man, a man whom the *Lord* sets himselfe against, a man whom the *Lord* is an enemy to, whom he puts all the strength and power he hath to confound, when he sees there is a man whom the Gospell curseth, which is more terrible than the Law, because the curse of the Law may bee repealed, there is a remedy for that in the Gospell: But the Gospell, if that curse a man, there is no remedy: This should homble us; for the Gospell should humble us as well as the Law. And there are sinnes against the Gospell as well as against the Law, and whatsoever is sinne should humble us, yea, the sinnes against the Gospell are greater than the sins against the Law: And therefore in this sense the Gospell is fitter to humble us. Now when a man comes to consider his sinnes, it may be possibly, hee lookes to sinnes especially against the morall Law; but you must learne to doe more than that; begin to thinke, Have I received the *LORD IESUS*? Have I beleeved in *Christ*? These are great sinnes against the Gospell: and these sinnes should chiefly humble us. If you thinke I presse this too hard, consider the words of the Apostle I named, *Let him bee accursed that loves not the Lord Iesus*: Let these words be sounding in your eares, compare your hearts to them, sometimes cast your eye on the one, and sometimes on the other, and see if it bee not absolutely required to love the *LORD*. And againe, reflect on your hearts, and see if you bee in in the number of those that doe love him.

6. Tryals of love to *God.*

And take heed herein that you deceive not your selves, for it is the manner of men, when we presse the love of *Christ* upon them, they are ready to say, I hope I love the *LORD*, I hope I am not such a miscreant as not to love him; yea, but consider whether thou doe or no: it is true, thou maist deceive me or another man when thou professest love to *God*; but in this thou canst not deceive thy selfe; for a man knowes what he loves, love is a very sensible and quicke affection. When a man loves any thing, when he loves his wife, loves his friend, loves his sonne, loves his sport, his recreation, he knowes he loves it, he hath the sense of that love in himselfe. Therefore consider with thy selfe whether thou hast any such stirring affection towards the *Lord Iesus* or no; dost thou feele thy heart so possessed with him? Art thou sicke of love, as the Spouse saith in the *Canticles*, *I am sicke of Love?* That is, are you grieved when he is absent? Are you glad when you have him? when you can get into his presence? For there is a kind of painfulnesse in love: and all painfulnesse is of a quick sense. When it is said, the Church was sicke of love, sicknesse is painfull: And therefore when you want the *Lord*, when there is a distance betweene him and you, when he doth not looke on you as hee was wont, there will be painfulnesse in it, and griefe.

1. Triall of love by the affections.

1. By griefe

2. By joy.

Again, there will be much joy and gladnesse when you have him. Therefore, let it be one way to examine your selves, if you feele such a love towards him or no.

him

Besides that, let me aske thee if thou walke with the *Lord*, if thou converse with him, if thou be perfect in his presence, if thou doe as *Enoch* did, walke with the *Lord* from day to day; as it is an argument of an evill man, that he walkes not with the *LORD*, that he *restraines prayer from the Almighty*, that is, that he doth not converse with him: So is it a great argument of love, to desire *GODS* company, to desire to be with him, to walke with *GOD* (to use that phrase.) You will say, What is that to walke with him? To walke with him is to observe the *LORDS* dealing with you, and to observe your carriage and dealing to him againe, that there may be continuall commerce and intercourse every day, that continually every houre, every moment, you would consider and thinke what the *LORD* doth to you, what his carriage is to you, what passages of his providence concerne you. Againe, consider what you doe to him, what carriage there is betweene you: I say, this conversing is an argument of love. Shall a wife professe love to her husband, and never come where hee is, never bee within doores, and never be in his company? So, will you say you love *Christ*, and not be frequent in prayer, or neglect and slight that duty, seldome converse with him, and seldome speake of him? When you love your friend, you are with him as much as you can, you love to speake with him, and to speake of him: So it is with the *Lord*, if you love him, certainly you will love his company, you will love his presence.

2. Triall, by walking with the *Lord*.

To walke with *God*, what.

3. Tryall, by the diligence of Love.

Besides, if you love the *Lord*, you know, love is a diligent thing: and therefore it is called diligent love, 1 *Thes*. 1. 4. *Effectuall faith, and diligent love*: that is, when a man loves a thing, hee is diligent to obtaine it, he spares no labour, no cost, he cares not what he doth so he may get it; much labour seemes little to him, many yeares seeme a few dayes, he cares not what he doth, so hee obtaine it, he is diligent and laborious. Doe you take this paines to draw neere to GOD, to get grace, to excell in it? Are you willing to put your selves to it, to deny your selves in your ease, to take some time from other businesses, and to bestow it this way? are you content to put your selves to a harder taske, to forbeare things that are pleasant according to the flesh, to take paines for the *Lord*? If you love GOD, it will make you diligent. A man will take paines to get the thing he loves.

4. Tryall, desire of present enjoyment of the thing beloved.

Besides, love is an affection that would enjoy presently the thing it loves, it cannot endure deferring. And therefore when a man professeth hee loves the *Lord*, and yet will deferre to come in, saying, I will serve the *Lord* perfectly, but not yet, not till my youth bee a little more over, not till things be thus and thus with me, then I will; it is certaine thou lovest him not: for it is true of every affection, that which is a true and right affection, that which is an hearty affection, it is present. If a man desire any thing, he would have it presently, hope would bee presently satisfied: and therefore *hope deferred is griefe*, and love deferred is a great griefe:

griefe: So that if you find a disposition to put it off in your selves, I will doe it, but not yet, certainly you love not the *Lord*. It may be if you were sure to die within a week or a moneth, what men would you be? how perfectly would you walke with *God*? how would you have your hearts weaned from the world more than they be? Well, if you love the *Lord*, you will doe as much presently, though much of your life remaine; for love is a present affection, it cannot endure deferring, but it would have full communion, and that speedily and presently: so is it with that affection where you find it.

Againe, if you examine your selves further, if you have this love in you, you may know it by this, Love is a thing that is well pleased with it selfe; as we say, *Love desires no wages*, that is, it carries meat in the mouth of it, it is wages enough to it selfe, it hath sweetnesse enough in it selfe, it desires no addition: So it is when a man loves, Love paies it selfe, I say, it is its owne wages. And therefore if you love the *LORD*, you shall know it by this; you serve him, and serve him with all your might, with all your strength, though he should give you no wages. *Iacob*, as you know, served for *Rachel*; the very having her was wages enough: So if you love the *LORD*, the very enjoying of the *LORD*, the very having communion with the *LORD*, the very having the assurance of his favour, that you might say, *My Beloved is mine, and I am my beloveds*: this is wages enough to a man that loves indeed;

5. Tryal of love; it is its owne wages.

deed; to ſuch a man, though there were not heaven to follow, though there were not a preſent reward, nor a future, yet he would love the *LORD*; and if he love him, there will bee a delight to ſerve him: and enough to him is the *LORDS* fauour, as *Chriſt* ſaith, *It is my meat and drinke to doe my Fathers will:* that is, though there were no other meat and drink, though there were no wages, yet this was as pleaſant to him as eating and drinking. Aske thine owne breaſt, whether in any thing thou loveſt, if the very enjoying of that, though there were no other wages ſuperadded, if that were not motive enough, if it were not comfort enough, and wages enough to cauſe you to doe it.

6. Triall of love by its conſtraining to pleaſe *God*.

But beſides all this, to name one more, If you love the *Lord*, it will make you, it will conſtraine you to pleaſe him, it will put ſuch neceſſity upon you to obey him in all things, to doe what hee requires, whatſoever is for his advantage, that you cannot chooſe but doe it; as the Apoſtle ſaith, 2 *Cor.* 5, *The love of Chriſt conſtraines us:* What is the meaning of that? That is, I cannot chooſe but doe it, it makes a man doe it where he will or no; it is like fire in his breaſt, he cares for no ſhame, it makes him goe thorow thick and thin: the love of *Chriſt* conſtraines us. It is true, I confeſſe I may loſe my reputation, you may reckon mee a mad man, ſome men doe thinke mee ſo; but that is all one, I muſt doe it, the love of *CHRIST* conſtraines me. So that where love is, it is ſuch a ſtrong impulſive in the heart, it carries one on to ſerve and

pleaſe

pleaſe the *Lord* in all things, that he cannot chooſe but doe it. As a man that is carried in a ſtrong ſtreame, or as one that is carried in a crowd, or as one that is carried in the hands of a ſtrong man, ſo a man is carried with this affection, that hee cannot chooſe.

Object. You will ſay, This is ſtrange, that love ſhould compell, it doth nothing leſſe.

Anſw. How love is ſaid to conſtraine. It is true, you muſt know, when the Apoſtle ſaith, *The love of Chriſt conſtraines mee*, it is a *Metonymie* from the effect, that is, love makes me doe it in that manner as a man that is compelled, that is the meaning of it. So it hath the ſame effect that compulſion hath, though there bee nothing more different from compulſion than love. And therefore know that of love, that it is ſuch a change as drawes one to ſerve the *Lord* out of an inward attractive. Thence I take that note of love, ſuch a thing as puts it on, ſuch a thing as riſeth from an inward inclination of the mind; from an inward principle, ſo that there is no other ſpurre, no other attractive, but the amiableneſſe of the object.

Now when a man ſhall find this in himſelfe, that he hath all theſe, hee findes that hee hath ſuch a ſenſible love, that he knowes hee loves the *Lord Ieſus*: Againe, he finds an earneſt deſire to bee in company with him, to walke with the *Lord* from day to day: Againe, he is exceeding laborious and diligent to get this love, to get this aſſurance of favour, and to excell in that grace, without which he knowes he cannot pleaſe him: Againe, when the affection is present, you would have communion with the *Lord*, and you would not have it deferred: Againe, when a man shall be well pleased with that he doth, it is enough that he hath the *LORD* himselfe, though there were no other wages: And when he finds such a strong impulsive in him, in his owne heart, that carries him on to serve the *Lord*, that hee cannot choose but doe it; when you love the *Lord*: And if you love the *Lord*, you are in *Christ*.

But if these things be not in you, you doe not love him: and then, what is your condition: You know what the Apostle saith, *Hee that loves not, let him bee accursed, let him be had in execration to the death.* I should prosecute it further, and shew the reasons why we should love the *Lord*, as there is great reason: But that I must deferre till the afternoone.

* * *

FINIS.

OF LOVE

The second Sermon.

GALAT. 5.6.

For in Iesus Christ, neither circumcision availeth any thing, nor uncircumcision, but Faith which worketh by Love.

THE last tryall of our love to *Christ* was its constraining vertue. Love will constraine you to serve him, you cannot choose but doe it, it so constraines a man, as the weight of a stone compelleth it to goe to the center, as the lightnesse of the fire compels it to ascend up: for such a thing is love, a strong inclination of the heart, when the soule puts it selfe on any thing from an inward principle, from a bottome of its owne, when it is carried on with no other motive but the amiablenesse of the object. *Simile.*

Now to conclude this, we must beseech you to

An exhortation to search if we love *Christ.*

consider your owne condition, and examine your selves by these rules, that you may be able to say as S. *Peter* said, *Lord thou knowest I love thee* : that is, to have such an assurance, that your hearts may bee well affected towards *Christ Iesus*, that you may love him, that you may be able to say to *God*, who knowes our hearts, searcheth our reines; that knowes all the windings and turnings of our soules, *LORD* thou knowest that I love thee. Since it is a matter of such moment, we should be carefull to examine, if we find that we have not yet this love: for we must know, that all that we have, all that we doe, it will nothing availe us, but *faith which worketh by love.* And if you object, why doe ye preach damnation to us? doe you tell us we are in an evill condition for want of this love? I answer, It is profitable for you, while you are in such a condition, to have it preached, it is good for you to speake this damnation to your selves, that while yet there is hope, you may seeke to be healed, that you may be translated into another condition, that you may not perish in the evill day; when there shall be neither hope nor helpe for you. For you must know, that when wee deliver you these signes of examining your selves, our end is not to grieve you, this doctrine tends not to destruction, but to discover to you your owne hearts, that you may know your owne condition, that if you want it, you may seeke after it. If therefore you find a want of this love, that we will doe next, shall bee to shew you what reason you have to love the *Lord Iesus* : for there is no

Quest.

Answ. It is profitable to preach damnation to men out of *Christ.*

no better way to get it in you, than to describe him to you, to shew you what cause there is of loving him: if we were able to present him to you as he is, wee should effect this thing, but that must be the work of the holy Ghost; notwithstanding we will briefly open to you such reasons as wee find used in the Scriptures. 7. Motives to love *Christ*.

And first, let this move you to love him, that he is worthy to be beloved, as *David* speakes, *Psal.* 18. 3. *The Lord is worthy to be praysed:* so we may say, the *Lord* is worthy to be loved: for what is it that makes any thing worthy of love? it is the excellency that we find there. Now in the *Lord* there is all kind of excellency: whatsoever there is that is amiable under the Sunne, all that you shall find in him more abundantly: If ever you see any thing in any creature, any thing amiable in man, if ever you saw any beauty, any vertue, any excellencie, all these must be more abundant in him that made these creatures. And therefore if you have a love, as there is no man without some love or other, some creature seemes beautifull to you, thinke with your selves, this is more in the *Lord*. If ever you see excellencie in any man, if ever you see any noblenesse, any holinesse, any excellencie of disposition, know that it is more abundantly in the *Lord Iesus*: Let these Rivers lead you to that Ocean, to that abundance of excellencie that is in the *Lord*. And if you love any creature, let it be with a little love, let your affection be proportionable to the object, as it exceeds in the *Lord*, so let your love exceed towards him,

He is worthy of our love.

All excellencie in *God*.

him, to *love him with all your soule, and all your strength.* And know this, that hee hath not onely that in an omnipotent manner, that is but sprinkled among the creatures, (they have but a sparke, but a drop of it;) but also there is this in the *LORD*, that there is nothing in him but that which is amiable. Every creature hath some imperfection in it, there is somewhat in it may cause aversation in you, there is no man but hath some weaknesse, but hath some infirmitie, there is no creature but it hath some want, some defect in it: but in the *Lord* there is no want, there is nothing to put you off; but as the Church saith, *Can.5. Hee is wholly delectable:* that is, there is nothing in him but that which is amiable. It would be a very profitable thing for us in this case often to thinke on the *Lord Iesus*, to present him to our selves in our thoughts, as the Spouse doth, *Cant.5.* she considers her *Welbeloved is the fairest of ten thousand:* so we should behold the person of our husband. You know it is but a harlotry love to consider what we have by our Husband, to consider what riches he brings, what honour, and not often to contemplate upon his person, and upon his vertue and excellencie: wee should learne to doe this with the *Lord*, that wee may love him. Therefore that we may helpe you a little in this contemplation, we will shew you how the *Lord* hath described himselfe: *Exod.34.6.* when the *LORD* describes himselfe to *Moses*; thus he declares his own name, *The Lord Iehovah, strong, mercifull, gracious, long-suffering, abundant in kindnesse and in truth, reserving*

Imperfection in every creature.

Exod.34.6 opened.

ving mercies for thousands, forgiving iniquity, transgression and sinne, &c. We will a little open to you this description that the *Lord* gives us of himselfe, that so you may learne to know what he is; for the way to love the *Lord*, is to know him: and indeed therefore we love him not, because wee know him not: there is no other reason, why in heaven, when we shall come to be present with him, we shall love him so abundantly, but because we shall know him *face to face*; that is the reason the Angels and the Saints love most: And of every man amongst the Saints, he that knowes most, loves most. Therefore it should be your labour to know the *Lord*. But to open, as I say, this description unto you.

Why we love not the Lord.

The excellencies of *God* in Exod. 34.

First, he is *Iehovah*, that is, he is a constant friend to whomsoever he is a friend, he is alway the same; for that is another name, by which the *Lord* describes himselfe to *Moses*, when hee sends him to Egypt, *I am that I am*, saith he, and *say, I am hath sent me:* I take this word, that it comes from the same root, *Iehovah* is described by that *I am*, and by that it is best understood, when the *Lord* calls himselfe *I am:* whereas every man may say, I was, and I shall be, this every creature may say; but the *Lord* saith, *I am:* that is, whatsoever the *Lord* was from eternity, the same he is to eternitie, there is no change in him: And that is a great excellency in him that may move us exceedingly to love him. You know when we meet with a friend that is constant, that hath no alteration in him, that is a sure friend, have him once and have him for ever, it sets an

IEHOVAH.

I AM.

an higher price on him. When wee can consider what the *Lord* is, that he hath dealt thus and thus with us, that he hath loved us; and when wee consider hee is constant in it, that hee embraceth them with *the sure mercies of David*, as they are called, that is, *his compassions faile not*, but when he hath once begun to love, he loves for ever; it is not so with men, if they love us at one time, they forget us againe, as the Butler forgot *Ioseph*; when they are in prosperity they forget us, but the *Lord* knows us in all our conditions; *thou hast knowne my soule in adversity*. When we are in a strait, friends oft-times are backward to helpe us, but the *Lord* in such an exigent, he is the same; he appeares in the Mount when there is no helpe in man; marke then his constancy, that hee is alway the same to us, that his mercies are sure, for they are called *the sure mercies of David*. He shewed mercies to *Saul* too, but they were another kind of mercies; *Saul* was not one he had chosen to himself, and therfore his mercies continued not, for indeed he never loved *Saul* with that unchangeable love: But when he loves a man as he loved *David*, his mercies are sure as they were to *David*. *David* was ready to step aside often as well as *Saul*; he let *Saul* goe, but hee carried *David* along: they were sure mercies, and such hee shewes to all those that he hath begun to love. That is the first, *I am*, or *Iehovah*.

God a constant friend.

Secondly, he *is strong*; *Iehovah, strong, mercifull and gracious, &c.* that is, *Almightie*. What is the meaning of that, that he is Almighty? The meaning

2. Almighty.

ning of it is this, that the *Lord* hath all the excellencies; those which wee call graces and vertues, and qualities in men, all these abound in the *LORD*; for what serves any vertue for, or any qualities that you have, but to enable you to doe something? If a man hath any science or art, that is but to enable him to doe that which without it he cannot doe: if a man hath the art of Arithmeticke, hee is able to number, or if he hath the art of Logicke, he is able to dispute: come to all morall vertues, What is temperance, but that which enableth us to doe such and such things upon such and such occasions? What is patience, but that which enableth us to endure afflictions? So all that is excellent in man, all those amiable, those beautifull qualities wherewith the soule is adorned, are but so farre good as they enable a man to doe this or that. Now when the *Lord* is said to be almighty, the meaning is, he hath all excellencie in him, and he hath it in the *highest* degree, for in this sense *GOD* is able to doe more than any man, in regard of excellency; whatsoever a man is able to doe, you know how infinitely the *Lord* hath it beyond him, he is able to doe so much more, as he is beyond any man; For that power, that attribute, that qualitie that is in man, it is not a quality in him, he hath it beyond any man. Againe, when a man is able to doe one thing, yet hee is not able to doe another; one creature is able to do this, another that: But the *Lord* is Almighty, therefore he is able to doe all things. And therefore this is a kind of excellency: that is the second description,

Almighty, what.

The creature can do but some things.

on, hee is *Iehovah,* and hee is Almightie.

Object. But now when you heare that the *Lord* is thus constant, and thus exceeding in excellency, a man will be ready to say, what is this to me? I am a sinfull man, there is nothing in me but that which may turne away the *Lord* from me, and cause him to abhorre me.

Answ. 3. Mercifull.

Well, saith he, to comfort you, know that I am *mercifull,* exceeding pittifull, exceeding ready to forgive; though your sinnes bee exceeding many, though they be exceeding great, yet the *Lord* he is merciful, he is ready to passe by all your infirmities. And that is another of his excellencies. You know wee reckon it a very amiable thing in a man when we see him pitifull. This doth more abound in the *Lord,* than in any creature, there is no man in the world so ready to forgive as GOD. If he were not *God,* if he were as man, my brethren, could he beare with us as he doth? Let us doe to a man injuries and injuries, againe and againe, and never give over, what man can beare it? doth he not in the end withdraw himselfe, and will no more bee reconciled? But it is not so with the *Lord,* when we have done all, *Yet returne to me saith the Lord, Ier.* 3.2. Well, but if we have such sins in us, suppose the *Lord* bee mercifull and ready to forgive, but yet there is no goodnesse in us, wee have nothing in us why hee should regard us, and why he should looke after us:

None so ready to forgive as *God.*

4. Gracious.

To that it is answered, the LORD is *gracious,* that is, though there be no worth found in you, yet he is ready to doe you good: as grace you know is pro-

per

per to a Prince or a great man, that is said to be gracious to his subject, or to one that is very inferiour; because he can doe nothing to deserve it, it is called grace. For grace, you know, is nothing but freenesse, and to bee gracious is to doe things freely, when there is no motive, no wages, when there is nothing to winne him, but of free grace he doth it. So the *Lord* doth what he doth of his free grace, *hee hath mercy on whom he will have mercy*, that is, when all men did stand before him alike, though there were nothing, when there was no cause why the *Lord* should regard one more than another, yet *Hee will have mercy on whom he will have mercy*, that is, he is gracious, though there be nothing in us to winne that love at his hands. Well, but yet we may be ready to object, It is true, the *Lord* hath beene thus to me, he hath beene very mercifull to forgive me my sinnes, he hath been very gracious to me to shew me favour when I never deserved it, but after I was put into such a condition, I provoked him to anger by relapsing into sin again and againe; after I have been in a good estate, I have broken the covenant with him, I continued not in that good estate that out of his mercy he hath put me into. To be gracious, what.

To this he answers, *Hee is long-suffering*, that is, though you provoke him out of measure, though you have done it againe and againe, hee continues patient, you cannot weary him out, but *his mercie endures for ever:* you know that if there were an end of his mercy, that, on your sinning, he should give over to be mercifull, his mercy did not endure 5. Long-suffering.

for

for ever; therefore it is ſaid, *Hee is long-ſuffering*, becauſe though your ſinnes be often repeated, yet the *Lord* as often repeates his mercy, therefore there is a multitude of mercies in him, as there is a multitude of ſinnes in you, there is a ſpring of mercy in him, that is renewed every day, hee opens a ſpring for *Iudah, and Ieruſalem to waſh in*: it is not a *ciſterne* but a *ſpring*, that is renewed as much as your ſinnes, that as you are defiled daily, ſo the *Lords* mercy is renewed to waſh away thoſe ſinnes; he is long-ſuffering. But beſides all this, hee goes yet one ſtep further; he is *abundant in kindneſſe and in truth*: that is, if you would know the *Lord* yet further, whereas you may thinke *Hee is a terrible God*, becauſe of his great Majeſtie, and power, and therefore that thoſe diſhearten you, as whereſoever you find terribleneſſe, that (you know) puts off, it is contrary to love: and therefore the *Lord*, to win us the more, tels us; that though he bee ſo great a *God* as he is, yet he is *abundant in kindneſſe*, that is, *Hee is exceeding ready to beare with us*, that looke what you find in a kind Husband, in a kind Father, or in a kind friend, that you ſhall find in the *Lord*, he is exceeding kind to you, he is not harſh, hee is not ſtiffe, he is not ready to obſerve all that you doe amiſſe: if you will aske any thing at his hands, if you want it, (as therein kindneſſe doth conſiſt) hee is ready to doe it, whatſoever it is, hee is a *God hearing prayer*, he ſaith, whatſoever you aske at his hands, he will doe it, can you have a greater kindneſſe than this? If kindneſſe be an attractive to win love,

6. Abundant in kindneſſe.

Kindneſſe wherein it conſiſteth.

love, he is kind, and he is abundant in it. If you will not beleeve this assertion, this affirmation, this description of himselfe, he tels you hee hath promised, and hee will be as good as his word, hee is *abundant in truth*, that is, as if he should say; I am not onely of such a nature and disposition as I have described my selfe to be, but besides this, I am engaged to you, you have many promises I have made you, I have sworne I will doe thus and thus: Therefore I will adde this to this disposition, *I am abundant in truth*, that is, you shall find me as good as my word; and not so only, but I will be better than my word: *I am abundant in truth*, that is, his performances exceed, they runne over, whatsoever he hath said, he will surely doe it. Consider this, consider how many precious promises you have, consider what the *Lord* hath said hee will doe for you, how full the Scripture is of promises every where; remember this, the *Lord* is abundant in truth, he will doe them and overdoe them, hee will fulfill every word that he hath said. And that hee may give you a proofe of it, he addes, that *Hee reserves mercie for thousands*, that shewes he is abundant in kindnesse and in truth: as if hee should say, when any of you doe mee service, when you are faithfull as *Abraham* my servant was, I am bound no more but to reward your selves; but I am abundant in mercy and forgivenesse, reserving mercy for thousands: The *LORD* cannot content himselfe to doe good to a mans owne person, but to his children, to his generation. As *David* when hee

7. Abundant in truth.

8. Reserving mercy for thousands.

loved *Barzillai* and *Ionathan*, it extended to their posterity, when his love was abundant: so the *Lord* reserves mercy for thousands.

Lastly, because the objection still comes in, when you have such a description of the *Lord*. I, but my sins are still repeated; he addes in the conclusion, he is a *GOD* still *forgiving iniquity, transgression and sinne*. Why are those three words put in? That you may know that he forgives sinnes of all sorts; for every man is ready to find some peculiarity in his sinnes, he thinkes such and such sinnes cannot be forgiven, sinnes that I have committed thus and thus: Nay, saith the *LORD*, what sinnes soever they are, of what nature soever, he forgives iniquity, he forgives naturall corruption, hee forgives lesse infirmities, hee forgives greater rebellions; and he is still doing it, for so the word signifieth, he is still and still forgiving iniquitie, transgression and sinne. So wee have shewed you what the *LORD* is, that you may learne to know him: therefore we will conclude this first, and say to you as the Spouse saith, *Cant*. 5. Such a one is the *Lord*, and *such a one is our welbeloved, oh you daughters of Ierusalem*, that is, *he is wholly delectable*, if we were able to shew him to you, it must be your labour to consider him, that you may learne to know him, and to love him.

9. Forgiving iniquity, transgression and sin.

Secondly, when you know this and consider what the *Lord* is, and what excellency is in him, consider in the next place the greatnesse of the *Lord*, and know that this great *God* is a suiter to you for

2 *Motive*. His greatnesse.

your love, that is, he that makes towards you. If a great King, or if your potent neighbour should sue to you for love, would not that move you? You know the weaker should seeke to the stronger, men of meaner condition should seeke to him of higher place; when the great *God* beseecheth us to be reconciled to him, when hee desires to bee at peace with us, and to be friends with us, I say, the greatnesse of *God* is a great argument to move us to love him: as you have that *Deut.* 10.17. When the *Lord* reasons there with the people to perswade them to love him, saith he, *I am the God of gods, the Lord of lords, mighty and terrible*: as if he should say, This great GOD hath done all this for thee; and this he requires at thy hands, that thou shouldest love him: when he shall desire but this, refuse it not. If one that we contemne, one that is beneath us, should seeke our love, we are not so ready to returne love againe; for we say he is below. But when we consider *God* in his Majestie and greatnesse, that hee should seek to be reconciled to us, that should move us, that should win our hearts to him.

Besides, consider what the *Lord* might have required of you; you know you are his creatures, you know what a distance there is betweene the *Lord* and you; if he had put you on a harder taske, you ought to have done it. if he had said to us, you shall offer your children to me in sacrifice, you shall give your owne bodies to be burned, you shall bee my slaves, who could have said any thing to that? for he is the *Lord*, the great GOD, our Soveraigne

2. Motive. The easiest conditions he requires of us.

 Creatour:

Creatour: But now when the *Lord* comes and askes no more at our hands but this, you ſhall love mee, will you deny it him? This is effectually urged in the ſame Chapter, *Deut.*10.14. where *Moſes* (marke the manner of urging it) had deſcribed to them what the *Lord* had done for them, that he had *brought them into that good land, &c. And now,* ſaith he, *What doth the Lord require of thee for all this, but onely this, that thou love the Lord thy God?* As if he ſhould ſay, the *Lord* might aske much more at thy hands; if he had, thou hadſt no reaſon to deny it: but all that hee requires is that thou love him: and wilt thou deny this unto him?

4.Motive. God bath planted love in us for this end.

Beſides, conſider who it is that hath planted this love in thy heart, is it not the *Lord* that gives thee this very affection? And when hee calls for this love againe at thy hand, doth he call for more than his owne? Shall he not gather the grapes of his owne Vineyard? and ſhall hee not eat the fruit of his owne Orchard? Hath not he planted in us theſe affections? and ought they not to be returned to him, to ſerve him, and to pitch on him?

5.Motive. We are ingaged to him.

Beſides, conſider you are engaged to love the *LORD*, and that ſhould be a great motive to us: in *Ioſh.*24.12. *You are witneſſes that you have choſen the Lord this day to ſerve him: And they ſaid wee are witneſſes:* that is *Ioſhua's* ſpeech to the people: As if hee ſhould ſay to them, You are not now to chooſe, you are now engaged, you cannot goe backe, you have poſſeſſed, you have choſen the *Lord* to ſerve him, therefore you are witneſſes against your selves. So I may say to every man that heares me, you are engaged to love the *Lord*: Why? Because you have chosen him for your husband, you are baptized in his name, you have taken him for your Master, and for your Father, therefore he may challenge it at your hands as right, for *hee is your Father: and where is his honour then? Hee is your Master, and where is his feare then?* That is, you are engaged, he may challenge it justly, you are his, hee hath bought you, yea hee hath over-bought you, he hath paid a price more worth than we, he hath bought us with his bloud: And what hath he bought us for, but to be his, that is, to love him? Therefore when we love him not, wee robbe *GOD* of our selves, wee doe an unnaturall thing, it is treacherie and injustice in us. As you know, it is one thing in a woman that is free from her husband to neglect a man that is a friend, but when shee hath engaged her selfe, and the match is made, now it is adultery. So every one of us that loves not the *Lord*, sins the more, because he is engaged to him: *Deut*. 32. 13. *Thou forsookest the strong God of thy salvation*, thou forsakest him to whom thou art engaged, he is the strong *GOD* of thy salvation, hee hath done thus and thus for thee. Therefore consider this, for seeing you have such an affection as love is, you must bestow it some-where, somewhat you must love: and you must know againe it is the best thing you have to bestow, for that commands all in you; and where will you bestow it? Can you find any creature upon whom to bestow it rather

If we love not *God*, we rob him.

Love is the best thing in a man.

than the *Lord*: Will you bestow it upon any man? the *LORD* exceeds them, as *David* saith, *Who among the gods is like thee?* That is, take the most excellent among them, that therefore are reckoned as gods, yet who among them is like unto thee? or whom will you bestow your love upon, your wealth, or your pleasures, or your phantasies? You must thinke the *LORD* will take this exceeding evill at your hands, that you should bestow this affection else-where, than on him whom you are engaged unto, to whom you are bound so much, who hath done so much for you.

6. *Motive.* What the *Lord* hath done for us.

But that which moves us most is particulars. If a man consider what the *Lord* hath done for him in particular, remember what passages have beene betweene the *Lord* and you, from the beginning of your youth: *Ier.* 2. *Neither said they, where is the Lord, that brought you out of the land of Egypt, through the wildernesse? I remember thee from the land of Egypt, &c.* That is, let a man consider GODS particular dealing with him; for when the *Lord* would stirre up *David*, and melt his heart, and bring it to a kindly sorrow for his sinnes, hee takes that course: 2 *Sam.* 12.7. It is *Nathans* speech to him; saith he, *Did not the Lord doe thus and thus? Did he not make thee King of Iudah and Israel? Did not hee give thy Masters Wives and thy Masters houses into thy bosome?* And if that had not beene enough, he would have done thus and thus. So let every man recount the particular kindnesses, and mercies hee hath received from the *Lord*; and when wee consider

der that it is he that doth all, that it is hee that feeds us, that it is he that clothes us, we have not a nights sleepe but he gives it to us, wee have not a blessing but it is from his hand, there is not a judgement that we escape, but it is through his providence: I say, the consideration of these particulars should be as so many sparkes to breed in us a flame of love towards the *Lord*, to thinke with your selves, when you have done all, how unreasonable a thing it is, how unequall a thing thtt you should forget this *God*, that you should never thinke on him, that you should not love him, he that hath done thus much for you.

And last of all, consider that the *Lord* loves you, for that is the greatest motive to winne us to love him; for as the fire begets fire, so love begets love. This was the cause that S. *Paul* loved the *Lord*. *Gal*. 2. 20. *He that loved me and gave himselfe for me*, saith he; I will not live any more to my selfe, but to him; he hath loved me, and gave himselfe for me; he hath loved me, and there was that testimonie of his love, he gave himselfe. I say, consider this love of the *Lord*, and let this beget in you a reciprocall affection towards him: Put all together, and consider, the *Lord* is worthy to bee beloved, and he that is so great sues to you for your love, that he that is *God*, that planted that love in your hearts, and therefore he doth but call for his owne, that he that hath done you so many kindnesses, that you are so engaged to him, that you are now bound unto, you are not now to choose; at the least come

7. Motive. The *Lord* loves us.

to this, to ſay he is worthy to bee beloved, bring your hearts to this, to deſire to love him.

Object. You will ſay, we may deſire long enough, but how ſhall we be able to doe it?

Answ. Meanes to enable us to love *God.* 1. Prayer.

I will tell you in a word, and ſo conclude. Firſt, you muſt pray for it; it is a lovely ſute, when wee come to the *Lord* and tell him, that we deſire to love him, that we would faine doe it if wee could, and beſeech him not to deny us that requeſt, that wee know is according to his will: doe you thinke that the *Lord* will refuſe you in that caſe, eſpecially if you beg it importunately at his hands?

Object. *Answ.* But if you object and ſay, We have prayed and have not obtained it; Know, that to love the *Lord* is a precious thing, and therefore the Apoſtle reckons it ſo.

Object. *Answ.* Prayer workes love 4. wayes. 1. It obtaines it.

You will ſay, How doth this prayer doe it? I ſay that it doth it partly by obtaining at *GODS* hands; for when you cry earneſtly, he cannot deny you: But as hee did with the lame and the blinde when they were importunate, hee never neglected any, but healed them. When you crie to the *LORD* and ſay, I would faine love thee, but I cannot, will he not be as willing to heale thy ſoule, to give thee legges to runne after him, and eyes to ſee him, as he was to heale the lame and the blind? certainly hee will not deny thee.

2. It brings us to communion with *God.*

But beſides that, Prayer doth it, becauſe it brings us to converſe, and to have communion with him; by Prayer we are familiar with *God*, by that meanes love growes betweene us: as you know when you

converſe

converse with men, it is a meanes to get love.

Againe, Prayer doth it, because when wee are much in calling upon *God*, the *Lord* delights to shew himselfe to such a man, yea at such a time, for the most part; as he shewed himselfe to *Christ* when he was praying, as he did to *Moses*, and to *Cornelius* and others. 3. In prayer *God* shewes himselfe.

And againe, Prayer it exerciseth this love, it blowes up the sparks of this love, and makes a flame of it; therefore much Prayer begets much love: If you would be abundant in love, be fervent and frequent in this duty of Prayer; pray much, and you shall find this effect of it, it will beget love in you. 4. Prayer exerciseth love.

Quest. You will say prayer is a generall meanes for other things; Why doe you put it as a particular meanes to get love?

Answ. The reason is, because love in an especiall manner, is a gift of the Spirit, a fruit of the holy Ghost; and it is true, it must be a peculiar worke of the Spirit to beget love. It is true, faith comes by hearing, and hearing begets faith; it is done likewise by the Spirit: but love is more peculiarly than other graces, the gift of the holy Ghost. And therefore 2 *Thes*. 4. saith the Apostle, *You are taught of God to love one another*: That is, it is such a thing as GOD teacheth, or else our teaching will never doe it: that which he saith of love to the brethren, we may say of the love of GOD; the LORD hath put love into man, man loves many times, and knowes not why: many times hee hath reason that hee should love, and yet he cannot, because it is a peculiar gift of Love a most peculiar gift of the holy Ghost.

of *GOD*. That naturall affection for a man to love his children, all the World cannot doe it, all the arguments in the World cannot perswade a man: for if arguments could doe it, wee might perswade others to doe so; but none can love so as the father doth his child: and why? But because the *Lord* workes that in men. So the love of *GOD* is a peculiar worke of the holy Ghost, none are able to love *Iesus*, but hee in whom the *LORD* hath wrought it, in whom the holy Ghost hath planted this affection: Therefore the way to get it is earnestly to pray, to acknowledge the power of the holy Ghost, to goe to him, and say, *LORD*, I am not able to doe it: this acknowledgement of the power of the holy Ghost is the way to prevaile. Besides, you know the power of *God* is so transcendent beyond the pitch of our nature, that except the holy Ghost worke more than nature, we shall never be brought together in agreeablenesse and sutablenesse; we are no more able to love the *Lord*, than cold water is able to heat it selfe: there must be somewhat to breed heat in the water; so the holy Ghost must breed that fire of love in us, it must be kindled from heaven, or else we shall never have it.

2. Meanes to consider our sins.

Secondly, another speciall meanes to enable you to love the *Lord*, is to consider your owne condition, to consider your sinnes, what you are, what hearts you have, and what lives you have led.

Object. You will say, how doth this beget love?

Answ. Yes, this is a great meanes: *Mary* loved much, because much was forgiven her, that is *Mary Magdalen*

dalen had great ſenſe of her ſinnes, the *Lord* had opened her eyes to ſee what a one ſhee had beene, what ſinnes ſhe had committed: And becauſe ſhee had that ſenſe of her ſinnes, her eyes were open to ſee her owne vileneſſe: hence it is that he ſaith, *ſhee loved much.* For when we are humble and poore in Spirit, when we are little in our owne eyes, then the *Lord* will come and ſhew mercie on us; when a man ſhall ſee his ſinne, and ſhall thinke with himſelfe, *I am worthy to be deſtroyed,* I can expect nothing but death, then the *Lord* ſhall come ſuddenly, as it were, and ſhall tell us, you ſhall live; and ſhall reconcile himſelfe to us: this will command love. We ſhall never receive the Goſpell ſo as to love *CHRIST*, till we come to povertie of ſpirit, till we be thus humbled: as in the firſt of *Luke,* it is the ſpeech of *Mary*, *My ſoule doth magnifie the Lord:* and why? becauſe *hee had reſpect to the poore eſtate of his hand-maiden:* when ſhe was little in her owne eyes, and made no account of her ſelfe, and thought not her ſelfe worthy to be looked after, the *LORD* comes and takes her, and vouchſafes her ſuch an honour as to cauſe his owne Sonne to bee borne of her: now ſhe could not hold, but that was it that enflamed her heart with love to the *LORD*, *My ſoule doth magnifie the* Lord, *becauſe hee had reſpect to the poore eſtate of his handmaid:* So we ſee in *David*, you never find a greater expreſſion of love in *David,* than at that time when hee was moſt humbled: when the Prophet came to him, and told him what the *LORD* would doe for him, that he would build

We cannot love *Chriſt* till we be poore in ſpirit.

build him an house, *David* begins to consider what he was: what is *David,* saith he? *What am I, or what is my Fathers house?* That is, I am but a poore miserable man, I am but thus borne, what have I done that the *Lord* should respect me so farre? If *David* had not beene so little and so vile in his own eyes, those great mercies had never so wrought in his heart. And therefore, I say, the way to make us abundant in love, is to consider our sinnes, to bee humbled, to consider what we are, and to conceive from thence the kindnesse of the *Lord*: you know how it affected *Saul,* when he came into the hands of *David,* that he had power to kill him; he considered what he had done to *David,* how he had carried himselfe to him, and he saw *Davids* kindnesse againe to him, (unexpected and undeserved it was) but it melted his heart, it dissolved him into teares. So the love of the *Lord,* when we consider how we have behaved our selves to him, and yet hee hath offered us peace, and yet hee saith, Returne, and I will forgive you; I say, this should worke on the hardest heart: And therefore consider your sinnes; it is not enough to say, I am a sinner, perhaps you are ready to doe so: But come to particular sinnes, consider wherein you have offended the LORD, say you have done thus and thus, as S. *Paul* reasons with himselfe, *I was a blasphemer, I was a persecutor, an oppressor, and yet the Lord had mercy on me:* so be ready to say, I have committed such and such sinnes, it may be uncleannesse, it may bee Sabbath-breaking and swearing, &c. yet the *Lord* hath been merci-

mercifull or willing to receive me to mercy: as that place, *Ier.3.1. If a mans wife play the harlot, will hee returne to her?* No, he will put her away, and give her a Bill of Divorcement: *but you have done it*, and done it oft, and *with many lovers*; and *yet returne againe to mee, saith the* Lord: So I say, when *Christ* shall come to you, when you have committed such and such sinnes, and the *Lord* shall say to you, though you have done this, though you have done it often, yet returne againe to me, and I will receive you to mercy: I say, this should melt our hearts, and cause us to love the *Lord*.

I should come to the Third, that is, *To beseech the* Lord *to shew his owne selfe to you:* for indeed you shall never come to love him, till the *Lord* shew himselfe to you. It is one thing when wee preach him to you, and it is another when the *LORD* shewes himselfe: For as the Sunne is not seene but by his owne light; there is no way in the world to see the Sunne, all the Candles, all the Torches cannot doe it, except the Sunne shew it selfe: So I say of the *Lord*, all the Preachers in the world, though they should speake with the tongues of Angels, they were not able to shew the *Lord Christ Iesus* what he is: But if the *Lord* shew his owne selfe to you, if he open the cloud and shew you his glory, and the light of his countenance, then you shall know the *Lord* after another manner than we can shew him to you, with another knowledge more effectually: And when you have seene him thus, you shall love him, without this you shall not love him.

3. Meanes to beseech the *Lord* to shew himselfe to us.

And

And therefore pray the *Lord* to ſhew himſelfe to you, as it was *Moſes* prayer, *Exod.* 33. *Shew mee thy glory.* What is that? That is, *Lord* ſhew mee thy excellency which is exceeding glorious: You muſt thinke *Moſes* asked not this in vaine, it was for ſome purpoſe, he asked not meerely to ſatisfie his fancy; for the *LORD* would not then have heard him: But what did he aske it for? Surely that he might love the *LORD* the more, by knowing him better. And when *Moſes* came to aske it at the hands of the *Lord* he did aſſent, he proclaimed, that is, hee revealed himſelfe more than ever he did before. So I ſay to every one of you, if you would be earneſt with the *Lord*, deſire him to ſhew you his excellency, that you might love him more, ſerve him more, and feare him more, hee could deny you no more than he did *Moſes*: for you muſt thinke, that this is no extraordinary thing for the *Lord* to ſhew himſelfe. That which he did miraculouſly to *Stephen*, when he opened the heavens, and ſhewed himſelfe to the outward view, that he doth ordinarily to the Saints, he ſhewes himſelfe to their mindes and inward affections. When we preach at any time, except the *Lord* ſhew himſelfe to you at that time, then our preaching is in vaine: for the word that we ſpeake is but a dead letter, it will worke no more upon you than a dead thing that hath no efficacie. But when the Spirit goes with the word, and hee openeth to you the thing that we ſpeake, then it is effectuall. Therefore S. *Paul* to the *Epheſians*, when hee had opened thoſe great myſteries, hee concludes with this,

Why *Moſes* deſired the *Lord* to ſhew him his glory.

this, *The Lord give you the spirit of wisedome and revelation, to enlighten the eyes of your understanding, that you may know what the hope of your calling is, and what is the glorious inheritance of the Saints, &c.* As if he should say, When I have said all this, it is nothing, it will not doe it; but hee beseecheth the *LORD* to give them the Spirit of revelation, and then it is done. And so to conclude all, when wee have said all wee can to move you to love the *Lord*, it is all nothing, except the *Lord* give you the Spirit of wisedome and revelation to open your eyes to see what is the exceeding greatnesse and excellency of his power.

* *
*

FINIS.

OF LOVE

The third Sermon.

GALAT. 5.6.

For in Iesus Christ, neither circumcision availeth any thing, nor uncircumcision, but Faith which worketh by Love.

OUT of these words wee have formerly delivered this point to you, that,

Whosoever loveth not, is not in Christ.

The last thing (in the prosecution of this point) was the meanes whereby this love is wrought in our hearts, which we did not then finish: notwithstanding we will not proceed in it at this time, but rather alter the matter, and doe that which I did not then intend; because there are many this day that are to receive the Sacrament, and you know when wee come to receive the Sacrament,

ment, our chiefe buſineſſe is to examine our ſelves. *Let every man examine himſelfe, and ſo let him eate of this bread, and drinke of this cup.*

We have often preſſed on you the neceſſity of theſe two things:

First, that you may not omit the Sacrament when it is adminiſtred in the Congregation whereof you are members: for if they were to bee cut off from the people that neglected the Paſſeover, why ſhould not this be accounted a greater ſinne, and to deſerve a greater puniſhment, to neglect the receiving of the *Lords* Supper, which is come in the place of the Paſſeover, and is farre beyond it?

The Sacrament of the *Lords* Supper is not to be omitted.

Reaſons.

1. The neglect of it is a great ſin.

The *Lords* Supper beyond the Paſſeover in two reſpects.

Firſt, becauſe it is more cleare, and it is more cleare, becauſe the doctrine is more cleare: for it doth more lively repreſent *Chriſt* now exhibited in the fleſh, than that which onely repreſented *Chriſt* which was then to come.

5. It is more cleare.

And ſecondly, becauſe the mercy that you are now to remember, is your redemption from ſinne and from hell, a greater mercy than that which they were to remember in the Paſleover, which was their deliverance out of Egypt (though that was not all;) therefore the neglecting of this muſt needs be a greater ſinne than the neglecting of that.

2. The mercy remembred in it is greater.

Now you ſee how ſtrictly *GOD* layeth a charge upon them, that no man ſhould omit the Paſſeover, unleſſe ſickneſſe or a journey hindred him. Now conſider this, you that have been negligent in comming to this holy Sacrament; for it is a great ſinne, and provokes *God* to anger, when he ſhall ſee that this ordinance which himselfe hath instituted, and which he hath laid such a charge upon you to doe, is neglected.

2. It is as great a sin as to neglect the word.

Besides, doe you thinke it is a sin to neglect comming to the word? And is it not as much to neglect this ordinance.

3. We need all helpes.

Besides, doe we not need all helps of grace? and is not this among the maine helpes?

2. Man ought not to come negligently to it.

Againe, as you ought not to omit it, so to come negligently to it, to come without examination, to come without a more solemne and extraordinary renewing of your repentance, is to receive the Sacrament unworthily, *to eate and drinke judgement and damnation to your selves*. Now there are two sorts that receive the Sacrament unworthily.

Two sorts receive the Sacrament unworthily.
1. Those that are out of *Christ*.
2. Those that are in *Christ*.

First, those that are not yet in *Christ*.

Secoddly, those that are within the Covenant, but yet come remissely and negligently, and take not that care they should in examining their hearts: for though you ought to renew your repentance every day, yet in a more speciall manner you ought to doe it upon such an occasion. As women doe in scowring their vessels; they make them cleane every day, but yet there are some certaine times wherein they scowre them more: so wee should scowre our hearts in a more speciall manner upon this occasion. Now because this is the businesse that wee have to doe this day, we will therefore handle the more fully that we touched lightly before, which is this examination, whether we love the *Lord Iesus* or no: for if you love not the *Lord Iesus*, you are

not

not in him; for whatsoever you doe availeth not, if you have not faith and love. Therefore if you find that you have not this love to *Christ*, that you are not *rooted and grounded in love*, you have nothing to doe with *Christ*, and if you have nothing to doe with him, you have nothing to doe with the Sacrament. And therefore we will shew you what properties of love we find in the holy Scriptures.

10. Properties of love.
1. It is bountifull.

This is one property of love set downe in 1 *Cor.* 13. *Love is bountifull, and seeketh not its owne things:* that is, it is the nature of love to bestow readily and freely any thing a man hath, on the party whom he loveth. We see, *Ioseph*, that loved *Benjamin*, as his love was more to him than to all the rest of his brethren, so he gave him a greater portion than the rest. It is the nature of love to be bountifull. What a man loveth, he cares not what hee parts with to obtaine it. *Herod* cared not to have parted with halfe his Kingdome to please that inordinate affection of his. The *Converts*, in the Apostles time, how bountifull were they, laying all their goods at the Apostles feet? *Zacheus*, when hee was converted, and his heart was inflamed with love to *Christ*, he would *give halfe his goods to the poore*. But in generall, it is a thing that you all know, that love is of a bountiful disposition. If you would know then whether you have this love to the *Lord Iesus* or no, consider whether you be ready to bestow any thing upon him, whether you be ready to part with any thing for his sake. *David*, when he abounded with love to the *Lord*, you see how he expressed it in his provision for the Temple, you see how hee exceeded in i, *An hundred thousand shekels of gold, and a thousand thousand talents of silver:* this, saith hee, I have done according to povertie: As if hee had said, If I had beene able to doe more, I would have done more, but this was as much as I could reach unto: herein he shewed the greatnesse of his love to *GOD* in the greatnesse of his bountie. Take it in the love which we have one to another: where a man loveth, he denieth nothing. *Sampson*, when he loved the harlot, hee denied her nothing that shee asked of him. If you love the *Lord Iesus*, examine your selves by this; are you ready to bestow any thing for his advantage? are you ready to take all opportunities to do somewhat for his glory? consider how many opportunities you have had, and might have had, wherein you might have expressed and manifested this love to the *Lord Iesus*. Might you not have done much to the setting of a powerfull Ministery here and there? have you not had ability to doe it? Would it not much advantage the glory of *Iesus Christ* to make bridges (as it were) for men to goe to heaven by, and to make the highway that leadeth thither? A greater worke of mercie than these externall workes that appeare so glorious in the eyes of men: to have blessed opportunities, and not to use them, because we have streight hands and narrow hearts, is a signe wee want love to *Christ*.

To neglect opportunities of doing good argueth want of love.

In the passages of your life there is many a case, that if you were of a bountifull disposition, you might

might doe much good in. You know what S. *Paul* ſaith, which was a great teſtimonie of his love, *Act*.20.24. *My life* (ſaith he) *is not deare unto me*, ſo I may doe any thing for *Ieſus Chriſt*, *ſo I may fulfill the courſe of my miniſtery*. So, examine your ſelves, whether you can ſay thus upon any occaſion; So that I may doe any good, ſo that I may helpe forward any good cauſe that may tend to the glory of GOD, my life is not deare unto me, my libertie is not deare, my eſtate is not deare, my friends are not deare to me. You that have to doe in government, many caſes there are, wherein, if you will doe any ſpeciall good, you muſt part with ſomething of your owne; GOD lookes to you and ſees what you doe, and how your hearts ſtand affected in all theſe paſſages; aske your ſelves now whether theſe things be not deare to you: if there were love in you, it would cauſe you to doe more than you doe. It was *Davids* great wiſedome, when water was brought to him that was purchaſed at ſo deare a rate, when ſo high a price was ſet upon it, hee would not drinke it himſelfe, but poured it forth to the *Lord*; and therein he ſhewed the greatneſſe of his love, that he was willing to part with that which hee ſo exceedingly longed for, which was bought at ſuch a rate.

The like hee did when hee bought the threſhing floore of *Araunah* the *Iebuſite*: he might have had it given him for nothing; *No*, ſaith he, *I will not offer to the Lord of that which coſt mee nothing*: As if he had ſaid, I ſhall ſhew no love to the *Lord* then, and if I ſhew no love to him, what is my ſacrifice worth? For *David* knew well enough that *GOD* obſerved what he did, he obſerved what it coſt him. The *Lord* obſerveth all that you doe: Beloved, he knoweth your hearts, and ſeeth what motions you have, and prizeth your actions accordingly. If you find any action for him, that coſt you ſomething, he obſerveth that likewiſe, *Rev.2.2. I know thy workes and thy patience:* ſo doth the *Lord* ſay of every man, I know what ſuch a ſervice coſt thee, I know what loſſe thou ſufferedſt when thou didſt part with ſuch a thing for my ſake. Therefore if you would ſhew your love to the *Lord*, and would have a teſtimony in your hearts, that you have this love wrought in you, bee not backward to beſtow any thing upon *Chriſt*. The woman that brake the boxe of precious ointment, you ſee how the *Lord* accepted that worke of hers, ſo much, that hee put it downe that it ſhould never be forgotten. For love, whereſoever it is, will open the heart, and open the hand, and beſtow any thing upon *Ieſus Chriſt*, that is in our power.

God obſerveth what his ſervice coſts us.

Now, if we examine whether love bee amongſt men by this ſigne, we ſhall find but little love, and we may juſtly take up the complaint of the Apoſtle, *Every man ſeekes his owne things, and not the things of Ieſus Chriſt.* That is, when any thing is to be done, men are ready to enquire thus, it is the ſecret inquiſition of their hearts; What is this to me? What profit will it bring me? Wherein will it bee to mine advantage? And if they find it is a thing

that

that will cost them something, and a thing that they shall get nothing by, how cold and backward are men to doe it? It is from this that men seeke their owne things.

But here every man will be ready to professe and say that he is not so strait handed, but he is ready to doe many things for *Christ*, that he is bountifull, and seekes not his owne things. *Object.*

My beloved, let us try this now a little: thou thinkest thou art so bountifull for the *LORD*, I would aske thee this; Doest thou doe it purely for the *Lord* in such a case, when there is no profit nor praise with men, nor advantage redounding to thy selfe? Art thou as forward then, as when there are all those respects? Art thou as abundant in it, as diligent and as ready to doe it? This discovers the falshood of mens hearts for the most part. *Answ.* Tryall of the bounty of our love. 1. When it crosseth advantage to our selves.

And besides, take it in the case of selfe-love, consider what thou doest, when thine owne selfe-love shall come in competition with this love to the *Lord*: for in that wee shall know our love to the *LORD*, when we deny our selves, when wee crosse our selfe love, and reject and refuse it: for otherwise it is no thanke to us, when there is no inward crossing in us, no contrary affection drawing us another way. Therefore if you would know whether you love the *LORD* or no, trie what you doe in the things that are dearest to you, consider what you doe in those things that of all others you are most unwilling to part with: for indeed herein is the tryall, as the *Lord* said to *Abraham*, when hee 2. When it crosseth selfe-love.

would have offered up his Sonne, *Now Abraham I know that thou lovest me*: As if he had said, This is a sure testimonie that thou lovest mee, because thy sonne is not deare to thee. So I say, when you are to part with something that is deare to you, consider what you doe in such a case, consider whether you can say generally, *I account all things but as losse and dung for Christ*. It may be thou art willing to part with something that thou carest not much for, but this is nothing. Some man will not lose his credit, that is deare to him; Examine thy selfe now, if thy credit be deare to thee, art thou content to lose the praise of men for *Christ*? When thou art put to a hazzard, art thou content to suffer the losse of thy estate?

Every man hath some particular temptation.

Every man hath some particular temptation, young men for the most part are *lovers of pleasures more than lovers of God*, and old men are lovers of their owne wealth more than of *GOD*. Therefore consider what you will doe now in your severall cases. *Christ*, you know, requires this at every mans hands, that his Wife and Children, that his Father and Mother, and whatsoever is dearest to him, that he should neglect it all for his sake; and herein a mans love is seene.

3. When it is done chearfully.

And when you have done all this, I will adde that further, Though you doe bring your hearts to doe it, yet are you willing to doe it? Doe you doe it chearefully and readily? For why doth the *Lord* require that as a necessary condition, that whatsoever is done to him, might be done chearfully and willingly?

willingly? For no other reason than this, but because he regards nothing but that which commeth from love; and if it comes from love, we know, we doe it chearefully. Therefore consider, whether thou art willing to doe this chearfully, and with a full hand, not niggardly and pinchingly; and by this you shall know whether you have this love to the *Lord Iesus* or no, whether you bee bountifull, whether you seeke the things of the *Lord*, and not your owne things.

Why God requireth a chearfull service.

In the second place, you shall find this to bee one propertie of love (by which you may trie your selves) it will bee content with nothing but with love againe from the partie whom we love. If one love another, let him doe never so much, let him be never so kind in his actions towards him, let him be never so bountifull to him, yet except hee have love againe, hee is content with nothing. Indeed when we doe not love a man, wee can be content to receive profit from him, and it is no matter though his heart goe another way so we enjoy it, but it is the nature of true love to desire to bee paid in its owne coine. Now if thou love the *Lord Iesus*, if thou mightest have all the blessings that hee could bestow upon thee, if he should open his hand wide, and compasse thee about with abundance, yet if thou lovest the *Lord*, thou wouldest not be content with this, but thou wouldest have assurance of his love, thy heart would be at no rest else.

2. It is content with nothing but love againe.

And this you may see in *David*, *Psal.* 51. *David*, you know, was well enough, hee hath health and wealth,

wealth, and abundance of all things, yet you see how miserably he complained, because he wanted that joy that he was wont to have, because he was not in those termes with the *Lord* that he was wont to bee; and till he had that, his bones were broken with sorrow, and he tooke it so to heart, that nothing in the world could content him, till hee was assured of *Gods* favour: And it is certaine, that if thou love the *LORD*, nothing will satisfie thy soule, but the assurance of his loving countenance to thee againe. Therefore that which *Absalom* did, we may make use of upon this occasion; hee had that wit, to make a right pretence, whatsoever his intent was: when hee was called from banishment where he lived well enough, and enjoyed all things, hee wanted nothing, but had as much as hee could desire, yet, saith he, what doth all this availe me, *so long as I may not see the Kings face?* It was but his craftinesse: Yet thus much we may observe out of it, that this is the property of love, that till a man see the face of *God*, that is, till he enjoy a neere and close communion with *God*, untill hee can have the love of *God* witnessed to his soule, hee cares for nothing in the world besides: As you have it in 2 *Chro.* 7.14. where that condition is put in: *If my people* (saith he) *when they are in distresse, shall humble themselves, and seeke my face, then I will doe thus and thus.* As if he should say, it may be they may seeke libertie when they are in captivitie; it may bee they may seeke health, when they are in sicknesse; it may be they may seeke deliverance from enemies, under whom

whom they are enthralled; but that is not the condition that I put them upon, but *if they humble themselves, and seeke my face, then I will heare in heaven,&c.* So I say now, if you will trie whether you love the *Lord Iesus* or no, consider whether you seeke his face, that is, whether you seeke grace or no, whether nothing in the world can content you but his favour. For it is the propertie of one that is truly sanctified, mercie alone will not content him, but he will have grace as well as mercie: Another man that loveth not the *Lord*, it is true, it may be he is pinched with a sense of his sinnes, but let him have mercy, it is enough hee thinkes; but now take a man that hath his heart right towards *God*, except he have grace, it contents him not; for that is the propertie and nature of true love, that it careth for no wages, all that it desires, is the love of the partie that what it doth may be acknowledged and accepted; and there is a great difference in that: You know, a Nurse doth much unto the child as well as the mother, and it may be more, but notwithstanding the Nurse never doth it but when shee is hired, but the mother doth it for nothing, and she doth it more abundantly, because she doth it out of love, and it is wages enough to her that shee hath done it, because shee loves her Child: So I say if you love the *Lord Iesus*, it is not wages that you seeke, but if you may have the light of his countenance to shine on you, if you may have his favour, if you may have opportunity to doe him service in your place, it is enough for you, you care not for the

A Christian seekes grace aswel as mercy.

Simile.

the present wages nor for future. Therefore herein you may know the nature of your love, the rightnesse and ingenuitie of it, if it be so that all that you doe is out of love to the *LORD*, and if you can content your selves with love againe from *God*, it is a signe that you love the *Lord Iesus*.

3. It desires the second comming of *Christ*.

Againe, (to proceed) if you love the *Lord Iesus*, you will also love his appearance: as you have it in 2 *Tim*. 4. 8. *A Crowne of righteousnesse is laid up for me, and as many as love the appearance of Iesus Christ*: and in *Heb*. 9. *ult*. *He was offered for the sinnes of many, and shall appeare the second time to such as looke for him, &c.* For whom was hee offered? and to whom shall he appeare? To as many as looke for his comming againe. So in 2 *Pet*. 3. 13. *What manner of men* (saith the Apostle) *ought wee to bee in all godlinesse and holy conversation, looking for, and hasting to the appearance of Christ? &c.* So that it is certaine every man that loveth the *Lord Iesus*, he loves his appearance, he hasteneth to the comming of the *Lord*, he looks for his comming againe: and it must needs be so in reason. For if you love any, you know, you must needs love their presence; will you professe that you are loving to any, that when you heare of their comming towards you, there is no newes more unacceptable to you? If a woman had a Husband in the *East Indies*, and report of his comming home should be the worst newes that she could heare, shall wee thinke that such a woman loves her husband? So if you did love the *Lord Iesus*, you would be glad to have his appearance.

Simile.

And

And(beloved) seeing the Apostle hath chosen out this note, why should not we presse it in our examination of our selves, whereby we may know whether we love the *Lord Iesus* or no: whether wee desire to be with the *Lord?* whether we can say, as the Apostle S. *Paul, We desire to be at home, and to be with the Lord?* If we examine the love of men by this rule, we shall find that there is exceeding little love to the *Lord IESVS*, men are so exceeding backward in desiring to be at home, and to be with him; and we may know that by our backwardnesse to be in the *Lords* presence upon earth: Shall wee thinke that men are desirous to bee in his presence in heaven, and yet are so unwilling to draw neere to him upon earth? But you will object,

How to know men desire not the second comming of *Christ*.

Object.

Many of those that love the *Lord*, that are men truly sanctified, yet are affraid of death, and the newes of death is terrible to them: and therefore surely this is a rare signe, even in those that have faith and love, to desire the appearance of *Iesus Christ*.

Answ. There may be backwardnesse in the Saints to die.

Simile.

I answer, it is true, there may be a backwardnesse even in the Saints, but you must know upon what ground it is. A Spouse that is to marry a Husband, no question but she would be glad to be handsome, and to bee prepared for his comming; and though she may desire his company exceedingly, yet because things are not so ready as shee would have them, or for feare that he may find that which may divert and turne away his eyes from delighting in her, perhaps she desires not his comming at that time.

time. There is a certaine negligence and unpreparednesse in mens hearts, which breeds an unwillingnesse in them sometimes, and makes them afraid of seeing the *Lord*, and yet there may bee a true and inward love after him,

1. That they may be better fitted.

Besides, you know, there is flesh as well as spirit, and the spirituall part desires, as S. *Paul* did, to be at home, and to bee with the *Lord*, and to enjoy his presence, but that flesh that is in us is alwayes backward to it. Therefore in *Rev.* 14. 13. *Blessed are those that die in the Lord, so saith the spirit:* but so saith not the flesh the voice of the flesh is contrary to it, but it is the voice of the spirit, and the regenerate part that is in us. So that this I may boldly say to you, that every man that hath this faith and love wrought in him by the Spirit of *God*, he hath that in him which doth earnestly desire communion with *Christ*, to live with him for ever, to bee in his presence continually, although there may be some reluctancie by reason of the flesh that is there. Take a man that hath sore eyes; you know, to the eye the light is exceeding pleasant, but looke how much sorenesse and defect there is in the eye, so much the light is burdensome to it; but so farre as the eye is right, so farre as it is perfect, so far is the light pleasing and delightfull to it; so is it with the heart of the regenerate man, looke how much faith, looke how much spirit there is, so much desire there is of the presence of *Christ*, and it is most pleasing and acceptable to him, as the light of the Sunne is to the eye, but looke how much sorenesse, that is, looke how

2. Because there is flesh in them.

Simile.

So much faith, so

how much flesh there is in him, so much reluctancie, so much unwillingnesse there is in him: and that he must strive against: But still the rule yoldeth good, that wheresoever the heart is right, there is alwayes an earnest desire and longing to bee with *Christ*. And indeed this is onely found in the Saints; for evill men, if they knew what heaven were, they would not desire it: for they desire heaven in another notion, they would bee well, they would bee freed from miserie and discontent which they meet with in the World, they would have whatsoever the flesh desireth, and that is it they looke after; but to desire heaven as it is, that is, to desire an excellency in grace, to be alway praising *God*, to be continually in his presence, to bee freed from the practice of sinne, this is a thing that if men aske their owne hearts, they doe not desire in this manner; for they desire it not here upon earth, when they are in the communion of Saints. When they are in places where there are holy speeches, and holy exercises, it is burthensome to them, they are out of their element, they are as men that are not upon their proper Center; these men desire to bee in heaven, but they desire another kind of happinesse than there is in heaven, the felicitie there is presented unto them under another *Idea*, they desire no more than the flesh desires: but to desire heaven indeed, as it is heaven, to desire *God* there in his purenesse and holinesse, to desire it so as thereby to be sequestred from all worldly, carnall and sensual delights, this a carnall man desires not. Therefore this is a distin-

much desire of *Christs* presence.

In what sense wicked men desire heaven.

distinguishing note and signe, that *hee that loves the LORD will love his appearance.*

4. It delighteth to speake of the party beloved.

Fourthly, you shall find this to be the propertie of love, he that loveth, is very readie to speake of the party loved; love is full of loquacitie, it is ready to fall into the praises of the partie beloved, and to keepe no measure in it, to abound in it, that is the disposition of every man that loveth. So is it in this love to the *Lord Iesus*: You may see in *David*, as he abounded in love to the *Lord*, so he could never satisfie himselfe in praising the *Lord*: In *Psalme* 105. which is repeated 2 *Chron.* 15. you shall find that he hath never done with it, but is alwayes singing praises to the *Lord*: *Sing praises to the Lord, and be alway talking of his wondrous workes.* And againe, *Remember his marvellous workes that hee hath done of old, and all the wonders, &c.* As if he should say. If you love the *Lord*, shew it in praising of him. Doe you professe to love the *Lord*, and yet never delight to speake of him? nor delight to heare others speake of him? My beloved, this backwardnesse that is amongst us to holy and gracious speech, to speeches that tend to the setting forth of the *Lords* praise, shewes that love to the *Lord Iesus* is wanting among us.

You know, it is naturall for every man to abound in the speeches of the things they love, of what nature soever they bee. Mariners are delighted to talke of their voyages, and souldiers of their battell, and Huntsmen of their games. If you delight in the *Lord*, certainly your tongues will be much in

speaking

ſpeaking of him, you will be ready to doe it upon all occaſions. *Out of the abundance of the heart, the mouth ſpeaketh:* and if love to the *Lord* do abound in your hearts, this love will bee expreſſed in your tongues, upon all occaſions: And therefore, at the laſt, you may judge of the meaſure of your love by this. He that ſpeakes much of loving *God*, and yet hath his ſpeeches emptie, vaine, and unprofitable, ſurely we may gheſſe that he loves not him at all: and this is a marke that will not deceive us.

And now what will you ſay for your ſelves, that you ſpeake no more upon thoſe ſeverall occaſions, that you meet withall in the world? Is it becauſe you are aſhamed, becauſe you are baſhfull, and fearefull to expreſſe your ſelves, and to make an open profeſſion of that holineſſe that is in your hearts? Certainely it is a ſigne that you love not the *Lord Ieſus*: for hee that loveth, is never aſhamed, becauſe whom a man loveth, hee magnifieth, he prizeth much, he hath a high eſteeme of: And therefore that baſhfulneſſe and fearfulneſſe that you object, will not keepe you backe, if you did love the *Lord* in truth and ſinceritie. Or elſe, why is it that you ſpeake of him no more? Is it becauſe you cannot ſpeake? Is it becauſe your underſtandings are weake and dull? becauſe you are not able to do it aſwell as others, and therefore you are loth to expreſſe your ſelves?

Love is not aſhamed.

You know, when you love any, that love will teach you to ſpeake, it will quicken the dulleſt wit and invention; love ſharpeneth, and maketh the

Love makes eloquent.

rudeſt tongue eloquent. It is the nature of love to ſet the heart on worke, and when the heart is ſet on worke, the *tongue will be as the penne, of a ready writer.* You know how the Apoſtle ſets it forth, *Our heart is enlarged to you:* Love openeth the heart wide: and the heart openeth the tongue wide: Therefore if you love the *Lord* much, you will be much in ſpeaking of him. Conſider therefore what your ſpeeches are concerning *God*, whether you your ſelves are ready to ſpeake much, and to delight to heare others ſpeake alſo: whether you bee glad of any occaſion, as thoſe that love are glad to heare thoſe that they love to be ſpoken of.

5. It wil do much and ſuffer much for the party beloved.

Fifthly, love will doe much and ſuffer much for the partie loved: S. *Paul*, as hee was abundant in love, ſo was he abundant in labour likewiſe; whoſoever aboundeth in love, will abound in workes alſo. Therefore ſee what you doe for the *Lord IESVS*, ſee what you ſuffer for his ſake. When *Chriſt* came to S. *Peter*, and asked him that queſtion, *Peter loveſt thou mee?* hee puts him upon the tryall upon this fruit of his love, *Feed my Lambes:* As if hee ſhould ſay, *Peter*, if thou wilt ſhew that thou loveſt me, expreſſe it in doing ſomething for my ſake, *Feed my Lambes:* herein thy love ſhall bee diſcerned; doe not ſay thou loveſt me, and yet art negligent in doing for me, *Feed my Lambes.* Wee ſhall not need to preſſe this much in this Congregation, becauſe it belongs to the Miniſterie: Although you have ſomewhat to doe in it for the Magiſtracie alſo; whereby they may expreſſe their love to the

Lord

Lord Iesus, to helpe the feeding of *Christs* Lambes.

It is true, we are as the Vines that bring forth the Grapes, but you are as the elmes that hold up those Vines: the Magistrates feed the people aswell as the Ministers: therefore that phrase is applied to *David*, he was a shepheard. Therefore in your severall occasions, when you meet with that which may tend to the feeding of the people of *God*, when you shall labour so farre as may lye within your compasse, that the *Gospel* may have a free passage, that there may be more faithfull and laborious Ministers set up in the severall places of the kingdome, the more you doe this, the more you feed *Christs* Lambes. And if you will shew that love you have to the *LORD*, shew it by feeding his people, that is, by doing that which lies in your power, tending to that end, by doing of it zealously, with all your might. And as that was the worke that *Christ* put *Peter* upon for the triall of his love, so I may say to every one of you, If you will shew that you love the *Lord IESVS*, doe the workes that belong to your particular place; for every calling hath a particular worke in it: if you love the *Lord*, bee diligent in that way, in that calling which *Christ* hath given you to doe him service in: and herein you shall shew your love, as it was *Christs* owne speech, *I have glorified thy Name*, that is, in that particular worke, in that charge which thou gavest mee to performe: so you must shew your love to *God* in doing the actions of your particular callings diligently. You know, when that womans heart abounded in love

Magistrates Shepheards.

Diligence in our particular calling, an argument of love.

to *Christ*, how it found out away wherein it would shew i. selfe presently in breaking the boxe of oyntment, &c.

As it is said of faith, *It is dead without workes*, so love is dead without workes, the *Lord* regards it not, it is a dead carkasse, without motion. We know, it is the nature of love to be diligent: if you do love *Christ*, it will make you diligent.

Suffering is doing but with difficulty.

And as you will be ready to doe much, so you will be ready to suffer much also: these two I put together, because suffering is a kind of doing, onely it is a doing of things, when there is difficultie and hardnesse. Now if you love the *Lord Iesus*, see what you will suffer for his sake; those that we love, we are exceeding ready to suffer for. A Husband that loves his Spouse, is exceeding readie to suffer any thing to enjoy her love, he is willing to suffer any displeasure of parents, of friends, to suffer the losse of his estate, he cares not for discredit in the world, hee is ready to breake through thicke and thin, and to doe any thing, so hee may obtaine her love at the last: So, if you love the *Lord Iesus*, you will suffer any thing for his sake. It was an excellent testimony of *Davids* love, in 2 *Sam*. 6. 21. when *David* there dancing before the Arke, was scoffed at by *Michal* his Wife, see what an answer he gives her, *It is*, saith he, *before the Lord*: as if he should say, I am willing to beare this at thy hands, for *it is the Lord who hath chosen mee rather than thy father and all his house*: As if he should say, seeing it is the *LORD*, for whose sake I endure this rebuke

buke at thy hands, I care not for it, I am willing to doe it, yea I will doe it more, and *bee more vile in mine owne eyes*, and expose my selfe yet to more scorne and derision, since it is to the *Lord*, who hath chosen me rather than thy Fathers house; So I say, when any thing comes to bee suffered for any good action, for any good cause (as indeed commonly such actions have sufferings joyned with them) if you love the *Lord* you will be ready to goe through it, and that with cheerefulnesse, because it is the *Lord* who hath chosen you, and passed by so many thousands. And therefore it was the commendation of those in *Heb.*10. it was an argument of their sinceritie, that they *suffered the spoyling of their goods with joy*. Whence came this, but from their love to the *Lord*? They were so farre from being backward to suffer, as that they were glad to have the opportunitie to suffer somewhat for his sake.

But you will say, I am readie to doe much for the *Lord*, and I hope I am not backward to suffer for him. *Object.*

It is well if it be so, but let me adde this to all that I have said, In what manner doest thou doe that thou doest? You know the caution that the Apostle puts in, in 1 *Iohn* 5.3. *Herein is love manifested, that we keepe his Commandements, and his Commandements are not grievous*. Indeed herein is the reality of love seene, that wee keepe the Commandements of *God*. It is true, a man may doe much for *Christ*, and yet not love him; an Hypocrite may *Answ.* 1.Ioh. 5.3. opened.

goe farre in performance, and yet though hee doe much, he may not love much: therefore you must examine your selves by that, in what manner you doe that which you doe. Therefore, it is added, if we *keepe his Commandements, and they bee not grievous:* as if he should say, the manner of your doing is all in all, you must both doe much, and suffer much, but they must both be done willingly. You know, the wife and the servant, they both serve the husband, and doe much for him, both are alike diligent, yet notwithstanding, there is this difference, the Wife doth it out of love, she doth it in another manner, proceeding from another affection, ayming at another end than the servant doth. So two men may be diligent in keeping the same Commandement of the *Lord*; the one doth it as one that loves the *LORD* earnestly, being desirous to please him, as one that delights in the *Lord*; nothing doth more content him, than when he is in an opportunitie wherein he may expresse his love to the *Lord*, all his Commandements are not grievous to him, it is not respect to the reward, it is not an eye to the punishment that moves him.

We must doe and suffer willingly.

Simile.

A man indeed may doe much for the *LORD*, when it is the respects that he hath to hell, and to judgement; to heaven, and the reward that moves him: Not, but that these may be motives; but yet you must remember this, that, if these be the principall, and if these onely move you, you doe it not out of love, you take but an aime from your selves. When a man hath a businesse of his owne to doe, you

Wee may use motives to duties, from reward and punishment.

you know how carefull hee is in it, and with what diligence he doth it, how often and how seriously he is devising with himselfe to bring his matters to passe. Now if you love the *Lord*, the actions that you doe, you will not doe them as those that are his slaves and servants, that doe things for other regards; And indeed, such is the love for the most part that is among us now adaies, there is much formalitie in our actious, we *have a forme of godlinesse, without the power of it:* even as in our love towards men, there are many complements, and much profession of love one to another, but wee find that there is little true love: So we may take up a complaint against men in their love to *GOD*, there is much formalitie, men are much in outward performances, which is well, I confesse, but alas, the power is wanting; it is all but complementing with *GOD*, as it were, when you come and doe these duties of *Gods* worship, when you keepe the Sabbath, and present your selves at Prayers and at Sermons, it is well you do so, but yet when *your hearts are going after your covetousnesse*, and after your pleasures, after this or that particular humour, the *Lord* lookes upon this as upon a formall performance: It is another kind of doing that the *LORD* requires at your hands. It may be you doe duties in secret and private, and it is a good propertie that you doe so, but yet that is not enough; you may doe them as a taske, that you are glad when the businesse is done and it is well that it is over: but when you will doe things out of love, you must know

A man may performe private duties and yet want love.

that you must doe it in another manner, not in this formalitie. If you will serve the *LORD* out of love, it is not the praying to him Morning and Evening that will content you, but it is the working upon your hearts, it is the beating upon your affections till you have brought them to a good frame of Grace, till you have wrought upon your selves a sound and through renewing of your repentance; you will never give over till your hearts bee quickned in prayer, till you have found that *GOD* hath answered you, till you have had experience of his mercy and loving kindnesse towards you.

What kind of prayer comes from love.

So when you come to heare, is this all (thinke you) that *GOD* requires of you, to sit here and lend us your eares for a little time? No, my beloved, unlesse you doe it from love, unlesse you bee moved to it from an inward principle, from an entire and holy affection to *GOD*, it is nothing. You must labour to have the Word wrought upon your hearts, you must observe how you practise, and how you bring forth into action that which you heare; for you doe not learne a thing here, when you come to heare the Word, till you practise it, till your hearts be transformed into it: Doe not thinke that you have done the worke, when you have sate here and heard us, when you have gone home and repeated the Sermon, and understand it: To heare as *GOD* would have you heare is another thing: It is like your lessons in Musick, you say you have never learned them till you be able to practise them, so you never have learned the word of *God* aright,

What hearing of the Word *God* requireth.

Note.

aright, till you have an ability in you to practise it.

To shew you what Love is, and what Faith is, and what Patience is, and to make you understand and conceive of it, it is nothing; but to have Faith, to have Patience, to have Love, to have your affections inflamed to the *LORD*, this is the right hearing. As it is in Physicke, the understanding of the Physicians Bill is nothing, it is the taking and applying of that which is there written that doth good to your bodies: so is it with the Doctrine that we preach, you may understand it, and apprehend it, and conceive of it aright; but except you bring it forth into your lives and actions, you learne it not. Therefore this slight and overly performance is not a true testimony of your love to the *LORD Iesus*, but the doing of it to purpose, so that *God* who searcheth the heart may accept of it, the doing of it throughly, that your hearts may bee wrought upon, this is a signe that your doing and suffering comes from *Love*. *Simile.*

***

FINIS.

OF LOVE

The fourth Sermon.

GALAT. 5.6.

For in Iesus Christ, neither circumcision availeth any thing, nor uncircumcision, but Faith which worketh by Love.

THE last thing that wee did was to shew you what were the properties of true love, that by them you may trie your selves whether you love the *LORD IESUS* or no: wee went through five in the morning, now wee proceed.

6. Property of love it is like fire in 4. things.

Another propertie of love is this, it is full of heate: Therefore in *Cant*. 8. it is compared to *coales of Iuniper*: and that phrase is used in *Mat*. 24.5. *Iniquitie shall abound, and the love of many shall waxe cold*. That Antithesis shewes that love is a hot thing,

thing, hot as fire. Therefore if you would know whether you love the *Lord Iesus* or no, consider what heat and what fire there is in you.

Now what are the properties of fire? Wherein doth love and that agree?

Fire, you know is the most active of all the Elements; cold benummeth a man, and is the greatest enemie to action: If thou love the *Lord IESVS*, thou shalt find thy love will have that property of fire, to set all on worke in thee, it will set thy tongue on fire, and thy hands on fire, and thy head and heart on fire, every thing that is within thee will be working, and doing some service or other to the *Lord*. When a man wanteth love, hee is as a Man benummed, as a Man frozen in his dregges, not apt to any thing; the more a thing is like to fire, the more aptnesse, and the more activenesse; so the more love, the more aptnesse and readinesse to every good worke: where there is no love, there men are *reprobate to every good worke*. 1. Love is active as fire.

Besides, love as it is very active, so it is very quicke, as fire is of a quicke nature. Therefore we say that love hates nothing so much as delaies; and it is in this like to fire, which is the quickest of all other Elements. Consider of this therefore; Art thou speedy in thy execution? If thou love the *Lord*, thou wilt not deferre and put off from day to day any thing that is to bee done, thou wilt not say with thy selfe, I will change my course of life, but not yet: No, if thou love the *Lord*, thou wilt doe it presently.. 2. Loue is quicke as fire.

Besides

3. Love is vehement as fire.

Besides, love agrees with fire in this, that it is earnest and vehement: and indeed I take it, that in that regard it is chiefly compared to fire. For fire, as it is of a quick, so it is of a vehement nature, and so is love. Looke what a man loves, upon that he bestowes the top of all his affections, and the maine strength of his intentions runne that way. Examine by this therefore whether thou love the *Lord* or not? If thou love the *Lord Iesus*, thou wilt looke upon other things, as things that thou regardest not much, thou wilt grieve for them *as if thou grievedst not, and rejoyce as if thou rejoycedst not: thou wilt use the World as if thou usedst it not*; thy heart will be taken up about *Christ*, and about the things that belong to the Kingdome of *God*, thy intentions will bee set upon the things that belong to the service of *God*, and thy owne salvation. This is a thing by which you may plainly discerne the truth of your love: examine therefore what it is upon which you bestow the maine, and the top of your intentions. Indeed, my brethren, the greatest things that the world hath, are not worthy of the toppe and strength of our affections; for they are but trifles. Therefore if you love the *Lord IESVS*, if you prize him aright, and bee rightly affected towards him, you will esteeme nothing great, but the enjoying of his favour, and nothing of worse consequent than the losse of it, nothing will bee of any great moment to you, but onely sinne, and grace; sinne that displeaseth him, and grace that brings you into favour with him: as for other things

things, you will looke upon them as trifles, you will not put the strength of your mindes to any thing else; this is the nature of love, it is vehement toward the thing it loveth.

Moreover, it hath also this property of fire, that it is still aspiring, it is still enlarging it selfe, still growing on, assimilating, and turning every thing into its owne nature, it is overcomming and is not ready to be overcome: Which propertie of fire is noted in that place I spake of in the Morning, *Much water cannot quench it, it is as strong as death:* Now death you know overcomes all; so will love, it will breake through all impediments. Consider whether you find this disposition in your selves; that your hearts are still drawing neerer and neerer to the *Lord*, that they are still aspiring up towards Heaven, that you are still going onward and thriving in the worke of Grace. 4. Love powerfull as fire.

But that which of all other things will manifest most to us this affection of love, is those affections which depend on it; you shall know it, I say, by the affections that hang upon it. It is true that all the affections depend upon love, but, for this time, I will instance but in two, namely, 7. Property of love, it commandeth the affections, especially anger and feare.

Anger, and

Feare.

Looke whatsoever it is that a man loveth, where hee findes any impediment in the prosecution of it, he is angry, hee desires with as much earnestnesse to remove that impediment, as hee loves the thing. 1. Anger.

Take

Take any man even of the mildest disposition, if in any thing that hee loveth much, and intendeth much, there bee an intercurrent impediment that shall interrupt him, he is angry, though otherwise hee be of a meeke disposition. For anger is but earnestnesse to remove the thing out of the way that hinders us: whatsoever a man loveth, hee is angry with the impediments that hinder him in it. Come now and examine your love to the *Lord* by your anger: that anger that proceeds from love to the LORD, wee call zeale: Will you professe that you love the LORD, and yet your hearts are not moved when he is dishonoured? Thinke with thy selfe when thou art wronged in thy name, or some body miscalleth thee, misreports of thee, and prosecutes thee with evill speeches and revilings, is not thy wrath kindled in thee against such a one? Well, if thou love the *Lord* IESVS as thy selfe, as thou oughtest to love him above thy selfe, why are not thy affections stirred in thee, when thou hearest him dishonoured, when thou knowest that his Name is ill spoken of? If a man should take from thee thy wealth, or any thing that is deare to thee; If a man should come and violate thee with ill termes, thou wouldest bee angry with him, and bee ready to flie in the face of such an one. If you bee thus affected to the *Lord*, and to his Glory, why doe you not the like for him? You know, *David* did the same: *Mine eyes gush out* (saith hee) *with Rivers of waters, because men keepe not thy law.* Therefore know, that if you find not

Anger what.

Zeale what.

not your hearts affected with the things that belong to *GOD*, that there is no anger ſtirred up, it is a ſure argument that you love him not. It is obſervable that is ſayd of old *Eli*, 1 *Sam*.4.3. when newes was brought him that the Iſraelites were fled, that moved him not ſo much; when it was told him, moreover, that there was a great ſlaughter among the people, that ſtirred him not neither; when it was told him yet that his two Sonnes *Hophni* and *Phineas* were ſlaine, yet this did not ſo much affect him: but when it was told him that the Arke of the *LORD* was taken, the text noteth ſomething more than ordinarie, that hee was ſo ſtirred with it, that hee fell from his ſeate, and it coſt him his life. Can you find this affection in your ſelves, that you are not moved with the death of children ſo much, or for the loſſe of your goods, or for your owne particular diſcontents, as when you ſhall heare that *the glory is departed from Iſrael*, that Religion ſuffers an Eclipſe in any place, that the Goſpell of *IESVS CHRIST* is hindred? This is a thing that will try your love to the *Lord*. If you find that you can heare of the deſolation of the Churches, and of the increaſe and growing of Poperie, and yet you doe not take it to heart to be affected with it, you doe not grieve for it, it is a ſigne that you want love to the *Lord*. You know what is noted of them in *Ierem*. 36.24. When the King had done an abominable action, that hee had cut the Roll in ſunder that *Ieremiah* gave him, and caſt it into the fire that was upon the hearth before him, it is ſaid

ſaid that thoſe that were about him, *did not rent their cloathes,* nor petition to him, &c. As if hee ſhould ſay; in this they diſcovered a wonderfull want of love to the *LORD*, and to this cauſe, that they were not moved with this diſhonour, that was offered to *GOD*, and to his ſervant, and to the cauſe of Religion at that time. You know what diſpoſition S. *Paul* had in this caſe, *Act.* 17. He obſerved, that the place, where he was, was given to *Idolatry*, the text ſaith, *His ſpirit was ſtirred in him*, his zeale and his anger was kindled in his breaſt. Therefore conſider what your affections to the *Lord* are by this holy anger that is in you. *Moſes*, you know, was the meekeſt man upon the earth, and yet you know how hee was moved, how his zeale was kindled in his breaſt, when hee ſaw the idolatry of the people.

2. Feare.

In the next place conſider your feare: For if you love the *Lord*, it will cauſe you to feare and tremble at his word, and at his judgements, for whom a man loves much, hee regards much, and when a man regards another much, hee is much affected with that he doth; Now when the *Lord* ſhall ſhew ſome tokens of his wrath, thoſe that love him and eſteeme of him, thoſe that prize him, cannot but be affected. *Shall the Lyon roare, and ſhall not the beaſts of the field tremble?* Conſider how you are affected therefore, when the *Lord* ſhall diſcover any expreſſion of his wrath, and what doth hee elſe in this ſtroake, which is now upon this place? is there not wrath gone out from the *Lord?* You know the Plague

These ſermons were preached in the time of the great peſtilence, 1625.

Plague is more particularly *Gods* hand, than any other affliction: Therefore *David* saith when hee chose the Plague, that he would choose to *fall into the hands of God*, intimating that, in that businesse, *God* was in a more peculiar manner the doer of it. As the thunder is said to be the voyce of the *Lord*, so the Plague may properly bee said to bee the stroake of the *Lord*, more peculiarly than any other affliction. Consider therefore what your affections are in this case; for, my beloved let it not be in vaine to you, that the *Lord* stretcheth forth his hand as hee doth now at this time among us. It is but yet in the beginning, and what is the *Lords* meaning in it? Is it not as a Messenger sent upon an errand? If it had its answer, if that were done for which the *Lord* had sent it, would hee not remove it againe? Would he not bid *the destroying Angel* to put up his sword into his sheath? Doubtlesse he would, if you would doe that at the beginning of this sicknesse, that must be done before the *Lord* will remove it from you.

Object. You will say, what shall wee doe then? *Answ.* I beseech you consider what commonly is the cause of a plague among us. Consider what hath beene the cause of the plague in former times. You shall find in *Numb.* 25. two causes of the Plague. One was the superstition and Idolatrie of the people; they began to bee yoaked with Idolatry, *They joyned themselves to Baal-Peor.* I confesse that sinne was not yet growne to any great height, it was but yet in the beginning, in the seedes, and

Causes of the Plague.

1. Idolatry.

yet you know how the *Lord* was offended with them.

2. Fornication. And the second was fornication, the ſinne of uncleanneſſe that was committed. It is not likely that all the people fell into that ſinne of *Idolatry*, or into the ſinne of *fornication*, but yet the *Lord* was offended with the whole Congregation for thoſe that did it, as his manner is to be. So here you ſee two cauſes of a plague, *Idolatry* which was but beginning, and the very admitting it into the Campe; and the *Fornication* of the people.

3. Security and pride. Another cauſe of the plague you ſhall find in *Davids* numbring the people, it was their ſecurity and pride, and truſting to themſelves, and the creatures: for ſurely it was not *Davids ſinne only*, (who had ſomewhat forgotten *God*, and truſted to his mountaine, and thought that that was ſtrong enough) but it was the ſinne of the people.

Security double. It is good (my beloved) to be ſecure out of confidence upon *God*, and therein, the more ſecurity the better: but to be ſecure for any outward helpe, either in the number of men, or ſhips, or ſtrength, or policie, or becauſe wee are compaſſed about with the walls of the Sea, or whatſoever it is wherein we thinke our ſafety conſiſteth, the more confidence in this the worſe. The *Lord* ſmote the people for this ſecurity in *Davids* time.

4. Unworthy receiving of the Sacrament. Another cauſe is, the unworthy receiving of the Sacrament. *Many are ſicke among you* (ſaith the Apoſtle) *and many are dead*, becauſe you receive the Sacrament unworthily. The *Lord* is pleaſed to puniſh

nish that particular sinne of receiving the Sacrament unworthily), with some sicknesse or other, whether the plague or no, wee cannot say, but this wee may be sure of, that this was the cause why so many were sicke and dead. You know that passage in the Booke of Chronicles concerning *Ezechias*; when the people had not prepared themselves aright as they ought, he prayed to the *Lord*, and it is said, *The Lord healed the people*: wee cannot say what the *Lord* healed them of, but yet it makes it evident that the *Lord* had some way smitten them. *Moses* for the omission of the Sacrament, the *Lord would have slaine him*; that is, hee would have sent something upon him, whether some disease, as is most probable, or some other thing which should have taken away his life in the end. The omission and negligent receiving of the Sacrament I put together, both which move GOD to anger, and to inflict plagues upon a people.

I will name yet one more besides these, and that is the coldnesse and deadnesse of their hearts who belong to the LORD, from whom hee expects better things, and more zeale; which I gather hence: What was the reason that the zeale of *Phineas* stayed the plague? *Numb.* 25. Because his love was hot, and his anger was kindled in a holy manner against that *Israelitish man*, and the *Midianitish woman*, that had committed fornication among the people. If the zeale of *Phineas* was the cause of staying that plague, and of with-holding the *Lords* hand, then surely the coldnesse of those from 5. Coldnesse in Christians.

whom the *Lord* lookes for much heate, for much fervency of ſpirit, whom GOD expects ſhould ſtand in the gap, I ſay, that is the cauſe that the *Lord* goes on in puniſhing.

Queſt. But what ſhould we doe now to remove it?

Anſw. Amend the things that are amiſſe, Repent and Amend, and hee will returne from his fierce wrath, which hee not onely intendeth againſt us, but is alſo already upon us; Labour to cleanſe your hands from idolatry and ſuperſtition, and cleanſe the Land from the crying ſinne of uncleanneſſe and fornication, and every man labour to purifie his owne heart.

How to remove a Plague. 1. Repentance.

2 To take heed of ſecurity.

And againe, to turne to the LORD, to take heed of ſecuritie, which is a forerunner of a ruine, as a great Calme is a forerunner of an Earthquake.

3. To take heed of receiving the Sacrament unworthily.

Againe, take heed of receiving the Sacrament unworthily; many of you this day have received, therefore I ſhould ſpeake ſomething particularly to them, but in truth this concernes all among us; but chiefly let me ſpeake to thoſe a little that are able to pray, that have ſome fire in them, that have had the worke of Grace in their hearts wrought by the Spirit of GOD, that have ſome ſparkes, if they were blowne up, that are men fit to ſtand in the gappe; It belongs to you, my brethren, to doe ſomething that the LORD may ſtay his hand: and remember that when the *Lord* begins to ſend forth tokens of his wrath and diſpleaſure againſt a Nation, it is a time wherein he expects and lookes for

What the *Lord* expects, whē he ſends forth judgemēts.

Humilia-

Humiliation and Repentance: Therefore take heed of neglecting that in *Isay* 22. *In that day* (saith the *Lord*) *when I called for humiliation, behold killing of fatlings and Oxen*, &c. Therefore know what your dutie is, and learne now to see what belongs to you to doe, shew your love to the *Lord* in trembling at his judgements, in being zealous for his Names sake: as indeed where there is abundance of love there is alwayes exceeding much zeale: So it was with S. *Paul*, so it was with *Elias*, so it was with *Moses*, so it hath been with all the Saints. And so much for this.

Where there is love, there is zeale.

8. Property of love, it doth things freely.

Another property of love is this, that it doth not play the Huckster with the *Lord* (as we say) it doth not bring things to an exact account, but when a man loveth, hee is willing to doe what offices of love and friendship he can, and hee doth not stand to looke for an exact recompence; (for that is to play the Huckster, to make a bargaine with *God*). but the nature of love and true friendship, wheresoever it is found, is this, to bee free in doing that it doth, and not to stand to examine how much they should doe, and how much they shall receive for doing of it; but to doe it with libertie and with freedome. And so it will be if your love bee right to the *LORD*, you will not stand halfe penny-worthing, you will not stand considering what you are bound to doe of necessity, whether you are bound to pray in your families or no, or whether you are bound to keepe the Sabbath so exactly and precisely as is commanded; whether you are

1. It will not limit it selfe to duties.

 bound

bound from giving so much liberty to your selves in vaine speeches, &c. But love will rather say, what shall I doe to recompence the *Lord*? It will bee devising what to doe, it will be glad of any occasion of doing any thing that may bee acceptable to *God*. When you set limits to your selves, and are affraid of going too farre, and doing too much, it is a signe that what you doe commeth not from love to the *LORD*, but from some naturall principle, it comes from your selves, and not from the spirit. For if you love the *Lord IESVS* aright, why doe you not labour to exceed in the duties of obedience? Why doe you blame those that goe further than your selves are willing to goe? Why doe you quarrell with that exactnesse, and precisenesse, and strictnesse which is required in walking in the wayes of *GOD*? Love is abundant in the worke it doth, and if you love the *Lord*, you will not set limits to your selves, you will not have such thoughts as these; I will doe as much as shall bring mee to Heaven, and no more, I will take so much paines as that I may not be damned: but to exceed, and doe more than needs, this I hope may bee spared, and I may goe to heaven notwithstanding well enough, though I goe not so fast as other men. No, beloved, if there be love in you, you will strive to doe the utmost of your power, it is the nature of love so to doe.

To limit our selves in *Gods* service argueth want of love.

Againe, you will not bee so exact, nor indent with the *LORD* what hee will doe to you; but though the *Lord* bee slow and slacke in rewarding you,

2. It will not indent with *God* for reward.

you, though hee stay long, and suffer you to goe on without taking any notice of you, as it were, nay perhaps hee gives you many afflictions and persecutions, povertie, trouble, sickenesse, &c. though the LORD doth not doe what you expect, yet your love will bee free, it will goe on, you will bee ready to say as S. *Paul* did, *I know whom I have trusted*: that is, hee was resolved to serve the *Lord*, to doe his utmost; though the LORD did reserve himselfe and the recompence of reward to a further time, yet hee was content. Such a disposition will bee found in those that love the *Lord Iesus*.

Againe you may judge of your love to the *Lord Iesus* by another propertie of love, which is a hatred of sinne, by your hatred of that which is contrary to him; for love is not better knowne by any thing than by hatred; for all hatred is properly rooted in love: for you hate nothing but because you love the contrary; therefore if you love the *Lord* IESVS, you will hate sinne. Examine your selves by this, for it is a sure rule, if you love the LORD, you will hate that which is evill. 9 Property of love, hatred of sin.

You will say, I hope I doe that. *Object.*

It is well if you doe, but let us consider that: it may bee you may bee angry with sinne, but doe you hate sinne? That was the commendations that the *Lord* gives to the Church in *Rev.* 2. *Thou hatest the works of the Nicolaitans, which I also hate.* Therefore, if you would know whether you love the *Lord Iesus*, trie it by this, doe you hate sinne? *Answ.* Many are angry with sinne, but hate it not.

Object. You will say, how shall wee know whether wee hate it or no?

Answ. Three differences betweene hatred and anger. In these three things you shall find wherein hatred differs from anger, and thereby you may examine your selves.

1. Hatred is more generall. First, hatred is more of generalls; a Man hates all drunkards if hee hate drunkennesse: hee hates all Toads and all Serpents, if hee hate poyson. A Man is angry with this or that particular, but hatred is of all. I would aske thee, doest thou hate all sinne, every thing that is called sinne, all that belongs to sinne? If it be this or that sinne that you make against, you are but angry with sinne, you doe not hate sinne: for hatred falls away upon the generall. Examine therefore if you find this disposition in your hearts, that you hate every sinne, that your hearts rise against every thing that is sinfull, whatsoever is contrary to the *Lord,* whatsoever you apprehend under the notion of sinne, that you hate, and resist, and strive against; this is a signe that you love the *Lord.*

2. Hatred is more cruell. Secondly, hatred desires the utter destruction of the thing it hates, anger doth not so: Anger desires but a revenge proportionable to the injurie: therefore we say there is a kind of Iustice in anger, it would not have the party that it is angry with, to be destroyed, but it would have him sensible of its displeasure, it would have something done that might answer the injury that is offered; but hatred desires the destruction of a thing utterly. Now doe you so with your sinnes? Doe you desire to have them

them wholly extirpate and rooted out of you? to have your lusts throughly and perfectly mortified? Are you willing to have sinne so cleane taken away, that you may have no libertie to have dalliance with it in any kind? Doe you hate it so as that you cannot endure to come neere it, nor to have it within your sight? It is a signe you hate it indeed.

Lastly, Hatred differeth from Anger in this, that it is implacable: Hatred comes from judgement, and it continues, and therefore hatred is not a passion, but we call it an affection; it is a bent, a disposition and frame of the will; Anger is a passion that dies, and flittes away after a time; but hatred continues. Is your disposition such to your sinnes? examine your selves; nothing is more frequent, my brethren, than to be humbled for some sinne, which amazeth you for the present, but doth your hatred continue? If not, you doe but fall out with your sinnes onely, and grow friends with them againe. If you did hate them, as you should, you would never returne to amity with them more.

3 Hatred is implacable.

Returning to amitie with sinne againe, a signe we hate it not.

Many a man takes resolutions to himselfe, I will bee drunke no more, I will be a Gamester no more, I will not commit such and such grosse sinnes, as I have done, any more; perhaps some shame, or some feare hath followed him, some deepe apprehension of wrath and judgement, which set him upon this resolution for the present; but if the heart be right, that thou hatest sinne as thou shouldest, thou wilt continue hating of it. Therefore consider.

der, whether you love the *Lord Iesus* by this triall, whether your hearts hate sinne in your constant resolution or no. This was the disposition that was in *Lot*, *His righteous soule was vexed with the uncleane conversation of the Sodomites*, that is, he did not only abstaine from the acts that they did, but his soule wrought against them, he was vexed with them, as a man is vexed with a thing that is contrary to his disposition.

So it is said of *Moses*, *Hee stood in the Doore of the Tabernacle, and hee wept as hee stood:* his heart was moved in him. It is not enough to abstaine from sinne, but to hate sin, and that is an argument of our love to the *Lord Iesus*: take this therefore for another tryall of your love.

10. Property, it loves the Saints.

Againe, there is one more, which wee cannot leave out; though it be a thing knowne unto you, yet because the Scriptures give it as a peculiar signe by which we may judge of our love to the *Lord*, it must not be passed by, and that is our love to the Saints; and there is good reason given of it, if wee consider well, 1 *Ioh*.4.20. Wilt thou say thou *lovest God whom thou hast not seene, and yet lovest not thy brother whom thou hast seene?* The meaning is this, for a Man to love the *Lord* who is is immortall, invisible, who dwelleth in light inaccessible, is a more difficult thing than to love thy Brother whom thou seest. For why doe we love the *Lord*, but because wee conceive him under such a notion? We thinke of him as such a *God*, having such and such attributes: Now saith the Apostle, whatsoever thou con-

1 Ioh. 4.20 opened.

They hate *Gods* image.

Why we loue the *Lord*.

conceivest of *God*, that very image and disposition is stamped on Man like thy selfe, thou shalt see the very same disposition in a holy Man that is in the *Lord* himselfe. Indeed it differeth in the degree exceedingly, there is but a glimpse of it, yet why is it said that the image of *God* is renewed, but that there is in holy men a disposition like the nature of *God?* Now this is in a more remisse degree in man, and therefore more sutable to our weaknesse; as you know, difficulty comes from disproportion, it is a harder thing to love the *LORD*, than a man like our selves. If therefore wee doe not love men like our selves, in whom is stamped a disposition like the nature of *GOD*, and his Image, in some degree, surely we cannot love the *LORD* who is so farre above us. *Note.*

Againe, a Man like our selves is visible, wee see his actions, we heare him speake, wee know more plainly the frame of his disposition, and therefore it is more easie to love a holy Man than to love the *Lord*: For so is the Apostles argument; Doe not thinke that thou lovest the *Lord* whom thou never sawest, when thou dost not love thy brother whom thou seest daily. Therefore we may conclude thus much, If we love not the Saints and holy men, it is certaine we love not the *Lord*. 2. They are visible to us.

I confesse every man is ready to say (in this case) he loves holy men.

I would put you to this tryall, and aske you but this question; you shall know it by this: Doe you love *all* the Saints? You shall find that the Apostle 4. Trials of our love to holy men.

S. *Paul*

1. To love all Saints.

S.*Paul* still in his Epistles puts in that cautino, ***Love to all the Saints***. If thou love grace and holinesse, thou wilt love it wheresoever it is. Many men will love some particular grace, especially when it suiteth with their disposition, and is agreeable to them, and to their constitution; but to love all grace, to love all holinesse in all the Saints, wheresoever it is found, it is an infallible signe that thou lovest the *Lord Iesus*.

2. To love none but them with a love of complacencie.

Againe, doest thou love none but them; that where grace is, thou lovest, and where it is not, thou withdrawest thy love?

But you will say, would you have us to love none but the Saints? I answer, it is true, wee ought to love all others with a love of pittie, wee should shew abundance of this love to all mankind; but then there is a love of complacencie and delight, and with this love wee ought to love none but the Saints.

3. To love those that excell in grace.

Againe, thirdly, doe you love them as they excell in holinesse? Many men can love one that hath but some degree of grace; but if it be one that hath more exactnesse than ordinarie, that hath proceeded higher in holinesse than hee thinkes requisite, here his heart is ready to quarrell, and to rise against him.

4. To company with them.

Lastly, doe you manifest your love by delighting in their company, and by the fruits of love towards them? You may professe much, and say much, but of all other things, company is the worst dissembled. Will you professe that you love the Saints, and that you delight in them, and yet desire to bee in any Company rather than in theirs? That when you are among them, you are as if you were out of your element, yea more as if you were out of your owne Center? it is impossible but that those that are moved by the same spirit, should bee best pleased when they are in one and the same society. Put all these things together, and by these you may judge whether you love the Saints or no.

Object. You will object, I doe love the Saints, but who are they? I love not hypocrites. And so it is made a notable excuse.

Answ. I will not wish thee to love hypocrites, onely take heed thou suffer not the impes and instruments of the Divell to paint out the true Saints unto thee in the colour of hypocrites: thou must consider that it hath beene the usuall manner to cast that aspersion upon all the Saints, upon all holy men in all ages, as the Apostle saith in 2 *Cor. Wee are as deceivers though true*: that is the common esteeme that the world hath of the Saints, they judge them to be deceivers, and to be men that professe themselves to bee otherwise than they are. You know what was said of IESVS CHRIST, *some said of him, hee was a good man, others said, nay, hee was a deceiver of the people.* You know what was said of *David*, that he was a subtle man, one that went about to deceive others. S. *Paul*, you know, was reckoned the great impostor of the world: this was alwayes laid upon the Saints: therefore let not the Divels instruments deceive thee in that.

Men hate the Saints under pretence that they are hypocrites.

Besides,

Besides, why are they Hypocrites? Is it because there are some shewes of holinesse in them? Surely that is not argument enough.

Thou wilt say, because they doe not answer that which in their profession they make shew to be.

Religion hated under other notions.

If that be the reason, why doest thou not pitch thy hatred upon those that are found to bee so? And to conclude this, you must know, that no man speakes against Religion, or hates Religion under its owne notions, under its owne name, but something else must be put upon it, the name of Hypocrisie, or the like.

And it is the common condition of men whose hearts are not upright, that they are not able to judge aright of the wayes of *God*; a man that hath not grace himselfe, cannot possibly judge aright of grace in others: but I hasten. I must now proceed in the point I formerly began to insist on, namely, in shewing you the meanes of getting this love, and of increasing it.

These two meanes are in Serm. 2. beginning pag. 49.

I shewed formerly some meanes to get this love and to increase it.

As first, Prayer, for it is the gift of the Spirit.

Secondly, to beseech the *Lord* to shew himselfe to you.

3 Of means to love, to remove impediments.

We will adde but one now at this time, to shew you the way more fully to obtaine this love.

If you would love the *Lord*, remove the impediments.

What are those?

Two impediments

They are two.

Strange-

Strangenesse, and uncircumcision of heart, or worldly-mindednesse. of the love of *Christ*.

First, strangenesse is a great impediment to love. It is an observation that the Philosopher hath, that strangenesse, when we doe not salute, and converse one with another, is a meanes of dissolving friendship; so in this case, when there growes a strangenesse betweene *God* and us, it unties and loosens that love and communion that should be betweene us. Therefore, if you would preserve your love to the *Lord*, suffer not your hearts to sit loose from him, suffer not a strangenesse to grow betweene *God* and you. For strangenesse breeds fearfulnesse, and fearfulnesse looseneth love, as boldnesse is the Parent and Nurse of love, and which increaseth it.

1. Strangenesse, it dissolveth love.

Boldnesse the parent of love.

Besides, when there growes a strangenesse betweene *GOD* and us, wee begin not to know the *LORD*, there growes an ignorance, and so there is an intermission of those reciprocall offices of love betweene us; that even as it is among the Saints, the forsaking of their fellowship looseneth their love, and so stoppeth the intercourse of good duties that should bee among them: so it is with the *Lord*. And therefore if you would maintaine love with the *Lord*, *draw neere to him, and hee will draw neere to you.*

2. It breedeth ignorance.

How shall we doe that? *Quest.*

By speaking much to him, by hearing him speake to us, by retyring to him upon all occasions for consolation and comfort. *Answ.*

How to draw neere in acquaintance with *God*.

If thou receive any injurie from men, wrangle not

not with them, but doe as *David* did, betake thy ſelfe to prayer, take heed of ſinne; for that of all other things will breed a ſtrangeneſſe betweene *GOD* and thee, and if you doe fall out, ſeeke to be reconciled againe as ſoone as may be, labour to entertaine a continuall commerce betweene *God* and thy ſelfe, obſerve conſtantly his dealing with thee, and obſerve againe thy carriage towards him, this will breed a familiaritie betweene *God* and thee.

And above all, bee much in prayer; for that in a ſpeciall manner maintaines and increaſeth this communion and familiaritie betweene the *LORD* and thee.

2. Vncircumciſion of heart.

Againe, the other thing that hinders, is uncircumciſion of heart, or worldly-mindedneſſe; in *Deut.* 30. 6. *I will circumciſe your hearts, and you ſhall love mee with all your ſoules, and with all your hearts.* As if hee ſhould ſay, that which keepes you from loving mee, from delighting in mee, is the uncircumciſion of your hearts, that is, your worldly luſts, and worldly cares, and worldly deſires, when theſe abound in your hearts, they keepe you from loving the *LORD*: Therefore in 1 *Iohn* 2. *If you love the world, the love of the Father is not in you.* Come to any particular, and you ſhall find it ſo if you love wealth, you cannot love the *LORD*, if you love pleaſures, if you love praiſe with men, if you love honours, &c. you cannot love the *Lord*, the love of *GOD* and vaine-glory, the love of *GOD* and covetouſneſſe will not ſtand together. Therefore if you will love

love the *LORD*, you must have your hearts circumcised, that is, you must have these sinfull lusts cut off; for nothing quencheth love so much as these. You know, the love of an adulterer quencheth the conjugall love of the Wife to the Husband: your love of the world is adulterie, the Scripture calls it so; therefore if you love that, it quencheth your love to the *Lord*.

You will say, may we not love the things of the World? *Quest.*

Yes, my brethren, only take heed that it bee not an adulterous love. *Answ.*

How shall we know that? *Quest.*

You shall know it by this, if it doe lessen your love to *GOD*: you may know whether your love to any creature, to any sport or recreation be adulterous or no. A chaste Wife may love many men besides her Husband; but if it once begin to lessen her love to her Husband, that is an adulterous love: Therefore if you would love the *Lord* aright, bee sure to cut off this, for it breedes a distance betweene *God* and you. As it is said of *Absalom*, when the hearts of the people went with *Absalom*, they fell from *David* the King; so when our hearts are stollen away with the love of earthly things, our love to the *LORD* is lessened with it. Therefore I say, if you will love the *Lord* aright, you must be carefull to remove this: for the cares of the world, the lusts and divers pleasures, these choake the love of the *Lord*, they are the greatest quench-coales of any other.

Answ. When love to the creature is adulterous.

Note.

Note. Love, you know, is of an uniting quality, when any thing lyeth betweene *God* and us, that, you may be sure, will hinder our love. Now there are many things that lye betweene *God* and us.

What lyeth in the understanding between *God* and us that hinders love.

Some things lie in our understandings, temptations to Atheisme, temptations to thinke that the Scriptures are not true, temptations to judge amisse of *God* in any thing, temptations to doubt of the favour of *God*; These lie in the understanding betweene *God* and us, and are contrary to love: for love uniteth.

What in the Will.

But in the Will there lyeth much more, sometimes vaine hopes, sometimes vaine feares, sometimes one thing, sometimes another. If there bee any inordinate lust after any creature, after any thing in the World, it lyeth betweene *GOD* and us, and makes a separation betweene us; and till that bee removed, *GOD* and wee cannot come together, till there bee an union, wee cannot fully love. Therefore if you would love the *LORD*, have your hearts circumcised, that is, have those things removed out of your understanding, and out of your will. Take away those obstacles that lye betweene *GOD* and you: And if you cannot doe it your selves, goe to *CHRIST*, it is hee that Circumciseth us *with the Circumcision made without hands*.

Knowledge of *God* a speciall helpe to make us love him.

Againe, when you have done this, that you may grow in love to the *LORD*, learne to know the *Lord*, for the more you know him, the more you will love him. What is the reason that the

Angels

Angels in Heaven ſo love him? Becauſe they know him. What is the reaſon that wee ſhall love him more in heaven than wee doe now, but becauſe wee ſhall know him more? Therefore when you reade the Scriptures, and obſerve the workes of *Gods* Providence in every particular, learne by this to know *God*: as you know a man by his actions and carriage, learne to have ſuch an *Idea* of *God*, as he hath deſcribed himſelfe in his word; that hee is true of his word, that hee is full of goodneſſe, that hee is abundant in long-ſuffering and patience, that he is exceeding mercifull beyond meaſure, &c. Labour to ſee his wiſdome, his goodneſſe, and his mercy, labour to know *GOD*: for when we come to know him aright, by that wee come to love him. Why doe wee love one Man more than another, but becauſe wee conceive him under ſuch a notion, wee conceive his heart to bee of ſuch and ſuch a frame, wee thinke him to bee a Man of ſuch and ſuch a condition? When wee thus conceive the *LORD*, it will teach us to love him more. Therefore this you muſt know, that for you onely to looke upon things that are beneficiall to you, as forgiveneſſe of ſinnes, and adoption, and an inheritance in Heaven, that is not love to the *Lord*. It is true, you ſhould doe all this, but that which you are principally to doe, is to looke to the Eſſence of *God*, to ſee ſuch excellencies in him, that thereby you may bee led home to him: and therefore that you may know him the better, you muſt be taught of him. Againe, you muſt not onely know him,

Wee muſt principally love *God* for his excellencies, not for our owne advantages.

but you must likewise have assurance of his love to you: for when you know the excellencies of the *Lord*, unlesse you have assurance of his love to you, it is not sufficient. Take a man of the highest place, and of the most excellent quality; if thou conceive that hee hath a hollow heart towards thee, thou canst not possibly love him: Thou must bee perswaded of the love of the *Lord* to thee. Therefore in the Text it is said to be *Faith which worketh by love*. The increase of the assurance of *Gods* love therefore is the meanes to increase thy love to him.

* * *

FINIS.

THE

OF LOVE

The fifth Sermon.

GALAT. 5.6.

For in Iesus Christ, neither circumcision availeth any thing, nor uncircumcision, but Faith which worketh by Love.

THE last thing wee did was to give you the properties of love to the *LORD IESVS*.

Now that which remaines to be done at this time, is to apply that which hath beene said, that is, to bring your hearts and the rule together, and to exhort you, that what you have heard in this, it may not passe like ayrie notions, and never bee brought home to your particular practice. For, my beloved, the word that wee deliver to you should be like *Nailes*, driven home to the head, *fastened by the Masters of the assembly*, as the Wiseman speakes, that they may sticke and abide in the Soule, as forked arrowes doe in the bodie, that they may not easily fall out againe. Therefore the maine businesse that wee have to doe in preaching the Word, is to fasten these words thus upon your hearts. That which wee will doe therefore at this time shall bee to exhort you to question your owne hearts, and to *examine them upon your beds*, whether these characters and properties of love which have beene delivered, doe agree to you or no. For, as the Apostle saith, *Vnlesse you bee in CHRIST*, that is, unlesse you bee knit to *CHRIST* in love, *you are reprobates*: it concernes every man therefore that heares mee at this time, to examine this strictly with himselfe.

Wee will expostulate the matter a while with you at this time, and you must expostulate the matter betweene *GOD* and your owne consciences, whether this love be in you or no. And although indeed this needeth not any distinct dividing into branches, yet that wee may helpe your memories, we will put it into a number.

Vse. Examination. And first wee will make this expostulation, You that professe you love the *LORD*, (as who will not bee readie to doe that, to say hee loveth *CHRIST?*) but yet, as the Apostle S. *John* speaketh of love to the brethren, that men love them in shew, and not in truth; so it is with most men, they love the *LORD* in word, and in profession, but they love him not in deed, and in truth:

truth: therefore first let mee aske you this.

You that professe you love the *LORD*, doe you not grieve him, and vexe him from day to day, and provoke him by your words, and by your workes? If this bee your case, it is certaine you love him not indeed. Some there are that professe much love to the *LORD IESVS*, but yet spend their time idly, are diligent in no calling, but waste their precious opportunities in sports, in idle visitations, in gaming, in doing nothing that is profitable, either to themselves or others, but eate and drinke, and rise up to play: It is the case of many of your young Gentlemen; a shamefull thing before men, and abominable in the sight of GOD,] that men should live like beasts, and make their soules like the soules of Swine, serving for nothing but to keepe their bodies from putrefaction, doing so much the lesse worke, because they have the more wages; burying so many precious talents, whereof their time is the chiefe, because it helpeth to improve all the rest: of which they shall give an exact account at that day, *When GOD shall judge the secrets of mens hearts according to our Gospell.* Doe you professe that you love the *Lord IESVS*, and doe you neglect him thus?

1. *Tryall.* If wee grieve him wee love him not.

Time a precious talent.

Besides this mocking of the *Lord*, and dissembling with him, you deale most foolishly with your selves: for all the comfort that you shall ever find in this life, it will bee from working, from being serviceable to *God*, and profitable to men;

emptie lives cause but emptie joy. Therefore if any man shall find this to bee his case, examine it, it is but a false profession of love. And as I speake to those that are young, that spend their time, *Nihil agendo*: So I may say the same to those that are of more yeares, that waste their lives in doing something indeed, but it is not that which they should doe, or in doing it in another manner than they ought; those that are so drowned in businesse, so overwhelmed with emploiment, so occupied with outward things abroad, that they have vacancie to feed their Soules within, to cloath them with graces. For you must know, my brethren, that your soules have need to bee trimmed every morning, as well as the bodie; they have need of breakefast, and dinner, and exercise, as well as the bodie: and as you faile in giving this due respect to the Soule daily, so you shall find that proportionably in that degree the inward man will languish, and grow faint. But to speake a word unto you likewise: Doe you thinke that you love the LORD IESUS in good earnest, and yet have scarce leisure to thinke of him from morning to night; that you cannot take time to speake to him, to seeke him, nor to prepare your hearts for him?

The soule hath need of respect as well as the body.

Besides this generall, come to particular sinnes, Sabbath-breaking, neglecting of private prayer, vaine-speeches, concupiscence and sinfull lusts, secret courses of uncleannesse, swearing, if not by greater, yet by lesser oathes, which indeed in this exceed

Wherein lesser oathes exceed greater.

exceed the greater, because in the other you sweare by the Creatour, in these by the creature. You that doe these things, will you say you love the *LORD?* You must know that it is a contradiction, it is impossible: For, *If you love mee keepe my Commandements:* If you keepe not the Commandements of *GOD*, certainely you love him not.

Object. But, it may bee, you will say that your meaning is good, that you are well affected to *CHRIST*, and therefore surely you doe not hate him.

Answ. He that neglecteth Gods commandements, loves him not.

My brethren, you are deceived in this, your meaning is not good; for while you cast the commandements of *God* behind you, you cast him away: and let mee say to you in this case, as you have it in *Ierem*, 3.4. You professe well in saying, *Thou art my Father, and the guide of my youth*, but you *doe evill more and more*. So, I say, when you professe you love the *Lord*, and that you reckon him your Father, and your Husband, thus you say indeed, but you doe evill more and more; and that is a certaine argument you love not the *LORD*. Therefore examine your selves by this rule: For if you love the *Lord*, you will reverence him. You know, whom wee love, wee reverence, and whom wee reverence, wee dare not doe any thing unmeet in their sight. Take any one whom we love, whose good opinion wee seeke for, wee had rather that all the world should see us doe an unseemely thing, than that he should; and certainly if you love the

LORD,

LORD, you would not dare to provoke him to anger. Therefore this carelesnesse in serving of him is a certaine signe of want of love to the *Lord IESVS*, this fearefulnesse, and carelesnesse, when you dare not shew your courage for him, when you account it a small matter to commit sinne against *GOD*, this ariseth from the defect of your love.

2. *Tryall.* By our sorrow after we have offended him.

In the second place, as you may trie your love by your taking care not to offend *GOD*, so likewise you may trie it by your sorrow and griefe after you have offended him. For you must know this, that love, as it hath the greatest joy of any thing else, when it obtaines that which it would have, so it is attended with the most exquisite griefe, when it is disappointed. As when one loveth another earnestly, if any breach fall out that shall make a separation betweene them, if any strangenesse grow betweene them, if they love, they will never bee at rest, it will trouble and disquiet them; but as the Scripture speakes, they are *sicke of love*, that is, they cannot bee quiet while there is such a condition, while there is any alienation, while there are breaches and offences between them: for you know that nothing is so sweet as love; as you have it in *Cant.*1. *Love is better than Wine*, and, as *David* expresseth it, *Psal.*63.3. *Thy loving kindnesse is better than life.* So sweet (I say) is love, as sweet as wine, and better than life. Now, by the rule of contraries, then, to have a breach made, to have a barre, and an interruption in this loving

loving kindnesse of the *Lord* towards us, or in our love towards him, it is bitter as wormewood, and sharpe as death. Therefore you may examine your selves by the offences you offer to *God*, when they are past: if you love him, it is certaine they will trouble you exceedingly: for so much sorrow for sinne, so much love. And you may take it for a sure rule; in what measure any man desires to please the *Lord*, in that measure hee will be grieved that hee hath displeased him. Therefore examine thy selfe, Hast thou sinned against him many times, and doest thou looke backe upon those sinnes in a carelesse manner? Bee sure that thou lovest him not. Examine this by that which passeth betweene man and man: When a Father or a Husband hath any thing committed against them by a Child, or a Wife, if they shall withdraw themselves, and professe themselves displeased, and yet the Child or the Wife, in the meane time, bee never troubled at this, but bee at rest, well enough content it should bee so, and are not disquieted for it; will not the parent or husband take this exceeding ill at their hands, when hee seeth his displeasure sleighted? For this is much greater than the offence it selfe. So I may say, whatsoever the sinne bee that you have committed, this hardnesse of heart, this negligence after the sinne is committed, when you are not disquieted for it, when your hearts are not troubled for it, it is a greater signe of want of love to the *LORD*, it is a greater signe of an evill and untoward disposition, than the sinne it selfe. Therefore this

So much sorrow for sinne, so much love.

Want of sorrow for sin, a greater argument of want of love, than the sin it selfe.

this want of sorrow for sinne, is a sure argument that you love not the LORD. You may take that for one signe of want of love, that you commit sins against *God* from day to day. For, doe but goe to your neighbours, and professe your love to them, and yet injure them againe and againe, not caring what wrong you doe to them, will they thinke that such a profession as you make is true? And will the LORD regard when you say that you love him, if you provoke him to anger, and renew your sinnes, and relapse into them againe and againe, and when you have sinned, take it not to heart? No, my Brethren, if you doe love him, you will doe as it is said, *Zech.* 12. when you have sinned, you will *mourne as hee that mourneth for his onely sonne*; your hearts will melt, as *Iosiahs* did; your hearts will smite you, as *Davids* did him: thus it is with all that love him in deed and in truth. Therefore in *Levit.* 16.29. and likewise *Levit.* 23. 27. (they are both one and the same) the LORD appoints a feast and a meeting together for cleansing of sinnes, it was the feast of attonement; saith hee, In that day when you come together to offer sacrifice unto mee, and to make an attonement, you shall *humble your soules, and whosoever doth not afflict his soule on that day, hee shall bee cut off from his people.* As if hee should say, At that day you come to reconcile your selves to the *Lord*, you make profession of your love to him, and of the desire you have to bee friends with him: Now if you come and make this profession, and doe not humble

humble your selves, nor afflict your soules on that day for those breaches that have beene betweene GOD and you, all your profession is but dissimulation; and such a man as will thus dissemble with the *Lord*, shall be cut off from his people. So, I say, when you professe that you love the *Lord*, and yet have hard hearts, that there is no softnesse there, that your hearts doe not melt towards him, but when you have sinned, you can looke backe upon your sinnes without any disturbance at all; know that it is but dissembling with the *Lord*, and you are worthy to be cut off from his people.

I come to a third tryall: If you love the *Lord Iesus*, have you your hearts after his owne heart: that is the disposition of all those that love him. *Acts* 13. 22. the LORD saith to *David*, *I have found a man after my owne heart, that will doe whatsoever I will:* That is, looke how the *Lord* himselfe was affected in any businesse, so was *Davids* heart affected, and so is it with all those that love the LORD; (for this is proper to the Saints:) if you love the *Lord*, you will be of one heart with him: If wee have hearts after his heart, as every Christian must have in his measure, (though perhaps hee reach not *Davids* measure) in all the turnings of our lives, upon all occasions, in the divers disposition of our wills, we will bee conformable to the *Lords* will, we will be like *God*, affected in every thing as he is affected. 3. *Tryall.* To have hearts after Gods own heart.

But, you will say, this is a hard thing, how shall we discerne it? *Quest.*

You shall discerne it by these two things: if you be *Answ.*

How to know our hearts are so.

be affected as he is, you will doe whatsoever hee will; as those words are added concerning *David*, *I have found a man after mine owne heart*, for *he will doe whatsoever I will*. You may examine your selves by that; Doe you doe whatsoever hee will? Are your affections aright, that you love what he loves, and hate what he hates? For your actions are the immediate fruits and effects of your affections, and as every man is affected, so he doth.

1. By hating that God hates *& è contra*.

2. By loving those that feare the Lord.

And besides, as that is one way to discerne it, so this is another, which you shall likewise find in *David*, that hee loved those that feared the LORD; and *those that love vaine inventions, doe I not hate them*, saith hee: &c. And that you may discerne this, consider whether you love all those that feare the LORD, and hate all those that are enemies to the *Lord*. For while there is nothing but nature in a man, so long those that are of good natures, that are faire in their carriages, and kind and loving to us, those wee love, and those that are contrary wee hate and dislike; but when you love the *Lord*, and are after his heart, and have another nature in you, it raiseth you above this nature of your owne, and then you will love those that are like the LORD, whosoever they are, though perhaps they are not so sociable, nor of so faire a naturall disposition: but if you have a new nature, and are become new creatures, now you have common friends, and common enemies.

Object.

Doe not object now, that you are willing to doe so, if they were sincere and upright, but they are hypocrites.

I say,

I say, doe not deceive your selves in this: for as they rejected *Christ* under the person of a counterfeit, and of a Wine-bibber, so thou maist persecute CHRIST under the person of an hypocrite. *Paul*, you know, he thought he did *God* good service in persecuting of those whom hee persecuted, yet though hee did it ignorantly, he confessed of himselfe that *hee was a blasphemer, and a persecutor*. So, I say, though you doe it ignorantly under the person of an hypocrite, yet that is the judgement, and the censure that will be upon you, and in so doing you are persecutors.

Answ. Men may persecute Christ under the name of an Hypocrite

And if you shall say, that if the *Lord* himselfe lived amongst us, if *Iesus Christ* were here, I hope I should shew that I doe not hate him.

Object. 2.

You shall see what the *Lord* himselfe saith, *In that you have done it to these, you have done it to mee.* As he speakes there in the matter of giving, so may I say to you concerning this case, In that you have despised those that feare his name, in that you have spoken against such as are his, you have done it against the *Lord*: in this thing you have shewed your hatred against him. Examine your hearts therefore seriously by this marke.

Answ. Those that persecute Christians would persecute Christ if he were on earth.

Againe, fourthly, wee will bring you to that expostulation which is grounded on 1 *Iohn* 2. 15. *Love not the world, nor the things of the world; for if you love the world, the love of the Father is not in you.* Now question with your owne hearts about this, whether you love the world, and the things of the world; for if you doe, the words are

4. *Tryall.* By loving the world.

are cleare, *The love of the Father is not in you.*

Quest. You will say, how shall we know this?

Answ. You shall know it by these three things.

Three trials of our love to the world.

1. By too much delighting in the things of the world.

First, by your delight in the things of the world, and your griefe and sorrow for the losse of them after you have enjoyed them; for if you find that you are over-much affected about them, it is certaine that you love the world, and the things of the world: Intemperate and excessive griefe, and complaint for worldly losses and crosses, is a sure argument and evidence that you love the world.

Whereas when you love the *Lord*, you will bee indifferent in those things; if a worldly losse befall you, you will grieve as if you grieved not, if any worldly advantage happeneth, you will enjoy it as if you enjoyed it not: A man will bee thus affected, If I have *God* sure, I reckon him onely my portion, all other things are by accident, hee onely is essentiall to my happinesse.

Wee doe not denie that a man may grieve upon such occasions, but it is a lighter kind of griefe; and therefore it is expressed well by the former phrase, *As if hee grieved not*: Hee knoweth all this while the maine is sure, and so long his heart is stedfast within him: but when a man shall fall into excessive griefe, when the affection shall bee exceedingly stirred about worldly things, it is a signe that you reckon not *GOD*, and the assurance of his favour to bee the maine thing in your happinesse: you should be affected to the World with a remisse affection.

affection. Now when your affections are so much taken up about them, it is a signe you love the world, and the things of the world. It is true, you may doe the things of the world, and enjoy them, and follow after them, but in a remisse manner; but when your affections are so much stirred about them, when you come to excessive love in the having them, and excessive griefe in the losing them, it is signe that you love the world, and the things of the world.

Secondly, you shall know it by this, when worldly things shall come into competition with those that belong to a good conscience, and the service of GOD, you shall find this one way whereby you may discerne your love to the world. When *Christ* would make a tryall of the young man, whether hee loved the world or no, he puts him to it by this, *Goe* (saith he) *and sell all that thou hast, and come and follow mee, and thou shalt have treasure in heaven.* When it came in competition once, whether hee were best to follow *Christ*, and sell all that hee had, and that hee must either forsake *CHRIST*, or forsake his riches, hee went away sorrowfull, and would not doe it. So we shall find in *Iohn* 12.42. when the matter came there into competition, that if they confessed *Christ*, they should bee cast out of the Synagogue; saith the Text, though they beleeved, *They confessed him not, for they loved the praise of men more than the praise of God.* Their carriage there towards *Christ*, when their confessing of him came in competition with

2. When worldly things come in competition with a good conscience.

their applause and honour among men, it was an argument that they *loved the world and the things of the world.*

You shall see in *Abrahams* case, when the *Lord* would put him to the triall, and bids him *come from his kindred, and from his Fathers house, and from his countrey,* this in *Heb.* 11. is taken as an argument of his love, that when he was put to doe either the one or the other, he made his choice to obey the *LORD,* though it stood with the losse of his countrey and friends. So, I say, consider with your selves, and you shall find many cases wherein your conscience will dictate to you, this you must doe, this you ought to performe, this you ought not to doe. Perhaps it shall bee said unto you againe, if you doe it, you shall lose such a friend, you shall lose such credit, you shall suffer such losse in your estate, you shall expose your selfe to such and such danger, you shall incurre such and such inconveniences to your selfe; consider what you doe in such a case: Many businesses fall out every day, wherein the like case is offered to you, many times you thinke it were best to doe so, and if it were not for the losse of something, or for the discredit, you would doe it. By this you may examine your hearts whether you love the world or no.

3. By being busie in them,

Lastly, you shall know whether you love the world, and the things of the world, by your actions; for where your love is, there your tongue, and your hand will bee, and all your endeavours: Now trie your selves by this, Are you occupied so so about the world, and the things of it, that all your endeavours and all your actions are taken up about them? Some about matter of pleasure, in hunting aud hawking, in gaming and sporting, your thoughts are there, and your speeches there; others againe in seeking wealth, and worldly greatnesse: Are you taken up about these? I say, the actions of a Man are a sure signe: for the *Lord* judgeth us by our actions; therefore wee may judge our selves by them. Consider in what element you live, if you bee so busied about worldly things, that you are never well but when you are there, and as for heavenly things, you doe them but by the by, and when you are doing them you are wearie; this is an argument that you love the world, when a man shall turne the streame of his endeavours all that way, when hee shall turne all his projects, all his actions, all his labours into that. As when the bodie hath a wenne or a wolfe in it, all the nourishment is drawne to that, and in the meane time the body is leane and poore: so is it when a mans heart is taken up with the World, it eates up and devoures all the thoughts, all the intentions of the mind, all his care, and endeavour, and striving runnes this way; and *the hidden man of the heart,* in the meane time, is left starved and pined within. This is a signe that you love the World, this so much intending the things of this world: as *Christ* speakes, *The lusts of your Father will you doe, Ioh.* 8. What is the meaning of that? That is, looke to your actions, to your doings, to your executions

Simile.

and performances, and you ſhall find that they are according to the luſts of your Father the Divell, thoſe actions they did were a ſigne that they did affect thoſe things that the Divell affected.

Object. But you will object, the holieſt man, hee that is moſt regenerate, yet is inordinately affected to the world, is too readie to grieve, and to rejoyce inordinately, is too readie to faile when theſe things come in competition with GOD. Therefore how ſhould we examine our hearts by this?

Anſw. The Saints doe mind the world too much, but they allow not themſelves in it.

I anſwer in a word, that it is true in the Saints, there is ſomething in their hearts that doth all this that you have ſpoken; but it is not they that doe it: as the Apoſtle ſpeakes, *It is not I, but ſinne that dwells in mee.* Wee cannot deny but that there is fleſh and worldly-mindedneſſe even in them; but yet this they doe, theſe worldly luſts and deſires they are ſtill checking them, and reſtraining them, and keeping them downe, ſo that though they bee there, yet they doe not *walke after the vanitie of their mindes,* they are not left by it, but they are *led by the Spirit, that walke by the Spirit.* Indeed ſometimes they fall, when they are tranſported with temptations, and through incogitancie, and infirmitie; yet their conſtant *walking is not after the vanitie of their mind,* for that is proper to thoſe that feare not GOD. Therefore know thus much (my brethren) that though the Saints doe theſe things ſometimes, yet their purpoſe, and their deſire and care is to croſſe and reſiſt them as much as they can, that though they have theſe inordinate worldly

worldly desires in them, yet they are not Midwives to themselves, to *bring forth fruit to the flesh*, they are not stewards, to provide for these before-hand, as it is in *Rom.13. Put yee on the Lord Iesus, and take no care for the flesh, to make provision for it:* I say, they are not stewards for their lusts, but they resist them, and strive against them. But to conclude this also, examine your selves by this rule, whether you love the world, and the things of the world.

And if we take an examination of men by this, how few are there that love the *Lord?* Wee may truely say as the Apostle saith, *The love of God is not in them*, for *men seeke themselves, and their owne things, and not the things of Iesus Christ.* One followes this particular, another that, every man fitting and plotting a garment to himselfe, composed of such vices as doe suite every mans humour. This is a signe that you love not the *Lord,* when you mind the World, and goe with the world, and let your whole body and soule follow it, with all the actions, and all the strength and endeavour thereof. *The love of many shall waxe cold, because iniquitie shall abound.* What is the meaning of that? That is, because the men of the world, those that are in place, because they shall countenance iniquitie, because the streame of the times shall goe that way; for this cause *the love of many shall waxe cold:* that is, because they mind the world, whereas if they did not love the world, and the things of it, though iniquitie did abound, yet their love would waxe

 hotter.

hotter. When things are so that iniquitie abounds, some will not take the paines, they love their ease, and contentment; others want courage to doe it, they are faint-hearted, and dare not adventure. Now whence doth this come, but from the love of the world? for no man is fearefull, but because there is something that hee is in love with, and is loath to part with. If a man did not love the things of the world, he would have courage for the truth. This is therefore an argument that men doe love the world, and consequently the love of the Father is not in them.

5. Tryall. By a readinesse to please him.

Let us come yet to another expostulation. In the fifth place therefore, if you love the *LORD*, you will find in your selves a readinesse to please him in all things, you will doe it naturally: As the Apostle speakes of *Timothy*, *I know no man like minded, who will naturally care for your matters*. So if you love the *Lord* aright, you will doe it with a naturall affection, you will love him naturally: For what is this love to the *LORD*, if it be right, but that which himselfe hath planted in us? Wee are *taught of him* to love him. It is like the naturall affection which Parents have to their Children; such a kind of affection will it bee: if you love the *LORD*, you will doe that which is good in his sight with a kind of naturalnesse and readinesse; you will bee carried to the duties of his service, as the fire is carried upwards, and not as stones are carried upwards, with the force of another, but you will doe them readily and chearfully; you will

not

not doe good duties as being haled to them, and put on to doe them, but you will bee *zealous of good workes*, that is, you will have a burning desire in your hearts, longing after them, you shall not need to have them forced upon you, but you will bee forward to doe them, you will bee affected to good workes as you are, out of selfe-love, to your owne businesse. You know, when a man naturally loveth himselfe, when hee is to doe something that concernes his owne good, how solicitous hee is about it, and how provident, fore-casting how to bring it to passe, and if any rubbe bee in the way it troubleth him; if there bee any faire passage, and likelihood of atchieving it, he rejoyceth. Now, if you love the *Lord* naturally and truely, you will goe about his businesse as you goe about your owne, if there bee any businesse to bee done. Magistrates in their place, Ministers in their place, and every man indeed shall find some businesse to doe wherein hee may bring glory to *Gods* name, and advantage to his cause. Consider now how you are stirred about it, doe you goe about this businesse, are you so industrious and laborious, doe you project it, doe you mind it as your owne? you will not stand expostulating the matter, to say, must I doe it? and is it of necessitie? But if it bee a thing that tends to the advancing of the glory of *GOD*, you will doe it with all readinesse, you will not so much stand upon this, what wages shall I have? and what profit shall I gaine? But as a loving woman to her husband, shee is glad to doe any thing for her husbands good, shee is satisfied with this, that shee hath an opportunitie to doe something; so it will bee with you, if your hearts bee rightly affected, you will then doe things after this manner.

Quest. You will say, how shall wee know this love? this is a nice and curious point to love the *Lord* thus naturally.

Answ. You shall know it by these two things:

Naturalnesse of love to the *Lord* is knowne by two things. 1. By our even carriage towards him.

First, by the evennesse of your carriage towards the *Lord*; for what a man doth naturally, hee doth with a kind of equalitie, with a kind of evennesse: so that, as we say, an uneven pulse is a signe of a deadly and dangerous distemper within; so I say, when you find an unevennesse in your carriages to the *LORD*, that you are off and on with him, that sometimes you doe a thing for him, and anon you will doe for your lusts, this is a signe that you love not naturally. Feigned things are for the most part unequall: because when a man doth not doe a thing naturally, hee cannot hold out; a man cannot dissemble so well, but at one time or other hee will discover himselfe; what a man doth naturally, and heartily, hee is like himselfe in it still. Therefore when there is such an unevennesse in your wayes, (some will be very forward in a good cause, now in a good moode, and then out of it againe) it is a signe you love not the *Lord* thus naturally, for then you would be even in your carriage towards him.

Adde to this the continuance of it, for if you love

love the *Lord* with a naturall affection, you will hold out, and bee constant in it. The second and third ground went farre in their profession, but their inconstancie shewed that they loved not the *Lord* with a naturall love; this discontinuing is a signe that your love is not true. I beseech you examine your selves by these things whether you love the *Lord*; remember what I said the last day, doe you desire that your sinnes should bee vtterly destroyed? doe you not dally with sinne? Would you not have some remainders within you? Nay, I will goe a step further with you, doe you not hate the *Lord*? — 2. By a constant carriage.

Object. You will say, *God* forbid wee should doe so, I hope we are not in that condition.

Answ. My brethren, first you must know, that there are many that doe hate the *LORD*: *Rom.* 1. amongst others, those are reckoned up, *Haters of God*: Therefore it is certaine that there are many, and many of those that come to Church, many that thinke well of themselves, and that others thinke well of too, that yet are haters of the *LORD*. *Quest.* You will say, how shall we know that?

Answ. I will aske you but this (to bring this likewise into examination, and so to conclude) I say, examine your selves by this:

Foure signes of hatred of God.

1. If we desire that he were not.

Doe you not desire that there were no *GOD*? examine your hearts whether if this newes were brought that you might live at liberty, that you might doe what you would, that you might satisfie your lusts in all things, that there were no *GOD*

to

to call you to account, to reward you according to your doings, whether it would not bee acceptable newes to many of you. Now it is certaine, if you would not have the *Lord* to be, you hate him; for whomsoever you would have taken out of the way, such a man you hate.

2. If wee looke on him as a Judge onely.

And besides this, consider whether you doe not looke upon the *Lord*, as upon a Iudge, whether you doe not all that you doe to him as one that lookes upon a Iudge: If you feare the *Lord* in this manner, it is certaine you hate him, for those whom you thus feare, you hate; and that you shall find in 1 *Iohn* 4. if you feare, saith hee, you love not; for *perfect love casts out feare*: when you looke upon *God* as upon a strict Iudge, and that is it that puts you on to doe all that you doe, that is it that makes you keepe a good conscience in secret: (for this you may doe, and yet looke upon *God* as a Iudge) to feare with this kind of feare is a signe you hate the *Lord*, for whom you feare, you hate.

3. When wee looke on *God* and his wayes as contrary to us.

Besides this, Doe you not looke upon GOD and upon his wayes, as contrary to your hearts? that your hearts, and the wayes of GOD are in an opposition; your hearts, and sanctifying the Sabbath will not agree; the *Lord* would have your speeches to bee good and holy, hee would have you not onely abstaine from evill, but to hate it, to have your hearts rise up against it: Are not these Commandements contrary to you? Consider but that holinesse that is expressed in the booke of GOD, and that is expressed also in the lives of the

the Saints, who carry his Image ſtamped on them, and is there not a kind of contrarietie betweene your wayes and theirs, betweene your hearts and them? If there be, it is a certaine ſigne of hatred: for whereſoever there is contrariety, there is hatred. Examine your ſelves by this, and ſee whether you doe not hate the *Lord*.

And yet, to come to one more, if you *love pleaſures more than God*, and wealth more than GOD, you hate *God*: For ſo you have it, *Math.6. No man can ſerve two Maſters, but either hee muſt hate the one and love the other,&c.* That is, when you love other things, though you thinke you doe not hate the *LORD*, yet, I ſay, in that you love pleaſures, and love the world, and the things of the world, in that you love your luſts, and the objects of them, in doing this, you hate the *Lord*. Now, if this be your caſe, if upon theſe expoſtulations that I have propounded, if upon theſe rules of examining your ſelves, you find that you doe not love the *Lord*, if this bee your condition, (as it is your wiſdome to deale ſtrictly with your ſelves; for hence it is, brethren, that the ſoules of men periſh, becauſe they will not ſee and ſearch into their eſtates, they will not come to this examination of themſelves, it is a painfull thing to them, men are backward to examine themſelves, in private; what is the reaſon of that phraſe in the Pſalme, *Examine your ſelves upon your beds*, but becauſe examination ſhould bee when a man is moſt retired?) I ſay, if you find it to be ſo, as it is the caſe of many, then it

4. When we love pleaſure more than *God*.

it ſhould open a window to you, to ſee what you have deſerved at the *Lords* hands, how juſt it were that the *Lord* ſhould caſt you off: For when you are enemies to the *Lord*, can you thinke much at it? My brethren, what a condition is that man in, that hath the great *God* of heaven and earth to bee his enemy?

And beſides this, have you not reaſon to juſtifie *GOD* in his juſt judgements upon others, when you ſhall ſee *GOD* ſharply plaguing them? It may ſeeme to you that it is a hard thing that men ſhould be ſo puniſhed; but when we conſider that they are haters of *GOD*, that they are enemies to him, you may juſtifie *GOD* in that he doth.

But, to conclude, you ought to humble your ſelves, if upon theſe tryals you find your ſelves to be lovers of the world, and not lovers of *God*. And you that are young and put off repentance, it ſhould move you to come in betimes: For if this be required of you to love the *Lord*, and you ſhall not bee exempted from death when it comes, though you bee never ſo able, and never ſo ſtrong and luſty; what condition doe you thinke you will bee in, if you die enemies to *GOD*, and haters of him, as you needs muſt bee, if you love him not? And if you thinke you have time enough hereafter to ſettle your affections; Conſider, is it in your owne power, though you have warning before death, to have this affection of love? You may doe many good duties, you may bee ſorry and repent for your ſins; but though you doe this, and a thouſand times more,

more, yet if you have not this love wrought in you by GOD, if it come not from heaven, if it be not the fruit of his owne Spirit, all your repentance, and all your forsaking of sinne, all your doing of duties, the change of your courses is nothing, the *Lord* regards it not, unlesse you have this naturalnesse of love. I have stood therefore the longer upon it, and upon this part concerning examination, because it is a matter of great moment. Wee should have come to the next part concerning exhortation, which wee would not dis-joyne, because it is very usefull and profitable; but we cannot doe it now, but reserve it for the after-noone.

* * *

FINIS.

THE

OF LOVE

The sixth Sermon.

GALAT. 5.6.

For in Iesus Christ, neither circumcision availeth any thing, nor uncircumcision, but Faith which worketh by Love.

AND before we leave this point, one thing I must adde. For what reason doe wee put upon this disposition, upon this examination, whether the love of *GOD* be in your hearts or no? The reason is not that you should bee discouraged, that you should bee put off from comming to *God*, that you should be grieved with the sight of the want of your love, but the end of it is to stirre you up to get it if you want it. You know, wee have formerly delivered some meanes of getting it, onely there is one which we will wil comend unto, you which we gave a little touch * on, but could not handle it, and it consists of these three branches. If you would love the *Lord*,

First, you must know him, for otherwise you cannot love him. As it is in naturall love that is bred betweene man and man, you say love ariseth from sight, they must see before they can love, so you must know the *LORD*, there must bee a sight of *GOD* by faith, before you can love him. And every man that sees him and knowes him as hee is, will love him, hee cannot chuse, for that is the *Lords* worke to all the Saints. *Ierem.* 31. *You shall bee taught of mee, and you shall know me from the greatest to the least.* It may be in some manner they knew *GOD* before, but although a man have never so exact knowledge of him, yet till hee bee a regenerate man, hee never knowes him indeed, it is an other kinde of knowledge that hee hath, when a man is regenerate; when *God* teaches him to know him, hee lookes on *GOD* with another eye, every thing is presented to him after another manner, hee sees now another beautie in *GOD* than ever hee saw before, hee sees another excellencie in him: for that knowledge hee had of him before bred not love. But when a man is once within the Covenant, the *LORD* will teach him such a knowledge of himselfe, as withall will worke the love of him. Such a knowledge you must have of the *LORD*, and you may helpe your selves to love him by reasoning, if ever you saw any excellencie in any man, or in any creature, it did helpe

* Pag. 108

The last helpe of the love of *God* consisting of three branches.

1. The knowledge of *God*.

helpe you to love that creature. Thinke with your selves there is more in *God* that made that creature; *Hee that made the eye, shall hee not see?* So hee that wrought that excellencie, shall not hee have it in himselfe in a greater measure? Besides, you may consider how the *Lord* hath described himselfe, that he is *most wise, most mercifull, and full of kindnesse, and gentlenesse, and abundant in truth,* as you know that description in *Exod.* 34.

Goe through all the vertues, and excellencies that are amiable, if you looke in the Scripture, you shall find them to bee in the *Lord.* This serious consideration will helpe you to increase your knowledge of the *Lord,* and by consequent your love of him. So that, if you would come to love a man, what is it that causeth you to love him, but because by his speech, and by his carriage and behaviour, you come to have such an apprehension of his disposition, hee hath a mind thus framed, thus qualified, thus beautified? When you conceive such an *Idea* of him, you love him. So, when you apprehend the *Lord* aright, when you observe him as he is described in his Word, when you observe his doings, when you consider his workes, and learne from all these together a right apprehension of him, I say, when you have such an *Idea* of him, such an opinion of him, then the will followes the undestanding, and the affections then follow, then you come to love him, and to delight in him. Therefore learne to know the *LORD* by his former carriage towards your selves, how kind hee

hath

hath beene, how exceeding patient, how exceeding ready to forgive, how much kindnesse he hath shewed; how he hath in mercie remembred you, though you have forgotten him; how you have recompenced him evill for good, yet hee hath not broken off the course of his mercie towards you. Consider his dealing with you, and learne by this, to know the LORD, and this will be a meanes to encrease in you the love of the *Lord*.

2. A looking upon *God* as one suitable to us.

This is not all, there is another thing, which is the second branch that I told you of; that is, to looke upon GOD as one suitable to you, and to your disposition. For if you should find never so much excellency in him, if hee be not agreeable to you, you love him not. A woman may see a man that she thinkes is very excellent in many respects, yet he is not a fit husband for her. It is the suitablenesse and agreeablenesse betweene GOD and our owne condition, that causeth us to love him. Therefore when you put these two together, consider the *Lords* mercy, and see that, and looke on your selves as sinfull men needing that mercie; when you see the LORD exceeding powerfull, and looke on your selves as very weake, needing that power; when you looke on him as the *Lord* of life, and see your selves subject to death, and needing that life; when you see your owne folly, and his wisedome, (goe through all in him, and then againe looke upon the contrary weaknesse in your selves) this is that which will make you apprehend *God* as one that is suitable, as one that is agreeable to you; and till you come to this, you ſhall never love him, and long after him, till the heart (namely) bee thus framed, till a man is humbled, till hee comes to the ſight of himſelfe: for as you muſt know GOD, ſo you muſt know your ſelves before you can love him. I ſay, when a man comes to that, hee begins to looke on GOD as upon one agreeable to him: As, take a man who is touched with a ſenſe of his ſinnes, whoſe heart is broken, who hath an apprehenſion of GODS wrath, and of his owne unworthineſſe, ſuch a man now will bee ſatisfied with nothing in the world, but the aſſurance of *Gods* love and his favour. As you ſee in naturall things, let a man bee very wearie, the daintieſt meat in the world, whatſoever you give him, will not helpe him; but hee muſt have that which is fit for that particular defect, nothing will helpe him but reſt. Againe, let a man bee hungry, and faint for want of meat; all the muſicke, the beſt aire, or whatſoever you can give him will doe him no good, it muſt be meat that muſt helpe him. If a man have a diſeaſe, it is not ſleepe, it is not meat and drinke, it muſt bee a medicine that is fit for his diſeaſe. So it is with the heart of man, when his heart is ſo broken, ſo humbled and touched with the ſenſe of his ſinnes, that he longs after nothing but remiſſion, nothing but the aſſurance of *Gods* favour, the aſſurance of his love and kindneſſe, nothing will ſatisfie him but that: it is ſo in naturall defects, and ſo it is in the ſoule, when the heart of a man is ſo faſhioned that it lookes upon

To a man ſenſible of his ſins nothing is acceptable but *Gods* favour.

God as one agreeable to him, and there is nothing else suitable but onely the *Lord*, and his favour, and his love; that is required, to breed this love in you towards him. What is the reason else, that it is said, *Hosea* 5.*ult*. *When they are afflicted they will seeke mee diligently?* But because afflictions teach a man to know himselfe, it teacheth him to know his owne weaknesse, to see his owne sinne, his owne impotencie, his owne unworthinesse; and when hee hath done this, then hee lookes upon *God*, as one who onely is fit for him, as one who is onely able to helpe him. Affliction doth but discover what was there before: For man is a weake and impotent creature, made for the *LORD*, he is nothing without the *LORD*, it is the conjunction with *GOD* that makes him up, onely hee knowes not this, he understands not this. Therefore when *GOD* opens a mans eyes, either by the immediate worke of his Spirit, to teach him to know himselfe, or by affliction, then hee comes to seeke after the *Lord*; when they are afflicted, they will seeke mee diligently. If thou shouldest have such an offer as was made to those, *Act*. 2. S. *Peter* tells them there, they should have remission of sinnes, they should receive the gift of the holy Ghost; if this had beene offered to them before they knew themselves, before they had beene humbled and *pricked at the heart*, as it is said they were, would they have regarded such an offer as this? No, they would not, although they had understood that offer never so well. So, I say, though you know his

Afflictions teach a man to know himselfe.

name, and his excellent attributes never so perfectly, yet till you come to know your selves too, you will never love him, you will never desire him, you will never long after him: for both these must goe together, the knowledge of *God*, and the knowledge of your selves, to teach you to love him. The knowledge of *God*, without the knowledge of your selves, is a fruitlesse speculation: And againe, the knowledge of your selves, and your owne misery, without knowledge of him and his mercy, is a miserable vexation. The knowledge of *God*, without the knowledge of your selves, is, as if a man should know a medicine, but should not know what defect it were fit to suppply: And to know your selves and your owne case without him, is to have the disease discouered, and not to know how to helpe it. And therefore learne to know both *God* and your selves: If you will love him, then you must learne to studie those two. Wee say, Schollers studie bookes, and Polititians studie men; but a Christian should studie GOD and himselfe, to learne to know *God* and himselfe better, by this meanes hee comes to know the *Lord*: as wheresoever you find any love to the *Lord* expressed, you shall find these two going together, as *David* oft, *Psal.* 18. and *Psal.* 116. *I love the Lord*, &c. Why? *For I was in distresse*, I was in griefe, the grave overtooke mee, and I was compassed about with death, and cried to the *Lord*, *and hee healed mee, and set mee at libertie*, *hee is my fortresse*, &c. That is, when *David* saw himselfe to stand in need, hee

The knowledge of *God* and of our selves must goe together.

A Christians studie.

hee ſaw his weakneſſe, and looked on *God* againe, as one that would helpe him, and heale him, as one that could ſet him at libertie; this cauſed him to ſay, I love the *Lord* dearely. So S.*Paul*, when hee ſaw theſe two, *I was a blaſphemer, I was a perſecutor*, and looked on *Christ* (who had beene mercifull to him) with faith, this was that which cauſed S.*Paul* ſo to abound in love towards *Christ*. And ſo *Mary*, *Luke* 1. *My ſoule doth magnifie the Lord*. And why? *For hee had reſpect to the low estate of his handmaid:* I was poore and meane, and loe hee hath raiſed mee to a high degree. This ſuitableneſſe, this knowledge of *God* and of our ſelves, is that which breedes in us a love of him. But is this enough now to know *God* and our ſelves? This is a faire ſtep to beget in you this love of him; for as you heard before, love is an inclination of the heart to ſome good thing agreeable to us.

But yet you muſt have a third, or elſe this will not doe, that is, aſſurance of the *LORDS* love to you, for if you long after him never ſo much, if you thinke him worthy to bee deſired; on the other ſide, yet if for all this you are not perſwaded of the *Lords* love to you, you cannot bee affected towards him. Wee cannot love any man whom wee conceive to bee ill affected to us: And therefore you ſhall ſee in the courſe of the Scriptures, love proceedes from faith, faith muſt beget love, that is, the aſſurance of *GODS* love muſt goe in: That is the third ingredient to make it up. 3. Aſſurance of the *Lords* love to us.

Object. You will say to me, we doubt not of this, but if we be perswaded of *Gods* love, we shall love him; but how shall wee come to this perswasion? how shall we assure our selves of his love?

Answ. Those to whom I should speake now, are of two sorts; either such as are out of the Covenant, or such as are already within it. For you

1. Such as are without.

that are without, to you I say, you may (if you will consider it) come to the assurance of his love towards you.

Meanes whereby men may be assured of *Gods* love to them.

1. *God* the Father offers his love.

For first, the *LORD* hath made knowne his owne willingnesse to take you to marriage. There are but two that are to give their consent, the Father to give his Sonne, and the Sonne to give his owne consent: The Father, you know, hath given his consent, *Isay 9.6. A Son is given: Hee so loved the World, that hee gave his Sonne.* Therefore certainly you have your Fathers consent, hee hath given *Christ*, as a father gives his sonne in marriage. But now whether wee have the Sons consent or no, of that we make question; saith the Apostle, *He loved us, and gave himselfe* to us, and *for us*; Yea, he not onely gives his consent, for his part, but he hath purchased his Wife with his owne bloud. And therefore you cannot doubt but that hee is willing to marry with you, to take you, and to receive you if you will come in. Why then, what is required now? Nothing at all but thy consent, if thou give thy consent to the *LORD*, thou needest not to question his favour, thou mayest assure thy selfe of his unchangeable love in *Iesus Christ*; for hee hath

2. So doth *God* the Sonne.

revealed

revealed it on his part, in his Word, you have his sure Word for that, *Heaven and Earth shall passe*, rather than that Word. This is the sound consolation that will not faile you, when you come to examination, and thinke with your selves, upon what ground am I assured of *Gods* affection towards me, that he loves me; I have his Word for it, hee hath said it, and he cannot recall it; yea, hee hath added his oath, that by two immutable witnesses you might have strong consolation; that is, you might have the greatest degree of assurance that can bee. Why, now, why doest not thou give thy consent? Why doest thou no more rest on it? You will say, alas! I am willing to give my consent, if that would doe it.

Object. But first, I am unfit to marrie the *Lord*, I am not prepared for such a match as that is, my heart is too bad, and my life hath been too sinfull to thinke of such preferment and advancement.

Answ. Vnfitnesse should not discourage us from taking Christ.

Take thou no care for that, the *Lord* knew thy unfitnesse, when he made that promise to thee, when he gave his Son, and the Son gave himselfe to thee, he was well enough acquainted with thee and with thy nature, he had an intention to marry a Blackmoore, he justified the wicked, hee knowes thou art so, and yet he will doe it, he will put a fairenesse, hee wil put a beauty upon thee, when thou art his Wife; therefore let not that hinder, thy unfitnesse.

Object. 2. You will say againe, it may belong to such and such, it doth not belong to me; my case is such, I have provoked him in this manner, my sinnes are of such a nature.

Answ. No sinnes exclude from *Christ*.

This shall not shut thee out neither. For why shouldest thou make exceptions where the *Lord* makes none? *Goe preach the Gospell to every creature under heaven.* What is the meaning of that? That is, goe tell every man, without exception, whatsoever his sinnes bee, whatsoever his rebellions bee, goe tell him this glad tidings; that is, to preach the Gospell to him, that if hee will come in, I will accept him, he shall be saved, his sinnes shall bee forgiven him, if he doe no more but come in, and take me, and receive mee. Therefore to conclude this, doubt not thou that that shall bee a hinderance on *Gods* part. And for thy owne part, there is no more required of thee but sinceritie, that thou take him, sincerely resolving with thy selfe, I will serve him for the future, I will bee contented to bee divorced from all my former loves, from all the sinnes that I have delighted in before, I am willing now to take him, and to serve him, and to love him, and to give my selfe wholly to him; I say, this sincerity of resolution is enough, there can bee no hinderance if this be found in thee. Therefore doe not thinke with thy selfe, I want sorrow for my sinnes, such a degree of sorrow, my heart is not broken enough, and therefore I am not fit: for thou must know thus much, that the promise is made to the comming, and not to the preparations. If thou canst come and take the *Lord*, it is enough, if a man have so much sorrow, so much heart-breaking as brings him home to *CHRIST*, as makes him willing to match with the *LORD*; if he have that

wrought

wrought in him, hee need not doubt of the other.

But now I come to the other, those that are already within the Covenant, to you I say, you may much more easily and fully come to this assurance, because yee have the fruits of the Spirit in you, which are the seales of his love; you have cause to trust perfectly through the grace that is revealed in IESVS CHRIST: you know that exhortation, *Trust perfectly to the grace revealed,&c.* that is, in the free offer to every man by CHRIST; trust not in that by halves, remissely, and unperfectly, and weakly; but trust perfectly, bee confident in that, that the LORD will thus receive you, trust perfectly in the grace revealed. 2. Such as are within the Covenant.

But, you will say, I commit many sinnes from day to day, I am negligent in many duties, I find much unevennesse in my life, many distempers in my affections, &c. *Object.*

What if you find all this in your selves? Yet so long as your hearts are sincere, you must know this, that every breach, every offence doth not breake the band of Wedlock between the LORD and you, you must not thinke there is a breach of covenant betweene *God* and you upon every sinne that is committed, but know that the Covenant holds good, till you come to choose another Husband, the *Lord* continues your Husband still. Therefore when thou art married to the *Lord*, it is not for thee to thinke then of questioning the match, but studie to please thy Husband, and to do thy duty. You know there may be many offences, *Answ.* Daily infirmities breake not the Covenant.

and many ſlight breaches betweene a Man and his Wife, but the bond holds good, there is no Bill of divorcement, except it be in caſe of Adulterie, that ſhee chuſe another Husband : ſo thinke, in ſuch a caſe, the bond is not broken upon every offence, and every ſinne that is committed. Learne to know this for thy comfort, for it is a great matter to have this aſſurance full.

Anſw. 2. Weake grace muſt not bee accounted none.

And beſides, conſider this, thinke not with thy ſelfe, becauſe I have not attained ſuch a degree of holineſſe as another hath, therefore I have none at all, that is an evill reaſon, that diſcourageth the Saints, diſcourageth many times thoſe that ſhould bee incouraged, that are already within the Covenant; hee lookes on another, and ſees hee cannot reach him, hee propounds to himſelfe ſuch a meaſure of grace, and of holineſſe, and of mortification of his luſts, and hee cannot come neere it; and hee thinkes, becauſe I cannot doe this, I have no ſinceritie in me. Not ſo, there are degrees; when a Man is within the doore, hee may goe further and further, and though all may be within, yet one may be further in than another.

Anſw. 3. The *Lord* is faithful, though we faile.

Beſides all this, know that the *LORD* is faithfull, hee cannot denie himſelfe, though thou faile on thy part, yet hee continues the ſame, and reneweth his mercie to thee, as thou reneweſt thy Repentance. But, to conclude this, if you would love the *Lord*, labour to doe theſe three things:

Labour to know him more:

Labour to know your ſelves more, that ſo

you

you may long after him as after one that you need.

And thirdly, labour to get this assurance, for it is this assurance that breedes the Love, that seales it up. When a man shall looke on GOD as one who may hate him for any thing hee knowes, who may bee an enemy to him one day, hee can never love him heartily. When a man hath no ground to set his foot on, hee will doe it tenderly and warily: but when hee lookes upon GOD as one whom hee may trust, whose love he is sure of, that he builds on that as a Rocke; this is that which makes his heart perfect to him, when hee can say, as *Paul*, *I know whom I have trusted:* If a Man have never so much excellencie in him, if you conceive him to bee hollow-hearted to you, your affections are not perfect towards him: So is it, if you looke on *God* as one that may bee your enemie. As wee say, friendship with Princes, it is like that familiaritie that those men have with Lyons that keepe them. A Lion, you know, will suffer a Man to play with him as long as hee lists, and when hee lists, hee will rise and devoure him, and rend him in pieces: so I say, the love of a Prince may be, and the love of men may bee: but the love of the *Lord* is not such, when hee loves, hee loves perfectly. It is true, he hath the strength of a Lion, hee is able to doe it, you are weake creatures subject to him, but hee hath that constancie in him, that when he loves once, it is alwayes perfect, and unchangeable. Let all these bee well condesired and wrought on your hearts,

Friendship with great men, what.

hearts, and it will bee a meanes to beget this love in you: even as fire begets fire, so will this beget love in your hearts towards him againe. So much for this.

Exhortation to love Christ.

The second point, which I intend to handle at this time, is this; another consectary, another use we are to draw from this Doctrine, *Hee that loves not, is not in Christ*.

The next use is to exhort you to come in, if it be a thing of that moment, now our businesse is to exhort to love the *Lord Iesus*. And is there not much reason to move you to it? If you had this love in your hearts, would it not bee a ground of much comfort to you? For if you were able to beleeve in *Iesus Christ*, and love him, you should have your salvation sure, if once you could find this disposition in your selves, as it must be in you, if ever you be saved, that your hearts long after him; still you are growing towards him, hanging that way, as a stone to the Center, as the Iron to the Loadstone: there is such a lingring after him, the heart makes towards him, and will have no deniall; but, as the Woman of *Canaan*, it breakes through all impediments, no barre can keepe it from him: as those that love, they are not easily put off; but are importunate till they have obtained reciprocall affections of the party beloved.

I say, if thou find this disposition in thy heart, it is the greatest consolation that thou canst have in this world: for if this bee thy case, thou maist boldly looke that *the gates of Hell shall not prevaile*

against

against thee: and if thou love the *Lord* in this manner, Heaven and Earth shall passe rather than thy salvation shall be hindred: it is impossible, because then thou hast a good ground of hope, and *hope will make thee not ashamed*; but be assured that *God* is thine, and all that hee can doe, and all that is his is thine; as *Saul* tels us, his power and his wisdome and all is thine: *Hee is a Sunne and a shield* to thee; thou shalt want nothing that is good, nothing that is evill shall hurt thee; the *LORD* brings all with him: this is your case if you love him, this is your consolation, this is that which may inflame your hearts with a desire of this affection. For, know this, that there is scarcely any thing else that wee can instance in, but an hypocrite may goe cheeke by jowle with a good Christian in that; he may do all outward duties, hee may abstaine from sinnes, there may be a great change in him; (you know how farre the third ground went, and those, *Heb.6.*) but this they cannot counterfeit, to *love the Lord*. Therefore, if thou find that thou love the *Lord*, thou hast this consolation, that thou art now sure, and indeed thou art never till then sure. And as reason differenceth a Man from a beast, so Love makes the great difference betweene a Christian and another. Indeed wee say it is Faith, but you know that Faith is differenced by love, that is, such a faith that breeds love, and so love is it that breeds that great consolation: And therefore this is thy comfort, if thou canst once bring thy heart to love the *LORD*, hee will beare with any thing, hee will

An hypocrite can counterfeit duties, but not love.

When we love God, he beareth with many infirmities.

will beare with many infirmities, as, you know, he did with *David* when he saw that he loved him. *David* had many great infirmities, as we see in the whole story, the whole relation of his life, yet because he loved the *Lord*, the *Lord* passed by all, and in the end he gave him this testimonie, that hee was a Man *after his owne heart*. So I say, love the *LORD* once, and he will beare with much in thee. On the other side, if thou doe not love him, doe what thou wilt, the *Lord* accepts it not. As wee see in the case of *Amaziah*; it is said that *Amaziah* walked in all the wayes of his Father *David*, and of the good Kings, he did as much as they, he was as great an enemie to idolatrie, he did all the duties of Religion, onely this was wanting, hee did it not with an upright heart, that is, he did it not out of love, and therefore the *Lord* regarded it not. And therefore let this move you to get this affection; there is much, if I could stand to presse it, that might inflame your hearts with a desire of it: only it is this love that sets a price on all that you doe, that makes all that you doe currant. As this stampe is set on your actions more or lesse, so they are more or lesse acceptable. This was that which set a price on the widowes mite, that set a price on a cup of cold water: this set a price upon *Abels* offering, and made it more aceptable than his brothers. The meanest service when it hath this stampe on it, is currant and good in *Gods* sight, hee accepts it: againe, the greatest performance without it, is nothing. *And if thou give thy body to be burned*, if thou

Motives to love.
1
It sets a price on all we doe.

suffer

ſuffer Martyrdome, if thou give all thy goods to the poore, doe what thou wilt without love, it is nothing, thy labour is loſt : this love ſets a price on all thou doſt.

We loſe not by this love.

Beſides this, conſider, this is that that muſt ſtirre you up above all other arguments, that if thou love the *Lord*, thou ſhalt bee no loſer by it: in all other love a Man ſeemes to bee a loſer; for when you love another, (as you know it is no love except it bee fruitfull and active,) when you beſtow on another your time, and your paines, and your Money, you know you have ſo much the leſſe your ſelfe. And therefore it is that men are ſo full of ſelfe-love, because that ingroſſeth all, a Man in that keepes all to himſelfe; but when hee comes to love another, hee parts with ſomething of his owne. And hence it is that men are ſo backward to love, in truth and in good earneſt. They love in ſhew and in complement, that is eaſie, but to love in deed is difficult, becauſe it takes ſomewhat from them. But in loving the *Lord*, it is not ſo, there is a difference betweene that and other loves : when you give the *Lord* your hearts, and beſtow them on him, hee will give you them every jot againe, and reſerve not any for himſelfe. You will aske mee, what is the meaning of this. My meaning is this, whatſoever you beſtow on the *LORD*, all the love that you give to him, it reflects and redounds to your advantage, you gaine by it all : as wle ſee, *Iſa*. 48. 17. *I am the Lord that teacheth thee to profit; for if thou keepe my Commande-*

mandements, thy reward, thy prosperitie shall bee as a flood, and thy rejoycing as the waves of the Sea. Markeit well, as if hee should say to them, When I command you to serve mee, and to love mee with all your Soule, and with all your strength, know, that all this is for your owne profit, it shall all redound to you. For, if you keepe my Commandements, your prosperitie shall bee as a flood, that is, it shall runne over the bankes, it shall bee so large, and so great; and your righteousnesse, that is, the reward of your righteousnesse, as the waves of the Sea; that is, one reward should follow upon the necke of another, as one billow followes upon the necke of another. This should bee your case, saith hee, if you love mee and keepe my Commandements, and serve mee. And therefore, saith hee, when I require your love and your service, herein there is a difference betweene that, and that which any man requires at your hands. All this is for your owne profit, it redounds to your selves, your selves fare the better for it. As it is said of the Sabbath, so I may say of this commandement, and all the rest, It was made for Man, and not Man for this; that is, for the profit of Man, for the advancement of Man; thy loving the *LORD* is for thy advantage, thou gainest by it: as it is, *Deut.* 5.29. *Oh,* saith he, *that there were a heart in this people, to love me, and to feare me, as they have promised; then it should goe well with them, and their children after them.* Not that I might bee a gainer, and you lose, but that it might goe well with you and your children

Difference betweene our service to God and service to men.

children for ever. So, if you love the *Lord*, when you thinke with your selves, I shall be a loser by it, I am perswaded that I shall lose much liberty, and much contentment and delight, I shall lose the giving satisfaction to many of my desires and lusts. No, thou shalt lose none of this, though a man seeme to lose this when he gives his heart to the *Lord*, but thou gainest all this; that is, the *Lord* gives thee thy heart againe, and gives thee leave to dispose of it, he gives thee leave to love thy friends, to love thy Wife and Children, and even to love thy recreations: hee gives thee leave to dispense and to distribute thy heart to this or that, as long as thou dost it lawfully, onely thou must doe it at his command.

Yea, when we give our hearts to the *Lord*, he gives us not them againe onely, but hee gives them much better than he received them, new painted, new beautified and new furnished, hee gives them in a farre better condition. There is no man that loseth by giving his heart to the *Lord*, but he gives it him again much better. As we say of vapours that arise out of the Earth, the heavens returne them againe in pure water, much better than they received them; so will the *Lord*: if thy heart ascend to him, thy impure, thy sinfull heart, the *Lord* will give it thee better. As wee say of earth, when the Earth receives the Sea-water, and puddle-water, it gives it better than it received it, in the Springs and Fountaines; for it straines the water and purifies it, that whereas when it came into the bowels of the Earth, it was muddy, salt, and brinish, it returns pure, and clean, and fresh, as you know

When we give our hearts to God, he gives them to us again better.

Simile.

Simile.

I the

the waters of the Springs and fountaines are : so the *Lord* doth with us. If thou wouldest give thy hearts desire, thy affections to him, thou shouldest have all againe, onely with this difference, thy affections should be more pure, thy thoughts, all the faculties of thy soule should be renewed, and cleansed, and beautified, he would restore them better to thee, but yet thou shouldest have them, let it be thy comfort. So that here is all the difference, take a man now that loves himselfe, and that thinkes with himselfe, Well, say what you will, I will go mine owne wayes, I wil provide for mine own contentment in this life, I know not what I shal have after, I will look to mine owne profit. I say, compare this Man with another, that resolves thus with himselfe, Well, from hence I will deny my selfe, and crosse my selfe, and will seek no more mine own contentment, nor to satisfie mine owne desires and lusts, but I will give my heart wholly to the *Lord*. The question now is, which of these are gainers? I say, the latter hath as much liberty & as much power of his owne heart, hee shall have as much use of all that is within him, as the other hath, that takes it to himselfe: all the difference is, the one is an unjust owner, the second, the *Lord* hath made the steward of his owne heart. So that the *Lord* hath thy heart, and yet it is thine owne heart, thou maist dispose of it as a Steward under thy Master, thou hast it as before, onely now thou doest it by his appointment, before it was at thine owne, Let all this therefore stirre you up to love the *Lord*.

He that gives his heart to God, hath as much liberty as he that followeth his lusts.

Object. You will say, indeed this is enough to perswade us to to come in, to love the *Lord*, and we are contented to doe so; the answer wee have frommost men. But now, what kind of love shall we have at their hands?

Answ. My Brethren, we must adde this for a conclusion, that it is not every kind of love that the *Lord* accepts: but your love must have these conditions in it, I will briefly name some of them, and so conclude.

First, you must love him *with all your hearts, and with all your soule*, you know, that is every where required in the Scriptures. That is, the *Lord* will have the whole streame of your affections, and desires and intentions, and your endeavours to runne to him, there must not any rivelet runne out of it, it must not bee drained away, but the whole streame must all be bestowed upon him, there must bee no division there; you must not say here as he saith, My Countrey, and my Father, my Children, and my Friends have a part in my love, but the *Lord* must have all, and there is good reason for it, because he bestowed all on you. It is in this love, as it is in marriage, in that there is no corrivall admitted, but there must be all in all; for the Husband must bestow himselfe wholly on his Wife, and the wife on the Husband: so if you love the *Lord*, if the match be made betweene you, there is all in that equality; if the *Lord* bestow all on you, and you bestow but halfe on him, there is no equality, but unevennesse. But when you bestow all on him, when you love him, with all your heart, & with al your soule, that makes the match betweene you.

5. Requisites in the love of God.

1. It must be with all the heart.

Why God must have all our love.

Object. You will say, the Lord doth not bestow himselfe wholly on me, he bestowes himselfe on many others, on many thousands besides me, and why should not I bestow my selfe on another?

Answ. I answer, it is not so, the *Lord* bestowes himselfe wholly on thee, *Hos.* 3.3. it is a borrowed speech, I will be to thee alone, and I will have thee to be so to me; so the *Lord* saith to every man, I will be alone to thee, and thou shalt be alone to me. *I am my beloveds, and my beloved is mine.* This is the match that must be betweene you. And when you say the *Lord* is not wholly yours I say, he is, though he bestow himselfe on many thousands besides. *Quest.* You will aske, how can that be? *Answ.* I say, that may be by reason of his infinitenesse; for that which is infinite hath not parts, and therefore he bestowes not himselfe partly on one, and partly on another, but he bestows all upon every one; for he is infinite and hath no parts. *God is to us alone how.* *Simile.* To expresse my selfe by a similitude, a point hath no parts, it is one indivisible, let a thousand lines come to one point, every one hath the whole, and yet there is but one that answers all, because it is indivisible, and every one hath all: So is it with the *Lord*, though there be many thousands that *God* loves, yet every one hath the *Lord* wholly he is to them alone, and expects thee to be to him alone, to bestow thy selfe wholly on him; therupon all those words are put in, *Thou shalt love the Lord with al thy mind, with al thy heart, & with all thy soule.* The meaning is this, when al that is in a man is set on work to serve the *Lord*, when he looks to the *Lord*, when he inclines towards the *Lord*, that is, when the mind is set on worke to think on him, to remember his glorious workes to have a right knowledge and opinion of him:

him: Again, when the memory is set on worke to remember him, and not to forget his benefits, his statutes, and his ordinances, and so the rest of his faculties. And therefore, if we love the *Lord*, wee will not doe this with our selves, to thinke I love him, and yet I wil suffer my mind in the mean time, to be exercised in contemplating of fornication; nor to thinke I love the *Lord*, and yet will suffer my memory, in the mean time, to be recollecting injuries, & breeding of them, and recalling my pleasant sins that are formerly past, that I should abhorre, thou canst not love him and do this. Againe, thou must not say, I love him, and yet let thy affections run after this and that, but thy whole heart must be bestowed on him: Thou must not think to love him, and to reserve thy affections for this or that particular thing that thou lovest inordinately, but thou must bestow all these on the *Lord*.

Love of God and contemplating of sin cannot stand together.

The second thing required in this love, wherewith I will end, is this, that *you love the Lord with all your might*. You will say, what is the meaning of that, to love the Lord with all my might, and with all my strength? For the understanding of this, you must know, that *God* hath given different might and different strength to men; as a rich man hath more might than another: for he can rule more, and sway more, and command more than a poore man can. Againe, a Magistrate, he can restraine by his power, and encourage men by his authority, and win them, yea compell them by his example. Againe a learned man, that is of great parts, that is of a stronger wit than another, hee hath more might than another, he is able to do more than a man of

2. Requisite in love, it must be with all our might.

Object.

Answ. What to love the Lord with all our might.

of weaker parts. Now to love the Lord with all our might, is to improve all the meanes we have, all the ſtrength, all the abilitie that we have above others, to improve it ſo, that we may ſerve the Lord with it more than others, that even as thou exceedeſt any in theſe abilities, ſo thou muſt goe beyond them in ſerving the Lord: This is to love the Lord with all thy might, that is, to love him ſo much more than a poore man, to beſtow more on him, to do more for him, as thy riches make thee more able, and more ſtrong than another. For thee to love him now as another man doth, that hath leſſe might, the Lord wil not take this love at thy hands; but will ſay to thee as Land-lords ſay to their Tenants, when they bring them leſſe rent then they ſhould, leſſe than is due, they will receive none; for they ſay, ſo much is due. The Lord will require this, that you love him with all your might. If thou be a rich man, if thou be a Magiſtrate, if thou be a man of ſuch and ſuch opportunities to ſerve the Lord, and doe but a little, he will not accept it at all: thou muſt love the Lord with all thy might, for *God* requires this at thy hands, hee leaves it not arbitrary. He ſaith, *To whom much is given, of him much ſhal be required*. He ſaith not, I leave it to him to do more or leſſe, but I require it, that is, I wil exact it, according to the meaſure he hath received. Therefore conſider with thy ſelfe, what means thou haſt, what power *God* hath put into thy hands, what ability thou haſt more than others. When you ſend a ſervant to market, as you give him a greater price, as you put more money into his hands, ſo you expect he ſhould bring home more

Simile. (margin, beside "ſay to their Tenants")

Simile. (margin, beside "you give him a greater price")

more than another that hath a lesse price put into his hands: So the Lord doth with men, he sends men into the world, as men are sent into the Market, he gives a larger price to some, to some he gives five Talents, to some three, to some two, the Lord expects that they should bring home according to the price they have in their hands, that is according to the might, according to the strength and opportunity he hath given them. For you must know, the Lord observes an exact difference betweene man and man. It may be, thou livest under better means than another, thou hast had better education than another, thou hast more knowledge in the wayes of *God* than another, the Lord hath helped thee more by the inward suggestions of his spirit than another, he looks that thou shouldest bring forth more fruit than another. And so againe for al other abilities and advantages: the Lord expects at our hands that we love him with all our might, otherwise, saith he, you might have given my money to the exchangers, and they would have made use of it. Marke that in the Parable of the Talents; for a man will be ready to say, if I bestow some love on the Lord, why should he exact and require the utmost, why doth he require so much at my hands? Yes, saith he, if another had this might, if another had this strength, & this opportunity that thou hast, he would have don as the exchangers do, he would have brought it in with profit; so if that ability were given to another, he would make use of it: And therefore think not much, if he require it at thy hands, for there is losse if he should not. Therefore know that the Lord requires

God is a loser when we are negligent.

quires this at thy hands. It may be that thou art more composed, and more disposed then another, it is nothing for thee to abstaine from drinking, to abstaine from swearing, because thou art framed this way by naturall ingenuity, and naturall temper that *God* hath given thee, it is not that the Lord requires no more, but that thou live soberly, free from grosse sinnes: no *God* lookes for more, he requires of every man according to his strength and ability. As, you know, a child may runne, and another man may walke, the Child takes more paines, the man lesse; if the reward were to be given according to the endeavour, the Child should have it, though hee that walkes come to the goale, before him.

Similie.

Note.

A man that is weake may not doe so much as another that is strong, and able to do ten times as much work as another man that is weak; though thou doe more worke than he, this is not accepted, because he looks that every man should doe his utmost, he requires that you should love him, and serve him, and set your selves to improve all your ability according to the might, according to the Talent, according to the price he hath distributed and measured to you.

FINIS.

OF LOVE.

The Seventh Sermon.

GALAT. 5. 6.

For in Iesus Christ, neither Circumcision availeth any thing nor uncircumcision, but Faith which worketh by Love.

THe last thing that wee entred upon was the conditions that *God* requires in our love to him, wee went through two of them the last time, wee come now to that which remaines.

Thirdly, you shall finde this to bee another condition in our love to the Lord, to love him *above all*, that is, incomparably above all: For, my brethren, wee may love many things in the world, wee may love our selves, wee are commanded to love our brethren as our selves; But this is

3. Requisite, to love him above all.

is peculiarly required to the love of *God*, if it be right in us, and ſuch as the *Lord* expects at our hands, that we love him above all, for otherwiſe we doe not love him as *God*, we love him as a creature: for to ſay we love him as *God*, and yet not to love him above all, is a contradiction.

1. Elſe we love him not as *God*.

Beſides, if we ſhould not reckon him as the chiefe good, and ſo prize him above all, ſome thing would offer it ſelfe one time or another to us, and draw our affections to it, and then we ſhould leave the *Lord*, and take that: Therefore, I ſay, it is required that we love the *Lord* above all. For every kinde of love is not ſufficient: as we ſee it in other things; that love that will ſerve a ſervant, or a common friend will not ſerve for a wife, it is another kinde of love; that love that will ſerve for one, will not ſerve for another: A Parent, a King, and a Maſter, as they have different relations, ſo they muſt be loved with different kinds of love. Now then conſider what love it is that belongs to the *Lord*, he muſt have all, he muſt have a love that anſwers him: otherwiſe, if thou come with a little pittance of love, and ſay, *Lord*, I am willing to beſtow this upon thee, the *Lord* will refuſe it; he will anſwer, I will take none of theſe things at your hands: Even as Land-lords do with their Tenants, when they bring not all the Rent, they refuſe it and reject it, because it is not that which they require, and which is due. Even ſo the *Lord* deales with us, as he did with the young man in the Goſpel, ſaith he, *Go and ſell all that thou haſt*: My brethren, it was not the act of ſelling, but it was the affection that was required.

2. Elſe we ſhould not love him conſtantly.

Simile.

quired. Therefore *Christ* did but try his affection by it; and it was performed by the wise Merchant that sold all, this the *Lord* requires that we should love him above all.

And there is good reason for it, for he is most excellent and most amiable of all.

Besides, I am sure he hath done for us more than all, as S. *Paul* speaks, *Was Paul crucified for you?* hath not *Christ* bought you, hath not he redeemed you, hath not he deserved more then all? and should he not therefore be loved above all? Why we must love the Lord above all.

Againe, is he not the uttermost end? are not all natures else subordinate? *God* as he is above all, so should we have a love answerable unto him.

But you will object, what, to love *God* above my selfe, how can I do that? *Object.*

Answ. Why we must love God above our selves. Yes my brethren, and there is good reason for that too, because in so doing we provide best for our selves; it is not so with the creature, if you set your love upon it, if you love any creature above your selves, it may be the destruction of your selves: But the *Lord* can provide for you, and repaire you againe, when the creature is destroyed for the *Lords* sake; when a man is a loser of any thing that he doth for the *Lord* he is a greater gainer by it; for it is the rule that *God* hath appointed the creature, and the perfection of every creature is in comming neere to the rule. Now when the *Lord* hath appointed this, to love him above our selves, in so doing we cannot cause but provide best for our selves, because therein lies our excellency and perfection. This is therefore another

another property of this love, we must love *God* above all, above all riches, above all profits, above all honour and credit, above all learning and delight, above our selves and our lusts: Therefore you shall find it in the phrase of Scripture how it runnes, those that love *pleasures more than God*, those that *love the praise of men more than God*, those that love wealth more than *God*, you see how they are excluded.

Not to love pleasures more than God, what

You shall see what it is not to love the praise of men more than *God*, it is this, when they come together at some times in competition, as they will ever and anon, still to preferre *God* before them. As for example, the Lord hath commanded you to sanctifie the Sabbath, to pray continually, the least thou canst doe, is to doe it Evening and Morning, and to doe it diligently. Now when thy profits and thy businesse, or thy ease shall come and thrust thee off from such a dutie, now they come together, and here they meet upon a narrow Bridge as it were; if thou shalt now preferre thy profits and thy businesse before the service of the Lord, thou art a lover of thy wealth more then of him. You may bring it to many such examples.

So againe, the Lord hath commanded to be diligent in your callings, to improve the time to the best advantage, for you shal give an account for it, it is one of the most precious Talents you have: Novv, if pleasures, and sports, and recreations shall come in and allure you, and call you, to dravv you avvay to spend time amisse, novv they come in competition; if ye do this ordinarily, ye are lovers of pleasures more then lovers of God.

So

So againe, God hath commanded thee that thou shouldest not commit adultery, that thou shalt not kill, that thou shalt forbeare to revenge, and the like: Now if any lust shall stand in opposition to such a command, if thou preferre this before it, thou art a lover of thy selfe, and of thy lusts before God.

In a word, go through any such thing, wherein God and thy lusts, thy pleasures or thy profits come in competition, when thou shalt in thy ordinary course be ready to preferre that before him, thou lovest that before him, thou lovest that before the Lord; and though thou thinke that thou lovest God, yet notwithstanding, know this, that that love is not sufficient, thou must love him above all.

And if you say, who is able to performe this? Who is it that doth not at some times preferre his pleasures and profits before the obedience to a command? *Quest.*

I answer, it is a thing that hath been done and is done by al the Saints: Therfore if you look into *Deu.* 30.6. saith the Lord, *I will circumcise thy heart, and the heart of thy seed, and thou shalt love me with all thy heart:* He speakes it there of a thing that is acted indeed, of a thing that is to be done by those that are regenerate: I will circumcise you, and then you shall doe it. And, my brethren, a man that hath the least measure of grace, if he be once in Christ, he loves God above all; that is, let a man be himselfe at any time, let not his lusts get the upper ground of him, as sometimes they doe when he is in passion and transported; indeed then feare may prevaile as it did with *Answ.*

with *Peter*, and lusts may prevaile as they did with *David*: But the meaning is, let a man be himselfe in his ordinary course, and still he preferres the Lord before any thing in all his actions.

Object. You will say, this is a thing that no man can do, to love *God* above all.

Answ. Yes, my beloved, therefore you must understand it thus; that comparatively you may reach it; all those that are sanctified, doe love him above all: although there be many degrees of Love you cannot reach unto, yet you love him above all. Even as it is in Marriage, a man may love his Wife with such a degree of love as is meete for her, yet there may be a greater degree of love, continuance of time may increase that love upon further knowledge, &c. So we may love the Lord above all, and yet come short of that degree that we may have after longer communion, and greater familiarity. So much for this third condition, to love him above all.

4. Requisite to be rooted & grounded in love.

But yet this is not enough, we finde another condition required in this Love, in *Ephes.* 3. 17. *That yee be rooted and grounded in love*, that is, that as yee must not love the Lord by halves, so yee must not love him by fits and by starts, it must be a fixed love, a permanent love, you must be rooted and grounded in it, otherwise, as it is said of him that is unstable in the Faith, as *Iam.* 1. 12. *He is as a wave of the sea tossed to & fro*, the same may be said of him that wavers in love, he is tossed to and fro, that is, sometimes he commeth with great purposes, with abundance of promises and resolutions, that seeme as

bigge

bigge as Mountaines, but ſtay a while, and they come to nothing, they vaniſh away. Suppoſe it were thy owne caſe, that a man ſhould come to thee, with an expreſſion of as much love, as that there could be no more for a day or two, but preſently afterward, hee is as ſtrange as if hee had never ſeene thee, wouldeſt thou regard ſuch a love as this? No ſurely, but as wee uſe to doe with franticke men, though that they be ſober for a while, yet we reckon them franticke, becauſe they are more conſtantly franticke; ſuch account doth the Lord make of ſuch as doe love him by fits and by flaſhes.

Our love to *God* not alwayes in the ſame degree.

But you will ſay, who is there that is alwayes at the ſame ſtay? It is true, my Brethren, I denie not but that the beſt of the Saints have their love ſometimes in the full tyde, and ſometimes in the loweſt ebbe; but you muſt know that there is a great deale of difference betweene theſe degrees, and that love that is as the morning dew and preſently dryed up againe, therefore you muſt alwayes remember, that this muſt be added to that which formerly hath beene ſpoken, that ye muſt be rooted and grounded in love.

How to be rooted in love.

1. To be rooted in faith.

You wil ſay, how ſhall we doe that?

Remember but theſe two things: Labour to be rooted and grounded in Faith, and then you ſhall be rooted and grounded in Love, as in that place I named before in *Epheſ.* 3.17. he prayeth that *Chriſt may dwell in their hearts by faith, that ſo being rooted and grounded in love, they may comprehend, &c.* Let a man conſider well upon what ground he hath perſwaded him-

himselfe of the Lords favour and love to him, let him not build upon a hollow sandie foundation, but let him build the assurance of his salvation upon a Rocke, that is, let him examine his grounds to the bottome, let him search it well, let him consider all the objectio is that may be made against his assurance, and not give over till hee be fully convinced, that the Lord his heart is perfect with him, and when he is thus rooted and grounded in faith, he will likewise be rooted and grounded in love.

2. pitch our love on his person.

Againe, remember to pitch your love upon the person; not to love him for by-respects, for other matters, but set your eye upon the very person of *Christ*, to behold him in his glory, in his purenesse, in his attributes, in all his excellencies, and so to love him, for that will continue; for if you love the Lord because he deales well with you, because you have hope, he will save you, because you have escaped such and such judgements through his providence, if any of these be the ground of your love, these are mutable; but if you love him for himselfe, because of that amiablenesse that is in him; for, my brethren, he is the same, *there is no shaddow of change in him.* Therefore if you love him thus, your love will be constant; this was the case of *Iob*, his love was right, he loved the very person of *God*, therefore he was willing to take good and evill at the hand of *God*, and yet his love remained sure. Take another man that hath not knowne *God*, that is not acquainted with him, it may be when the Lord hath brought him into prosperity, he will forget the Lord, as *De-*

mas embraced the present world; the prosperity of such a man drawes him from *God*. Another man, when persecutions and tryals come, he forsakes the Lord, because indeed he pitched not his love upon his person, therefore he loves him not constantly. But to goe on.

The next is that property ye shall find in 1 *Thess*. 1. 3. *Diligent love*: that is the last which I will name to you. I say, it must be a diligent love wherewith you love the Lord, and not an idle and negligent love, not a love that is in shew onely, but a love that is operative, for that *God* requires.

5. Requisite, it must be diligent.

You will say, wherein should our love be diligent?

Wherein our love must be diligent.

I answer, you must be diligent in preparing for the Lords comming, that you may receive the *King of glory*, that he may enter into your hearts, for there is a diligence of love in that; to doe as *Iohn Baptist* came to doe, to *prepare the way of the Lord*. What was that? to bring downe the mountaines, and to raise up the Vallies, that is, those high thoughts, those high lusts that stand in opposition against the Lord, that barre the Doore against him, that will not let him enter into your hearts, bring downe those mountaines: againe, the vallies must be raised up, that *God* may come and dwell in your hearts; the diligence of love is shewed in opening to the Lord when he knockes, that when a thing shall be suggested to you, it is for the Lords advantage to embrace it, for it is the nature of true love, it enlargeth and wideneth the heart.

1. In preparing for Christs comming.

2. In adorning the Soule.

Againe, love is diligent in adorning it selfe, and beautifying the Soule for the approach of the Lover, such is this love that we speake of, it will make you make your selves new creatures: expresse your diligence therefore in labouring to adorne your hearts with graces, that the Lord may take a delight to dwell in you; be diligent also in cleansing your selves *from all pollution of flesh and spirit*, that when the Lord commeth, hee may finde no sluttish corner within you, for the Lord hateth these: As the *Israelites* were to goe with a paddle, and cover every filthy thing, because saith the Text, *The Lord walketh among you:* So must we doe, keepe our hearts cleane if wee will have the Lord delight to dwell with us, we must be diligent to remove out of his sight whatsoever he hateth.

3. In keeping his Commandements.

Lastly, wee must be diligent in keeping his commands, wilt thou say thou lovest *God*, and yet doest disobey him and rebellest against him from day to day? The Lord careth for no such love, for indeed love cannot be otherwise judged of than in obeying: to say thou lovest him, and keepest not his commands, it is but a dead love, and a picture of love, it is not love indeed; it is, but as the Apostle saith, to doe it in word, and not in truth; for when you love him indeed, you doe the thing he would have you to doe: Therefore so much diligence in keeping his commands, so much love, hee that doth most, loveth most. And so you see the conditions that are required in this love, what a kind of love it is that *God* will have at your hands, or else he will not take it of you.

Now

Now my brethren, there remaines but one thing more, wherewith we will conclude this point, that is; now I have been so large in shewing you what this love is, (wherein you cannot blame us if we presse you to it, because it is one of the greatest and most radicall vertues, Faith and Love, therefore we have been the larger in describing it to you;) I say, now you have heard what it is, what remaines but this, to shew you the great danger in not loving? And that we will make to be the last consectarie that we will draw from this Doctrine.

I say, consider how dangerous a thing it is to neglect it, the Lord you see requires it upon pain of damnation, whatsoever you have, yet notwithstanding if you have not this love, you are not in Christ, and so you shall be excluded. Let no man think that this is exaction, that it is a hard thing that the Lord requires it with this exaction, for what is it that he requires? If he had required of you to offer sacrifice, as he did in the old Law, then the poore man might have objected, he had not wherewithall; if he had required us to fight battels, the weak man might have said he could not doe it, he was not able: but now young and old, rich and poore, all can love.

God deals not hardly with us in requiring love; because,

1 It is that which every one may give.

2 He that requires this, might have required harder things.

Besides, if we consider who it is that requires this love, is it not the great God of heaven and earth? Is it not the Sonne? If he had commanded thee the hardest thing in the world, if he had said, thou shalt cast thy selfe into the fire, thou shalt sacrifice Children to me; you are his creatures, and you must obey him:

him: But when he requires this onely at thy hands, to love him, is it not equall?

3. It is for our owne benefit.

Besides, when he requires this, it is for your benefit, for when you have given the Lord your hearts, the Lord gives you them againe; even as the Earth, the Water it receives from the sea, it returnes it better back againe in springs and fountaines, and pure streames; So doth the Lord give you your hearts back againe, when you have bestowed them upon him, and withall he gives you leave to bestow them upon other things, to love all things that you may and ought to love, and which is good for you to love. Therefore the Lord may require it upon this penaltie, for he askes but his owne, and what he hath deserved at thy hands, therefore it is a most reasonable and equall request. *For what doth the Lord thy God require of thee,* saith *Moses, but onely that you love the Lord your God?* So I say to you, what else doth the Lord God require of you?

The danger of not loving the Lord.

But againe, know this, that as it is a command full of equitie and reasonablenesse, so the danger is the greater if you doe it not; and what that is, I will shew you but by one place, 1. *Cor.* 16. 22. *Cursed is he that loves not the Lord Iesus, yea let him be had in execration to the death.* That is the place I would have you to consider, that now when you have been acquainted with this whole Doctrine of love, you might know the danger of not performing and doing of it; whosoever loves not the Lord Iesus, let him be *Anathema Maranatha,* he curseth him in two languages, to shew that it is a peremptory curse.

But

But what is that to be cursed?

My Brethren, to be cursed is to be separated, to be set apart, or appointed unto evill, so that all that love not the Lord Jesus, they are men separated and set apart to evill, so that no man may meddle with them, no man may touch them to doe them good: as the Saints, and those that love the Lord, they are set apart that no man may touch them for hurt; so it is here, when a man is cursed, the meaning is this, hee is set apart secluded from all good things, that none are to meddle with him, hee is set apart for evill, all things shall concurre together to doe him hurt; this is when the Lord curseth any man, and this is the case of every man that loves not the Lord Iesus. To be cursed, what.

Our businesse when we preach the Gospell, is but to offer the Lord Iesus to you, that is all that we have to doe; and all that you have to doe that heare us, is to take Iesus Christ, to beleeve in him, to love him: Now saith the Lord, if yee will not doe this, if you will not love him, every such one let him be accursed. Now, when the Lord shall curse a man, as *Isaac* said, *I have blessed him, and he shall bee blessed*: so whom the Lord curseth, he shall be cursed, and it is a feareful thing if you consider it; and therefore wee will a little open it, and shew you wherin this curse consists.

Which I urge the more, because it is an usual thing among men, when they come to consider their sinnes in particular, wherewith they have provoked *God* to anger, they look upon this or that grosse sin, but this defect and omission of love they scarce put into the number of their sinnes. But that you may know now what it is not to love him, you may consider by the greatnesse of the punishment; and that you see here is a curse: Now that you may know what this curse is; know that it consists in these foure things.

The curse of God in foure things. 1. Separate from grace.

First, it consists in this, he shal be separated from grace and goodnesse, from holinesse; and this is the curse upon his soule in this respect, in regard of exclusion from grace, which is to the soule as an obstruction in the liver is to the body, as a theefe in the candle is to the candle, which causeth it to waste and consume, and weare away; so it is in this curse, when *God* shall lay it upon the soule of any man, he shall not thrive in grace, his inward man shal not prosper at al, he shall be still in the wearing hand, & the *Lord* shall take away from him thatwhich he seems to have: when the Lord shal say to thee as to the fig-tree, *Never fruit grow more on thee*: that is a fearful curse, when the *Lord* shall curse, and say to a man, though thou hast some leaves upon thee, there are som things that seem to be good in thee, yet because thon hast not love, never fruit shal grow upon thee more. What a curse is it thinke you, that shal make the soule of a man to wither, as the fig-tree withered after the speech of *Christ*? that is, when every thing shall drive a man off from that which is good, and carry him on to destruction; whatsoever befalleth him in poverty, in prosperity, riches, and friends or enemies, every thing shall breed his hurt: he shall have riches when hee is most ready to abuse them, he shall have adversity then, when it is worst for him to bee in adversity, that shall bee to him as the lopping of trees out of season:

ſeaſon: hee ſhall be as an unthrifty ſonne, ſet him to a trade in the Citie, there he goes downe the wind; put him to husbandry in the Countrey, that thrives not with him: ſuch is the caſe of every one that loves not *Chriſt*. So my brethren, when *Chriſt* is preached to you, when you will not receive the doctrine, but refuſe it, you ſee the doome here, ſaith the Apoſtle, let him be accurſed: this cauſeth men to goe away from the Lord. *Becauſe they receive not the love of the truth*, therefore hee gives them up to beleeve lies; becauſe that men receive not *Chriſt* in the love of the Goſpell, he gives them up to a reprobate ſenſe, from one degree to another, till there be no remedy. We ſee by experience, are there not many that are given up to the ſinne of drinking, and idleneſſe, and company-keeping, and others to other ſins? you ſee many plod on in an old tracke of ſin, ſome lying a long time in a dead ſottiſh courſe, ſo as the moſt powerfull Miniſtery in the world will not ſtirre them, which is an evidence that the Lord hath curſed ſuch, therefore the Miniſtery can doe them no good. And this is the firſt curſe upon men that love not the *Lord Ieſus*.

But perhaps thou regardeſt not this curſe, becauſe thou regardeſt not grace and holineſſe from which it ſequeſtreth thee, but yet there is another branch of it, thou ſhalt be ſeparated from the preſence of the Lord, that is, from the joy, from the influence, from the protection of *God*; and this is a very fearefull curſe. You know what it was to *Cain* in the fourth of *Geneſis*, when the Lord had curſed him,

2 Separation from the preſence of God.

him, saith he, *I am hid from thy face:* that was the great curse that was laid upon him, of which he was most sensible, that he was separated from the presence of the Lord. And my brethren, this is no small thing, because *God* is the *God of all comfort*, and to be separated from his presence, is the worst thing that can befall us in this life.

It was *Sauls* case, when the Lord had once cast him off, he was separate from the presence of God, so that when he came to aske counsell, the Lord would answer him no more, he would have no more to do with him: you know how fearefull and how bitter this was to *Saul*. On the other side, see how much *Moses* magnifies this presence of God. *Lord*, saith he, *if thou goe not with us, carry us not hence:* as if the presence of God were the greatest comfort in the world, as indeed it is. This is another thing wherein ye shall be cursed.

3. A curse on the outward estate.

Againe, there is yet another branch of it, ye shall not onely be separated from grace, and from the presence of the Lord, but there shall be a curse upon your outward estate. It is said of *Cain* in the same Chapter, *Thou shalt be cursed from the earth:* it may be many that heare of being cursed from grace, and of separation from the presence of the Lord, are of that minde that they care not for it, that they regard it not: it may be you care not to be cursed from heaven; but to be cursed from the earth goes neere to you, and that is a thing which the most earthly-minded man in the world is sensible of. Now you must know, that whosoever loves not the Lord Iesus shall be be cursed from the earth, that is, there shall be a curse upon you in all earthly things, in all things that belong to this present life whatsoever they are.

Object. But you will say, we see it quite otherwise, we see such men as they, described to be men that abound in outward wealth, in outward blessings.

Answ. It may be so in outward shew, but yet there is a curse upon them notwithstanding. *Abimelech* had the Kingdome, yet there was a curse that never ceased till he was rooted out of the Kingdome: The *Israelites* had the Quailes, but yet there was a curse with them: *Ahab* had the Vineyard, but it was a curse to him. So all these things that are of themselves blessings and mercies in their owne nature, yet if the Lord will mingle them with a curse; ye shall find no ease from them at all: and this is a thing that is well known by experience, if the hearts of men will speak what they know. This is the case of those that love not the Lord; *The earth shall not give her increase*, you shall not have that sound comfort, that sweetnesse, that influence of comfort from earthly blessings; though you have the creatures about you which naturally have blessings in them, yet they will not give downe that milke for your comfort, you shall not be satisfied with them, you shall see a constant emptinesse in them, they shal be to you as the shel without the kernell; and so much more shall ye be miserable, because ye shall find the least comfort in them when you most expect it: the Lord meets thus with those that love him not in earthly blessings.

A man may be cursed in outward things in the midst of plenty.

But last of all, there is one branch of this curse which

4 The eternall curse at the day of judgment.

which exceeds all the rest, and that is the eternall curse that shall be upon men for ever: while ye live here in this life, there is a certaine shew, a certaine twilight of comfort that the Lord sometimes affords even to evill men; but then there shall be a perfect midnight, then the Sun of comfort shall set upon you altogether, and rise no more: in that day, saith the Apostle, it shall be *the day of the manifestation of the just wrath of God:* in that day when the Lord shall open the treasures of his wrath, those which have beene so long time a gathering. While we live here, the clouds of Gods indignation are but gathering, then they shall grow thicke and blacke, and fasten upon you to the uttermost, then all the great deeps shall be broken up, then the flood-gates of Gods judgements shall prevaile and over-flow you; that case shall be yours at that time, and this is a time which is to be considered by you now. In *Eccles.* 1. 7. *Remember the dayes of darkenesse, for they are many.* My brethren, eternitie is another thing than we consider it to be while we live in this world. In *Psal.* 78. 38. *The Lord called backe his wrath, and stirred not up all his indignation:* but at that time the Lord shall stirre up all his wrath; ye do here but sip of this cup, but then ye shall drinke up the dregs of it for ever. This shall be the case of those that love not the Lord.

Men may be cursed, though the curse be not executed.

But you will say, this is a farre off, and therefore the lesse terrible: it is not neere at hand.

Well, though this curse in which we have shewed these foure branches, be not presently executed, yet remember this, that when we preach the Gospel to you,

you, as we doe from day to day, and are still offering you Christ, beseeching you to come in, and take him and love him, but yet you will not, know that there is a thunderbolt alwayes following this lightning: when *Iohn* the *Baptist* came and preached the Gospel, he tels them presently of the curse that was to follow. You doe not know the time when the Lord will execute this curse; *Cain* was cursed many yeares before he died: and so *Saul*, when the Lord had rejected him, and had made a separation between God and him, (for a curse is but a separation, when a man is cast aside and set apart for such a purpose, so *Saul* was set apart for evill) yet he reigned many yeares after, notwithstanding he was under the curse. So those that the Lord sware in his wrath they should not enter into his rest, there was a curse upon them, yet they lived many yeares in the wildernesse: Therefore though the execution be not presently, and though thou be in prosperitie for the present, yet it is but *Cains* prosperity; though he had his life continued, yet the curse lay upon him notwithstanding: therefore I say, take heed of refusing and deferring, lest he sweare in his wrath that ye shall not enter into his rest; it is a dangerous thing to refuse the Lord Iesus, when he is offered the first, second, third and fourth time, and still you will not come in. Take heed and remember that speech of the Apostle that we named to you, *Whosoever loveth not the Lord Iesus, let him be accursed.* When the Apostle looked upon the men to whō he had preached and written, You *Corinthians* to whom the Gospel hath been plentifully preached and made

knowne

knowne, those among you that have heard me, and have been made acquainted with this doctrine of the freenesse of Gods offering grace to you; if you will not take Christ in good earnest, if you will not love him, let such a man be accursed: and brethren, S. *Paul* was stirred up by the Spirit of God to pronounce this curse. So I say, let these words continue in your minds, that whosoever loves not the Lord Iesus, let him be *Anathema Maranatha*; and *he that hath eares to heare, let him heare what the Spirit saith:* for happy and blessed are those that love the Lord Iesus, but miserable and cursed are those that doe not love him.

***

FINIS.

OF

OF LOVE.

The Eighth Sermon.

GALAT. 5. 6.

For in Iesus Christ, neither Circumcision availeth any thing nor uncircumcision, but Faith which worketh by Love.

HAving ſpoken of Faith and Love, it remaines that we adde to them good workes; for which we will goe no further than this Text: we cannot have a fitter, for, ſaith the Apoſtle, when you come to have to doe with *Chriſt Ieſus*, to be ingrafted into him, to make your ſelves firſt acceptable to *God* through him, all the workes you can doe are nothing, they are no more than the omiſſion of them; circumciſion is the ſame with uncircumciſion: But what is of moment then? Faith (ſaith he:) But what faith

faith must that be? Such a faith as begets love: And what love must that be? Such a love as sets you on worke: so that you have a chaine here consisting of these three linkes; faith which when it is right, will beget love, and love when it is right will set you on worke; faith which works by love. So the point we will deliver to you out of these words, shall be this.

We are to be judged not onely by our faith and love, but by our workes.

That we are to be judged not onely by our faith and love, but also by our workes; that no man hath faith and love, that none are new creatures, that none have sincerity, but workes will follow.

This is a point which I doe not meane to handle at large as we have done the other, but will endeavour to finish it at this time: it is a very necessary point, because men are ready to applaud themselves in their knowledge, in their good meaning, in their honest desires, and in the meane time they faile in their lives and actions; therefore as those are the radicall vertues which indeed make up the new creature, *Faith* and *Love*, so you must know that good workes are never dis-joyned from them, wheresoever there is sinceritie and a new creature, good works will follow.

The Scripture you know is evident in this, *A good tree bringeth forth good fruit*, *Math.* 7. that is, it cannot bee, that a man shall have a new heart, it cannot be that a man should bee regenerate, but that his workes will be also new; looke how farre the heart of any man is holy, looke how farre his heart is put into a new frame of grace, in that measure his works will be good, and his life sanctified. In *Acts* 14.22. it it is said of *David*, *I have found a man after mine owne heart, who will doe whatsoever I will:* and in *Mat.* 23. 26. *Make the inside cleane, that the out-side may be cleane also:* As if he should say, if the inside be right, if the heart be set right within, if that be well moulded, the outside will be cleane, they cannot be dis-joyned.

If a man have a treasure within, there will be silver in his speeches and actions; but if his heart be nothing worth, his words and actions will be but meere drosse: It is the scope of that, *Prov.* 10. 20. *The words of the righteous are as fined silver, but the heart of the wicked is nothing worth:* That is, when his heart is nothing worth, his speeches and actions are nothing worth too, but the good man that hath his treasure in his heart, there is silver and gold in his speeches and actions, that is, they are likewise precious. Therefore let no man say he hath faith and love, and as good a heart as the best, though his actions be not so good, though hee be not so strict in his carriage; for it cannot be my brethren.

For first of all, if a mans heart be good, hee hath the spirit of *God* dwelling there: now, saith the Apostle, 2 *Tim.* 1. 6. *The spirit is not a spirit of feare*, or a spirit of weakenesse, a spirit that onely makes attempts, and is not able to bring things to passe; but it is *a spirit of power, a spirit of a sound minde:* That is, doe not thou pretend thou meanest well and desirest well, and thinke it is sufficient, but stirre up the gift that is in thee, set thy selfe on worke, doe the actions that belong to thee in thy place, and doe

Reason 1. Because every Christian hath the spirit, and that is strong.

not

not say I am not able to doe it, for we have not received a spirit that is weake, but a spirit of power: the same I may say to every Christian, If ye be in *Christ*, ye have the spirit, which is a spirit of power. So you have it likewise, *Gal.* 5.25. *If you live in the spirit, walke in the spirit*: that is, if you have so much of the spirit, as to make you living men, shew it by walking in the spirit, by following the spirit, by doing that which the spirit guides you to; therefore it is impossible that man should have a right minde, but that his workes also will be good, because grace is strong; in 2 *Tim.* 2.1. *And thou my sonne, be strong in the grace received, &c.* As if he should say, grace is a strong thing, it strengthens every man that hath received it; if thou professe thou hast received the grace of *Christ* to regenerate thee, to change thee, and to make thee a new creature, let that appeare by shewing thy selfe strong in thy actions, able and ready to doe every thing that belongs to thee in thy place. Indeede flesh is weake; so much flesh, so much weakenesse: for that is weake, and fading, and withering, and mutable; it is grasse, and all the purposes of it, and the desires of it are no better: but the spirit is strong, and grace is strong, quite contrary to the flesh: as the Prophet speakes, *Isay* 31.3. *Ye are men and not Gods, flesh and not spirit*, when he would shew their weakenesse; as if weakenesse were a concomitant of the flesh, and strength a concomitant of the spirit: Therefore if you have the spirit of *Christ* in you, there will be strength to goe through good workes, not onely to intend them,

and

and purpose them, and resolve on them, but you will put those resolutions and purposes in execution.

Secondly, it must needs be so, because there is a chaine, betweene good workes and the inward rectitude of the heart, a chaine that cannot be dis-joyned; for ye shall finde that these three things alwayes goe together.

2 *Reason.* Inward rectitude and good works alway goe together.

First, as that indeed is the beginning of every mans renewing, there must be a knowledge, a man must be enlightned, he must be renewed in the spirit of his minde, as the Apostle saith. Now if the knowledge be right, if it be a convicting knowledge, a sanctifying knowledge, a knowledge to purpose, it will draw on affections, it cannot chuse, they are never separated; you are never truly enlightened by *Gods* Spirit, but affections follow necessarily, and then if the affections be right, if knowledge draw on holy affections, love, and feare, and desires, &c. Affections are the immediate principles of actions, there is no man that hath right affections, but good workes will follow: so that these three are never disjoyned: sanctified knowledge draweth on holy affections, & they draw on good actions: as ye have it in *Matth.* 13. 5. *Their hearts are waxed fat, and their eares are dull of hearing*, and why? you shall see the chaine there, *lest seeing with their eyes, they should understand with their hearts, and bee converted, and I should heale them:* Marke it, if they should see with their eyes, the Lord hath given them up to judge amisse of things, that seeing they doe not see, that is, they see not to purpose, they are not convinced, they doe not judge; for if they did see with their eyes, that is, if they did see indeed, they would have understood with their hearts, their affections would follow in their hearts: and if they were set aright, then they would be converted, that is, their lives would be turned to *God*; and if these three were done, hee must needs heale them: but saith *God*, I am resolved not to heale them; therefore they shall see as if they did not see: for these will draw on one the other. So I say, if the heart were right, if there were faith and love, good workes would follow: therefore let no man say he hath grace, hee hath love and faith, except his life be also holy and good.

3. *Reason.* Because there is a new creature.

Lastly, wheresoever there is faith and love, there is a change of nature; for you know that wheresoever they come, faith that is effectuall, and love that followeth from faith, it makes a man a new creature, they are the very things wherein a new creature consists. Now when a mans nature is changed, it must needs be active: for that which is naturall to a man, he doth without unevennesse, there there is no inequality in his doing it, he doth it constantly, where there are naturall principles of actions, the actions flow like water from a spring: indeed where the nature of man is not changed, that is, where there is onely good purposes and good desires, and no alteration of nature, there actions doe not come as water from a spring, but as water from a pump, that is forced and extorted: but where there is a change of nature, there is no difficulty, a man

man doth it with facility and with desire; it is his *meat and drinke to doe the will of God.* Therefore I say good workes will follow, there will be the same degree of holinesse, of rectitude in your lives, in your actions, as there is of grace, as there is of faith and love in your hearts. And this is enough to make the point plaine to you; the maine businesse will be to make use of it, and to apply it to your selves.

Vse 1. Not to be content only with good meanings.

And first let us make this use of it, not to content our selves with good meanings onely, as it is the fashion of men to say, my heart is as good as yours, and my meaning is as good as yours, though I bee subject to infirmities, though I cannot make such a shew, though I cannot doe so much as others doe: this is the common objection, and though men say it not constantly, yet they thinke it, otherwise they would not content themselves in such a condition as they doe. But I say, deceive not your selves in this; for, my brethren, you must know that you may have good purposes and good meanings: wee will not deny you that you may have these, and yet have no true grace; for you must know that good purposes and desires may arise from these two things, which every unregenerate man is capable of.

Good purposes whence they arise. 1.

There may be knowledge, as you know an evill man may have knowledge of all the mysteries of salvation as well as the most holy. I doe not say hee hath the sanctified knowledge, but the law of *God* is partly written in his heart; the Lord hath taught every man somewhat.

2

Secondly, in an evill and unregenerate man there

may be not onely knowledge, but an approbation of what is good in it: they can approve that which is good; so farre they may goe. I doe not say they can delight in it, for that is another thing, they do not love and delight in it, that is not sutable to them, yet they may approve it. Now from these two principles, to know that which is good, and to approve it, they may goe so far as to purpose and desire to serve God; they may have good meanings, but yet if actions follow not, if there be not reformation in their lives, if a man deny not himselfe in his beloved sin, if he come not to that outward profession of holinesse that is required in Scripture, and is seene in the lives of the Saints, he hath nothing to comfort himselfe withall; these good meanings will not serve the turne.

2. Approbation of that which is good.

For know this, though it be true as we see there may be actions where there is no sound heart, as the second and third ground brought forth a kind of fruit when there was neither of them aright: hypocrites you know may goe farre, they may make a blaze, as your comets doe more than the true starres: though this be true, that there may be abundance of good workes where there is no rightnesse and soundnesse, no sincerity, no purenesse within, yet againe also on the other side, wheresoever there is sincerity, there are good workes, and though many times the outside be cleane when the inside is not, yet the inside is never cleane, but the outside is cleane too, and that is the thing we must examine our selves by. Though it bee not a good rule to say, I have good workes, therefore my heart is right: yet it is a good rule to say on the o her

Though there may be good workes where the heart is unsound, yet where ever the heart is sound, there are good workes.

other side, I want good workes, therefore my heart is not right; except there be a generall reformation in your lives, except things be reformed that you know to be amisse: Indeed when it is not revealed to you, then there is something for you to say, but when you know that such a duty is to bee done, that your speeches should be holy, that they should bee seasoned with salt, that you ought to abstaine from sinnes of all kindes, from al appearance, that you ought not to admit any kind of dalliance, not the least touch of any sinne. Now not to set your selves with all your might to reforme this, this is a sure argument you are not right: for if the generall frame of the heart be good, there will be a generall reformation of the life. Therfore let no man say, I purpose well, but in this particular infirmity I must be spared, to such a thing my nature is prone, and I am given to it, I cannot tel how to refraine it, and I hope it is not so great a matter: Say not so, for if the heart be right, the actions wilbe right and unblameable.

For though you see sometimes a man may have a good colour from flushing and painting, when the constitution of the body within is but crasy and unsound: yet again it is true, there is never any that hath a sound and haile constitution, there is never a healthfull body, but the complexion is good; the heart is never right, but you shall see it without: though you have leaves without fruit, yet you never have fruit, but there are leaves, there are actions appearing. Therefore learne to judge aright of your selves, content not your selves with good purposes; only you see the com- *Simile.*

 plaint

plaint of the Scripture of the lacke of this in people. What is the reason the Lord cals for *obedience rather than sacrifice*? Because that is the touchstone that every man is tryed by. *I an weary, saith he, of your fat of Rammes, I am burdened with your sacrifices, Esa.* 1. The thing that I desire, is that you *cease to do evill, and learn to doe well*; that is the thing that the Lord lookes for at every mans hand: these outward performances are good, they must be done, and these good meanings must be had, but yet that is not enough, you are not to judge your selves by that.

Object.

But it will be objected, that the best men have their failings, those that have a good heart, yet doe we not finde them subject to infirmities as wel as other men? And if this be the rule we are to be judged by, who shall be saved?

Answ. Holy men have faylings. 1 Whē they are suddenly transported. *Simile.*

To this I answer first, it is true that the most holy men may many times do that which is ill, but it is by accident; it is when they are transported, when they are carryed besides their purpose. As a man is bound for such a place, sayling such a way, his compasse stands still right, he alters not that, though the wind carry him violently another way, yet hee lookes still to the right way, that is his intent stil, and it is known by this, when the wind is over, and the gust is past, hee returnes againe, and sayleth to the haven he intended to goe to at the first. So is it with al the Saints, they saile by a right compasse, their intents are still good; whensoever they doe otherwise, it is by accident, it is when they are overborne by some temptation, by some passion, when they are not perfectly themselves

Againe

Againe you must know this, that every holy Man, as he hath grace in him, and a principle of holy actions, so he hath also flesh in him, and a principle of evill actions; now that principle may sometimes prevaile and get ground of him, yea it may prevaile mightily sometimes, and make him doe as evill actions as the worst man. For that is a true rule, a man that excelleth in grace may sometimes excell in ill doing; you must take me right, that is, a man that hath a more impetuous spirit than another, so that none excelleth such a spirit when it is set aright, hee may be as impetuous in evill-doing for a fit, for a time, when that evill principle within him shall get the better. Therefore though you see a good Man sometime unlike himselfe for a fit, yet it is at that time when the flesh prevailes, for now grace though it be there, yet sometimes it is laid asleepe, it is not alwayes acted: as the Philosopher was wont to say, It is one thing to have knowledge, and another thing to use it alway: so is it with grace, sometimes the Saints doe not use that grace and holinesse, and hence it is that they are subject to great failings; but I say it is by fits and by accident, the constant course of their life is right, because the constant frame of their heart is right. 2 Holy men have flesh in them as well as spirit.

But againe, there is another objection on the other side, that evill men sometimes do well, as well as good men do sometimes ill. *Obiect.* 1.

Answ. To this I answer, that it is true they doe so, but yet we must know that it is not they that doe it, but the good that dwelleth in them, as the Apostle speakes The good that evill men doe, it cannot be said that they doe it.

in *Rom.* 7. which may be implyed on the contrary. When any regenerate man sinneth, it is not he that doth it, but the sinne that is there; that is, it is not the Master of the house, but a rebell that is crept in by accident: So I say of every evill man that doth that which is good and right, it is not he that doth it, but some good that is there. For it is one thing for a man to have good things in him, and another thing to be a good man, hee may doe some things sometimes for a fit that are good, *Gods* spirit may be there to helpe him to doe much; I say, not that the Spirit dwels there, but he may take up his lodging for a time, and from him hee may have common assistance, common gifts that may enable him to doe much: therefore I deny not but those may have many good flashings of lightning that may enable them to doe much; onely this we say, *The day spring from on high* never visited them; that is, the Morning never riseth upon them, to guide their feete in the way of peace, for that is proper to the Saints; they never have any constant light that leadeth them so farre as to bring them in: they have some lightnings indeed that guide them in this or that particular, to helpe them in a step or two, to enable them to doe many good actions by fits, but not to bring them to perfection.

A man may doe good, and not be good.

Use 2. Christians better taught than great learned men without grace.

Secondly, if this be so, that we are to be judged by our actions, then this will follow from it, that poore Christians are better taught than the greatest Clerkes: they are better taught I say, because they doe more, therefore indeed they know more. For all

all the knowledge we have, all the sincerity, whatsoever is right within us, if it be to be judged by the actions, then he that doth most, he knowes most; for no man knoweth more than hee practiseth, because what knowledge soever a man hath that hee practiseth not, marke it, and know certainely it is a dead knowledge, it is an inefficacious knowledge. When things are dead and inefficacious, wee say they are not, as leaven that doth not leaven the dough, it hath but the name of leaven and no more, the thing it selfe is wanting; it is not knowledge if it bring not forth practise. As we say of drugges, they are not true when they doe not worke, but they are false and counterfeit. Every man is to be judged by what he doth. Therefore, I say, those that doe most, those are knowing men, *Those that seeme to know*, as the Apostle saith, *know nothing as they ought*: A man may know much, a man may have a large extent of knowledge, yet this is true of him, if his life be barren, if he bring forth nothing into action all the while, hee knowes nothing as hee ought to know, though hee know much. On the other side, the other sort, though their extent be never so small, yet what they know they know as they ought. Therefore vvhen you looke upon men in the vvorld, vvhen you vvould make a judgement of them, I say, those that know most, they are not the best, you must not put them in the highest degree, when you come to matters of Religion; but men are to be judged by their actions. When men have knowledge onely to know, as they have money to account with, and not

to

to buy and ſell with it, it is but dead, a man hath no good by it, that money makes him not the richer: ſo men that have knowledge onely to know with, not to make them more uſefull in their lives, more ſerviceable to *God*, and profitable to man, it is unprofitable knowledge: therefore thoſe are the wiſeſt men, let them ſeeme never ſuch fooles, though they are not able to ſpeake ſo much as others; yet they know moſt that practiſe moſt. For there is that difference betweene Art and Wiſedome; indeede it is true in matter of Art, he that omitteth wilfully may be the beſt Artiſt, becauſe there is no more required of him but skill, and it is but ſome error in him, it is the commendation of his Art that he erreth willingly. But now in matter of holineſſe and ſanctity, there he that knoweth and doth not, is the greateſt foole: For wiſedome conſiſts moſt in that. Wiſedome comprehends indeed theſe three.

Wiſedome in three things.

First, to invent, to ſee, to know and underſtand things.

Secondly to judge a right of things you know.

Thirdly, to put in practiſe that which you have concluded to be the beſt; and this latter is the greateſt part of prudence. Therefore thoſe men that know, that can diſpute well, that have cleare underſtanding, and yet doe nothing, they are the unwiſeſt: againe, thoſe that can ſpeake little, and perhaps have not ſuch a treaſure of knowledge as others, and yet can doe more, they know more than the wiſeſt. Therefore let us not miſeſteeme thoſe that are good Chriſtians, and holy men, and ſet too high a price

price upon others; for there is an errour under that, and it hath an ill consequent to judge of Religion by the opinion of those that are onely knowing men in Religion: No, beloved, Religion is the Art of holy men, and not of learned men; and it was the custome of former times to judge of heresies not so much by disputes, as by the lives of those that have beene the professours of them: and that *Christ* directs us to, *You shall know them by their fruits:* and what are those fruites? Their fruits are their actions.

Religion an art of holy men not learned men.

We learne in Schooles what to say in such a controversie, how to dispute rather than how to live: and that is the complaint we may take up in these knowing times, where *knowledge* (I confesse) *abounds, as water in the Sea*, but practice is thin and rare, *like grasse upon the house top, of which the Mower cannot fill his hand:* and that is the burden of us that are Ministers, that we teach much, and see little fruit, wee see no amendment of mens lives, men doe the same things that they were wont to doe, the duties they were wont to be defective in, they are defective in still. Alas my brethren, the end of our preaching is not that you should know, but that you should doe and practise: as it is not the desire of the Shepheard that his sheepe should returne their meate in hay againe, but hee would have it in their milke and fleece: So it is not our desire that you should onely know, though indeed many come short of that, but that you should shew it in your fleece and milke, shew it in your lives, that all the world may see it there.

there. It is not enough for him that desires to write to see the copy, and to know it, and the fashion of the letters, but then he hath learned it when he can write after it: so you must know Sciences are of two sorts; indeed some there are, the end of which is only contemplation and knowledge: but some there are, the end whereof is action; and they are no further good than we practise them. What is Musicke, but the practise of it? What is Physicke? The knowledge of all will not heale a man, but the taking of it. So it is with Divinity, the knowledge that we teach is nothing worth; if you know as much as could be knowne, it were all nothing worth without practice, practice is all in all; so much as you practise, so much you know. It is a great matter to have your judgement true in this case, for when men shall applaud themselves meerely in this, that they know and have right purposes and honest desires, and shall esteeme their estates by this, it causeth men to content themselves with a loose and negligent life, but we must know that *God* judgeth us by our actions, and that is our best rule to judge by too, therefore we should learne thus to judge our selves.

Sciences of two sorts.

Object. If you object, But it is a rule that wee have heard often, that the will is often taken for the deed, and if the will be present with us, though the action doe not follow, yet we are accepted according to the will.

Answ. To this I answer in briefe; first, it holdeth onely then when there is some impediment which you

cannot

cannot remove: as for example, a Man hath a desire to doe good to such poore people, hee hath a compassionate heart, hee is willing to be bountifull, but hee wants meanes to doe it; in this case the Lord accepts the will for the deed, for upon that occasion is this delivered in this place by S. *Paul*: so it is in every thing else, when you have a desire, and there commeth some impediment, that it is not in your power to remove, then the will is accepted for the deed. As when a man hath a desire to move his hands, his legges or armes, but because of a palsie that hangs upon him, hee is not able to stirre them, here the will is for the deed, hee is not able to doe it, though the mind be right and the desire good; so when you come to such duties that are not in your power to do, when there are some impediments that you are not able to remove; here the will is accepted for the deed.

The will taken for the deed

1 When the impediment cannot be removed.

Sometimes a man is ignorant of some particulars, and he hath a desire to obey *God* in all things; here the will is accepted for the deed, though he be not come to that degree of perfection as others are. But as men apply it commonly it is amisse, for when a man thinks I have a good purpose to do this, but I cannot pray, I cannot be so strict in looking to my actions and speeches; here the complaint is not right. For if yee stirre up your selves and doe the utmost you can doe, the deed will follow the will, there is no such impediment here but that you may remove. Therefore our answer is, that the reason why you cannot doe, is not because of such impediments

2 When a man is ignorant of some things, & yet his desires are right.

pediments that you cannot remove, but because your will is not yet right, which the Schoolemen call an imperfect Will; it is but such a will as the Wiseman speakes of concerning the sluggard, hee willeth and *lusteth, and hee hath not:* and what is the reason? If it were a full, a compleate and perfect Will, it would draw action with it, hee would not be a sluggard any longer, but he would draw forth his hands to doe somewhat to bring his desires to passe, but indeed he hath but light wishings and no more. And so it is with men in Christianitie, they are as *Salomons* sluggard, they wish they had such sinnes mortified, that they had such graces, they wish they could attaine such a measure of Faith and Love; but they take no paines, no Man hath hight of grace without paines; doe you thinke to get the greatest excellency in the world without paines? It is true, the Lord must doe it, but yet he doth it by your selves, you are agents in the businesse. Therefore doe not say, I wish well and desire well; for if you would doe your uttermost that you ought to doe, if your will were full and compleate, and desires right and strong, you would doe more, you would excell more in grace, and would amend your lives more, you would have your lusts more mortified: therefore let not this deceive you. I should presse this further, but wee will come to the last thing, because I would conclude this point with this time, and that is,

No man hath a great measure of grace without paine.

Use 3. An exhortation to doing.

To exhort you to be doers, that your Faith may be *Effectuall Faith*, and that your love may bee *diligent Love.*

Love. This is the great businesse which wee have to doe, and the thing which for the most part we all fail in, that there is no doing, no acting, no working of our Faith: be exhorted now therefore to adde to your faith diligent love, especially you that professe your selves to be growne Christians, looke you to it, and know, that as in nature every thing when it is ripe brings seed and fruit; if not, it is but a dead thing, a dead plant that keepeth the roome idle. If there bee that ripenesse and maturity in you, shew it by bringing forth seed and fruit, shew it by doing something. For, my Brethren, we are called into the *Lords* vineyard for the same purpose; it is not for you now to stand idle, the time of your standing still is past, it is for you now to worke, for yee are now come into the day. That exhortation is excellent, 1 *Thes.* 5, 6, 7, 8. *Let us not sleepe* (saith he) *as do others, we are come out of the night.* Those that are still in the night, it better beseemes them to sleepe, and to sit still and do nothing, but let us not sleepe as doe others, for we are of the day; let it not be so with you as with others, to bee much in speech onely, but labour to be much in actions. As it was said of *Gideon, up and be doing, and the Lord will be with thee*: so I say to every one, up and be doing, and the *Lord* shall bee with you; that is, though perhaps you doe not find that vigour, that fervency and livelinesse of spirit, yet bee doing notwithstanding, it is your wisest way, for that doing will increase the grace within you. Exercise increaseth health, as well as health enables to exercise; so the use of grace will increase grace and other abilities

Motives to be workers.

The use of Grace increaseth it.

ties: motion causeth heat, as well as all motion commeth from heat; so every good action proceedeth from grace, and good actions intend grace, and therfore be still acting, and judge of your selves by that; for what is grace, what is that you call Christianity else, but to do that which another man cannot doe? Therefore if there be such a difference betweene you and others, as you professe there is, shew it by doing that which another man cannot doe, by exposing your selves to that danger, to those losses for any good cause, which another would not doe; by spending more time in prayer, by taking more pains with your hearts from day to day than others doe, by keeping the Sabbath better than others doe, by being more exact in looking to your wayes, that you may *be holy in all manner of conversation*, that other men will not doe. I say, shew your grace, shew your regeneration, by being new creatures, by doing more than others; this is that which will make the world beleeve that you are Christians in good earnest, and not in shew only, that your profession is in deed & in truth; and truely there is no other way, this doing is that which makes a man excellent. You heare men complain of the barrennesse of their grounds many times, we may likewise justly take up the complaint against the barrennesse of the lives of men.

A goodly sight when mens lives abound with good works.

How goodly a sight is it when a man lookes into the Husbandry, to see the vine full of clusters, to see the furrowes full of Corne, to see the trees laden with fruit! When wee look upon men, it is the goodliest sight wee can behold in *Gods* husbandry, to see men

men ful of actions & good works. I beseech you consider of it seriously, and now set upon the doing of it, while there is Sand in the Hower glasse, your life will not last long, the day doth not continue alwayes, the night wil come when no man can work. When a Candle is put out, you may kindle it again; when the sun is set, it riseth again; but when our life is past, when the glasse is run, it ariseth no more, it is turned no more, *it is appointed to all men once to die.* If yee might dye twice or thrice, it were another case, but now it is your wisedom, therfore while it is time, while this short day lasts, to do what you have to do concerning your salvation with al your might, because the time is short.

There is nothing that is a truer property of wisedom, than for a man to take hold of opportunities, not to lose the day, nay not an houre in the day; for time is most precious, it is like gold, of which every shred is worth somewhat: it is your wisedome therefore to be oft sowing seed to the spirit, there is none of those good works, not the least of them but wil do you good in the latter end: for alas, what are your lives but your actions? so much as ye do, so much you live: your lives are short of themselves, why do you make them shorter by doing nothing? For as we have said heretofore, one man may live more in a day than another in twenty, because he doth more: you live more as you act more.

A true property of wisedome.

Simile.

Besides, what is it a man serves for in al his labour under the Sun? What is it that he desires but pleasure, comfort & contentment? Now this consists in doing, in working; for al pleasure followeth upon operation: and further than there is working there is no delight.

Pleasure and contentment is in action.

Therefore it was a wise saying in that Philosopher, that the happinesse and comfort that a man hath in this life consistes not in abundance of wealth, in swimming in delights, but it consists in doing the actions of a living Man, which is the greatest comfort you can finde here in this life. Doe the exercises and actions of holinesse, and the more yee doe, the more comfort yee shall have; for even as light followeth the flame, so pleasure and contentment followeth action.

The end of our life.

1 To glorifie God.

And besides (my Brethren) what doe you live for? is it not to glorifie *God*? You professe so much, and how is it done? Not by your desires or good meanings, but by your actions, those are the things that men see and feele, and glorifie your heavenly Father. For when your actions shine before men, *Herein is my Father glorified*, saith Christ, *that ye bring forth much fruit*: The doing of much is that which brings glory to *God*, the more you doe this, the more glory you bring to him.

2 To doe good to men.

Againe, another end of your life is to doe good to mankinde: shall they be able to fare the better for your purposes, for your good resolutions? No, they fare the better onely for that you doe for them and to them; it is your actions that benefit men.

Lastly for your selves, what is it that helpeth you and doth you good? Onely your good deeds and your actions, it is that which furthers your reckoning and account. That place is much to this purpose, *Phil.* 4. 17. *I care not for a gift but I desire fruit, because it will further your account*. Marke the phrase,

Phil. 4.17

the meaning is this, every good worke that a holy Man doth from the time of his regeneration, (for till then no actions are spiritually good) it is put upon his score, it stands upon his reckoning, there is not a penny nor halfe penny lost; that is, the least good worke is not done to no purpose, but the Lord will repay him againe every penny and farthing. This (saith he) will further your account. And when will the Lord pay? Not onely in the day of Judgement, (then indeed you shall be paid to the uttermost) but you shall be paid even in this life: marke that too, *You shall have a hundred fold here*, saith Christ, *They that forsake father, or mother, or wife, or children, shall have an hundred fold in this life.* Therefore, Brethren, if there be any wisedome in the world, this is the onely wisedome, to be still doing, to be much in actions. Why doe you trifle out your time therefore to no purpose? *why sit you idle here?* Why doe you not rise up and bestirre your selves? Why doe you not fill your lives with many actions? You have good purposes in you, why doe you not stirre them up? It is true, indeed wee are becalmed many times, because the Spirit doth not blow upon us; but yet notwithstanding, if wee would pray for the Spirit, the Lord would quicken us.

But you will say, alas, what shall we doe? It may be our callings give us no opportunity to doe that which other mens callings doe: if wee might be Preachers, and have such and such businesse wherin we might onely minde the things that belong to salvation, then it were easie. *Object.*

Answ. In every calling men have occasion of doing good.

My Brethren, you must know that you shal find continuall occasions of doing good actions every day, whatsoever your callings are. It is an errour among the Papists, to thinke that to give almes, to crucifie the flesh and to use that hardly, to fast, and the like, that these are the onely and most glorious actions: They are exceeding wide; good actions are nothing else but to doe the will of the Lord, and to bring forth fruit; the fruit of every Tree in the Orchard is but as the actions of every man, and then are the trees good to the Husbandman, when they are full of fruit. Every action that you doe is that fruit which *God* lookes for, now that fruit is good works, that is pleasing to the Gardner, to the Husbandman: Therefore to doe the Lords will is to doe a good worke. Now by this you may see what a large field you have for good workes, in what calling soever you are set, though it be never so meane a place you have.

Good actions, what.

Good workes in suffering. In sicknes.

To suffer imprisonment and disgraces for good causes, this is a good worke; for it is a great worke to suffer, and in that you doe the will of the Lord. When a Man is sicke, and lyeth in his chamber upon his bed, sicke of a Consumption or a Feaver, that he is not able to stirre; yet to doe this with obedience, to submit then to the wil of the Lord, is a good worke: for to beare a burden is a worke, to beare sickenesse and calamity after this manner, is a work, to thinke the Lord hath put me into this condition; he might have given me strength to goe abroad as others doe, but hee hath laid sicknesse upon me; I

say

ſay the right bearing this burden is a good worke.

Againe, to take paines with our hearts, to maſter our unruly luſts and affections is a good worke. Doe not you reckon it a worke to breake Horſes, to maſter Colts? It is the trade of ſome men to doe ſo: and is it not a good worke for you to get victory over your luſts, to tame your unbridled natures, to curbe your unruly hearts and affections in all the variety of occaſions that ye paſſe through? It is a work to behave our ſelves as become Chriſtians, decently, and comely, and holily, in poverty, in riches, in honour, and diſgraces; to behave our ſelves under theſe things in a right manner, to carry our ſelves patiently and holily through them as becomes good Chriſtians, this is a good worke, and this belongs to every one, though his calling be never ſo meane.

In maſtering our luſts.

When *Paul* ſtood at the barre, and *Feſtus* reviled him, and ſaid, he was a *mad fellow*, the ſuffering of this was a worke in *Paul:* Marke his manner of carriage in it, *I am not mad moſt noble Feſtus:* there was a work in that. So I may inſtance in the things wherein you may ſeeme to doe the leaſt; the ſtanding ſtill in ſome caſes is a work: the Apoſtle (makes among the great workes that are to be done by Chriſtians) this to be the chiefe, *To keepe our ſelves pure and unſpotted of the world*, to paſſe through all occaſions, and to be never the worſe for them, to goe through all defilements of this preſent life, and not to bee tainted: and if this be a work, how much more is it then to be ſtill doing, to be in act and operation alwayes?

alwayes? Therefore do not ſay you want, when you ſhall alwayes have occaſion enough of that.

Queſt. But you will ſay, theſe generals are good to exhort us to be doing, but yet in particular what would you have us to doe now?

Anſw. Our workes muſt be ſutable to the ſeaſon. I will inſtance in ſome few things. There are certaine times of working; as husbandmen, ſometimes they have times of harveſt, and ſometimes they have ſeed times, wherein it is required that they worke more than at other times: So the Church of *God* hath times and ſeaſons, and the Common-wealth hath ſome ſeaſons and times when men ſhould be ſet aworke to doe more than at other times; and you all know this is ſuch a ſeaſon, wherein there ſhould be a working of every one in their ſeverall places; I ſay it is time now for men to be working more than ordinary.

Queſt. But you will ſay, what is it you would have us to doe?

Anſw. Duties ſuting the preſent times. 1. Contend for the Faith. My brethren, *Contend for the faith once delivered to the Saints.* Marke it, the worke muſt be to contend for it, this muſt be your eſpeciall care, you muſt be men of contention, let the world ſay what they will of you, it is a dutie that lyes on you, it is that which the Spirit calls for from you, that ye be men that ſhould contend; you muſt not doe it coldly, and remiſſely, but earneſtly to ſtrive for it. Let not pretence of indiſcretion hinder you, for diſcretion (Diſcretion.) when it is right, teacheth a man not to doe leſſe but more, and better than another man, diſcretion wee ſay doth not take metall from Horſes, but guides

thoſe

those Horses and puts them in a righter way, discretion makes no man lesse active, but it gives his actions a better tincture.

So againe, let us not say we must be moderate, for what is that moderation? Indeed the moderation that keepeth from actions, wherein is excesse, is good, but if you meane by moderation to goe a slow and easie pace in the wayes of *God*, that is coldnesse, idlenesse, carelesnesse; there is no excesse in any good way. Therefore that is your worke now to contend for the Faith, that is, for all the points of Faith; for every jot of that is precious: saith the Apostle *Iude*, it was but *once delivered to the Saints*: as if he should say, it is too precious a treasure oft to be dispensed, it was but once delivered to the world: if *Christ* did meane to come againe, and renew the Articles of our Faith, wee might be more remisse and negligent, for if we did lose them, he might restore them againe, but they are but once delivered, therefore your care must be to keepe them the better.

Moderation.

The faith once delivered.

Besides, it is the common Faith, therefore every Man hath interest in it; doe not say therefore, what have I to doe? it belongs to these and these men to looke after it. It is the common Faith, and every Man hath part in it, and should contend according to his place and power, and within his spheare, and remember it is a matter of much moment, for every part of the Faith or little matter of Faith (I speake now of the whole Doctrine of Faith) that you should be exceeding exact in keeping of it, that it receive

Common faith.

no

Error in opinion worse then error in practise

no detriment, especially in matter of opinion. For, my Brethren you must know, that it were better there should be great offences commited in the Land, great and notorious crimes, than there should be any losse in the matter of Faith; because where the opinions of men are set wrong, that is a principle that carries them still on. Great sinnes come from great passions, and men are able to see them, and when the passion is gone over, they are easily recalled againe; but errours in opinion are matters of great moment, therefore it belongs to every one to looke to it, to us that are Preachers in our places, to Magistrates in their places, to every Man to contend for the common Faith: and know this my brethren, that there are certaine opportunities which the Lord gives you, and you must take heed of neglecting them, it may be to let a thing goe sometimes, it will be never recovered againe. Therefore looke that you be diligent in it, stirre up your selves to doe it, while there is occasion offered. In other things, men are apt to be men of action, they would have imployment, and worke that they may be some body in the world; and it is very well, there is something in that, it is a noblenesse of disposition so to doe: but alas, what poore and weake reward have you for that? It may be a little vaine glory, it may be some applause from Princes or people, it may be some emptie ayry preferrement. To doe the will of the Lord, the worke hee hath given you to doe, it is no matter what it is for, a servant must not chuse his worke; I say whatsoever it is, though in never

so

so mean a thing, the greatest excellency is to do his will that makes us Kings and Princes to him, that makes us partakers of the Royall bloud, as *Christ* saith, *These are my Brother, and Sister, and Mother, that doe the will of my Father.* It is this doing of his will, this action that puts you into a high condition: I see not that *Paul* was ambitious of any thing but of this, that he might be doing, that hee might live an usefull, a profitable life. In *Rom.* 15.20. *I was ambitious*, saith S. *Paul*, *to preach the Gospell, even where it had never beene preached*, this is all my ambition to put my selfe upon the hardest taskes: so it should be your ambition to doe something for the Church. When you read the story of *Moses*, that *hee was mighty in word and deed*; of *David*, of the Iudges, and the Worthies of the Church, they should bee so many incentives to you, to stirre you up to be doing in your place.

2. Duty, Fast and pray.

But this is not all that we would commend to you at this time, to bee men of action, and to observe the opportunities, but there is another thing, and that is this, that likewise the season commends to you, that is, to fast and pray: as in husbandry, so in the Church, there are certaine seasons of actions, and those seasons must not be omitted. Marke what the course of the Scripture was in every calamity, *Ioel* when there was a famine begun, *Sanctifie a fast, saith the Lord, call a solemne Assembly*: when there is a plague comming, when there are great enterprises in hand, when there is any thing plotting for the advancement of the good of the Church, doe you not thinke now, that the omiſſion of opportunities are ſinnes for you to neglect this dutie, doe you not thinke the *Lord* will require it? It is true indeed, it is an extraordinarie: but doe not extraordinarie times and occaſions call for it?

Againe, is it not evill in ſuch extraordinary caſes to omit ſuch an extraordinary duty? As we find in Scripture, when the *Lord* would call for faſting, and they did it not: Indeed to turne it to jollity and feaſting is another thing, a ſinne of a greater nature; but now the very ſtanding ſtill and omitting of this dutie is diſobedience to the *Lord*, and to be guilty of the judgements that are upon a people; I ſay the ſtanding ſtill and not haſtening to the gap: What ſhall wee ſay then of thoſe that reſiſt this courſe, and thruſt men out of the gappe? Conſider it therefore ſeriouſly, this is a ſpeciall dutie required, the ſeaſon lookes for it that we ſhould humble our ſelves before *God*.

3. Duty, renew our covenants.

Againe, there is one thing more that wee will ſpeake of, but in a word; that is, that every Man for his owne particular renew his ſpeciall Covenant with *God* concerning the amendment of his life in particular: for I find that in all times when the *Lord* had ſtretched forth his hand againſt a Church and Nation, that this hath been required, that they ſhould come and enter into a Covenant with *God*: You ſhall find that *Aſa* did it, *Chron.* 16. that *Nehemiah* did it, that it was done in *Ieremiahs* time, when they had warres in hand: Wee have many examples of it in Scripture, every Man did

did it; and because every man could not come to doe it personally, the head did it for the rest. I say the *Lord* lookes for this from every man in private, that hee should doe this in a particular manner; to consider what have I done amisse in my life? What have I done to provoke the *Lord?* What sins of commission, and what of omission? Have I been cold and luke-warme? Have I been too much conformable to the times? For this is it that brings judgement upon a people; the Saints when they are not zealous; when they fall from their *first love*, may helpe forward a judgement as well as grosse sinners, yea and more too. Let every man therefore stirre up himselfe to doe his dutie. In a word, wee should strive and contend for the advancing of *Christs* Kingdome, for the furtherance of the Gospell, for the good of mankind, for the flourishing of the Church, wherein our owne good consisteth; and we should doe it earnestly, wee should contend for it, contend with *God* in prayer, contend with our Superiours by intreaty, with our adversaries by resistance, with cold and lukewarme men by stirring them up, by *provoking one another to good workes*. These are the workes that wee exhort you to, and thus you shall bee assured you have *Faith that workes by love*. Learne this, to joyne these together.

The sins of Gods children helpe to bring judgements.

And so much shall serve for this time, and this Text.

THE TABLE.

THE TABLE.

THE TABLE.

Direct.

Not

M.

If

FINIS.

Memorandum, that those which you finde with this (⊙) at the end of them, are most or all in the third part.